A Greek Priest. Engraving from Jost Amman, *Habitus praecipuorem populorum* (Nuremburg: Hans Weigel, 1577), Plate 186.

From Samos to Soho

Byzantine and Neohellenic Studies

Vol. 12

Edited by
Andrew Louth FBA and David Ricks

PETER LANG
Oxford · Bern · Berlin · Bruxelles · Frankfurt am Main · New York · Wien

John Penrose Barron

From Samos to Soho

The Unorthodox Life of Joseph Georgirenes, a Greek Archbishop

PETER LANG
Oxford · Bern · Berlin · Bruxelles · Frankfurt am Main · New York · Wien

Bibliographic information published by Die Deutsche Nationalbibliothek
Die Deutsche Nationalbibliothek lists this publication in the Deutsche Nationalbibliografie; detailed bibliographic data is available on the Internet at http://dnb.d-nb.de.

A catalogue record for this book is available from the British Library.

Library of Congress Control Number: 2016934653

Facsimile of *A Description of the Present State of Samos, Nicaria, Patmos and Mount Athos* on pages 235–266: Reproduced by kind permission of the Syndics of Cambridge University Library.

ISSN 1661-1187
ISBN 978-3-0343-1788-7 (print) • ISBN 978-1-78707-286-2 (ePDF)
ISBN 978-1-78707-287-9 (ePub) • ISBN 978-1-78707-288-6 (mobi)

Hochfeldstrasse 32, CH-3012 Bern, Switzerland
info@peterlang.com, www.peterlang.com, www.peterlang.net

This publication has been peer reviewed.

Printed in Germany

Contents

Figures

Maps

(Edited and drawn by Giles Darkes.)

Preface

When my husband, John Barron, died in August 2008, he left behind a nearly completed typescript of his biography of the seventeenth-century Greek Orthodox archbishop of Samos, Joseph Georgirenes. John had first encountered Georgirenes in the library of Balliol College, Oxford, when he was working for his DPhil on the history of Samos in the Archaic period. The archbishop's booklet, *A Description of the Present State of Samos, Nicaria, Patmos and Mount Athos*, had been published in London in 1677, but it still provided John with a useful guide to the geography of the island of Samos and the advantages of various harbourages. At that time John knew very little about the author. In 2001, however, when he was invited to give a paper at the conference held in Oxford to mark the 300th anniversary of the brief existence of a 'Greek College' within Worcester College, John began to explore the life of Joseph Georgirenes in more detail and he became intrigued by the twists and turns of the westward travels of this unusual Greek priest. Following his retirement from the mastership of St Peter's College, Oxford in 2003, John was able to spend more time in pursuit of the archbishop and he spent long hours in the Bodleian Library, the National Archives and the British Library, as well as making research trips to Ikaria, Samos, Patmos, Mount Athos, Volterra and Brussels. By the time of his death, eight of the nine chapters had been drafted.

When I came to look through the chapters, I found that they were largely completed and the footnotes were almost all in place. The missing chapter would have dealt with Georgirenes' time in Constantinople. I turned to my colleague, Professor Jonathan Harris, an expert in the history of Byzantium, and he very kindly agreed to supply the chapter. Peter Lang International Academic Publishers agreed to publish the book in their series of Byzantine and Neo-Hellenistic Studies, edited by Professor David Ricks and Professor Andrew Louth, both of whom have been extremely considerate and helpful.

Then, in 2012 my editorial work on John's text took an unexpected turn when I received an email from a scholar, then at Churchill College, Cambridge, Dr John-Paul Ghobrial. He had come across Georgirenes in the records of the Archive of the Indies in Seville, when the archbishop was washed up on the shores of Buenos Aires following a shipwreck in 1694. This discovery opened up a new perspective on Georgirenes and Dr Ghobrial kindly agreed to write an epilogue to John's book which has provided yet another, and unexpected, context for this versatile archbishop.

What has sustained and encouraged me in this difficult enterprise of preparing John's book for publication, has been the tide of goodwill and affection for John which has always carried me forwards. Whenever I was stuck, or in need of expert advice, all those to whom I turned were willing to go out of their way to help me: Dr Charalambos Dendrinos has assisted with Greek texts and helped me to understand the practices of the Orthodox Church; Dr Nicholas Richardson (and his wife Dr Jenny Richardson) translated Georgirenes' flowery dedication to the *Description*; and Helen Hughes-Brock read and improved several chapters and provided essential help in locating items of modern Greek historiography. Georgirenes' two wills in the National Archives in Buenos Aires were located by Dr Juan Pablo Artinian, transcribed by Dr Ariel Morrone and translated for me by Christopher Dove. Dr Jenny Stratford provided generous hospitality in Paris and helped to locate, in the Bibliothèque Nationale, the two volumes which Georgirenes gave to Louis XIV. Ruth Stungo meticulously compared Henry Denton's English text of Georgirenes' *Description* with the French translation made by Antoine Galland, and provided many helpful insights and much expert botanical expertise. Professor John Miller read through the chapters dealing with Georgirenes' time in England and eliminated several mistakes. Dr Claire Daunton helped to secure the microfilm of Georgirenes' booklet in the Cambridge University Library and Dr Eric Southworth and David Hogarth brilliantly translated texts from several languages. Dr Christian Steer kindly took a number of photographs for the illustrations in the book and Professor Joel Rosenthal not only allowed me to make use of his sixteenth-century engraving of a Greek priest, but took the trouble to ensure that the publishers were supplied with a photograph of appropriate quality. Giles Darkes expertly drew the maps which greatly help to elucidate Georgirenes' *Description*. Nigel Hope, himself a classicist, did a brilliant job of copy-editing a complex manuscript and ironed out inconsistencies. Many of these people knew John and helped me for his sake. Without this help and support I could not have completed John's book, nor prepared it for publication. To them all I offer my heartfelt thanks.

Caroline Barron
August 2016

Abbreviations

For full details of these publications, see Bibliography.

Acta	CPF, *Acta Sacrae Congregationis*
BL	British Library
CJ	*Journals of the House of Commons, 1667–1687*
Coll.Fr.	*Collectanea Franciscana*
CPF	Congregatio de Propaganda Fide
CSPD	*Calendar of State Papers Domestic*
Description of the Present State	J. Georgirenes, *A Description of the Present State of Samos ...*
Galland, *Voyages inédits*	A. Galland, *Voyages inédits ...*, ed. M. Couvreur and D. Viviers
HMC	Historical Manuscripts Commission
LJ	*Journals of the House of Lords*
Nouv. Biogr. Gen.	*Nouvelle biographie générale*, ed. M. Hoefer, 46 vols
ODNB	*Oxford Dictionary of National Biography*
Oxford, Bodl. Lib.	Oxford, Bodleian Library
SC	CPF, *Scritture riferite nei Congressi*
SOCG	CPF, *Scritture originali riferite nelle Congregazioni Generali*
TNA	The National Archives

Introduction

More than 300 years later, it is hard to assess the motives which led Joseph Georgirenes to leave his home on the Greek island of Melos and embark on a series of journeys which would take him, ultimately, to the New World. Was it ambition, wanderlust, self-preservation, curiosity or a simple Christian faith? Perhaps all these, at different times, played a part in his odyssey. Traces of his travels can be found in the archives, scattered across three continents, and the story that has been pieced together here is both intriguing and incomplete.[1] But there are sufficient pieces now in place in the jigsaw of Joseph Georgerines' life to map his travels, if not yet to be able to be certain about his motivation.

Joseph was born in the middle of the seventeenth century on the poor island of Melos where the population of Orthodox Greeks had been substantially interspersed by colonies of Italian Catholics. The two communities intermarried and lived in comparative harmony. This early exposure to Catholicism may well have predisposed Joseph to a tolerant attitude towards those who followed the practices of the Western Church. He left Melos to become a monk on Mount Athos, a very significant centre of Orthodox monasticism and learning. Here he became a priest as well as a monk; he did not remain, but moved on to Constantinople where Patriarch Dionysius IV appointed him (with the necessary approval of the sultan) to be archbishop of the islands of Samos and Ikaria. He remained in these islands for five years until circumstances (about which Joseph is very circumspect) led him to give up his post (although not his title) and to retreat to the island of Patmos where he became the keeper of the Cave of

1 For a comparable traveller who found his way, at almost the same time as Georgirenes, from Baghdad to the Spanish colonies of the New World, see John-Paul A. Ghobrial, 'The Secret Life of Elias of Babylon and the Uses of Global Microhistory', *Past and Present*, ccxxii (2014), pp. 51–93.

the Revelation. In Constantinople Joseph had met scholars, merchants and diplomats from the countries of western Europe, and now he left Patmos to exploit those acquaintances and to seek alms and support from the wealthy kingdoms of Europe for the struggling Orthodox communities of the Ottoman Empire.

From Venice he moved to Florence, Volterra and Rome and then on to Marseilles and Paris where he met a group of intellectuals who were in touch with English scholars all of whom were interested to know more of the beliefs and practices of the Orthodox Church. It was at the behest of these men that Georgerines wrote his *Description of the Present State of Samos, Nicaria, Patmos and Mount Athos* in 'vulgar Greek', which was translated first into French and then into English and then translated once more from the English version back into French. Although the second French version was not published until the twenty-first century, the English translation appeared in 1677 and is reprinted here.[2]

In Italy and France, Joseph seems to have been accepted, with some hesitation, as a Catholic, but in London he was courted by the Anglicans, and Henry Compton, the Bishop of London, gave him permission to raise money to build a Greek church. This he succeeded in doing, and Joseph was responsible for the erection of the first Orthodox church in Greek Street in Soho. Although the church was completed and consecrated in 1677, its finances were shaky and the patriarch in Constantinople was unwilling to accept the compromises that Joseph had made to accommodate the services to the practices of the Church of England. Caught up in the tangles of the Popish Plot and dogged by imposters and deceitful servants, Joseph finally left England in 1682.

It might have been expected that he would return to Patmos, or to Mount Athos, but, instead, he turned south to Spain and then westwards across the Atlantic to Brazil and Argentina. Shipwrecked off Buenos Aires in 1694 he arrived there with few companions and meagre possessions. But he seems to have owned the small fishing vessel in which he arrived

2 See below pp. 235–66; for the French version, see Antoine Galland, *Voyages inédits*, i: *Smyrne ancienne et moderne*, ed. Manuel Couvreur and Didier Viviers (Paris, 2001), pp. 247–325.

and he brought with him the impressive *berat* from the sultan in which he had been appointed to the archbishopric of Samos nearly thirty years earlier. When, in the following year, Joseph believed himself to be on his deathbed he drew up his will but, in fact, he seems to have recovered and lived for a further seven years, or more. Perhaps he set off once more on his travels: his final burial place is unknown.

Joseph Georgirenes has not found favour with members of the Greek Orthodox community who have branded him as a 'philokatholikos' and a trimmer.[3] Some recent writers, however, have been more sympathetic to the complex situations in which Joseph found himself.[4] One may view him as an unstable believer, willing to bend with the strongest wind, whether that was Orthodox, Catholic or Anglican. Others may believe that his commitment to the Christian faith transcended differences in religious practice, and that Joseph considered the threat from insurgent Islam as more serious than the varying practices that divided Christians from one another. Was he, perhaps, an ecumenist ahead of his time?

However one views the twists and turns of Georgirenes' odyssey, he remains remarkable for the range of his contacts and his journeys. He must have been a man of some learning to engage the attention of the sophisticated theologians of Paris and Oxford, even if, in the end, they were baffled by his opaque theology. His book about Mount Athos and Samos remains an important source of information for the life of these communities in the seventeenth century. Although, by his own account, Georgirenes was not a good-looking man, he must have had considerable personal charm to survive, and indeed to succeed, in the courts of Rome,

3 See, for example, E. I. Stamatiades, *Epistolimaia diatribē peri Ioseph Georgeirēnou, Archiepiskopou Samou 1666–1671* (Samos, 1892). This account given by Georgirenes to the authorities of the Italian church in Volterra in 1674 was written down in Italian, hence it is possible that Georgirenes was unaware of the exact wording (as opposed to the general drift) which was extremely hostile to Greek Orthodoxy.

4 For example, C. Mettis, 'Josef Georgerines o Melios, proen Archiepiskopos Samou, idrytes tes protes Ellenikes koinotetas tou Londinou to 1677', *The Orthodox Herald* (magazine of the Greek Orthodox Archdiocese of Thyateira and Great Britain), vol. ix (1997), July/August, pp. 11–17; September/October, pp. 10–19; November/December, pp. 18–24.

Paris, London and Madrid. He overcame the problems caused by his unfamiliarity with local languages, and the machinations of duplicitous hangers-on, and managed to secure the documents and support he needed to travel ever westwards. Tossed on seas of controversy and conflict, he sailed onwards, a remarkable witness to the intrepid courage and curiosity of an island Greek.

CHAPTER 1

Melos: Between Two Cultures (1630s and 1640s)

The future Archbishop of Samos, Joseph Georgirenes was born some time in the mid-1630s on Melos, a small and poor Greek island precariously divided between Greek Orthodoxy and Roman Catholicism.[1] It has to be confessed that we know virtually nothing of his early years, though his own later insistence on recording his Melian origin whenever he could may permit us to infer that his childhood was happy enough. His baptismal name is not recorded: Ioseph, of course, is the monastic name he received at his profession, when it was usual to take a name beginning with the same letter as the baptismal name, in this case therefore perhaps Ioannes or Iakobos or Ioacheim, among other possibilities. Of his family we know almost nothing, except that in his will he tells us that he had four brothers named Lawrence, Martin, Nicholas and Peter.[2] Presumably the family belonged to the Orthodox majority, since Joseph was to make his way to Mount Athos and pursue a career in the Eastern Church. But their surname is worth a moment's speculation. The name Georgirenes, so spelled, is first found on the title-page of the archbishop's book, as translated by Henry Denton from Antoine Galland's French. That is, of course, to be taken as a standard Anglo-Latin transliteration of the Greek GEORGEIRENES – which, however, is not otherwise found in Greece, and was certainly not to

1 For Joseph's date of birth there are indications. He may have been about thirty in 1667: see p. 73. In 1677 in Oxford he was judged to be aged about forty. And in 1680 his hair and beard were still black: below, p. 213.

2 See below p. 221. One brother, Lawrence, appears to have accompanied Joseph to England, see below p. 172. The fact that Joseph remembered all four of his brothers in his will drawn up in 1695 suggests that he may have kept in contact with them.

be found in nineteenth-century Melos.[3] Indeed *Georgeirēnēs* is not a naturally Greek formation, despite its apparent union of two Greek elements, *geōrgos* or *Geōrgios*, 'farmer' or '(Saint) George', and *eirēnē* or *Eirēnē*, 'peace' or 'Irene'. If it is not typically Greek, the alternative in this meeting-point of East and West may be that, like so many Cretan names of the period, it is a transliteration of the familiar Italian: *Giorgerini*. And there is evidence that this was indeed the case, for we do in fact have examples of the archbishop's own preferred orthography, in his inscriptions in the manuscripts which he gave to Louis XIV and in the foundation inscription which he composed for his church in London. The archbishop's name is there given in the two donation inscriptions in the demotic genitive as Georgeirēnē, or in the foundation stone, in the atticized genitive case, as GEORGERINOU, evidently implying a nominative *Georgerinēs*.[4] Joseph's family name was, therefore, probably Georgerines, Hellenized from the Italian 'Giorgerini', but Denton's version of his name as Georgirenes is, however, retained here since it is the customary spelling of his name in all literature from the late seventeenth century. There may have been an Italian element within the population of Melos and it may be relevant that, according to the English traveller Bernard Randolph, who visited the island in 1664, the majority of Melian women were Italian speakers.[5] It is not unreasonable to speculate further that, Orthodox as the

3 E. I. Stamatiades, *Epistolimaia Diatribē peri Ioseph Georgeirēnou, Archiepiskopou Samou 1666–1671* (Samos, 1892), p. 11: there was no information about the family to be found in Melos.

4 See Figure 3; cf. below, p. 177. (The name is wrongly transcribed in my earlier publication, 'Archbishop Joseph Georgirenes and the Prehistory of the Greek College', in Peter M. Doll, ed., *Anglicanism and Orthodoxy 300 Years after the 'Greek College' in Oxford* (Oxford, 2006), at p. 91.) It may be noted also that the name of the archbishop's brother is given in a contemporary English patent warrant as 'Georgerini': TNA, SP44/40A, fol. 223; *CSPD, 1677–78*, p. 508; see below, p. 172. Moreover the archbishop's French friend and translator, Antoine Galland, whose own French orthography is almost impeccable, gives his name as *Georgerine*.

5 See below p. 11 for Italian bishops on Melos. Bernard Randolph, *The Present State of the Islands in the Archipelago* (Oxford, 1687), pp. 32–4. His French contemporary Thevenot, however, describes the population as 'presque tous Grecs'; he adds that the women affected to be unable to pronounce the letter 'l', *Voyages de Mr de Thevenot en Europe, Asie & Afrique*, 3rd edn, 3 pts in 5 vols, i: *Voyage du Levant* (Amsterdam, 1727),

family must have been, it may nevertheless have carried in its background and in its memory some lingering hint of an Italian Catholic past, a heavy inheritance in that divided island.

The island of Melos was, clearly, among the poorest of the many poor Greek islands in the seventeenth century. 'Damned of the damned' was the verdict of that indefatigable Turkish traveller Evliya Celebi on the infidel people of Melos, when he visited the island in the mid-seventeenth century. As a sight, it was 'commanding and beautiful', even dramatic: 'On its southern flank are white cliffs. Its mountainous parts are smooth red rocks.'[6] But to a Turk the natives were at best hostile; at worst, they were the most accursed of all the peoples of the Archipelago.

For Ottomans and Venetians alike, engaged for the past quarter-century in the seemingly endless struggle for the mastery of Crete (1645–69) – and the Ottomans at that time preparing for an all-out assault on the Mani – the significance of Melos lay in its harbour, opening to the north-west but well sheltered, with 'room for two hundred ships'. That has always been its significance: two and a half centuries later, 'Milos', says Lawrence Durrell, 'is a damnably dull hole of a place, with a magnificent bay so large that it could welcome the whole Allied Fleet both during the Crimean War and the war of 1914–18.'[7] A great flooded volcano, spent and slumbering, the island was a landfall familiar to any naval commander, merchant or pirate who rounded the three prongs of the Morea, braving the perils of Cape Malea to enter the Aegean Sea; it was equally familiar to those sailing from the opposite direction who needed a safe haven in

---

pp. 342–3. See also J. Pitton de Tournefort, *Relation d'un voyage du Levant, fait par ordre du Roy* (Lyon, 1717). References herein are to the English translation by John Ozell, *A Voyage into the Levant: Perform'd by Command of the late French King*, 2 vols (London, 1718), who says that in 1700 the population contained 'none but *Greeks*, except the Judge, and he's a *Turk*' (i, p. 118).

6 E. Celebi, *Odoiporiko stēn Ellada (1668–71)*, ed. Dimitris Loupes (Athens, 1994), pp. 260f. On Evliya Celebi, see J. Freely, *Istanbul: The Imperial City* (London, 1998), pp. 221–36. See also below, p. 11 n. 17.

7 L. Durrell, *The Greek Islands* (London, 1978), p. 234. Cf. J. T. Bent, *The Cyclades, or Life among the Insular Greeks* (London, 1885), ed. G. Brisch (Oxford, 2002), p. 32: the harbour 'could hold all the navies of the world within it'.

which to await calm weather and a favourable wind. Not surprisingly, then, as Evliya Celebi recalled, its ownership was continually in dispute between the Ottomans and Venice. Nor did it serve only as a base for national navies. Bernard Randolph, who visited the island shortly before Celibi's visit, observed that: 'The Privateers had made this place their chief Rendezvous for several years, to almost the ruine of the Island.'[8] The identity of some, at least, of these western privateers is made clear by Thomas Coke, who visited Melos in November 1664:

> In the morning the wind continuing we saw Milo & Antimilo ... after dinner came to an anchor, where were 10 Corsale of Malta the one which [was] called Fama del Mare of 24 guns was commanded by one Cavaliere Du Tomps a knight of Malta a Frenchman, the other was a small barke of 8 guns. They had taken two good prizes off Alexandria, bound for Egypt to go to Mecha. There was an other Corsale with the banner of the Great Duke [of Tuscany], ... [added later:] We stayed 3 days at Milo.[9]

Half a century later, the French traveller Tournefort, chief botanist to Louis XIV who sent him to the Aegean, noted that though the corsairs had been reduced, the economy of nearby Argentière (Kimolos) had suffered still further as a direct result:

> This Island is become wretchedly poor ever since the King [of France] put down the *French* Corsairs in the *Levant*. *Argentière* used to be the place of their Rendezvous, where they spent in horrible Debaucheries the Booty they took from the *Turks*; to the great advantage of the Ladies, who are none of the coyest nor ugliest; ... the Women have no other Employment but making Love and Cotton Stockings.[10]

And then, on Melos itself, 'The Ladies likewise made no ill hand of it; they are as arrant Coquettes as at *Argentière*.'[11]

8 Randolph, *Present State of the Islands*, pp. 33–8.

9 London, BL, Add. MS 10130, fols 10v–11.

10 Tournefort, *A Voyage into the Levant*, i, p. 112. The purge was evidently incomplete, for Tournefort adds that the Turkish itinerant judge 'dares not talk big, for fear the Inhabitants should send him packing on board some Corsair of *Malta*'.

11 Ibid. p. 117.

Melos was no stranger to drama of this or any other kind. Its turbulent history – Byzantine, then part of the post-1204 Genoese duchy of Naxos, Byzantine again, Genoese again, then a Venetian possession, and since 1566 an insecurely Ottoman dominion – had left its Christian population a troubled religious heritage which perhaps meant little to most of those who passed by to try their fortune in the Archipelago or to take their business to the mainland ports of Smyrna and Constantinople.[12] But close and frequent contact between the islanders and western visitors had led a very few to stay longer and even to become settlers. Long established or newly arrived, the population was identifiably divided along religious lines, an Orthodox majority alongside a Catholic minority. Each group had its own bishop, the Catholic serving a mainly Greek-speaking flock, but with an admixture of Italians and French. From 1642 till 1662 or later, the Catholic see was held by one Antonio Serra.[13] For much of the time, but by no means always, the two religious groups maintained reasonably good relations. In 1655, for instance, the French traveller Thevenot reported that

> L'Eveque Latin celebre dans une chapelle qui est jointe avec une Eglise des Grecs; cet Eveque a beaucoup de decimes, qu' il partage avec l'Eveque Grec, en prenant deux tiers, & l'Eveque Grec l'autre tiers: l'Eveque Grec a plusieurs Eglises bien baties & bien entretenues, & plusieurs Pretres: les Habitans de cette Ile sont presque tous Grecs, qui sont fort a leur aise, civils, mais tres mechans, & perfides.[14]

> [The Latin bishop celebrates in a chapel which is held jointly with the Greek Church. This bishop has many tithes which he shares with the Greek bishop, he taking two parts and the Greek bishop the third part. The Greek bishop has several churches, well built and well maintained, and several priests. The inhabitants of this island are almost all Greeks who are greatly at their ease, civil but very ill-natured and dishonest.]

12 Both Randolph, *Present State of the Islands*, p. 33, and the French traveller Thevenot a decade earlier, *Voyage du Levant*, p. 343, assert that Melos was rarely visited by the Turks, provided that the taxes were duly dispatched to the pasha in Chios.

13 See P. B. Gams, *Series Episcoporum Ecclesiae Catholicae* (Regensburg, 1873–86; repr. Graz, 1957), p. 449, for the few names known from 1349 onwards.

14 Thevenot, *Voyage du Levant*, pp. 342f.; cf. Tournefort, *A Voyage into the Levant*, i, p. 119: 'The Episcopal Church ... was heretofore a *Greek* chapel, sold to the *Latins*'.

But there was an undercurrent of hostility between the two communities. Twenty years later, in 1675, John Covel, chaplain to the English ambassador at Constantinople, noted that many of the 'natives' were Roman Catholics and that about twenty or twenty-five of the most important families were of that 'persuasion'.[15] Apparently these leading men collected the dues owing to the Pasha but kept a significant percentage for themselves. Two years previously, Covel was told, one Georgio, 'a popular man amongst the Greeks yet a man of no great learning nor birth', had collected the dues instead, thereby saving the taxpayers as much as one third of the usual payment. The thwarted Catholics were outraged, and threatened to kill Georgio unless he paid them their usual profit. The commons rose in his defence, assigned him a bodyguard twenty or thirty strong, his constant companions, and gave him a gold chain which 'this proud loggerhead' wore to taunt the enemy. The next time the pasha came

> the great ones complain'd … that Georgio was a factious fellow, little than a rebell to the G. Sr. [Grand Signior]. The [Pasha] sends for him and the fool had the pride to come with his chain. The [Pasha] brought him [and] 8 or 10 more to St[amboul] and put them in the G. Sr's. Bagno; soon after by the Vicier's order he was hang'd at Casimbasha wth his Chain about his neck.

That was in 1675.[16] Only four years later, according to the account of a Frenchman, P. Sauger, the Catholic element attempted a curiously parallel takeover. Ioannes Kapsis, who had served as a fo'c'sle officer with the French fleet, made himself lord of the island, and was invested with a golden chain about his neck by the bishop, Dom. Antonio Camillo, in his cathedral, while the people roared their approval. Kapsis took up residence in the

15 London, BL, Add. MS 22914, fol. 65. The date is not altogether clear. The note occupies the upper half of the first page of a single *bifolium* mounted immediately following the first section of the volume, which records 'Our voyage to Nicomedia, Nice, &c', starting on 16 Feb. 1677 and breaking off at Chios on 14–16 May. On Covel, who had been chaplain since 1 January 1671, see E. Leedham-Green, in *ODNB*, xiii, pp. 726f.; it appears that Covel had hoped to be appointed secretary, rather than chaplain, to the ambassador, Sir Daniel Harvey.

16 BL, Add. MS 22914, fol. 65.

best house in the island, and surrounded himself with an armed guard of twenty-five, and double that number when he went out. He was popular, and his rule lasted three years (1677–80). It would have lasted longer had he not made the mistake of trusting the Turks. When word of him reached the Porte, plans were made for his removal. Three galleys were sent 'to collect taxes', and to deliver an effusive message of greeting from the sultan. Suspecting nothing, Kapsis boarded one of the galleys with only twelve of his guards and was at once arrested, exchanging (as Sauger put it) his golden chain for iron fetters. Ioannes suffered the same fate as Georgio: he was executed at the Bagno in 1680.[17] Tournefort, visiting Melos in 1700, was told the same story.[18]

By the time of Tournefort's visit the balance of ecclesiastical prosperity in Melos was no longer as Thevenot had observed it half a century before. Each community had its own bishop still; but the Catholic, who had depended on Candia in Venetian Crete, for much of his revenue, had become so impoverished since the Turkish conquest of that island in 1669 that his staff was reduced to a single priest, all he could afford out of the pension which the French king provided to the desperately poor Catholic hierarchy of the Aegean. 'The last Bishop died so necessitous, that he had pawn'd the Chalice, Mitre, and all the Ornaments of his Church: he had starv'd to death had not the King allow'd him a Pension.' The Orthodox bishop, in contrast, Tournefort found to be rich.[19] Perhaps he had managed to take advantage of Catholic political misjudgements such as Bishop Camillo's support of the upstart Kapsis to acquire rights to the whole of the

17 P. Sauger, account written in French in 1698, tr. A. M. Karales, as *Historia tōn archaiōn doukōn kai tōn loipōn hēgemonōn tou Aigaiou pelagous* (Hermoupolis, Syros, 1878), p. 199. For the Bagno as part of the sultan's very extensive prison system, situated near Tershane, the Kapitan Pasha's shipyard and naval arsenal at Kasimpasha on the northern, Pera, side of the Golden Horn, opposite the Phanar, see the nearly contemporary account of Evliya Celebi (Evliya Efendi *alias* Mehemmed Zilli ibn Dervis), *Seyahatnamesi*, tr. J. von Hammer as *Narrative of Travels in Europe, Asia and Africa in the Seventeenth Century*, vol. i, pts 1–2 (London, 1834–46; repr. New York, 1968), pp. 43–9, esp. 44.

18 Tournefort, *A Voyage into the Levant*, i, pp. 114–34, esp. pp. 115f.

19 Ibid. pp. 119–20, noting the discrepancy with Thevenot's account.

tithe income, not only the one-third which he had enjoyed in Thevenot's time.[20] Although the events described here belong to the last third of the century, they are symptoms of the long-established and intermittent, but deep-seated, tension between Catholic and Orthodox, whose roots extend back far earlier.

Life in seventeenth-century Melos was uncomfortable for other reasons too. Tournefort described the capital, now the ghost-town of Zephyria:

> This town contains near 5000 souls, and is prettily built, but abominable nasty; for when they make an erection of a house, they begin with the hogsty, beneath an arch even with the ground, or a little lower, and always fronting the street: in a word, it is the jakes of the whole home. The ordure that gathers there, joined to the salt-marshes on the sea-side, the mineral exhalations of the island, the scarcity of good water, so infect the air, that it breeds very dangerous distempers.[21]

Nonetheless, he goes on to say that the 'prettily built' houses are better than you would find in Candia: two-storey terraces, their masonry 'well performed'.

Outside the capital life was perhaps healthier, and income levels lower. It is idle to speculate about the Georgirenes family's standing in the Melian community, except that, as Orthodox, they are unlikely to have been numbered among the leading families. If their socio-economic position is otherwise unclear, the question of their address – coast, capital or country – is even more obscure. Nor does it matter. Short of his running away to sea, the island was neither so extensive nor so populous that the limited range of opportunities for betterment that it offered would be likely to remain for long undiscovered by Joseph or his parents. Randolph found the men of Melos 'industrious'.[22] Certainly there was plenty for them to do. The economy was based on agriculture, the universal Greek crops of olives,

20 Even before the fall of Crete, in 1658 an unnamed Catholic Bishop of Melos had been killed by the Turks, presumably in retaliation for some pro-Venetian initiative. Gams, *Series Episcoporum Ecclesiae Catholicae*, p. 449. This in itself might have led to confiscation of revenue and to the decline of the bishopric.

21 Tournefort, *A Voyage into the Levant*, i, p. 116.

22 Randolph, *Present State of the Islands*, p. 33.

grapes, figs and grain, together with cotton, and here encouraged by the fertile volcanic soil, and on the island's rich mineral deposits of salt, sulphur, alum, pumice, obsidian, and iron ore.[23] And the sea was still full of fish. Joseph had a brother, Lawrence, a layman who, in later life, was engaged in the fish trade; and this may well have been the family's occupation.[24] That is the only hint. Moreover the life of the sea provided other opportunities also. Tournefort observed that the 'Miliotes' were good sailors and could make a decent living as pilots.[25]

Contemporary western travellers may permit us a glimpse of Joseph's mother, at any rate in her youth. Randolph, for instance, notes that 'The women are equal in beauty with any in the Archipelago, and pretend to exceed them in breeding'[26] – in both of which qualities, however, Tournefort found them lacking when he visited the island a generation later:

> The ladies ... are as arrogant coquettes as at *Argentière*: they all make use of the powder of a sea-plant to beautify themselves; it gives a ruddiness to their cheeks, but it soon goes off and spoils the complexion, as well as destroys the upper skin. The ladies of both islands follow the same dress; it is a very disadvantageous one to the fair sex, and must needs look very odd in the eyes of all foreigners: it utterly mis-shapes them, and represents the prettiest of them with monstrous mill-post legs, fit for nothing but to be painted on skreens or fans.[27]

Two centuries later, Theodore Bent lent more towards Randolph, with an admiring description of the traditional dress of the island women.[28] On Sundays they affected a jacket of purple silk edged with fur, and a satin skirt spangled with white flowers, a stomacher of silvered brocade and a lace-edged silk gauze apron. Their padded headdress carried a muslin handkerchief, surrounded by gold lace. A pair of 'dainty little shoes' completed

23 See A. Philippson, *Die griechischen Landschaften*, 4 vols (Frankfurt a.M., 1950–59), iv: *Das Aegaeische Meer und seine Inseln*, pp. 185–94; Tournefort, *A Voyage into the Levant*, i, pp. 122–32.

24 See below, p. 172.

25 Tournefort, *A Voyage into the Levant*, i, p. 117.

26 Randolph, *Present State of the Islands*, p. 33.

27 Tournefort, *A Voyage into the Levant*, i, pp. 117–18.

28 Bent, *The Cyclades*, p. 31.

the ensemble – a very different impression from Tournefort's caricature. On weekdays the dress was simpler: a headdress known as the *kourli*, an intricately folded and tied veil of white muslin framed by two hanging curls on either side, the dress blue, sometimes with a stomacher. The men of the island evidently attracted less attention.

Whatever the visual appearance of the island, with its peculiar fragrances, Melos could sometimes be a frightening place for a child. Even in the nineteenth century Theodore Bent could find that 'all sorts of old superstitions survive'.[29] Many of these centred on cures for the legion of diseases to which the islanders were subject. There were spells to drive these evil spirits elsewhere – into animals, or trees, or simply over the cliff. Or a piece of the victim's clothing might be left on a stone in the hope that the disease could be tricked into migrating into the stone. Or a string might be tied about the neck of a fever patient, and then tied around a tree-trunk with appropriate spells designed to bind the illness to the tree. For a child, there was the risk of being thought emaciated, perhaps the work of malevolent Nereids who lurked around every corner. The remedy lay in a visit to a chapel dedicated to the epiphany of the Mother of God at Klima, near the modern capital at Plaka. Here was once the scene of a kill-or-cure ritual, already made illegal before Bent's visit, but no doubt still practised in Georgirenes' day. 'Conventional' medicine having proved ineffective, the child would be stripped naked and placed on the marble altar for the night. If it survived, then it could not have been Nereid-struck after all; the parents, relieved, if still baffled, would take it home for further nourishment. But if it died, that clearly was the will of God. Other rituals were more overtly pagan. For instance at the building of a new house it was usual to kill a bird and on the foundation-stone smear a cross in its blood. More terrifying, in Melos and Kimolos more than anywhere else in Greece, belief in vampires still flourished – not the sanitized shades whom Odysseus conjured, thirsty for nothing more than the blood of sheep, but spectres who stalked the earth at dead of night to strangle men as well as

29 Ibid. pp. 22f., 32, 36f.

beasts and to drink their blood.[30] By the nineteenth century a calming remedy had been devised, a libation of vinegar and hot water poured on to the grave with accompanying prayers for the compassion of God. But Bent recalls that the old remedy still held sway in the northern fastnesses of Andros where the practice was to disinter and burn the suspect's corpse, and scatter the ashes to the wind. Even in Melos in his day a vestige of the old ritual survived, as an exorcism not for vampires but for the dead who still cursed the living: the corpse was exhumed, the heart cut out and burned and the ashes scattered, the rest of the body put into a sack and cast into the sea – which, on one notable occasion, boiled obligingly. It might have been the world of the brothers Grimm, terrifying to an imaginative child.

We do not know much about the opportunities for education in the Melos of Georgirenes' boyhood. As elsewhere, such schooling as was available will have been in the hands of the churches. Martin Crusius, the learned professor at Tübingen who, in the sixteenth century, quizzed the Greek visitors to the University, noted that this was the case.[31] One visitor who stood out as more unusual was Iakobos Meloites, a forty-five-year-old born in Patmos and raised in Melos, who arrived in Tübingen by a circuitous route on 14 December 1587 bearing letters of introduction from a string of Orthodox patriarchs – Constantinople, Alexandria, Antioch, and Bulgaria with the Balkans – to say nothing of the King of Poland, or of the Cretan Constantine Corniactus at Leopolis in Russia, a member of the Greek congregation there. Meloites was full of information about the Greek islands – lovely but barren Patmos, its extensive property in Crete supplying the needs of the 150 monks, beyond what their little gardens could produce; Samos, well watered, fruitful and beautiful, uninhabited until a decade ago but now

30 For a lively modern account, see G. Horton, *Home of Nymphs and Vampires: The Isles of Greece* (Indianapolis, 1929), esp. pp. 109–21 (vampires), 122–34 (Nereids).

31 See *M. Crusius, Graecae et Latinae Linguae, cum Oratoria, in Acad. Tybing. Professoris, Annalium Suevicorum Dodecas tertia, ab anno Christi MCCXIII usque ad MDXCIIII annum perducta, adiecto paraleipomeno variorum plurimarumque rerum libro: in quo hodiernum quoque Turcicum Bellum, a 1590 usque ad 1596 Domini annum diligenter describitur* (Frankfurt, 1596), pp. 766–838; conveniently summarized by P. G. Zerlentos, *Sēmeiōmata peri Hellēnōn ek tōn Martinou Krousiou Souēbikōn Chronikōn, Historikē Bibliothēkē tōn apo Halōseōs Chronōn* (Athens, 1922).

resettled; Melos with its two centres of population, the castle, and Chora the capital, its agricultural output recalling that of Crete, and a major exporter of sea-salt. 'In these islands, and others too,' Meloites reported, 'there are little schools for boys, where they learn to read and discuss the Psalter and other texts.' He added that in many islands Italian was taught, to facilitate trade with Venice. Himself brought up in Melos, Meloites may safely be trusted when he includes that island in his general report on education in the Archipelago.[32] There is no direct evidence that the school known to Meloites in 1587 was still open half a century later, but there is no reason to doubt it. Moreover, the year 1645, when Joseph was probably some ten years old, saw the erection of a self-consciously fine double church of Christ and the Virgin (the date is to be seen over the door) in what was the chief town of the island, Chora, now renamed Zephyria. Even if the Orthodox school had not existed continuously, the consecration of this grand new church would be an obvious occasion to restore the provision.

The Orthodox Church was not the only possible source of education. Catholic missionaries were active here, both Jesuit and Capuchin, and for them the foundation of schools was an obvious means to long-term influence. Not many years before Joseph's birth Capuchin missionaries had entered on a sustained campaign among the Greeks which within a century was to lead many bishops and archbishops, and not a few patriarchs, to Rome, along with a multitude of Orthodox priests and monks and some tens of thousands of their flock.[33] To the benighted and stagnant faithful

32 Crusius, p. 805; cf. Zerlentos, pp. 25–8. If Crusius judged his age aright, he will himself have been of school age in the 1560s. See also H. Omont, 'Martin Crusius, George Dousa et Theodore Zygomalas', *Revue des Etudes Grecques* x (1897), pp. 66–70.

33 For the history of the Capuchin mission to the Greeks, see Ignazio da Seggiano, *L'opera dei Cappuccini per l'unione dei Cristiani nel vicino Oriente durante il secolo XVII, Orientalia Christiana Analecta* 163 (Rome, 1962). An earlier account, especially useful for Melos, is by Clemente da Terzorio, *Le missioni dei Minori Cappuccini*, 10 vols (Rome, 1913–38), iv, pp. 308–24. See also Rocco da Cesinale, *Storia dei missioni dei Cappuccini*, 3 vols (Paris and Rome, 1867–73). The primary source is the series of reports and other correspondence, mainly sent by the prefects and wardens based in Constantinople, to the *Sacra Congregatio de Propaganda Fide*, published

they brought the freshness of a newly opened window. On a practical level, they were better physicians and surgeons than could be found locally; skating easily over theological difficulties, they brought with them the new learning in philosophy, in mathematics and in astronomy. It was a heady mixture. The Capuchin initiative was almost exclusively French, and particularly from the province of Paris. It began early in 1623 with an appeal by the Parisian Père Pacifique to the *Sacra Congregatio de Propaganda Fide* (who knew him as Padre Pacifico della Scala) to send missionaries to win over the separated churches of the East. The Holy Congregation agreed at once, within three months plans were being made, and within three years an advance party of four, all from Paris, arrived in Constantinople with a letter of introduction from the French king to his ambassador there, instructing him to find them a house; two more Capuchins went on to Sidon.[34] Two years later again, on 1 December 1628, the energetic co-prefects wrote from Paris to the superior whom they had appointed to Chios, giving him his instructions: to study the local language, to preach, to hear confessions, and to teach the young –

> Nous mettons aussi l'instruction de la jeunesse entre les fonctions plus profitables. C'est pourquoy nous exhortons grandement les Peres, que vous y destinez, d'embrasser ce travail avec joye pour l'amour de notre Seigneur, se souvenans de ces parolles: *Sinite parvulos venire ad me, talium enim est regnum coelorum.*[35]
>
> [We also consider the instruction of the young among the most profitable activities. It is for this reason that we especially exhort the fathers, whom you intend to deploy

in extenso and in chronological order by Ignazio da Seggiano, 'Documenti inediti sull' apostolato dei Minori Cappucini nel vicino Oriente (1623–1683)', *Coll. Fr.* xviii (1948), pp. 118–244; xxii (1952), pp. 339–86; xxiii (1953), pp. 297–338). It must, of course, be remembered that these communications are designed to put the work of the Capuchins in the best possible light, and to justify the expenditure on it provided by Rome as well as by the French wing of the order.

34 *Coll.Fr.* xviii, pp. 118–25 and Docs I–III, cited as from *Sacra Congegatio. de Propaganda Fide, Archivio* (Rome, 1576–1680), respectively *Scritture riferite*, vol. 383, fol. 1; ibid. fol. 110; vol. 101, fol. 288.

35 *Coll.Fr.* xviii, pp. 127–31 and Doc. V, in Archivio generale dei Fr.Min.Capp.Rome.

> there, to embrace this work with joy for the love of Our Lord, remembering these words 'Suffer little children to come unto me, for theirs is the kingdom of heaven'.]

How long did Melos have to wait for a Catholic School?

By 1631 two more permanent stations had been established, in Smyrna and Naxos as well as in Constantinople and Chios, with the help of Kyrillos Kontares (intermittently Patriarch 1620–38), who was himself to go over to Rome in 1638. An important development in the context of the Catholic mission to the Archipelago was that at the request of the Greek Metropolitan of Paronaxia (that is, Paros and Naxos) one of the two Capuchins sent began to preach in demotic Greek. Two years later the two prefects were able to report to the Holy Congregation that the four stations were now secure, and that 'our fathers have begun to visit the islands of the Archipelago' – they mention invitations from the bishops of Syros and Andros – 'and there preach the word of God and hear confessions, to the great joy of the inhabitants'.[36] In 1636 the Capuchin superior at Constantinople in a report to Cardinal Antonio Barberini, prefect of the Holy Congregation, declared explicitly that in his two schools at Galata and Pera, the pupils were 'la gioventà del nostro rito *con alcuni del Greco*' [youth of our rite with some of the Greek]: the Capuchins expected to educate – and hoped to convert – the Orthodox, not only Catholics; and this was the case in Chios also. Extending their work to the islands of the Archipelago, they had begun to preach in Paros, where the demand for their words outstripped the capacity of the churches to contain the congregations they attracted; and Greek Orthodox priests and monks, though in the guise of laymen, were willing to make confession to them and to receive the sacrament of penance.[37] This, then, was the position about the time of the future Archbishop Joseph's birth in Melos – if, that is (and it is an important caveat), the somewhat rosy view of their own achievements promulgated by the Capuchins may be believed. But it is noticeable that Melos is not yet mentioned in their reports. Indeed, when in 1641 Father Thomas of Paris sent a very full

36 Ibid. pp. 135–9 and Docs VII and VIII, respectively Arch. Segreto Vaticano, MS Borghese I, vol. 469, fols 173–4; Bibl. Vatican., Cod. Barberini Lat. 4605, fol. 99.

37 Ibid. pp. 141–3 and Doc. X, CPF, *SC*. vol. 153, fol. 215.

account of the activities of the mission in Greece to Cardinal Barberini, he mentioned schools in Constantinople, Chios, Naxos, Syros, Andros and Smyrna; Melos is conspicuous by its continuing absence.[38] It is of course possible that, as occurred at Syros and Andros where the schools received pupils from Tenos and Athens respectively, Melian pupils may have travelled to be educated in Naxos, or even in Andros or Syros. It would have been worth the journey. But the first positive evidence for a Capuchin school in Melos belongs to the period when Joseph had already left the island.

Since Joseph was in later life so careful to preserve the memory of his Melian origin, he may have made a point of keeping up his local contacts, and the course of his subsequent career makes it worthwhile to follow a little further the story of Catholic schools at Melos. In 1661 the Capuchins at last established a permanent station on Melos, and in 1665 built there a convent consecrated on 25 June that year and dedicated to St John Baptist and St Anthony of Padua; a decade later it was claimed to be the only church in Turkey that the Capuchins had built *de novo*. In their report to Rome they did not mention an inconvenient aspect, noted by the traveller Randolph who had visited the island the previous year, namely that the convent was built with generous contributions from the locally based privateers, no doubt in the hope of saving their souls.[39] In 1670 the island at last appears by name in the annals of the Congregatio de Propaganda Fide, when Father Alessio da Sommovoire, in answer to a detailed list of specific questions, wrote from Smyrna and reported that at Melos the cathedral was at present in the hands of a vicar apostolic, Mgr Dom Giovanni Antonio Camillo, subsequently confirmed as bishop. Significantly, Melos appears to have

38 Ibid. pp. 178–93 and Doc. XV. Father Thomas gives the numbers of pupils as twenty in Galata (including some Greeks and English, and an Armenian), forty at Pera, sixty in Chios, an average of thirty in Naxos, in Syros 'very many' enjoying a broad curriculum, 'many' in Andros (including some from Athens), solely Greek clientele at Kusadasi, and an unspecified number at Smyrna.

39 See the report sent from Smyrna on 10 March 1675 by the highly experienced Father Urban, who had first come to Greece in 1648 and had served several terms as superior in Chios and Constantinople: *Coll.Fr.* xxiii, p. 320 and Doc. XXXIII, CPF, *SC*, vol. 454, fols 360ff. See also da Seggiano, *L'opera dei Cappuccini*, p. 90; Randolph, *Present State of the Islands*, p. 33.

had the fewest Catholics among its population of any of the other eight Capuchin stations, though it is impossible to reconcile Alessio's low figure – 'no more than eight or ten' (compared with 400 given for Naxos and more than 550 in Syros, and in Chios as many as 6,000) – with the number of Catholics given by Covel in 1675, 'about 20 or 30 families'.[40] The size of the Catholic population is not the only subject on which the Capuchins and the Protestant Covel appear at odds. In their reports to Rome, both earlier and later, the Capuchin prefects and wardens and the local superiors were keen to assert their overwhelming popularity among the Greeks they came to save. Father Urban, warden in 1675, was no exception. Of Melos he wrote that the Greeks there – the Orthodox, that is – allowed the missionaries to preach in all their churches, which in Lent they did every evening, going round the churches in turn: 'the Greek metropolitan is our great friend, and all the Greeks there wish us well'. That was the very year in which Covel wrote of unconscionable greed and oppression on the part of the Catholic minority, demanding a high premium on the tax they collected for the Turks, and calling down the wrath of the Kapitan Pasha on the Greeks when they demurred.[41] The two accounts are not, strictly speaking, incompatible; they certainly leave a very different impression of the relations between the adherents of the two rites.

Although the Capuchins had established their station in Melos by 1661, their school there is first mentioned only in 1670. How long it had been in existence, we cannot say: we have seen that it appears not yet to have been founded in 1641, but that was a generation ago. Father Alessio reported that the school, housed in the new convent, had about a score of pupils – that, as against twice the number in Syros, and thirty more in Naxos, where the Jesuits also maintained a school with twenty-three or so pupils, to say nothing of Chios, where Jesuit and Capuchin schools each boasted a hundred pupils.[42] The Melian school was evidently in scholarly hands;

40 *Coll.Fr.*, loc. cit. (previous note), pp. 373–86, esp. p. 374, and Doc. XXIX, CPF, *SC*, vol. 429, fols 81ff. For Covel's figure, see p. 10.

41 *Coll.Fr*, xxiii, pp. 318–24, esp. p. 320, and Doc. XXXIII, *Arch. Prop. Fid.*, *Scr.rif.*, vol. 454, fols 360ff.; Covel, in BL, Add. MS 22914, fol. 65.

42 For Alessio, see *Coll.Fr.* xxiii, p. 384, and n. 37 above; for 1641, see above and n. 35.

for the superior, Father Dominique, a fifty-one-year-old from Amiens who had served in Greece, though not necessarily in Melos, for the past eighteen years, was a theologian, now supported by a recently arrived young colleague of twenty-eight, Father Henri from Rethel, and a lay brother aged thirty-seven, Humile from Creil. They taught to the same syllabus as the more populous establishment in Constantinople: reading and writing, Christian doctrine and good behaviour, mathematics (the abacus), Latin and Italian. Five years later, when Father Urban encountered the French ambassador Nointel at Melos on the return leg of his triumphal voyage to Jerusalem, of which more later, he found that the school had split into a Latin and a Greek division: 'e numerosa in nostra chiesa ('and there are many people in our church').[43] It may be that the split was related to the hostility between Catholics and Orthodox of which Covel wrote. More probably, the change was dictated by the nature of the population of Melos, where Father Urban found a score of 'Latin' families and several Frenchmen, as well as 'Latin' corsairs coming and going daily. Certainly the arrangement lasted, for when Tournefort visited the island in 1700, he noted that not only had the Capuchins undertaken responsibility for Catholic education, as elsewhere in the Aegean, but that at that time there were still two French priests, of whom 'one keeps a School for *Greek*, the other for *Italian*'.[44] But in the course of a punitive expedition of the Kapitan Pasha, very likely a sequel to the Kapsis affair of 1677, the Capuchins had been expelled at three hours' notice and their church burned, perhaps as a punishment for their connections with the privateers. By Tournefort's time, however, the church had been rebuilt with financial support from Louis XIV as well as more from the privateers. The convent and its church, on the road from the old town to the port, still retains something of the air of a fortress, its curtilage protected by a high wall. By the late seventeenth century there may have been yet another school. When Pietro Coronelli came to compile his *Isolario dell' atlante Veneto* for publication in 1696, he observed that the Latin Bishop of Melos, though reduced to the support of a single priest and serving a congregation of not more than a hundred, nevertheless maintained

43 *Coll.Fr*, xxiii, p. 320.

44 Tournefort, *A Voyage in the Levant*, p. 117.

a Catholic school at his cathedral of St Peter.[45] Given the closeness in date of Coronelli's account (1696) and Tournefort's visit (1700), it seems likely that the bishop's Latin school operated alongside the Capuchins' Greek school, and was significantly different from theirs, perhaps in its syllabus, perhaps in the ages of its pupils. It is possible also, since the see predated the arrival of the Capuchins, that the bishop's school was older than theirs, perhaps already in existence in Joseph's childhood.

So the future Archbishop of Samos, who was later to be so comfortable in working alongside the Western Church, may have been the product of the Catholic school run by the Latin bishop. It seems unlikely that he was educated by the Capuchins, at any rate in Melos. For though their mission to the Greeks began in 1628, it appears that a permanent station on Melos was not established until 1661, by which time the young Joseph had grown up and gone; and there is in fact no direct evidence for a Capuchin school on the island before 1670. If Joseph did indeed receive any substantial amount of formal education in his early years, it will have been either in a school run by the Orthodox Church or, if in a Catholic school, then either in his bishop's diocesan school or in a Capuchin school overseas. Alternatively, he may simply have enjoyed some limited or informal teaching at the hands of his Orthodox priest – provided, that is (and it was not always the case), that the latter was himself literate. The truth is we have no more idea what formal education, if any, Joseph received on Melos than we have of any other aspect of his childhood. We know only that his early years were passed against the background of a society always uneasy with itself, sometimes torn apart by confessional loyalties, sometimes rising above them in their consciousness of a shared Christian community, within an empire whose masters showed little interest in the niceties of sectarian distinction among the infidels.

45 *Isolario dell' atlante Veneto, del P.Coronelli, Parte 1* (Venice, 1696), p. 240; ibid. p. 227, Capuchin school on Andros, the pupils exclusively Greek; cf. pp. 233, 238, Capuchins on Tinos and Syros; Tournefort, *A Voyage into the Levant*, p. 117; Randolph, *Present State of the Islands*, p. 33; Sauger, tr. Karales, *Historia ton Archaion*, p. 199. See also Zerlentos, *Sēmeiōmata*, pp. 20–3; A. E. Vakalopoulos, *Historia tou Neou Hellēnismou*, 4 vols (Thessaloniki, 1961–73), B.I, p. 250.

CHAPTER 2

Mount Athos (1650s)

Joseph Georgirenes seems, early in his life, to have manifested that *Wanderlust*, or spirit of adventure, which was to be a marked characteristic of his later career. He left Melos for the Holy Mountain of Athos. Here, at the heart of Orthodoxy, many of the twenty 'ruling monasteries' of Mount Athos found themselves accepting an influx of novices, and among them in about 1655 the young Georgirenes. When he wrote his *Description of the Present State of Samos, Nicaria, Patmos, and Mount Athos* some twenty years later, he allowed almost nothing of his personal experiences to creep into the text.[1] But that he did indeed make his way to the Holy Mountain we are assured by his Oxford translator, Henry Denton, who knew him in Constantinople in the mid 1660s: 'In all these places he liv'd, and writes nothing, but what he saw, or what he receiv'd from the constant Tradition of the places.'[2] And, indeed, his retranslator and close friend Antoine Galland records that he spent six years on Mount Athos.[3]

For the twenty monasteries and for their dependencies, the seventeenth century appears to have been a time of consolidation and slow reconstruction, in which, however, the gap between the poor and the more prosperous

1 Written 1676, licensed 1677, published 1678. Georgirenes' account of Mount Athos occupies pp. 85–112, and see Map 2, p. 382. The account was also reprinted with slight variation as a two-sided broadsheet, of which a copy is to be found inserted into BL, Add. MS 22912, fols 339v–340r. It carries neither the name of the printer nor the date or place of publication.

2 Ibid. 'To the Reader', fol. A 10v (immediately before p. 1).

3 Galland, *Voyages inédits*, p. 249; cf. E. Legrand, *Bibliographie Hellénique ... des ouvrages publiés par des Grecs au dix-septième siècle*, 5 vols (Paris, 1894–1903), ii, p. 346.

houses became even more glaring than previously.[4] By the mid-seventeenth century the oldest of the monasteries had already existed in something like their current form, as walled settlements of closely integrated communities, for some 800 years, insulated from any substantial change by their remoteness and by their devotion to their royal or aristocratic founders' statutes, their *typika*. Earliest was the Protaton ('Firstest'), in Karyes; and then came the Great Lavra, founded in 963. And even these were preceded by centuries of monasticism on Mount Athos when informal communities of monks, *lavrai*, of the Palestinian monastic tradition came and went, worshipped together or separately. The foundation of the *megistē lavra*, 'greatest of the

4 For the account of Mt Athos which follows, I owe a great debt to my friend Captain Nikolas Lemos, who took me there in October 2007 and introduced me to a number of *hēgoumenoi* and other custodians of the traditions of the Holy Mountain. Among the extensive literature on Mount Athos, I have profited most from A. Riley, *Athos, or the Mountain of the Monks* (London, 1887); P. Meyer, *Die Haupturkunden für die Geschichte der Athosklöster* (Leipzig 1894); G. Smyrnakes, *To Agion Oros* (Athens, 1903); F. W. Hasluck, *Athos and its Monasteries* (London, 1924); R. M. Dawkins, *The Monks of Athos* (London, 1936); E. A. de Mendieta, *Le presqu'île des caloyers: le Mont-Athos* (Brussels and Bruges, 1955), new and revised ed., trans. M. R. Bruce as *Mount Athos, the Garden of the Panaghia* (*Berliner Byzantinistische Arbeiten*, xli (Berlin and Amsterdam, 1972)); S. Loch, *Athos: The Holy Mountain* (London, 1957); P. Sherrard, *Athos, the Mountain of Silence* (London, 1960); S. Runciman, *The Great Church in Captivity* (Cambridge, 1968); S. Kadas, *Mount Athos* (Athens, 1998); G. Speake, *Mount Athos: Renewal in Paradise* (New Haven and London, 2002). Most paint a picture of Athos in the seventeenth century as labouring under a Dark Age. Apart from Georgirenes' own book, the most useful contemporary account is by Dr John Covel, chaplain to the English ambassador in Constantinople and a considerable scholar of the Orthodox Church, who spent about a week on Mt Athos in April 1677: B[ritish] L[ibrary], Add. MSS 22912, fols 335–51, and 22914, fols 38–46v; some parts edited and rearranged by F. W. Hasluck, 'The First English Traveller's Account of Athos', *The Annual of the British School at Athens*, xvii (1910–11), pp. 103–31; cf. John Covel, *Some Account of the Present Greek Church* (Cambridge and London, 1722). For further discussion of Covel, see below, pp. 104, 143. Covel's account was a major source for Paul Rycaut, *The Present State of the Greek and Armenian Churches in 1678* (London, 1679), pp. 215–63; on the latter author, see Sonia P. Anderson, *An English Consul in Turkey: Paul Rycaut at Smyrna, 1667–1678* (Oxford, 1989), esp. p. 222. See also J. T. Bent, *Early Voyages and Travels in the Levant* (Hakluyt Society, London, 1893), pp. 101–287.

lavrai', set a new pattern which prevailed, though it has never attempted to suppress the more informal houses and hermitages of the old tradition. For 500 years the monasteries grew and prospered, enjoying the favour of emperors and patriarchs.

Following the Ottoman conquest, however, and notwithstanding their prompt submission to the Turks which forestalled the threat of direct subjection, the monasteries had soon found themselves in economic difficulty. For though the sultans had left their internal arrangements largely undisturbed, and had indeed issued *firmans* confirming their right to enjoy their property without hindrance, their relative autonomy was conditional on their paying high levels of taxation, while the chief source of benefactions and subsidies, the Byzantine court, had been removed. Thrown back upon their own resources, they had suffered a century of steep decline. But by the mid-sixteenth century, when a contemporary French traveller estimated the population as 5,000 or 6,000,[5] the deficit began to be made good by the Danubian princes of Moldavia and Wallachia (now Romania), and occasionally even by the Russian Tsar, and a degree of renewed prosperity is to be observed in the building or rebuilding of churches at Iviron, Dionysiou, Koutloumousiou, Dochiariou, Karakalou, Stavronikita, Xenophon and elsewhere, and in the new flowering of their interior decoration at the hands of such outstanding artists as Theophanes and his Cretan school.

More generally, this reawakening betokens a new spirit of individual enterprise and initiative which led the monks of some houses – the free-spirited Greeks rather than the more acceptant Slav minority – to question the peculiarly Athonite 'coenobitic' pattern of communal living, as laid down in successive *typika* for the Holy Mountain and designed to replicate the life of the earliest Christians, who 'had all things in common' (Acts, ii 45). Indeed, this traditional system of a community living and eating together in poverty, chastity and obedience and in shared devotion to regular prayer, under a permanent *kathēgoumenos* or *hēgoumenos*,

5 Pierre Belon, *Les Observations de plusieurs Singularitez et choses memorables* (Paris, 1553), fols 34r–45r, esp. fol. 36, cited by M. E. Martin, 'Some Western Images of Athos in Early Modern Times', *Byzantine and Early Modern Greek Studies*, xxii (1998), pp. 51–74, esp. pp. 52f., 56, and n. 8.

their 'abbot', had almost ceased to have meaning for many of the monks. Some of the more austere had chosen the narrow path to holiness which the eremitic life provides; but more had turned their common houses into apartments of however many rooms individual monks could afford to run and to staff out of their personal resources, shunning the authority of an abbot for the looser regime of a changing *prohēgoumenos* or 'prior', and abandoning any pretence of community, usually eating at home, and only worshipping and dining together on Sundays and major festivals.[6] Even the greatest houses such as the Lavra and Vatopedi had intermittently adopted this less exacting way of life, characterized by those who disapproved of it as 'idiorrhythmic', 'individually' or 'privately regulated', that is 'self-regulated', and blind to both poverty and obedience.

From time to time efforts were made to restore discipline. At Christmas 1573 Patriarch Jeremias II, a determined reformer and enemy of corruption, on his way to a visitation of the churches and monasteries of the Peloponnese, was met at Thessaloniki by a delegation of leading Athonites who besought him to correct the wayward. To this end he asked his brother of Alexandria, Patriarch Silvestros, to perform a visitation of the Holy Mountain on his behalf, to put an end to notorious abuses and bind up the wounds of a torn community. Among his other achievements by the following September, Silvestros restored the coenobitic system at the Lavra, which had lapsed into *idiorrhythmia*.[7] How long this sterner regime was maintained, there or elsewhere, we do not know: by the early years of the following century most of the monasteries of the Holy Mountain, even perhaps including the Great Lavra, appear to have fallen back into *idiorrhythmia*, though it is not often easy to learn at what date the transformation took place.

6 For the Athonite system and its variants, see for instance Sherrard, *Athos, Mountain of Silence*, pp. 29–37; cf. de Mendieta, *Presqu'île*, pp. 78–91. For the three terms *kathēgoumenos*, *hēgoumenos* and *prohēgoumenos*, see Ph. Meyer, *Die Haupturkunden fur die Geschichte der Athoskloster* (Leipzig, 1894), index, s.vv. In the instructions for monastic organization attributed to the Lavra's founder, St Athanasios, the terms *hēgoumenos* and *kathēgoumenos* are used interchangeably, ibid. pp. 106–7.

7 Ibid. pp. 215–18, esp. 215, lines 27ff.

We are fortunate that the veil is perhaps lifted in April 1661, about the time when Georgirenes' six years on Athos must have been coming to an end, when 'the Great Council of the Holy Mountain', consisting of the *kathēgoumenoi* and *dikaioi* ('abbots' and 'stewards') and leading elders of each of the twenty houses, met as vendors to take part in a 'fire-sale' of *kellia* (monk's cells) in Messe – the 'Midst', that is at Karyes – the sale forced upon them by the extreme poverty to which low numbers and high taxes had reduced them all.[8] Clearly this was a last resort, and the seriousness of the crisis demanded that all should be represented at an authoritative level, by the head of house where possible, and at least by the steward. It appears that in each case the decision as to which *kellion* should be sold was taken on behalf of the monastery in question, in relation to the scale of its debt, by the other nineteen; documents survive which contain the signatures and offices of those present, including nine of the twenty heads. Although the titles used are sometimes ambiguous it would appear that at this time the Slavic houses appear to have been coenobitic, whereas among the Greeks both ways of life are to be found, the idiorrhythmic perhaps the more commonly attested.

Neither Georgirenes himself, nor his friend and editor, Antoine Galland, records which of the twenty monasteries (or to which of the several dependent *skētai*) the future archbishop became attached: he was not, of course, attached to any of the Slavic monasteries which he himself was to list as 'Bulgarian'.[9] And there appear to be no records of sufficient sensitivity to enable discrimination between one Joseph and another among those named in the Athos archives. Some monasteries recruited from particular regions; and those with possessions, *metochia*, outside the Holy Mountain might look in that direction for their novices. But Melos did not come into that category: the only known *metochia* on the island at

8 See P. Lemerle, ed., *Actes de Kutlumus*, *Archives de l'Athos*, II 2 (Paris, 1988), pp. 200–1, no. 71.

9 Hasluck, 'The First English Traveller's Account', pp. 92–6: Chilandar, St Paul (both in fact Serbian), Zographou and 'Burgarian' Xenophon (both Bulgarian).

this period belonged to the monasteries at Seriphos and Patmos and to the Patriarch of Jerusalem.[10] We are thrown back on the internal evidence of Georgirenes' book. There are a number of arguments, in the end not quite decisive, though they have sufficient cumulative force to justify the working hypothesis that Georgirenes was in fact a member of the Great Lavra. It is not simply that he begins his list of twenty-one houses (including the Protaton in the monastic capital at Karyes) with the Lavra, for that enjoyed primacy of precedence as the oldest and one of the largest, and is accordingly found at the head of most lists. The list of monasteries in Georgirenes' book is topographical, a well-remembered land-based trail beginning at the Lavra and proceeding up the north-east side of the peninsula as far as Esphigmenou ('Tousimenou') and Chilandar, which then crosses and returns along the south-west side to St Paul and thence into the homeland of the *skētai* and hermitages at the tip.[11] This may, but need not, make the choice of the Lavra as starting point more significant. And is it personal attachment, or is it simply history and precedence, that accounts for the disproportionate amount of space allotted to the foundation and early history of the Lavra and its relation to the *lavra* settlements at Bethlehem and elsewhere in early monastic Palestine, occupying two pages initially and four pages later in the book, whereas most houses rate no more than half a page and some only a couple of lines?[12] It is very striking that his historical perspective is Lavra-centred to the point of distortion. There is much emphasis on the achievement of St Anthony and the Egyptian hermits; this is common ground. Thereafter it is St Sabas of the Palestinian *lavrai* who takes centre stage. There is no mention of St Pachomios or of St Theodoros of the Stoudion in Constantinople, who might have been thought worthy of note since they were between them responsible for the peculiarly Athonite 'cenobitic' system. More significant, perhaps, is the fact that Georgirenes' full account of the founding of the Lavra by St Athanasios 'the Athonite' includes at least one detail for which there is no other source. He tells, as others do, of the founder's despair of completing

10 Cf. Tournefort, *A Voyage into the Levant*, p. 121.

11 *A Description of the Present State*, pp. 87–98 and see Map 2.

12 Ibid. pp. 87–9, 101–4; contrast for example Vatopedi, p. 91, with two lines.

his monastery, of his abandoning the site and retreating back along the road towards Karyes, until, half-way between the Lavra and Karakalou, he 'was met with by the Blessed Virgin, who took his staff from him, and smote a Rock, 'till it sent out a Spring of Water, that runs at this day'. Thus far the general tradition.[13] But 'then thrusting his staff into the Ground, it became a Tree, and sent forth Boughs and Leaves'. Only Georgirenes has this sequel. It was, however, the version current at the Lavra itself, where it is illustrated on one of the relief slabs which form a frieze below the west windows of the *exonarthēx*: outside the monastery Athanasios with a gesture of amazement watches as the Virgin strikes the rock with her staff and the waters gush forth, while behind him a dove watches from the safety of a notably lush and healthy tree.[14] Finally, it is only at the Lavra that Georgirenes shows any knowledge of the interior of a building: 'in their Hall, where they eat in common, there is a large Marble Table, where 600 Monks sit down together'.[15] It will be said that four weak arguments do not add up to a single strong one; but they are at least straws in the wind,

13 Covel has a charming version, BL, Add. MS 22912, fol. 342v: 'Ath. Pardon me if I do not believe till I see some signe for there are many delusions of the Devil.'

14 *A Description of the Present State*, p. 88; cf. Dawkins, *The Monks of Athos*, pp. 178 and 181. For the relief, see Kadas, *Mount Athos*, fig. 83 on p. 152, and for its placing fig. 78 on p. 147 (right edge). This version, of course, implies that Athanasios' staff was of wood, and not the iron staff still preserved in the monastery, with which he dispatched the demons who impeded his work of construction; see below, p. 229. Athanasios' *agiasma*, traditionally, is the spring that gushes from a fissure in the limestone, a little way above the coastal track leading to Iviron, near Morphonou Bay and the Amalfian tower. Cf. Covel, BL, Add. MS 22914, fol. 46; Hasluck, 'The First English Traveller's Account', p. 115.

15 *A Description of the Present State*, pp. 88f. It must be confessed, however, that the statement is, strictly speaking, untrue. The Lavra's memorable refectory contains not a single great marble table, like that at Iviron, but a multitude of smaller U-shaped tables of marble, as at Vatopedi, ranged at right angles to the walls: it is these that are indeed remarkable. It is possible that the mistake is the result of an easy misreading, *trapeza* (singular) for *trapezia* (plural), rather than misinformation; but in the absence of either Georgirenes' original or Galland's first translation it is impossible to assess the significance of the error presented by the English version.

and in the absence of any other evidence, they may be thought sufficient to allow a working hypothesis that the Lavra was indeed Joseph's home.

A skeleton account of the six years Joseph spent on Mount Athos can be reconstructed, both from what the future archbishop himself says of the Holy Mountain and from what he omits, and supplemented from our general understanding, such as it is, of Athonite monasticism in this period. From the latter it may be assumed that when he reached Athos he was visibly bearded, about eighteen years old, the age laid down as the minimum for entry; in a world without birth certificates this could only be an approximation, conventionally equated with the ability to grow a beard, as required by successive imperial and patriarchal *typika* (constitutions) for the holy community and designed to keep it unequivocally beyond risk of inadvertent contamination by the female sex.[16] We may imagine that the young islander arrived at Mount Athos by sea. If he came equipped with a letter of introduction, perhaps from his bishop in Melos, he will no doubt have gone straight to his chosen monastery, stopping only to transfer to a local boat. Otherwise, he perhaps landed at Daphne or elsewhere on the sheltered side of the peninsula, and took the path to Karyes, the monastic capital with its Saturday market and its ancient church the Protaton (his text calls it 'Porpat'), there to seek advice on a house appropriate to his needs and interests, and perhaps even the name of an elder monk, to whom he might attach himself.[17] The winding path from Daphne leads past nearby Xeropotamou steeply uphill for five or six miles through a thick forest of oak and chestnut – a novelty to a boy from the Kyklades – before plunging briefly to the agricultural and horticultural paradise of Koutloumousiou and so into Karyes. Here each of the twenty monasteries maintained a lodging and a representative, under the overall control of the Protos ('First'), whose absolute authority, perhaps already tottering, had not yet been abolished in

16 For the *typika*, Meyer, *Die Haupturkunden*, *Urkunden* I, IV, V, VII, XI, etc.

17 Or, with less care for calm seas, he might have landed at Stavronikita or Pantocratoras and so have taken a shorter path to Karyes. 'Porpat' would appear to be a misreading of Georgirenes' original Greek, πορπάτο for πορτάτο, on which see Covel, BL, Add. MS 22912, fol. 348v. In the broadsheet version of Georgirenes' account (see n. 1 above), it is 'corrected' to the strangely Latinized 'Protatumi'.

favour of a permanent committee of the four greatest monasteries (Lavra, Vatopedi, Iviron, Chilandar), with periodic consultation of the remainder.[18] Such struggles for power will have meant little to Joseph, faced only with a momentous and perhaps irrevocable decision about his own future. Nor will he have been delayed by contact with the civil governor, the Turkish *aga*, and his tiny staff of two or three, whose chief role will have been to watch for signs of political unrest among the monks and to ensure that taxes were duly paid; less realistically, Georgirenes says that the *aga* was there to defend the monasteries from Barbary pirates, and that was no doubt given out as the pretext for his presence, since it is repeated by Covel.[19] Advice received and the Lavra chosen (if indeed that was the outcome), the last stage of the journey could begin.

From Karyes there are two ways to the Lavra, by land or by sea, neither of them easy. By land the path descends sharply through more forests to the north coast and Iviron, an uncomfortable scramble of at least one and a half hours, skidding over scree and plunging down the watery steeps, until one emerges to come upon the originally Georgian monastery, walled

18 Covel notes a rather different constitutional position: 'There all the *Hegoumenoi* and deputyes of all the Monastrys meet commonly every Saturday, to hear and determine all controversys and deliberate on all difficultyes that arise amongst them, and to adjust all taxes or contributions which the Pasha of Salonicka or rather the G.Sig[r] shall lay on them.', Ibid. fol. 348v. See also J. Darrouzes, 'Liste des Protes de l'Athos', from *Le Millénaire du Mont Athos, 963–1963, Études et Mélanges* (Chevetogne, 1963), i, pp. 407–47. Darrouzes lists 101 *Prōtoi* from Andreas *c.*887 to Kallistos in 1593. Thereafter there is no coherent list, though the title and duties appear to have lasted to about the middle of the seventeenth century, to judge from a patriarchal letter of 1639 preserved at the Lavra, and another of 1641 at Philotheou: ibid. p. 445. The office of *Prōtos*, already obsolescent, appears at last to have disappeared in the upheavals which followed the end of the Cretan war in 1669; to replace him, the Turks had already installed a governor, to whom the monks appear to have accorded similar privileges: cf. *A Description of the Present State*, pp. 90–1. The title has since been revived.

19 Covel, BL, Add. MS 22912, fol. 344, 'Here is an Aga sent every year from the Bustangebasher … of Cple to govern them in all civil matters; and protect them from all violence of strangers or invaders. And he is maintain'd at their comon but publique charge.'

high against pirates as if drawing its skirts about itself. Refreshment here, perhaps even a night's rest, before continuing along the coastal path to the Great Lavra itself, some seventeen or eighteen miles, and seven hours, further on.[20] The alternative way to the Lavra is by sea, after retracing one's steps from Karyes to Daphne to await the next boat. It can be a terrifying and dangerous voyage, deceptively calm for the first couple of hours, south to Simonopetra, Grigoriou, Dionysiou and the then Serbian monastery of St Paul and the *skētē* of St Anne, outposts of civilization, before rounding Cape Pinnes (the ancient Nymphaion) at the southern tip of the peninsula, the cliffs of Karoulia precariously studded with hermitages, into rougher water. From here the experienced sailor keeps well off the evil shore under Kafsokalyvia which saw the destruction of Dareios' Persian fleet on its way to Greece in 491 BC, ripped open by reefs and ground to splinters on the rocks. To a sailor rounding the easternmost headland, Cape Prodromos, into the teeth of the north wind, eyes averted from the Cave of the Wicked Dead, the serenity of the Lavra's harbour and arsenal appears at last as welcome as a Cornish haven to a deep-sea fisherman.[21]

From the harbour and its fortress protected by a drawbridge, 'with a Sentinel perpetually standing to give notice of any *Corsairs*', Joseph would have made his way uphill into more open terrain than he had left behind in the chestnut forests, a leaner landscape of turkey oaks, holly and arbutus clinging to the skirts of the mountain peak, to the Great Lavra itself. At first sight more like a walled village than a monastery, it is an imposing place, the oldest as well as the proudest of the Athonite houses, founded in 963 by the hermit monk from the *lavra* at Bethlehem, Athanasios of Trebizond. The Blessed Virgin was the sole patron of the Holy Mountain that should for ever be her garden, her 'Paradise', and it was she who pointed out the site and helped from time to time with the construction. In return for this assistance, the Virgin demanded and received the title of 'steward'

20 For the approach by land, cf. for instance the vivid account of de Mendieta, *Presqu'île*, pp. 138–44, 236ff.

21 For the hazards of the voyage, see Loch, *Athos*, pp. 190–4. For the Cave of the Wicked Dead, see below, p. 56 and n. 72.

of the monastery; which is why the Lavra has no human *oikonomos*, but a heavenly *oikonomissa* for ever.[22]

On first arrival, Joseph may have found the Lavra formidable, entered as it is by a vaulted passage guarded by two sets of iron gates.[23] Inside the courtyard, two buildings stand out – and remained in his memory – among the apparently unplanned jumble: the church and the refectory. 'It hath likewise a very fair Church, and in their Hall, where they eat in common, there is a large Marble Table, where 600 monks sit down together.' The church, like two other ninth- and tenth-century foundations, the Protaton and Iviron, is dedicated to the *Koimēsis*, the Dormition of the Virgin. Though subjected to some renovation and reconstruction, it is essentially the building begun by Athanasios (who lies within it) and was completed in 1004, the pattern of all the Athonite *katholika*. From the outside it appears to be a domed basilica; in fact it is in the form of a Greek cross, with the transepts as well as the east end culminating in apses, the *naos* prolonged by an inner and an outer *narthex*. The rectangular impression it owes to its two flanking *parekklēsia*, actually smaller cross-in-square churches which communicate with the *katholikon* between them; that on the north side, dedicated to the Forty Martyrs, contains the founder's tomb, while that on the south commemorates St Nicholas. The complex remains as it was in Georgirenes' day, apart from a third *narthēx* added in the nineteenth century; and there is much fine fresco-decoration of the sixteenth century. The refectory, built or rebuilt for the monks by an archbishop of Serres in 1512, is the grandest on the Holy Mountain. A flight of steps up to a wide porch supported on pillars leads into a cruciform hall with a western apse containing the abbot's seat of honour, and a fine timber roof. Like the church, it too was improvingly frescoed in the sixteenth century, with a *Last Supper* in the apse, a *Tree of Jesse* in the south transept, and a *Last Judgment* at the east end to reprove the indulgent diner as he leaves, as well as cycles of martyrdom and monastic history in two registers of red-framed

22 *A Description of the Present State*, pp. 87–8. See Dawkins, *The Monks of Athos*, pp. 176–86.

23 For a full and sympathetic description of the Great Lavra, see Sherrard, *Athos, Mountain of Silence*, pp. 42–8.

scenes above a parade of saints and fathers on the long walls. Surrounded by all this decoration, and equally remarkable, are the forty-eight D-shaped marble tables, each designed for perhaps six or even eight monks, ranged on either side of the central gangway.[24] Between the two great buildings is the delicate *phialē* of 1635, a decorative fountain of water for consecration playing into a huge and ancient basin of white marble, surrounded by a circle of Byzantine reliefs punctuated by an arcade of eight Turkish columns which carry a dome frescoed with the *Baptism of Christ*. As if all this were not enough to overawe the newcomer with a sense of the Lavra's power and permanence, two towering cypresses nearby would draw the eye to heaven, planted (it was said) by St Athanasios the founder himself and by his steward Euthymios who went on to found Dochiariou.[25] Less formal structures complete the scene, on the north side the hospital of 1580 (later converted to a guest-house) and on the south the monks' cells, replacing the wooden galleried ranges which were probably of similar date.[26] In Georgirenes' day the east end of the courtyard beyond the *katholikon*, now occupied by the library and museum, was still an open garden, apart from the recently constructed chapel of St Michael of Synada, the gift of the *voivode* (local governor) of the Danubian principalities in 1643.[27]

24 And one in the apse for the abbot. The forty-eight would seat 300–380. For ease of cleaning, the tables have in their raised edge an aperture at the gangway end, designed to allow debris and water to escape onto the floor, which itself slopes towards the door. For similar marble tables in the refectory of Vatopedi, the second oldest of the monasteries, see Kadas, *Mount Athos*, fig. 77 on p. 145.

25 Euthymios' cypress (which was already giving concern in 1936, see Dawkins, *The Monks of Athos*, p. 184) is now gone, but traces of it remain in the ground alongside an established tree of more recent date. Athanasios' cypress continues to flourish.

26 For a convenient summary of the buildings and their dates, see Hasluck, 'The First English Travellers' Account', pp. 180–5. I am immensely grateful to the good-humoured *hēgoumenos* of the Lavra, Archimandrite Prodromos, who enabled me to explore the monastery in most congenial circumstances in October 2007.

27 For this chapel and the courtyard before development, see P. L. Theocharides, *Photography on Mount Athos*, 4: *Monasteries and sketes of the Holy Mountain ... 1870* (bilingual, Thessaloniki, 1996), pp. 22–3, 75, and pl. For a list of nineteen churches within the walls of the Lavra, and five outside, see Riley, *Athos, or the Mountain of*

If it is not hard to recapture the grandeur of the Lavra, which has struck all its visitors since the sixteenth century. It is much more difficult to recreate the way of life which awaited its new recruit from Melos about the middle of the seventeenth. Above all, was the monastery idiorrhythmic or was it coenobitic, as the patriarchs Jeremias and Silvestros had left it eighty years before? For on the answer to that question depends any reconstruction of Joseph's working day, whether it involved labour for the community as a whole, perhaps at some more specialized craft, or whether it was of a more *ad hoc* nature at the behest of his Elder. And was the monastery populous or not, poor or comfortably off? It must be admitted at the outset that no definitive answers can be given to these questions; but some answers are more plausible than others.

In the 1540s, the Lavra had contained some three hundred monks;[28] but when Patriarch Anthimos II visited this once great house in 1623, he found only five or six, living in the direst poverty, with whatever implications that may have had for their institutional structure. It is not unreasonable to conclude that – as happens from time to time in the long history of the Holy Mountain – in the latter part of the sixteenth century and the early years of the seventeenth vocations had plummeted to the point of catastrophe. Towards the middle of the seventeenth century, however, a modest revival of the monastery appears to have begun, with generous funding from the princes of the Danubian provinces of Moldavia and Wallachia. This gave rise to a new degree of self-respect, expressed in the construction of the *phialē* in 1635 and that of St Michael's chapel in 1643 – both dates almost certainly earlier than Joseph's arrival. These works presuppose a significant population. In 1676 Georgirenes gave a figure of 600; but it is not clear whether this is an estimate of the number of monks at that date or a memory of the population in his own time there, fifteen or twenty

---

the Monks, p. 166. Covel counted even more, BL, Add. MS 22912, fol. 342: 'at least 26 little chappels or oratorys, and candles burning in them day and night'.

28 L. Belon gives the total of all monasteries as 5,000–6,000, with no single house holding more than 300, *Les Observations*, fol. 36; he lists Vatopedi and the Lavra as the largest, ibid. fol. 36v. Cf. Martin, 'Some Western Images', pp. 53, 56 and n. 8.

years previously.[29] In April 1677 the English ambassador's inquisitive and well-informed chaplain, John Covel, homeward bound at the end of his engagement, visited Mount Athos and estimated the membership of the Great Lavra at 450, of whom only about 300 were resident, the remainder being engaged either in fund-raising abroad or seconded to the *metochia*. If Joseph was indeed of the Lavra, he will have found it not rich, but no longer destitute: Covel notes that the Lavra was assessed to pay more tax to the Turks than any other monastery.[30]

It is commonly, and perhaps rightly, supposed that the decline of a *koinobion* into *idiorrhythmia* is related to a decline in population. What is less clear is whether an increase in numbers or prosperity normally leads to a renewal of the common life. The Great Lavra seems to have enjoyed a revival in its fortunes around the time when Joseph is likely to have been there; and there is reason to believe that the monastery was indeed coenobitic at this time. We have seen that in 1623 Patriarch Anthimos II reconciled two factions within the monastery, one side numbering no more than five or six monks, who had found each other's company intolerable, and have noted the implication of a low population. It seems likely that the issue was of *idiorrhythmia* against *koinobia*, though that is perhaps the best guess; it is to be expected that imposition of the latter system would have been part of the patriarchal settlement.[31] And this may have been the incentive which led to the construction of a new kitchen attached to the refectory in 1625, coincidentally soon before Anthimos' death.[32] Near to the date of Joseph's profession, in 1643 and again in 1653, the monastery placed in the little church of St Michael of Synada, newly built in the south-east part of the courtyard, stones bearing the names of the *hēgoumenoi* Joseph and

29 *A Description of the Present State*, p. 89. This is the second highest population given, after the 800 at Slavic Chilandar, ibid. p. 92.

30 BL, Add. MS 22912, fol. 341.

31 See above, p. 35.

32 All the more surprising, then, that the inscription over the kitchen door carries by way of dating the building the name not of a permanent abbot but of the *prokathēgoumenos* (prior) Timotheos, normally to be taken as a sign of *idiorrhythmia*. Quoted by Smyrnakes, *To Agion Oros*, p. 391.

Joasaph respectively, as would be expected if the house were coenobitic.[33] But when Covel visited the Lavra in 1677 he reported that at the Lavra he and his party regularly had their meals with the retired patriarch Dionysios III, perhaps suggesting that the common refectory was not in daily use. To sum up: the Great Lavra was restored from *idiorrhythmia* to the coenobitic system in 1573, and that was probably the system which Anthimos left in 1623; in 1643 it was coenobitic and was still so in 1653; it may have lapsed again by the 1670s. Hence we cannot tell for certain whether it was as a *koinobion* or as idiorrhythmic that Joseph knew the monastery in the 1650s, if indeed that was when he was there.

His own account hints that it was in fact coenobitic for at least part of his time. It is not simply that the system which he describes in his book is plainly and solely the coenobitic, for none of the visitors to the Holy Mountain who have left accounts of its way of life mentions any but the coenobitic before about 1840. Georgirenes, like the others, spells out the formal position: the monks of Athos eat together, and they maintain a life of poverty, as well as chastity and obedience.[34] But he adds a telling circumstantial detail:

> For the better government of the Monastry, the Superiour goes in person to every man's Cell, accompanied with some of the elder *Caloirs* (monks), and if he find any man out of his Cell, or two or three together in another man's Cell, this is a Crime, after three reproofs very punishable. The younger *Caloirs* stand in great dread of this nocturnal Perambulation.

This reads like personal experience, and such a proceeding would have no relevance in the idiorrhythmic system: Joseph was then, probably for a time at least, a member of one of the few genuinely coenobitic houses, during the youthful stages of his stay on the Holy Mountain.

It is not always easy to know what the monastic life means to those who undertake it. Covel, writing about the Holy Mountain only a couple of decades after Joseph's time there, was given an account of what were then expected to be the essential qualities that defined a monk in the form of a

33 Ibid. p. 390.
34 *A Description of the Present State*, pp. 108–11.

somewhat whimsical recipe for 'A good medicine for the soul', which he quotes in the original Greek as well as in English translation:

> Take a root of spiritual poverty; and the flowers of humility; and the leaves of Patience; and the twigs of Prayer. And lay them on the sieve of good discourses; and put them all together and bray them in the mortar of Obedience; then put them into the pitcher of conscience, and moisten them with water from the drops of tears; and then under them kindle the flame of Divine Love; and when they have boiled a while, empty them into the platter of Discretion; and mingle them with Thanksgiving; Then soup them with the spoon of compunction, and wipe all clean with the towel of Confession; and thus you will empty and wipe away all the multitude of thy sins. Hear ye [adds the Protestant Covel] what little credit is to be given to what the monks say.[35]

Joseph's own account of the monastic life is more prosaic. 'They that enter into this profession, are kept six months Probationers; during which time they are put to all the Exercise they must undergo in their Profession.'[36] Today the novitiate lasts for about three years. Its much shorter duration in Georgirenes' time may indicate a greater intensity of training in those days, with correspondingly less time devoted to material affairs such as horticulture and the handicrafts. Or it may simply be that monks were less fully prepared for the life they were to undertake. Certainly one can understand that, with vocations perhaps at a low ebb in the early part of the century, and numbers at a catastrophic level for a generation or more, the Great Lavra will have set something of a premium on speed, even if there was some cutting of corners as a result. Whatever the explanation, Joseph evidently spent but six months as a probationer in training for the monastic life, and that was normal at the time. After that (though he says nothing of this first profession) he will have received his cassock (*rason*) and cap, and have entered the first level of Greek monasticism, that of the *rasophoros*. It is a level from which the more humble often do not aspire to rise, but may remain lifelong *rasophoroi*. The single ceremony of profession which Georgirenes describes, however, is not this, but corresponds exactly and verbatim to the service at which the *rasophoros* advances to the

35 BL, Add. MS 22912, fol. 345, heard at Chilandar.

36 *A Description of the Present State*, pp. 105–8, for both novitiate and profession.

intermediate level, that of the *mikroschēmos* or *stavrophoros*, 'wearer of the little habit', 'wearer of the cross'. The lower level he passes over in silence. Then, 'After the six months are expired, the Novitiat chuseth among the Old Caloirs a God-father to introduce him, and to instruct him in the Ceremony of his Admission.' Nothing is said about the duration of this next stage of the monk's training, from *rasophoros* to *mikroschēmos*. Today it is usually about three more years, but it has always been the responsibility of the elder in consultation with the abbot (or, in idiorrhythmic houses, the *prohēgoumenos*) to determine the appropriate moment. When the time is ripe,

> This God-father brings him to the Church door, where he is strip'd to his Shirt, and prostrates himself, then he makes a second prostration in the middle of the Church, and a third at the Altar, and a fourth to the Superiour. Then upon his knees he answers to all the Interrogatories made him by the Superiour, which are commonly these.

The first is the purely formal question why the novice has come to the altar in the presence of the assembly of monks: 'A desire to live a Monastick life'. The remaining inquiries are to satisfy the abbot that the new monk is here voluntarily and not under duress, that he will remain and obey the rules of the house, and that he will be prepared to take the customary vows of chastity, poverty ('Temperance') and obedience. After further similar questions, and after prayers, the abbot reverts to the issue of free will, this time requiring the novice to swear on the gospels that he has indeed come of his own volition. Satisfied on this point, the abbot proceeds to the tonsure, and then to the new monk's investiture in the unrelieved black of the lesser *schēma* (habit). To a threefold *Kyrie* at each stage, and with a commentary on the significance of each item, cassock and girdle, veiled bonnet and mantle are put upon him, epistle and gospel are read, and the symbols of cross and candle put into his hands. 'This done, the other *Caloirs*, every one salute him with a Kiss, and so the Ceremony is ended.'[37]

37 For comparison of the full service of the little habit, conveniently in English, see N. F. Robinson, *Monasticism in the Orthodox Churches* (London and Milwaukee, 1916), pp. 75–91: for the initiation of the *rasophoros* with only the tunic and cap without veil, ibid. pp. 71–3.

This description of the profession ceremony of the *mikroschēmos* is not of course intended to be specific to Georgirenes' own monastery, but to apply equally to all; local differences are not significant. There are, however, one or two elements peculiar to the Great Lavra. Here the new monk is required to wear about his neck the heavy penitential cross which Athanasios himself once wore. This, when not in use, is kept together with the founder's cross-headed staff and a second abbatial cross of iron. To wear the founder's nine-pound cross must have added considerable spiritual as well as physical weight to what was anyway a deeply moving experience.[38]

The *mikroschēmos* may be said, in modern parlance, to have reached the career grade. Of two other ceremonies which mark important but optional stages in the career of the Athonite monk Georgirenes says nothing. The first is the advance from the little *schēma* to the altogether grander habit of the great *schēma*, which calls for a further investiture including three more items of dress, and the renewal of vows in terms similar to those of the first profession. The second is ordination to the priesthood, a status to which relatively few of the monks aspire, and which can indeed be approached from one of the lower levels. It is only after six years from his profession that a monk becomes eligible for either of these steps, and even then the decision rests with the abbot. Georgirenes, in fact, himself spent only six years in all on the Holy Mountain, hence neither of the ceremonies is described in what is essentially an account of his own experiences. When he left the Holy Mountain, therefore, he was probably not yet a priest.

The religious life was of course demanding. In principle the monastic day is divided into three parts of eight hours each, for prayer, for work and for sleep. Within these notional totals, however, and given the dictates of light and darkness, the elements are considerably interwoven; and, as in any other walk of life, it is sleep that suffers.

38 Dawkins saw these relics in the separate chapel of St Athanasios, where he says the ceremony took place, *The Monks of Athos*, pp. 185f. He notes, however, the statement of Komninos, *Proskynētarion tou agiou orous tou Athōnos*, 2nd edn (Venice, 1864), p. 16, that the relics were kept within the *katholikon*, close to the founder's tomb. It is at any rate more credible that the ceremony belonged normally to the *katholikon*.

> Their constant morning Prayer is three hours before day; their evening Prayer at Sun-set. On *Sundays* they go to Prayers five hours before day in the morning, and before great Holy-days their Prayers continue all night. They have likewise other set hours of Prayer for the day-time. ... [And they are required] To be always ready to go to Prayers at the appointed Hours. At Midnight; before Day; at Noon; at Sun-set; and after Supper.[39]

Even then the religious day is not ended, for when the monks disperse to the silence of their cells it is the time for private prayer. Georgirenes describes what was presumably his own (or typical) practice, doing penance in the shape of sixty prostrations, each accompanied by 'a short Prayer', for the abbot and the other brethren, for benefactors and for all Christians. For many this was also the occasion for private study by candlelight, or perhaps for mastering difficult liturgical music, or recitation of the 'Jesus prayer', in its simplest form, 'Jesus have mercy on me', or, more elaborately, 'Lord Jesus Christ, Son of God, have mercy on me a sinner' – this said with head bowed, eyes directed towards the heart, breathing controlled, in the hope of inducing a trance-like vision of the Divine Light.[40] For those younger monks to whom the Divine Light proved elusive, this was no doubt the moment for congregating in each other's cells, and even for romancing over an unsanctioned drink, liable to be interrupted by the heavy footfall of the abbot and his senior colleagues, and 'after three reproofs very punishable'.[41] For most it was at last time for sleep, to rise again in time for the next day's midnight service of Orthros followed after an interval by Matins and the eucharistic Liturgy, lunch around dawn, the day's work on either side of the noon-time service, Vespers, dinner, and Compline.

It was – it is – a hard life, harder perhaps than the impression of it that Georgirenes gives. And the two meals which support it are simple fare: perhaps simpler today that in Joseph's time, for on four days in the

39 *A Description of the Present State*, pp. 104f., 109.

40 See, for example, *The Oxford Dictionary of the Christian Church*, 3rd edn, by E. A. Livingstone after F. L. Cross (Oxford, 1997), s.vv. 'Hesychasm', 'Jesus Prayer', and bibliography there cited.

41 *A Description of the Present State*, p. 111; cf. ibid. pp. 109f., for the prohibition of private refreshment.

week – Sunday, Tuesday, Thursday, Saturday – the monks were allowed to supplement their bread and olive-oil, pulses, home-grown vegetables and fruit and home-made wine, with eggs, butter, cheese and fish, the first three presumably imported, since 'they suffer no ... Female Creature of what kind soever ... to come within the Mount'.[42] The other three days of the week were fast-days, however: three, for even the Pharisees fasted on two days (Luke xviii 12). And the Orthodox Church observes a multitude of fasts throughout the year, as well as the continuous fasts of Advent and Lent. On fast-days

> They eat none of these, nor drink any thing but Water only; and those other days they have only a Dinner, at Night they eat a piece of Bread, and drink a little water at the Church-door, and so to Prayers, and thence to their Cells, where they remain in great silence.

Meat was universally forbidden, though sometimes quietly available in the idiorrhythmic houses. There was fish (except on the many fast-days), and monks went out to fish especially for tuna; if Joseph did indeed come from a fishing family in Melos, he may have had skills to offer in this direction.[43]

'One thing is very remarkable, that Idleness is utterly banish'd here, no man lives in the Isle, who is not some way employ'd.'[44] Georgirenes will have been no exception to this rule, though he gives little inkling what his own duties were. As a junior, he is perhaps unlikely to have held one of the very many offices, some of them little more than sinecures, required for the administration of the monastery, though some few – that of the gatekeeper, for instance – would not have been beyond the capacity of a monk who was young and able-bodied. And there was plenty of domestic work to be done, from assisting the *archontarēs* in the guest-house or the *trapezarēs* in the refectory, the *mageiras* in the kitchen or the *mangipas* in the bakery, to working with the *bordonarēs* (mule-keeper) in the stables, to say nothing of

42 Ibid. p. 110, cf. pp. 86–7.

43 Cf. above, p. 13. Locally caught fish was no doubt supplemented by the import of stockfish from northern seas – remembered by Dawkins, *The Monks of Athos*, p. 319, as 'the only really nasty thing that has ever been set before me'.

44 *A Description of the Present State*, p. 98.

spinning and weaving, tailoring and shoemaking.[45] The more responsible duties, however, such as the oversight of church, treasury, stores, library or archives, were entrusted to more senior hands, while a literate junior might be responsible for reading in the refectory at meal-times and helping the less fluent to find their places in their service-books in church. Each monastery aimed to be self-sufficient. There was always building-work to be done, whether repairs or remodelling or entirely new construction: we have already noted new works of the seventeenth century at the Lavra, the church of St Michael of Synada and the great *phialē*, and the coming of Wallachian and Moldavian funds will have given rise to other works also. And there were food and fuel to be grown or gathered.[46] The simple diet of the monks was heavily dependent on grain and on olive oil, as well as garlic. However, the prevalence of legends of the miraculous filling of granaries and oil-vats by the Virgin would seem to suggest that these staples were not grown locally in quantity but imported, like eggs, butter and cheese, presumably from a monastery's *metochia*, to which therefore monks were seconded as necessary;[47] Georgirenes says nothing of this, and as a junior may not have been regarded as suitable for this degree of independence.

Secluded though the life of an Athonite monk is, and is intended to be, experience of the outside world was not confined to service in the *metochia*. Georgirenes devotes considerable space to the dispatch of monks on fund-raising journeys beyond the bounds of the Holy Mountain, sometimes even overseas, the need for which he attributes partly to the rapacity of the Turks and partly to the need for money to buy what could not be grown or made: 'as the matter is order'd, they commonly want Money to pay their Haratch, or yearly Tribute of 3 Dollers per Poll, and

45 For a near-contemporary conspectus of offices held in the monastery, see Covel, BL, Add. MS 22914, fol. 39v; cf. Hasluk, 'The First English Traveller's Account', pp. 109–11, cf. Kadas, *Mount Athos*, pp. 26–9.

46 Cf. Dawkins, *The Monks of Athos*, pp. 319–31.

47 The Lavra's ten or twelve *metochia*, like those of most monasteries, were for the most part conveniently concentrated on the local mainland and north Aegean islands: cf. Covel, BL, Add. MS 22914, fol. 39; Hasluk, 'The First English Traveller's Account', p. 109.

buy themselves Cloaths and Furniture for tilling their Land'.[48] Georgirenes gives a highly detailed description of the fund-raising procedure, both the appointment of the mendicants and their conduct abroad, from which it is not unreasonable to suspect that he may have participated personally in such an expedition. This may indeed have lain behind his own later suggestion that the Abbot of Patmos send him abroad to raise funds for that monastery.[49] On Mount Athos it was all highly organized, with parties sent abroad each year. First the twenty monasteries agreed among themselves where should be their respective hunting-grounds, to avoid confusion and duplication of effort, and indeed annoyance of donors, for diminished returns. Then the abbot appointed the leader of that year's mission, who in turn chose his own team, all of whom acknowledged the authority of the abbot and of their leader by prostration and the kissing of hands. So they set off to work together in pairs, having first equipped themselves by a visit to a *skētē*, in search of

> such Hermits as live by Manufacture, as particularly, the making of Crosses and Figures that represent our Saviours Passion, and Seals and Marks proper for the consecrated Bread. The Caloirs that are sent abroad to confess People, and to gather Alms for pious Uses, buy up all these Manufactures to present unto people among whom they come.[50]

48 *A Description of the Present State*, pp. 99–101. (The *haraç* was the due of the Kapitan Pasha.) Covel, BL, Add. MS 22914, fol. 39, gives the annual expenses of the Lavra as 6,000 dollars, of which 2,500 comprise various taxes paid to the Turkish authorities, the rest maintenance. Elsewhere he gives the Lavra's total monthly assessment as 110 dollars, 1320 *p.a.* He also estimates the complement of monks at 450, which at 3 dollars *per capita* would generate for the kapitan pasha 1,350 dollars, a reasonably consistent figure. The remaining *c.*1,200 dollars of the 2,500 will then represent donations and dues other than the *haraç*, most obviously the 1,200 payable (according to Rycaut) to the *aga*. See BL, Add. MS 22912, fol. 341, cf. 22914, fols 39, 40v; Rycaut, *Present State*, pp. 220, 252. For difficulties in interpreting or reconciling the evidence for the *haraç* and other taxes, see Martin, 'Some Western Images', p. 72.

49 See below, p. 109.

50 *A Description of the Present State*, pp. 96f. See also ibid. pp. 42f. (on Samos), where Georgirenes says that monks, especially those of Mount Athos, enjoyed a virtual monopoly of the confessional.

Proper formalities were observed:

> When they go abroad, they first apply themselves to the *Metropolite* of the Diocese, and show him their Letters of Obedience from their Superiours. Whereupon the *Metropolite* gives them Letters of Permission to ask Charity, and confess Penitents throughout his Diocese. Where they Confess any, they exact nothing of them by way of pecuniary Penance, but only receive what in charity they freely bestow.[51]

The reference to the confession of penitents implies that the areas to which most of the confessors directed their steps were within the Orthodox world, and certainly the richest sources of support will have been Moldavia and Wallachia, and even Russia. As it happens, we have a further source of much the same date in Covel, who makes it clear that at the Lavra fund-raising had reached industrial proportions. Of the 450 monks of the Lavra, says he, *at least* 150 at any given time

> are abroad to beg alms, whereof they have some all over the Greek church and as they come home others go out as missioners, that being the first point of καλογερισμ [being a monk] to vow obedience to ye ηγουμενο [abbot] and fraternity, many go as far as Russia, Muscovy (I met two here that have been at Archangelo), Morea, Palestine, Stanbol, Smyrna.[52]

If they went to the Peloponnese (Morea), they are likely to have visited the Archipelago also and even to have canvassed support in the Catholic dioceses there, particularly those with a significantly mixed population, if the Capuchin account of the good relations between Christians of the two persuasions is to be believed. And they may have journeyed on to the long-established settlements in southern Italy, the old *Magna Graecia*, and in Sicily. Some may have travelled further still, for Georgirenes avers they 'continue ordinarily two or three years in their perambulation'. Much earlier, in 1628, Father Ignatios, a former head of the monastery of Vatopedi, went to Rome to the *Sacra Congregatio de Propaganda Fide*, 'being now instructed to solicit charity and having found certain indulgences given

51 Ibid. pp. 100–1.

52 BL, Add. MS 22914, fol. 40v; Hasluk, 'The First English Traveller's Account', p. 111. Cf. Rycaut, *The Present State*, p. 226.

to them by Eugenius IV [1431–47] and other Roman pontiffs, comes to Rome with them, and asks a contribution of the Holy Congregation, and a recommendation to leading Christians'; he went on to raise hopes that Vatopedi might be reconciled to Rome – but secretly, for fear of the Turks.[53] Nor was Rome the limit. Later, in 1715, the *hēgoumenos* of Pantocratoras visited the University of Oxford to seek charitable funds, both corporate and from individual members. The request was put into the form of a petition in English, and commended by the vice-chancellor. It appears to have borne fruit; and it was perhaps following a further donation a decade later that the University was recompensed for its generosity with a large watercolour of the monastery.[54]

On their return, their vow of poverty reasserted, the travellers handed over the proceeds of their mission to the treasurer, the *skeuophylax*. It might be a very substantial sum: when Covel was at the Lavra in 1677 an 'emissary' returned with 1,000 dollars.[55] The *skeuophylax* 'lays it out upon necessary occasions,' says Georgirenes, 'and what is left, is kept to defray the Charge of another Voyage', and so the cycle is renewed. Successful fund-raisers might receive special recognition. Covel wrote:

> those of years and standing, if they bring home good store of money are undoubtedly made ηγούμενος the year following. ... [But if] when they return they bring little or nothing, and give a sorry account of their time, they are turned by with disgrace.[56]

If Covel was right about the scale of the Lavra's operation, it is not at all unlikely that Joseph served on one of these expeditions of which he says

53 G. Hofmann, 'Athos e Roma', *Orientalia Christiana*, v/2 (no.19, 1925), pp. 165f, Document 14. Cf. below, p. 50.

54 Petition, Oxford, Bodl. Lib., MS Willis, fol. 52, fols 197–8; watercolour, MS Gr. Misc.a.1. I owe my knowledge of these episodes to the kindness of Mr Andrew Honey. The petition is valuable for the light it sheds on the Turkish taxation of the monasteries: Pantocratoras was then assessed to pay 1,000 of the 20,000 crowns assessed as the Kapitan Pasha's annual due, double the total demanded in Covel's time, and in addition a *per capita haraç* of 10 crowns to the sultan. See also Dawkins, *The Monks of Athos*, p. 324.

55 BL, Add. MS 22912, fol. 341.

56 BL, Add. MS 22914, fol. 40v; Hasluck, 'The First English Traveller's Account', p. 111.

so much. Two or three years of travel beyond the Holy Mountain will certainly have enlarged the mental as well as the visual horizons of those who took part, and may often have made it hard for them to readjust to the narrower life to which they would again be confined.

There was another kind of narrowness at which Georgirenes bridled, at least in later life, whether or not his sensitivity was kindled by the broadening experience of travel. This was the exclusion of women and of all female creatures whatsoever from the Mountain. It is the theme with which he begins his account, noting not only the steps taken by the monks to prevent feminine infiltration of their houses but the threat of excommunication directed even against the female members of the families of lay fishermen, should they happen to step upon the sacred shore. It is the theme with which he closes his account again: 'Thus much of Mount *Athos*, wherein is a thing remarkable, beyond all example, that in a space of ground, 160 miles compass, where no less than 6000 men constantly live, there should not be seen a Woman.'[57]

This traditionally obsessive rejection of women appears to have been a matter on which he felt strongly for, not long before his book was written, as will be seen, Georgirenes as archbishop had used his authority to promote equality of the sexes among a congregation of his own.

If the archbishop's subsequent career saw a reaction against discrimination on grounds of sex, he was to prove also to be an enemy of sectarianism, as we shall see in later chapters. Ever since the Fourth Crusade and the Latin occupation which followed, the Athonite monasteries had for most of the time maintained an unwavering opposition to any dealings with the Church of Rome. Whether this struck young Joseph as strange, we cannot say: as a native of the Kyklades, after all, he would have encountered

57 *A Description of the Present State*, pp. 86, 111–12; and see below, p. 230. Martin, 'Some Western Images', p. 69, observinsg that Georgirenes' expectation that his readers will find the exclusion of women 'remarkable' is more naturally a western than an Orthodox reaction, suggests it is an 'exclamation' interpolated by the English translator. One may agree with the observation without accepting the conclusion: it might rather be an indication of a western cast of mind in Georgirenes himself by the time he came to write his book.

strongly pro-Catholic sentiment among many of the Orthodox of his childhood, more than willing to accept both education and confession from the Capuchin missionaries. That he would have encountered implacable hostility to Rome among many of his fellow monks in his early years on Athos, however, is beyond doubt, and it was certainly a lively topic at the Great Lavra, where the attitude to Rome had from time to time shown a certain ambiguity.[58]

Inevitably, as was the case with Melos, almost all of the evidence for contacts between Athos and the Catholic Church comes from the latter, again largely contained in the records of the *Sacra Congregatio de Propaganda Fide*. Catholic interest in the Holy Mountain can be traced back at least as far as the early days of the Latin empire of Constantinople. In 1213 Pope Innocent III took the monasteries under the protection of the Holy See; and even after the Greek restoration in 1261 the emperor Michael Palaeologus and his patriarch Bekkos continued to work for the reconciliation of the Eastern and Western Churches.[59] In 1438–9 there were *hēgoumenoi* of Athonite monasteries present at the Council of Florence, and at least three signed the bull of union which emerged. By the early seventeenth century, in the deep shadow of Ottoman rule, contact between Athos and Rome had become unexceptional at all levels. In 1611 and 1620 monks of Athos were to be found studying in the school attached to the Jesuit church of St Benedict in Constantinople; in 1622 monks stayed in Constantinople as guests of the Jesuits, and one of them even took the opportunity to make his profession of the Catholic faith.

Reports of such contacts and conquests soon captured the interest of the Holy Congregation in Rome. The monks of Mount Athos, it was

58 The most useful collection of materials for the study of relations between Rome and the Holy Mountain is provided by Hofmann, 'Athos e Roma', pp. 137–83; cf. idem, 'Rom und Athosklöster', *Orientalia Christiana*, viii (1926), pp. 4–39. For a brief survey of relations between Athos and Rome over the past millennium, see M. Plested, 'Athos and the West: Benedictines, Crusaders and Philosophers', *Friends of Mount Athos, Annual Report 2007* (Oxford, 2008), pp. 43–54.

59 Hofmann, 'Athos e Roma', pp. 148f. and Doc. 1; D. J. Geanakoplos, *The Emperor Michael Palaeologus and the West, 1258–1282* (Cambridge, MA, 1959), pp. 264–73.

well known, were held in great respect by the Greeks and by their bishops, who were indeed for the most part selected from their number, and if the monks could be won over to Rome the road to reunion would be short and smooth: so, at least, the secretary of the Congregation, Mgr Francesco Ingoli, wrote in a memorandum to his masters. They were persuaded, and a Greek Catholic priest from Zante, Alexandros Vasilopoulos, a graduate of the Greek college in Rome, was sent to assess the possibilities. At the same time word of what was afoot was sent to Catholic bishops in Zante and Constantinople and to the Archbishop of Candia, with instructions to watch and report on Vasilopoulos' activities. He set off for Constantinople in January 1627 with letters to the bishop and to the Venetian envoy, stating explicitly that his brief was to work for the reconciliation of East and West. As early as 9 October the Holy Congregation received Vasilopoulos' report, which described the Holy Mountain and its monasteries, their relics and their manuscripts, gave an encouraging assessment of the prospects for winning the monks over to the cause of reunion, and recommended the establishment of a mission, initially to the Great Lavra, with himself as the first missionary. The Congregation became at once sufficiently excited by the prospect of luring Athos into the Catholic fold as to write the same day to a Russian metropolitan appointing him to steer the process – 'quod magnum patet catholicae fidei propagationi ostium aperiendum esse in ecclesia orientali' (since the opening of a door into the Eastern Church would be a great thing for the propagation of the Catholic faith).[60]

The following year the Holy Congregation received from another Greek Catholic priest, Kanachios ('Canachio Rossi'), a Peloponnesian from Nauplia, a very full description of sixteen of the monasteries, in which, he said, he had almost always been well received. At the Great Lavra he had met the ex-patriarch Anthimos II and at Esphigmenou (Tousimenou) a bishop, both of whom had spoken warmly of their desire for union with Rome, a feeling he had found to be widespread among the monks. There is nothing perfunctory about his report. At the Lavra he had had some discussion about the viability of reunion with the abbot, whom he characterizes

60 Hofmann, 'Athos e Roma', pp. 139ff, 150–7 and Docs 2–12; Geanakoplos, *Emperor Michael Palaeologus and the West*, pp. 264–73.

as a rather remote figure, sitting alone on his dais in the refectory, his silver-topped staff beside him. A tactful host, the abbot had said nothing against the Church of Rome; but he did note that the pope's design of bringing the monasteries over to the western rite ran the risk of making them an object of suspicion to the Turks. 'Pretty well all the other monks listened to me eagerly, and marvelled at the orthodoxy of the pope and his good will towards the Greek people.' Kanachios found himself at the Lavra for the feast of Pentecost, and spent the night in church with the monks, who sang like angels and read like bumpkins. Robed as a monk at the order of the abbot, and placed in the choir, the visitor was happy to expound many passages of scripture at the monks' request, and took the opportunity to add a Catholic slant to his remarks, to which they listened with pleasure, forever calling the pope 'most blessed' and 'all-holiest'. The master of ceremonies asked Kanachios to read out Saint Gregory Nazianzus's sermon on Pentecost, after which Anthimos, arrayed in his full patriarchal canonicals, read another, by Saint John Chrysostom. Kanachios was plainly impressed by Anthimos, and not a little flattered by the attention he received from the old patriarch and indeed from the monks also. Anthimos, patriarch for a year in 1622, frankly explained that he had sold his office to Kyrillos Lucaris (Cyril Lucaris) for an agreed sum, and told of his ambition to go to Rome to pay his respects to the pope, if only his advanced age would allow.[61] Death thwarted this hope, and Anthimos was buried in the Lavra.[62] That was the year, 1628, in which Father Ignatios, *prohēgoumenos* of Vatopedi, travelled to Rome to seek charity from the Congregatio; he came with a letter of introduction from Kanachios.[63] Mgr Ingoli, the secretary of the Sacred Congregation, eagerly seized upon Ignatios' offer to work for the reunion of Vatopedi with Rome, though he ignored Kanachios' advice that the best hope was to work through Ignatios alone and, instead, insisted on sending him back to the Holy Mountain with a companion. Ever ambitious, Ingoli urged Ignatios to try to win over not merely his own monastery but all twenty, and to negotiate with their abbots for the establishment of

61 Ibid. pp. 141, 158–65 and Doc. 13; esp., for Lavra, pp. 160f.

62 Cf. above p. 36, and n. 31.

63 Cf. above p. 46, and n. 53.

a Catholic school.[64] Ignatios appears to have had no immediate success, though the seed was sown.

Meanwhile Vasilopoulos was still at work, though with declining enthusiasm and nothing to show. Early in 1631 he was in Smyrna, on his way back to Rome. Here he found the Orthodox archbishop keenly pro-Catholic and eager for him to remain and give the Lenten sermons. Tired of missionary work, he agreed to give one only, for Septuagesima, and resumed his westward journey only to be seized as an infidel off the coast of the Peloponnese. It was only the intervention of a French captain and the payment of a ransom that saved his life – and allowed him to write to the Congregation proposing that the French king be asked to bestow lavish honours on the captain; now thoroughly disillusioned, he added his view of the corrupt characters of the monks, and their invincible ignorance.[65] Kanachios' determination, however, was evidently stronger, and it may be – we do not know – that Ignatios' advocacy had played a crucial part; for at last in February 1636, despite 'questo orribile freddo', a Catholic school opened in Karyes at the Protaton, where 'si ritrovano 20 persone come vicerettori degli monasteri', a ready target for hopes of reunion. The school had as master a nephew of Kanachios, 'Niccolo Rossi', who had studied at Rome in the Greek college of St Athanasius; by June it had ten monks as students. Two years later the number of students had doubled, following a curriculum which included secular learning as well as the Catholic doctrine of the sacraments. All was well for three more years. But in 1641 Turkish interference forced Rossi to move the school to Thessaloniki, where, though Athonite monks still attended, together with many laymen, it was bound to be less effective as a constant source of Catholic influence. Rossi died in 1643, and the school soon declined under his successors. Though the Congregation in Rome tried to have the school returned to Athos, not necessarily to Karyes, by 1646 it appears to have sickened, and it died soon afterwards.[66] But it had clearly made

64 Hofmann, 'Athos e Roma', pp. 141, 166f. and Docs 15–16.

65 Ibid. p. 168 and Doc. 17.

66 Ibid. pp. 141f., 169–75 and Docs 17–21. See also Hofmann, 'Rom und der Athos: Briefwechsel zwischen dem Missionar auf dem Athos Nikolaus Rossi und der

a favourable impression on the monastic representatives at the Protaton at Karyes, for in 1643 they dispatched an 'epistola synodica' to the Holy Congregation in Rome, petitioning to have a church and school allowed to them in Rome itself; in return, they offered to provide *and endow* a monastery for Catholic Basilians (i.e. monks of the Order of St Basil who followed the Catholic rite) on the Holy Mountain.[67] This was the high point in the Congregation's long and patient attempt to win over the twenty monasteries to be the centre of support for the drive for reconciliation and reunion. The proposal was greeted with excitement and warm enthusiasm. A reply was sent, offering an even better site than that sought, which was not 'in loco salubris aeris': the Athonite delegation would see this for themselves when they arrived. But nothing happened.

Disappointed of the prize which had for a moment seemed within their grasp, Rome turned to a more low-key, cautious approach, using western rather than Greek agents, and in 1646–7 attempted to secure a French educational mission to Mount Athos. The order chosen was not that of the Capuchins, well established as they were in Constantinople and the Archipelago, but that of the Minimi, the friars of S. Francesco da Paola. In their black habits they might perhaps mingle more readily with the Greeks. More significantly, they were committed to an austerity of diet which even surpassed the restraint of their monastic hosts, abstaining not only from meat but from fish also, as well as from the imported dairy products and eggs which the Athonites enjoyed when they could. The apostolic nuncio in Paris was asked to find the necessary personnel, the French ambassador in Constantinople to ascertain their tax position and to treat for the good offices of the 'Bostangi Bassi', who might not otherwise recognize the unfamiliar habit of the Minimi, in the assurance

Kongregation de Propaganda Fide, Quellenausgabe mit Einführung', *Orientalia Christiana Analecta*, 142 (1954).

67 Hofmann, 'Athos e Roma', pp. 142, 175f. and Doc. 23: 'cellam seu monasterium cum possessionibus et iurisdictionibus suis in eodem Monte Sancto'. In the text as transcribed, the request is for a church, but the word is crossed out and 'school' written.

that his expenses would be fully covered by the Holy Congregation.[68] Three friars were identified and appointed, their role being to teach literacy to the monks, so that they might become 'capaci delle verità cattoliche'. But there the story ends.[69]

The final attempt to secure the reunion of East and West in this period was not an undertaking of the Holy Congregation but of the Jesuits, who, as we have seen, had had a series of contacts with monks of the Holy Mountain since the early years of the century; it was very much a private initiative of a dedicated and enthusiastic French Jesuit, Père Isaac d'Aultry. In 1633 there had been an attempt, alongside the other approaches then being pursued, to establish a Jesuit mission on Athos. It had had the approval of the new patriarch, Kyrillos II Kontares, successor to the 'Lutheran' first Kyrillos (Cyril), Lucaris. But Kontares was thought too close to Rome – he was later, indeed, to accept the supremacy of the pope – and the Jesuit attempt appears to have failed when he fell before the year was out. Père d'Aultry was not one to accept a setback, and he evidently resolved to follow his chosen path alone. His own attempt to win the monks to the great cause of reconciliation occupied most of the period *c.*1645–60, and it centred on the Great Lavra.[70] The evidence begins with two letters from Père d'Aultry, written on an urgent visit to France when he judged that success was within his grasp if only he could gain access to a substantial sum of money. The first letter was a rather formal communication in Latin to the Society's General, Piccolomini, the second a more discursive account in French sent to the latter's *assistente* for France, Père François Annat. Writing from Marseilles to the General, he tells him that the monks of Athos have lately renewed their oft-repeated offer of a site for a permanent Jesuit mission, at a price of 1,000 *aurei*. It is, he admits, not a trivial sum. But all Greek confessors, preachers, bishops and metropolitans are drawn from the twenty-two [sic] monasteries and the 6,000 monks they contain, and whoever educates the

68 The bostangi bassi (bachi) was the head of the bostangis, a corps of valets who worked in the gardens of the sultan, see Galland, *Voyages inédits*, p. 314, n. 1.

69 Ibid. pp. 143, 176–8 and Docs 24–6. See G. M. Roberti, *Disegno storico dell' ordine de' Minimi*, 3 vols (Rome, 1902–22) ii, p. 689.

70 Hofmann, 'Athos e Roma', pp. 144–5, 178–80 and Docs 27–8.

monks controls the education of all Greece.[71] To Annat he wrote another letter from Paris on 13 January 1651, thanking him for an encouraging letter of 19 December, and outlining the position in more detail. He had always, he said, made a point of cultivating the *hēgoumenoi* of the Athonite monasteries, and while at Thessaloniki succeeded so well with the abbot and fathers of the Lavra that they actually gave him a small ruined church of their own in that city. He had spent 1644 and 1645 attempting to rebuild it, without the support of the French consul, to which he had felt himself entitled, but the work had been overtaken by the outbreak of hostilities between Turkey and Venice, and he had had to withdraw, having found himself the Society's sole representative there for more than a year. And now for the good news: the Lavra had offered him a site within their *enclos*, with a little church already there and enough land to provide bread and wine for three Jesuits. Admittedly this would not be a gift: the price was 1,000 *escuz* and it would cost a further 200 to build them a house. But what an opportunity! From that base they would be able to visit all twenty-two monasteries and their 6,000 monks, educate the younger of them and instruct the older, the source of the ecclesiastical hierarchy – though it would call for a certain patience and tact, for the older monks were usually ignorant and would obstruct the education of the younger, perceiving them as a threat to themselves. Nor should one overlook the potential of the Turks for obstruction: it would be necessary to win over the Bostangi Bashi to give permission. Finally, what was proposed cut across other Jesuit initiatives in the region, and might arouse opposition as a possible threat to scarce resources; no doubt a letter to Constantinople from Annat would do much to smooth the path. Having thus put his case, d'Aultry reverts to his own relations with the Lavra. While at Malta in the previous March, no doubt *en route* between the Aegean and France, he had told the Grand Master of the Knights of the Lavra's sympathetic support of the Jesuits

71 The twenty-two no doubt comprise the twenty 'ruling monasteries' together with the Protaton at Karyes and the *skētē* of St Anne: see *A Description of the Present State*, pp. 81–98, the monasteries numbered 1–21, plus St Anne. For the additional authority of the literate, cf. the mid-sixteenth-century observation of Belon, cited by Martin, 'Some Western Images', p. 53.

and of the monastery's sufferings at the hands of the omnipresent corsairs, and had obtained from him letters patent taking the monastery under his protection and forbidding all corsair vessels to molest the Great Lavra and its monks in any way whatsoever. He hoped, he wrote, to complement this initiative by obtaining a patent in the same terms from the Grand Duke of Tuscany, restraining the other great source of mischief, the corsairs of Leghorn (Livorno). 'Je croy,' he adds, 'qu'il y aura plus de difficulté à obtenir les douze cent escuz que ces deux patentes. Neanmoins nous avons à faire à un grand Maistre, à qui il sera facile s'il le veut ...' ['I believe that it will be more difficult to obtain the twelve hundred *escuz* than these two patents. Nevertheless, we are dealing with a Grand Master for whom it will be easy, if he wants it ...'].

Seven more years elapsed, and then the outcome of d'Aultry's long campaign was reported in two letters from the head of the Jesuit mission in Constantinople, Père François Martin, to the Society's general, Père Nickel, whose letter of 22 April 1658 had taken nearly six months to reach him, though prudently dispatched in two copies by different routes. Having previously received the General's approval, and (it would appear) having at last surmounted the financial difficulties, d'Aultry had left Constantinople for Athos on 17 March, only to find that, having had so long to reconsider, the fathers of the Lavra had lost their enthusiasm for his project and were no longer willing to agree to let him have what had been promised. This time the postal service appears to have been miraculously swift, for Martin's letter of 21 October was answered by Nickel barely a week later (if that can be believed), expressing his dismay at the failure of d'Aultry's initiative, though on this occasion his letter took almost a whole year to make its way east. It was a sad sequel that Martin had to recount. At the end of the year d'Aultry had been captured by one or other of the marauders who made Aegean travel so hazardous, and held prisoner for almost a month in the depth of winter. On his release, he had managed to reach Naxos, where he died of a fever on 16 January 1659. No one could have foretold such an outcome, Martin continues: d'Aultry was only sixty-four years of age, and of such a robust constitution that he might have been expected to reach his father's four score years. His life's work in ruins, it may be surmised that he died of a broken heart.

It will have been during the years of d'Aultry's prolonged *pas de deux*, and probably in its later stages, that Georgirenes reached the Lavra, one of the bright young monks whom the Jesuit hoped to educate as a counterweight to the engrained ignorance of the seniors. He will in all probability have been living there, and have taken part in the discussions, as opinion hardened against any facilitation of the Catholic dream of reunion, whether that was the result of changing theological perceptions or merely of a loss of nerve which must have become ever more debilitating as the Turkish siege of Candia dragged on.

There has always, moreover, been a substantial body of feeling among the monks of the Lavra and of Athos generally that remains implacably opposed to any compromise with the antichrist who occupies the throne of Peter. The swing of opinion against d'Aultry may have coincided with, and given new strength to, those who shared that way of thinking, which is reflected in one of the most arresting stories in the anecdotal tradition of the Lavra. Some of the Lavra monks had allowed a Latin mass, whereupon the monastery was wrapped in a black mist. Those of the monks who had joined in this sacrilege became a terrible example, for when they died their wicked bodies refused to decompose; and when, after the customary three years, they were exhumed for their bones to be gathered and transferred to the charnel house the bodies were found to be still incorrupt, though black and swollen like vampires, *brikolakes*. Still so, they were put away in what came to be called the Cave of the Wicked Dead in the face of the inaccessible cliff below Cape Prodromos. The story was still widely current in the 1930s, told – as oral traditions are – as if it had happened yesterday, and to be heard from the monks of Tousimenou and Philotheou, from an unidentified muleteer, and from a lay servant at the Lavra; it was thought too tactless, too hurtful, to have questioned the Lavra monks themselves.[72] Coming from Melos, all too familiar with the horror of vampires, the story would have struck a chord with the young Joseph. It was designed to warn

72 Dawkins, a visitor to Mount Athos since 1905, *The Monks of Athos*, pp. 304–6, referring to visits of 1931–5; cf. Loch, a frequent visitor to the monasteries from 1928, when he came to live in Ouranopolis, *Athos*, p. 201. For the location of the cave, see Dawkins, *The Monks of Athos*, pp. 305f.; Loch, p. 193.

and deter collaborators, yet to a more sophisticated hearer who had known the advantages of cooperation between Catholic and Orthodox in the Melos of his childhood, and who may have regretted the denial of opportunity for a Jesuit education at the Lavra itself, the story might instead have suggested that reconciliation of the Eastern and Western Churches was long overdue, for they shared a common enemy in a time of the increased confidence and success of Islam.

It was perhaps time to move on, to Constantinople.

CHAPTER 3

Constantinople (1661–1667)

Jonathan Harris

Georgirenes left almost no record of his time in Constantinople, but it is possible to imagine what his first impressions must have been on arriving in the city in the mid-1660s from the accounts of other seventeenth-century visitors. As he approached, whether by sea or by land, he might well have been inspired by what he saw only to receive a very different impression once he was inside the walls. The Venetian Pietro della Valle (1586–1652) who arrived in August 1614 wrote that,

> there is little level ground in Constantinople, because of the unevenness of the hills which, as well as creating many valleys in between them, overhang the seas on either side. This makes the city appear most beautiful to anyone approaching it or viewing it from afar over the sea ... Yet within there is nothing at all to match the beauty of the exterior, and indeed here it is very ugly. For the streets, which would be better if they were well maintained (as they must have been in other times) are today, through the negligence of the inhabitants, scarcely passable.[1]

The narrow, crooked streets with their tall, overhanging houses created a warren of darkness and disorder at odds with the distant prospect of the narrow peninsula surrounded by blue water. The Englishman George Sandys (1578–1644), who was there a few years earlier than della Valle, likewise complained that 'there is not in the world an object that promiseth so much afar off to the beholders, and entered so deceiveth the expectation ...'[2] For a young monk who had spent the whole of his life on the sequestered rural island of Melos and the monastic peace of Athos, the first experience of

1 *The Pilgrim: The Travels of Pietro della Valle*, trans. G. Bull (London, 1989), pp. 7–8.

2 G. Sandys, *A Relation of a Journey Begun in An. Dom. 1610* (London, 1615), p. 36. Cf. W. Lithgow, *The Totall Discourse of the Rare Adventures and Painfull Peregrinations* (Glasgow, 1906), pp. 124–5.

Constantinople's streets must have been more shocking than it was for della Valle and Sandys. They were, after all, seasoned travellers who were familiar with the equally chaotic and filthy streets of western European cities such as London, Rome and Paris. Indeed some travellers went so far as to compare Constantinople favourably to those places and to extol its streets as being safer and better policed.[3] Georgirenes, who had never experienced urban life before, is likely to have reacted in much the same way as one admittedly rather jaundiced nineteenth-century traveller who was clearly accustomed to more ordered urban conditions:

> The first thing for surprise is the squalid aspect of the streets, the pavement being formed of irregular blocks of stone of all sizes and all shapes that present a bewildering succession of sharp angles and treacherous cavities. You trip over the former, you slide with unpleasant suddenness into the latter. These pitfalls are full of black, fetid water; a swarm of pestilent flies broods there; and the pungent stench stifles you. A novice still, you give a side glance and look down at the mass of ordure that lines the thoroughfare; at rotting vegetables; offal over which dogs snarl and wrangle; here and there a cat with its head beaten in ...[4]

Pressure of population was largely to blame for Constantinople's unprepossessing urban landscape. The capital of the Ottoman Empire was a mighty metropolis of some 600,000 inhabitants, concentrated in the narrow promontory bordered to the north by the city's harbour, the Golden Horn. To feed the multitude two hundred tons of bread were baked in the city every day, twenty thousand oxen were slaughtered there every month and seven million sheep and lambs every year.[5] Consequently, as della Valle observed, 'within the circle of the walls there is no empty space whatever, nor any vineyards or gardens as in Rome: everywhere is packed tight'.[6] Through these thronged streets the doubtless rather bewildered Georgirenes would have had to have made his way.

3 *The Travels of Lord Charlemont in Greece and Turkey, 1749*, ed. W. B. Stanford and E. J. Finopoulos (London, 1984), p. 209.

4 K. Bey, *The Evils of the East: Or, Truths about Turkey* (London, 1888), pp. 21–2.

5 P. Mansel, *Constantinople: City of the World's Desire, 1453–1924* (London, 1995), pp. 118–19.

6 *The Pilgrim*, pp. 6–8.

Quite apart from the crowds and the cluttered streets, there was another feature of Constantinople that cannot have failed to have struck him. In the Christian enclaves of Melos and Athos, there were scarcely any Muslims to be seen apart from the Ottoman Kadi and his staff. Here by contrast, at the very heart of the Ottoman Empire, Islam was completely dominant. The great imperial mosques towered over the streets and their domes and minarets spread across the city's skyline. The muezzin's call marked the hours of the day. As an Orthodox Christian and a Greek, Georgirenes can hardly have failed to have felt a pang to see another religion so triumphant in a city which had once been the centre of his faith. After all, Constantinople had a long history that predated its current role as the seat of the Ottoman sultan. Founded in around 800 BC by colonists from the ancient Greek city of Megara, it had been known until AD 324 as Byzantion. It had then been refounded by the first Christian Roman emperor, Constantine (306–37), and renamed Constantinople or 'city of Constantine' in his honour. For the next 1,100 years it was the capital of the Christine Byzantine Empire until, on 29 May 1453, the Ottoman sultan Mehmed II (1451–81) had stormed its defensive walls after a six-week siege.

One of Mehmed's first actions, as soon as the city was under his control was to declare that the cathedral of the Holy Wisdom or Hagia Sophia should henceforth be a mosque. In the years that followed he and his successors had slowly erased the traces of the Christian past by building great new mosques of their own, each one surrounded a complex of religious, educational and charitable buildings. Mehmed's mosque of the Conqueror replaced the church of the Holy Apostles. The vast Süleymaniye, built by between 1550 and 1557 for Süleyman the Magnificent (1520–66), incorporated columns and paving stones from other demolished churches. The complex boasted a hospital, an orphanage, a soup kitchen, an insane asylum, a library, baths, a hospice for travellers, as well as the grand central mosque.[7] Opposite Hagia Sophia and on the same grand scale was the mosque of Sultan Ahmed, also known as the Blue Mosque, with its six minarets. Built between 1609 and 1616, it now provided the setting for the sultan

7 *An Ottoman Traveller: Selections from the Book of Travels of Evliya Çelebi*, trans. R. Dankoff and S. Kim (London, 2010), pp. 8–17.

and his court to attend Friday prayers. The most recently completed was the New Mosque, or Yeni Cami which overlooked the Golden Horn, Constantinople's broad harbour. Work on it had started in 1597 but it had not been completed and what was built had burned down in 1660. The sultan's mother, Turhan Hadice, saddened by the sight of the blackened ruins, had commissioned an architect to rebuild and complete the mosque, which opened for worship in 1664. It attracted the admiration of one western visitor, Lady Mary Wortley Montagu (1689–1762), who saw it in 1718 and described it in a letter to Lady Bristol as: 'the most beautiful structure I ever saw, be it spoke to the honour of our sex, for it was founded by the mother of Mohammed IV. Between friends, St Paul's church [in London] would make a pitiful figure near it ...'[8] Many Christian visitors, though, were much more interested in exploring Constantinople's Christian past than its Muslim present. George Sandys spent many pages of his account of his visit describing the religion of Islam but says almost nothing about the mosques and their surrounding buildings. Rather, he was fascinated by the former cathedral of Hagia Sophia, which he considered 'exceedeth all not onely the rest' of the mosques but even 'all other fabricks whatsoever throughout the whole universe'. Sandys was also drawn to the Hippodrome, known to the Turks as the At Meydani or 'horse square'. It was here that in Byzantine times chariot races had been run while the emperor looked on from his private viewing box, although the banks of seating that had once accommodated throngs of spectators had long since disappeared. The place reminded Sandys of Smithfield Market in London.[9] It is hard to believe that Georgirenes did not seek out some of the remains of Byzantium at some point during his stay.

Such antiquarian musings would soon have been punctured by contemporary reality for Georgirenes had arrived in Constantinople at a rather tense time. On the face of things, the Ottoman Empire was as powerful as

8 Lady Mary Wortley Montagu, *The Complete Letters*, ed. Robert Halsband, 3 vols (Oxford, 1965–7), i, p. 400.

9 Sandys, *Relation of a Journey*, pp. 31–2, 34; Jonathan Haynes, *The Humanist as Traveler: George Sandys's Relation of a Journey Begun in An. Dom. 1610* (London and Toronto, 1986), pp. 65–81.

ever. The conqueror's successors still ruled the city and the vast empire of which it was the centre. The sultan was Mehmed IV (1648–87), who was also the caliph or supreme leader of Islam, the representative of the Prophet Mohammed. Mehmed was an able enough ruler, but his main passion in life was hunting. Consequently he seldom visited Constantinople and spent very little time in the sultan's traditional residence there, the Topkapı palace. He preferred to base himself in Adrianople, which gave better access to the countryside of Thrace. Summer and winter he would sally forth two or three hours before sunrise, to the dismay of local farmers who had their crops trampled and ruined in the furious pursuit. Anyone wishing to curry favour with the sultan knew the way to his heart. The English ambassador presented him with four large mastiffs, which were then set to kill a lion and a bear, to the great delight of their new owner.

Fortunately Mehmed did not have to curtail his hunting too much, because he had an able pair of hands to whom he could delegate much of the business of government. From 1656, he was advised by Köprülü Mehmed, the first in a dynasty of energetic grand viziers. In 1661 Köprülü Mehmed was succeeded by his son Köprülü Ahmed Fazıl, who presided over the final completion of the Ottoman conquest of Venetian Crete.[10] Nevertheless, the younger Köprülü had inherited a difficult state of affairs, which could not be resolved overnight. As a result of the Cretan war, trade was languishing and taxes had been raised to fund an all-out effort to bring the conflict to a conclusion. Not surprisingly, there was discontent and, as one English observer recorded, in some areas of the Ottoman Empire the populace:

> openely in the streets rayled highly against the grand signor minding his hunting more than his subjects and sayed openly that their emperor was mad, and that speedily his brother who hath more braines and will take more paynes in the management of publike affayres, will be set up in the throne. That empire is at a very low ebbe, and

10 G. F. Abbot, *Under the Turk in Constantinople: A Record of Sir John Finch's Embassy, 1674–1681* (London, 1920), p. 25; A. C. Wood, 'The English embassy at Constantinople, 1660–1762', *English Historical Review* 40 (1925), pp. 533–61, at p. 542; John Freely, *Istanbul: The Imperial City* (London, 1996), pp. 241–2.

> must have strange changes in a little time; their weakness is apparent; they do not want only mony and men too, but braines to governe what they have.[11]

Georgirenes can hardly have been unaware of the discontent around him and it is likely that he spent most of his time in Constantinople well away from the main squares and centres of population safely among his own Orthodox co-religionists.

For all the disappearance of Byzantium and the overwhelming visibility of the symbols of Islam, Constantinople was not an entirely Muslim city. There were substantial Jewish and Christian communities and George Sandys reckoned that put together they amounted to about half of the city's population.[12] They tended to be concentrated well away from the centre of things at Topkapı and the Blue Mosque. The Jews, many of them Ladino speakers whose ancestors had been expelled from Catholic Spain, lived in the districts of Balat and Haskoy on either side of the Golden Horn. The Armenians had their church and patriarchate at the fishing harbour of Kumkapi on the southern shore of the city. Greek Christians, the descendants of the Byzantines, were accommodated in the district known as Phanar on the upper reaches of the Golden Horn. Here the church of St George acted as the seat of the ecumenical Patriarch of Constantinople, the successor of the patriarchs of the Byzantine Empire and the senior patriarch of the Orthodox Churches. It would have been to Phanar that Georgirenes would have made his way when he reached Constantinople in around 1664.

Like the Jews and the Armenians, the ecumenical patriarchate and the Christian Greeks of Constantinople enjoyed a broad tolerance under their Ottoman masters. After his conquest of Constantinople in 1453, Sultan Mehmed II had quickly realized that he needed to reconcile his Christian subjects to his rule and to ensure that they did not try to make common cause with the Christian powers of the West. He therefore saw to it that the vacant patriarchal throne was occupied by a candidate who was diametrically opposed to any union between the Orthodox and Catholic Churches. On

11 K. M. Setton, *Venice, Austria and the Turks in the Seventeenth Century* (Philadelphia, 1991), pp. 212–13, citing TNA SP97, XIX, fols 75–6.

12 Sandys, *Relation of a Journey*, p. 77.

6 January 1454, the monk Gennadios, formerly known as George Scholarios, had been enthroned according to the same rites and ceremonial as had prevailed in Byzantine times. Mehmed himself took the role in the ceremony that had formerly been played by the Byzantine emperor, of handing the new patriarch his staff of office. The patriarch thus became a protégé and servant of the sultan. The Ottomans allowed religious minorities to keep their own laws and customs, constituting a distinct *milet* or nation under the sultan's overlordship. The patriarch was now recognized as the head of the Greek *milet*, in charge of courts that had jurisdiction over all matters with a broadly religious dimension such as marriage and wills. There were, moreover, some forty Greek churches scattered throughout the city by the mid-seventeenth century in which the Greek Orthodox liturgy and rites continued unhindered. The main restriction on their activities was that they were not allowed to ring bells to summon the faithful to prayer, probably because it would compete with the muezzin's call.[13] Foreign observers concluded that the Greek Christians had a very easy time under the Ottomans: 'They have as great Liberty, save onely the use of Bels, as we have under our Princes ... There is free liberty of Conscience, for all kinds of Religion, through all [the sultan's] dominions ...'[14] Appearances were deceptive, however, for the Greeks were extremely vulnerable to arbitrary actions on the part of their masters. If a church was seized to be converted into a mosque there was, in practice, little that could be done about it, and the number of Greek churches in Constantinople tended to shrink as the years went by. In Byzantine times, the patriarch had, of course, resided next to the cathedral of Hagia Sophia. After 1453, with the cathedral having been made into a mosque, the patriarch was moved to the second largest of Constantinople's churches, the Holy Apostles. That, however, was shortly afterwards taken over too, as the sultan had decided to demolish it and replace it with his mosque of the Conqueror. The patriarch moved to the much more modest

13 J. Harris, *The End of Byzantium* (London, 2010), pp. 241–2; Steven Runciman, *The Great Church in Captivity: A Study of the Patriarch of Constantinople from the Eve of the Turkish Conquest to the Greek War of Independence* (Cambridge, 1968), pp. 161–71, 191.

14 Lithgow, *Totall Discourse*, p. 106.

church and monastery of the Virgin Pammakaristos in the north of the city overlooking the Golden Horn. That remained his seat until Sultan Murad III (1574–95) decided that he would dedicate a new mosque to commemorate his recent victories in Georgia and Azerbaijan. Rather than build anything new, he took over the Pammakaristos church in the spring of 1588 and it became the Mosque of Conquests (Fethiye Camii). The evicted patriarch moved to the new church of St George in Phanar.[15]

The Greeks were also vulnerable to manipulation of the patriarchal office for financial gain, for the Ottoman authorities could not resist making use of their powerful position. They had long ago come to expect a generous payment from a new patriarch to have his appointment approved. As time went by the 'gifts' became larger as rival candidates sought to outbid each other to obtain official backing for their election. Once they were elected, they were expected to pay regular gifts to the authorities to keep themselves in office. Much of this was raised through loans so that by 1678, the ecumenical patriarchate was reckoned to have debts totalling 350,000 dollars, which increased daily as the interest accumulated. The patriarch's revenues, on the other hand, were drawn from very limited sources such as admission fees paid by new bishops so there was never any hope of this vast debt ever being paid off.[16]

This state of affairs not only ensured that the patriarch was in permanent penury but also that patriarchs came and went with bewildering rapidity. The expectation of gain provided the Ottomans with a reason to see the incumbent of the patriarchate changed as often as possible and to find a motive for deposing him on any pretext. Sir Paul Rycaut (1629–1700), who was at the English embassy in Constantinople between 1661 and 1667, wryly observed that 'the Turks, finding this Fountain the fresher, and more

15 *Emperors, Patriarchs and Sultans of Constantinople: An Anonymous Greek Chronicle of the Sixteenth Century*, trans. M. Philippides (Brookline, MA, 1990), pp. 56–7; *Die byzantinischen Kleinchroniken*, ed. P. Schreiner, Corpus Fontium Historiae Byzantinae 12, 3 vols (Vienna, 1975–7), ii, p. 595.

16 P. Rycaut, *The Present State of the Greek and Armenian Churches in 1678* (London, 1679), pp. 93, 98, 113.

plentifully flowing for being drained, continually suck from this stream'.[17] At the time of Georgirenes' arrival, the patriarchal throne was probably occupied by Dionysios III, a man whose tenure typifies the seventeenth-century patriarchate. When his predecessor Parthenios IV had resigned in June 1662, Dionysios was quick to offer the phenomenal sum of 900,000 aspers and was duly consecrated. He enjoyed the office until October 1665 when he was unceremoniously ousted in turn and Parthenios IV returned for the second of his five periods in office. That was the norm throughout the seventeenth century. Between 1595 and 1695 there were sixty-one changes on the patriarchal throne but only thirty-one individual patriarchs, so often were they deposed and later reinstated. Not all patriarchs were simply dethroned: some were executed. Parthenios III was hanged in 1657 for supposedly conspiring against the sultan with foreign powers, Mehmed IV wishing to 'set an example to those who might wish to try that in future'. Gabriel II was hanged in 1659 after he had been deposed for trying to convert a Muslim to Christianity.[18] Rycaut summed up the position in which the patriarchate found itself:

> The contention between the Greek clergy for the Patriarchal Power at Constantinople hath begotten many troubles in the Church; for such whom Ambition and Covetousness excite with a desire for this Ecclesiastical Preferment, and having some riches of their own, and Credit to make up the rest at interest, seldom or never miss the prize that they pursue; for the arguments of Gifts and Benefits are so prevalent with the Grand Vizier and the other Turkish officers, that they can afford easie admittance to the most frivolous accusation that may be objected against the present Incumbant, by which means the Patriarch is often changed, and the Debts

17 Rycaut, *Present State of the Greek and Armenian Churches*, p. 98.

18 D. Kiminas, *The Ecumenical Patriarchate: A History of its Metropolitanates with Annotated Hierarch Catalogs* (Rockville, MD, 2009), pp. 40, 47; G. Podskalsky, *Griechische Theologie in der Zeit der Turkenherrschaft (1453–1821)* (Munich, 1988), p. 399; N. M. Vaporis, 'A Study of Ziskind Ms No. 22 of the Yale University Library: Some Aspects of the Ecumenical Patriarchate of Constantinople in the Seventeenth and Eighteenth Centuries', *Greek Orthodox Theological Review*, xii (1967), supplement, 1–40, at p. 31; Runciman, *Great Church in Captivity*, pp. 179n., 201–2; T. Papademetriou, *Render unto the Sultan: Power, Authority and the Greek Orthodox Church in the Early Ottoman Centuries* (Oxford and New York, 2015), pp. 19–36.

> of the Church increased, and the Election rather in the hands of the Turk than the Bishops ...[19]

Not all western observers were as sympathetic towards the Greeks of Constantinople as Rycaut. Several visitors to Constantinople compared them unfavourably to the ancient Greeks and denounced them as sadly lacking in the virtues of their forebears. George Sandys, who wanted to find out more about the city's Byzantine past, found them shockingly ill-informed about their own heritage: 'For not a Greek can satisfie the Inquirer in the history of their own calamities. So supine negligent are they, or perhaps so wise, as of passed evils to endeavour a forgetfulness'.[20] The Scotsman William Lithgow was scathing:

> They are wholly degenerate from their Auncestors in valour, virtue, and learning: Universities they have none, and civill behaviour is quite lost: formerly in derision they tearmed all other Nations Barbarians: A name now most fit for themselves, being the greatest dissembling lyers, inconstant, and uncivill people of all other Christians in the World.[21]

Such denunciations need not be taken too seriously. While classically educated westerners were fond of comparing the modern Greeks to the ancients, not all did so in such a negative way and many were sympathetic towards them as Christians living under infidel rule.[22]

It was during his stay in Constantinople that Georgirenes took the first steps to exploiting such sentiments, for his time there gave him the opportunity to come into contact with a much wider range of western opinion and thought than the Catholic missionaries that he might have encountered on Melos or Athos. He might have done so initially at the patriarchal academy of higher education, which had long been established near the church of St George in Phanar. In 1593 its curriculum had been updated to include

19 Rycaut, *Present State of the Greek and Armenian Churches*, p. 97.
20 Sandys, *A Relation of a Journey*, p. 36.
21 Ibid. pp. 36, 77; Lithgow, *Totall Discourse*, p. 105.
22 J. Harris, 'The Grecian Coffee House and Political Debate in London, 1688–1714', *The London Journal*, xxv (2000), pp. 1–13, at 5–6; T. J. B. Spencer, *Fair Greece, Sad Relic: Literary Philhellenism from Shakespeare to Byron* (London, 1954), pp. 119–22.

sciences alongside the obvious theology. There had even been an attempt to set up a Greek printing press there in the 1620s until the Ottomans decided that it was subversive and closed it down. The academy, however, survived and in 1666 was provided with a young and energetic director in the person of Alexander Mavrogordatos (1636–1709), who gave lectures on classical Greek, medicine and philosophy.[23] Mavrokordatos and several other teachers at the academy had studied in Italy, either in the Greek college of St Athanasius in Rome or at the University of Padua. There can be no doubt that what they had learned there was reflected in their teaching of non-theological subjects.[24] Georgirenes may well have attended some of the courses at the academy during his stay. If so, it would have given him an insight into the Christian world beyond the narrow confines in which he had moved so far.

Beyond Phanar, there was a much more direct way to come into contact with western European modes of thought, through the foreign embassies. The French had been the first to break ranks with a united Christian front against the Muslim Ottomans when they sent an ambassador to Constantinople in 1535.[25] There had been a chorus of disapproval at the French king establishing friendly relations with the infidel in this way, but slowly other countries had followed suit. The English had made a formal

23 N. Camariano, *Alexandre Mavrocordato, le grand drogman (1673–1709)* (Thessaloniki, 1970), pp. 14–15; N. Iorga, *Byzance après Byzance* (Paris, 1992, reprint), pp. 207–12; Runciman, *Great Church in Captivity*, pp. 114–15, 222; E. Layton, 'Nikodemos Metaxas: The First Greek Printer in the Eastern World', *Harvard Library Bulletin*, xv (1967), pp. 140–68; Vaporis, 'Study of Ziskind Ms No. 22', pp. 26–7.

24 On Greek students in Rome and Padua, see Heleni Porfyriou, 'La presenza greca in Italia tra cinque e seicento: Roma e Venezia', in D. Calabi and P. Lanaro, eds, *La città italiana e i luoghi degli stranieri XIV–XVIII secolo* (Rome, 1998), pp. 21–38, at pp. 22–3; G. Fabris, 'Professori e scolari greci all'università di Padua', *Archivio Veneto*, xxx (1942), pp. 121–65; Cleobulo Tsourkas, *Gli scholari greci di Padova nel rinnovamento culturale dell'oriente ortodosso* (Padua, 1959); C. Dima-Drağan, 'Le patriarche Chrysanthe Notaras et le docteur Jean Comnène – étudiants à Padoue', *Revue des Études Sud-Est Européennes*, vii (1969), pp. 691–3.

25 M. Heath, 'Unholy Alliance: Valois and Ottomans', *Renaissance Studies*, iii (1989), pp. 303–15; D. L. Jensen, 'The Ottoman Turks in sixteenth-century French diplomacy', *Sixteenth Century Journal*, xvi (1985), pp. 451–70.

treaty with the Ottomans in 1583 and established a permanent embassy. In 1660, Heneage Finch (1627/8–89), Earl of Winchilsea took up the post as representative of the newly restored monarchy and of the Levant Company. He installed himself in the embassy in Pera, across the Golden Horn from Constantinople proper where most of the foreign legations were now to be found.[26]

Not that the relationship between the Ottoman Porte and the Christian powers of western Europe was thenceforth particularly cordial. During the 1660s, there was considerable tension with the French because the Ottomans were well aware that they were sending help to the defenders of Candia, the last major Venetian stronghold on Crete. There were regular diplomatic incidents when French ambassadors considered themselves to have been slighted by the ponderous ceremony of the Ottoman court. On one occasion, the French envoy was roughly shoved outside by the palace eunuchs when he tried to march into an audience with the sultan without first having surrendered his sword. On another, the ambassador ended up in an unseemly tussle with one of the viziers over exactly where in the audience chamber his seat should be placed.[27] Nevertheless, the French maintained their presence in Constantinople and around the time of Georgirenes' arrival the ambassador was Denis de La Haye (1626–1722) who had been sent by Louis XIV with the task of improving relations with the Porte and securing better terms for French commerce. There is no evidence that Georgirenes had any contact with de la Haye, but in 1670, the office passed to Charles-Marie François Olier (1635–85), Marquis de Nointel. This was the man who did battle with the vizier over the seating arrangements as described above, and Georgirenes was later to meet him on Patmos.[28]

26 Wood, 'English Embassy', p. 542; S. P. Anderson, *An English Consul in Turkey: Paul Rycaut at Smyrna, 1667–1668* (Oxford, 1989), pp. 24–40.

27 D. Cantemir, *History of the Growth and Decay of the Othman Empire*, trans. N. Tindal (London, 1734), p. 424; A. Vandal, *L'Odyssée d'un ambassadeur: les voyages du Marquis de Nointel (1670–1680)* (Paris, 1900), pp. 229–30.

28 C. A. Frazee, *Catholics and Sultans: The Church and the Ottoman Empire* (London, 1983), pp. 100–1; Vandal, *L'Odyssée*, p. 55. See below p. 105.

Georgirenes did meet with at least one member of the English embassy during his stay in Constantinople. It was customary for an Anglican chaplain to reside in the English ambassador's palace with a salary of £100 a year paid by the Levant Company. In October 1664, a fellow of Queen's College Oxford, Henry Denton (*c.*1640–81), was appointed to the post. Described by Winchilsea as a 'modest, ingenious person', Denton was a keen student of languages and during his stay in Constantinople was said to have mastered Arabic, Syriac and Slavonic, and to have made impressive progress with Turkish. In the minute books of the Levant Company, though, he chiefly features for his complaints about the inadequacy of his salary.[29]

Denton was one of a small band of English intellectuals who were deeply interested in eastern Orthodoxy. Those Churches seemed, after all, to have a great deal in common with Anglicanism since they rejected the authority of the pope but maintained an episcopal hierarchy with apostolic succession. There had been some tentative contacts. Some decades before, Patriarch Cyril Lucaris had sent a fifth-century Greek manuscript of the Bible, the so-called *Codex Alexandrinus*, as a gift to King Charles I (r. 1625–49), and a number of Greek students had been dispatched to study at Oxford.[30] It was no doubt in pursuit of this interest in Orthodoxy that at some point Denton met Joseph Georgirenes. The only evidence for the acquaintance is Denton's own statement on the frontispiece of his English translation of Georgirenes' *Description of the Present State of Samos, Nicaria, Patmos and Mount Athos* that he had known the author in Constantinople. The two men probably communicated in Greek and it was no doubt from Denton that Georgirenes first learned something of England.

29 A. Hamilton, 'Henry Denton (c.1640–1681)', in H. C. G. Matthew and B. Harrison, eds, *The Oxford Dictionary of National Biography* 60 vols (Oxford University Press, 2004), xv, p. 853; J. B. Pearson, *A Biographical Sketch of the Chaplains to the Levant Company, maintained at Constantinople, Aleppo and Smyrna, 1611–1706* (Cambridge, 1883), pp. 15, 51.

30 H. Trevor-Roper, 'The Church of England and the Greek Church in the time of Charles I', *Religious Motivation: Biographical and Sociological Problems for the Church Historian*, ed. D. Baker (Oxford, 1978), pp. 213–40; Runciman, *Great Church*, pp. 289–93; G. A. Hadjiantoniou, *Protestant Patriarch: The Life of Cyril Lucaris (1572–1638), Patriarch of Constantinople* (Richmond, VA, 1961), pp. 92–3.

Nothing else is known about Georgirenes' stay in Constantinople except what he himself tells us. On 7 October 1666, by mandate of the sultan, he was consecrated Archbishop of the islands of Samos and Ikaria. The ceremony was performed by the ecumenical patriarch Parthenios IV, then still enjoying the second of his five brief spells in that precarious office.[31] The promotion brought Georgirenes' stay in Constantinople to an end.

31 *Description of the Present State*, pp. 32–7.

CHAPTER 4

Samos and Ikaria (1667–1671)

The new Archbishop of Samos appears to have been some thirty years old, his preferment not at all exceptional in an age of youth: his contemporary, Patriarch Dositheos of Jerusalem, was Archdeacon of Jerusalem at twenty, Archbishop of Caesarea at twenty-five and patriarch before he was thirty.[1] Under the Byzantine Empire Samos, like many of the Aegean islands, had been the see of a suffragan bishop under the Archbishop of Rhodes. But the Turkish conquest left the island desolate, not only without a bishop but without any substantial population at all. Eventually it was re-peopled from Mytilene, Vourla (ancient Klazomenai on the Turkish coast) and elsewhere, an event remembered still in the name of the village of 'Mytelenians', in the hills behind the then capital, Chora, and in that of 'Vourliote' on the north side of the island.[2] Well watered, agriculturally rich and densely wooded, the island soon regained its former prosperity; the patriarch in Constantinople appropriated the ecclesiastical revenues to his own church, and the Samians had to be content with the ministry of his vicar. According to Georgirenes, this state of affairs continued for a century, until the people demanded an archbishop of their own. The patriarch conceded their demand, and appointed the Bishop of next-door Ikaria to serve both islands. That was the arrangement which Georgirenes inherited. But it was not an altogether happy arrangement, for there was little love lost between the two islands. When Bernard Randolph visited Samos in Georgirenes' time, he found that 'they of *Samos* have a saying

1 For Georgirenes' probable age, see above, p. 5; Dositheos was aged 31 when he and Dionysios of Constantinople convened the Synod of Jerusalem (Bethlehem).

2 See J. Georgirenes, *A Description of the Present State of Samos, Nicaria, Patmos, and Mount Athos*, trans. H. Denton (London, 1677), pp. 2f., 25; M. Margarones, *Geographia Nomou Samou* (Karlovasi, 1966), pp. 66–71.

that when God made those Islands he order'd that all the rubbish should be cast upon *Icaria*' in the form of a barren and rocky mountain ridge – 'which they have no great reason to say, for they have their own share also of Mountains'.[3]

Following his consecration in Constantinople, the new archbishop made his way to Samos, to the then capital, Chora. Here was his cathedral of Hagia Paraskevi, and alongside it the archiepiscopal residence. It is hard now to form any very precise impression of this complex as it appeared in 1666, for both buildings were transformed by the great upsurge in Samian church construction in the following century. Hagia Paraskevi, no longer a cathedral since the transfer of the capital to Vathy during the years of independence (1834–1912), is built on a hillside site which slopes so sharply that the women's gallery overlooking the long nave is entered at the upper ground level. The archbishop's house, also entered at the upper level, was evidently rather grand, but all that now survives is a double flight of steps to a platform outside the front door, and the remains of a storeroom at lower ground level, of Melian form and so, perhaps, a construction of Georgirenes.[4]

Having reached Chora, the archbishop describes the procedure by which he took possession of the diocese. The first step was to make his

3 B. Randolph, *The Present State of the Islands in the Archepelago* (Oxford, 1687), p. 53. Ill-feeling between these islands was still noticeable up to the Second World War and later: A. J. Papalas, *Rebels and Radicals, Icaria 1600–2000* (Wauconda, IL, 2005), *passim*. For the geological and agricultural basis of the economy of the two islands, see A. Philippson, *Die griechischen Landschaften*, 4 vols (Frankfurt a.M., 1950–9), iv: *Das Aegaeische Meer und seine Inseln*, pp. 260–73.

4 For the typical Melian storeroom, see above, p. 12. The house of Georgirenes' time became obsolete, or was at least remodelled, in 1743, when the newly appointed Metropolitan Kallinikos built a new residence 'from the foundations up', behind the original house and entered at the lower level from a little square on the north side; it is now the Demarcheion. I am most grateful to Mr Ch. N. Landros, the director of the National Archives of Samos, and to the parish priest of Chora, Papas Demetris Papastamatiou, for their patience and care in guiding me around the town; and to Mr Landros for much further assistance with the *minutiae* of early modern and modern Samos, on which he is a leading authority.

way to the opposite end of town in order to exhibit the sultan's patent to the Turkish governor, the *cadi*, no doubt in a ceremony performed on the *loggia* which still survives, carried by an arch over the street at the end of the Turkish 'palace'. Next he summoned the head-men of all the villages to Chora – Greeks, indeed, but chosen by the Turks as safe – to whom the new archbishop read the patent before depositing it among the public records.

> This done, they all accompany him to the Cathedral Church, where after the Reading of his Institutions, given by the Patriarch, he is plac'd in the Archiepiscopal Throne, where every one comes to kiss his Hand, and he bestows upon them his Benediction; and then makes them a Speech (if he find himself of sufficient capacity to do't).[5]

There followed the handing-over of ecclesiastical dues – fifteen or twenty 'dollars' from the local priest in Chora, as an indication of the sum to be expected from the others. Regular income, of course, was much less: from the priests, four dollars in the first year, thereafter two; similarly from the Orthodox faithful forty-eight *aspers* (an *asper* is two fifths of a *piastre* or dollar) in the first year but only twenty-four in the second and subsequent years. Ordinations and weddings were to be the irregular source of the archbishop's remaining income. Marriages between islanders earned him a dollar, two dollars if the couple came from elsewhere, with a deterrent fee of three or four dollars against second or third weddings. All in all, these were no great riches. Bernard Randolph, indeed, found Samos 'the Seat of an Arch-Bishop, tho' of so mean an Estate, as it will hardly suffice to give him bread, when he has satisfied what is due to the Patriarck of *Constantinople*'.[6] No doubt it was this very poverty that made Georgirenes, poor monk though he was, acutely aware of economic factors in his account of his diocese.

If financial dependency on his flock might prove a source of friction, even less comfortable were relations with the civil power, the Ottoman officials, who, like the archbishop, resided in Chora.[7] The leading officer was the *cadi*, whose duties were primarily judicial, including the hearing of appeals against judgments of the archbishop, who exercised a delegated

5 *Description of the Present State*, p. 33.
6 Randolph, *Present State of the Islands*, p. 54.
7 *Description of the Present State*, pp. 6–12, 26–31.

jurisdiction to which many of the Greek population had recourse, especially the ecclesiastics. The duty of enforcing the *cadi*'s decisions lay with the second senior officer, the *aga*, who was also responsible for the collection of taxes. Apart from these two and their immediate associates – three or four families with the *cadi*, ten or a dozen men to assist the *aga* – there were very few Turks in the island: too few, in fact, for there to have been any pressure to *rebuild* the mosque, destroyed in a Venetian raid. In addition to the two resident officials, a third would visit every summer to collect the '*haratch*' (otherwise *kharadj* or *cizye*), the annual poll-tax levied by the Grand Signior on his male Christian subjects at the rate of three *piastres* a head – that is, fifteen times the sum they were required to pay to the archbishop. Exceptionally, among Samian residents only married men were subject to this tax, though an orphan incurred an obligation to pay on behalf of the family even if he were an infant; and all male Samians who were non-resident were required to pay. When the time came for the tax to be found, the *cadi* called a meeting of the village headmen to hear the warrant read and to be reminded of their responsibility for raising the money in accordance with a census to be compiled by the village priest, with severe penalties for concealment. No excuses were accepted by the collectors, and defaulters were clapped in irons until they paid.

In addition to this civil tax, and perhaps no more acceptable to the Orthodox of Samos, was a land-tax, the *vacouf*, levied for the support of the mosque at Tophane in Galata designed by the great Sinan in 1580 as a miniature of Aghia Sophia for the Kaptan Pasha, Kiliç Ali Pasha. The Kaptan Pasha, one of the few commanders to have emerged with any credit from the *debacle* of Lepanto in 1571, had been responsible for the resettlement of Samos, as Georgirenes noted, and had reserved land as an endowment for his mosque and *medrese*.[8] Finally, there was inheritance tax. This was levied on chattels by the *cadi* at a flat rate of 3 per cent. Moreover in cases where a man left no male heir, his land fell to the *aga*, who also had the right to seize and dispose of any land left uncultivated for seven years. Inasmuch as the archbishop was ultimately responsible for the smooth running of

8 Ibid. pp. 2–3, 8–9, 11.

the system and the enforcement of all these exactions, there was a perennial risk of his falling foul of one side or the other. Nor was that the only risk. His penultimate predecessor, as recently as 1660, had failed to raise the protection money demanded by a Venetian fleet during the struggle for Candia, 'Whereupon the Venetian Admiral, without any respect to his Religion as a Christian, or to his place and quality as an Arch-Bishop, did most Barbarously put him into the Gallies'.[9] And when Georgirenes arrived in Samos the struggle for Candia was still in progress.

In his five years on Samos, Georgirenes came to know the island well. Best of all, of course, he knew his archiepiscopal capital and its churches

> There are but six Churches, and those small ones. Nor is it expedient in that Country, that anything which concerns the Christian Religion should make any outward appearance of Magnificence, or costliness, least it should provoke the envy and avarice of their proud Masters to Sacrilegious Rapine.[10]

There are indeed six old churches to be seen in Chora, most of them now showing signs of eighteenth-century enlargement, in the later more settled times. Apart from the cathedral and its adjacent residence, there is the church of Agia Anna, which retains the unpretentious scale of which Georgirenes writes, still with its seventeenth-century iconostasis carrying a *Presentation in the Temple* dated 1677. At its west end a flight of steps leads up to a former hermitage, serving today as the entrance to the women's gallery. Agios Ioannes Prodromos and the Church of the Dormition, each with double nave, show signs of expansion; the latter has in its iconostasis a *Panagia* of 1718. Agios Demetrios was rebuilt *c.*1800, but a lintel of the earlier church survives, carrying the date 1605. The church of the Panagia Brontiane completes the half dozen.[11]

The town was well watered, says the archbishop, with two fountains, Platanos and Messaki, of which the former was judged 'sweeter to the taste'.

9 Ibid. pp. 36–7.

10 Ibid. p. 12.

11 This list, however, takes no account of two churches currently under excavation, said to belong to the seventeenth century: According to Papas Demetris, if modern churches are included, the number rises to forty-five!

One of them, which still flows a few yards below the cathedral, bears the date 1605; there is another, undated, in the street leading to the little church of Agios Nikolaos. This part of Samos, indeed, as Georgirenes notes, is particularly well watered – so much so that the lake at Glyphada, between Chora and Pythagorio (known as Tigani until 1955), the archbishop judged 'enough to furnish a whole fleet'. Georgirenes, of course, knew nothing of the thousand-yard tunnel cut through the walled hill above the ancient city in the sixth century BC, under the supervision of the Megarian engineer Eupalinos, in order to bring in a piped water-supply.[12] But he did know its replacement of Roman times, visible on the southern slope of the same hill, a little way below the monastery of Panagia Spiliani:

> Here is also an artificial Channel, six miles long, drawn from a River of a perpetual stream, which besides the Mills it drives, does water the Country in times of greatest drought. This water arising near the Village of the *Arnhauts* [i.e. Albanians, at Pandrosso] becomes large enough by new supplies of other Currents, to deserve the name of a River, and is that which the Ancients call'd *Imbrasus.*[13]

The archbishop's *Description* of his diocese includes an important topographical section in the form of a tour of the island (see map 3 on p. 383), noting the population of its villages and the number of their churches (the former sometimes calculated by rule-of-thumb, or so it would appear, a hundred families to a church), and often commenting on the characteristic local products which formed the basis of their economy.[14] From Chora he leads the reader southwards to the great plain, 'which by reason of the abundance of standing Water wherewith it perpetually stagnates, yields no benefit, but great nuisance to the neighbouring Inhabitants'. If it were drained, he implies, it could become richly agricultural, and no longer a sanctuary for the mosquito. 'Yet it is like to continue still a Fenny Marsh, so long as the Tyrannous Government of the Country gives so small Encouragement to the improvement of Lands.' There is no further

12 Herod. iii 39. See J. P. Barron, 'The Sixth-Century Tyranny at Samos', *Classical Quarterly*, n.s. xiv (1964), pp. 210–29.

13 *Description of the Present State*, p. 5.

14 Ibid. pp. 12–26.

lingering on the plain, and the next stop is at its western end, a mile or so from the ancient site of the Temple of Hera, at the mouth of the Imbrasus. Here the archbishop describes an estate watered by the river, belonging to the monastery of St John in Patmos, 'giv'n by a *Greek* architect, one of the first Planters [i.e. settlers], who dying without Issue, left all he had to the said Monastery' – to which, in fact, this *metochion tēs Kolonas* still belongs. It is a large estate of some 3,500 *stremmata*, that is upwards of 860 acres. The 'planter' was evidently the Cretan Nikolas Sarakenes, navigator to the fleet of Kilic Ali. The double church of St George and St John (named by Georgirenes as 'the Theologian'), was built by Sarakenes as part of the bequest to Patmos made in his wills of 16 February 1581 and 18 September 1590, shortly before his death on 11 October in the latter year. Curiously Gerogirenes says nothing of this church although it still today looks just as it did when he was archbishop.[15]

Further upstream is Milli, 'the mills', its economy based on the power of the river and the ability of its soil to deliver unusually heavy crops of oranges and lemons. Today the Imbrasus is a stream rather than a river, which would be hard put to turn a mill-wheel, except perhaps in the depth of a particularly wet winter. But the oranges are still there.

Because Georgirenes took the southern coastal road, he failed to mention two of the largest and most prosperous monasteries on the island, and so added them as a postscript at the end of his circular tour. The first of these was the monastery of the Cross known as the Stauros monastery and founded in 1592 which lies just a little way to the north of the road from Chora to Pyrgos. It appears still to be a wealthy and impressive monastery

15 See the very full discussion by H. J. Kienast, 'Der Turm des Sarakini auf Samos', *Deutsches Archäologisches Institut: Archäologischer Anzeiger* (2001), pp. 525–57; cf. the account of the former ephor of antiquities, K. Tsakos, *Samos: A Guide to the History and Archaeology* (Athens, 2003), pp. 102–3. The wills and other documents, for which see Kienast, 'Der Turm des Sarakini', p. 556, n. 63, are in the monastic archive in Patmos, no. 33. The date of 1602 over the door of the church of St John evidently relates to reconstruction or repairs undertaken by Patmos and recorded in the same archive. Kienast's account supersedes that of P. Hetherington, *The Greek Islands: Byzantine and Medieval Buildings* (London, 2001), pp. 278f., who wrongly dates the churches to Samos' Genoese period in the fourteenth century.

with an opulent church rebuilt in the nineteenth century surrounded on three sides by a walled enclosure, but the southern side is open to wide views across the water to the island of Ikaria. Georgirenes tells us that there were thirty monks living off rich agricultural land farmed by lay brothers and, in addition, that there was another monastery (which he does not name) attached to this house where the sole occupation of the brothers was to make cloth and carry out all the other labour necessary to maintain the Stavros monastery.[16] Further west, lying just south of the same road, is the impressive monastery dedicated to the Great Mother of God, but also commonly known, as Georgirenes points out, as the house of the Blessed Virgin of the Five Houses. This name may point to an earlier form of monasticism in which small individual houses clustered together, and their communal life followed later. The monastery was clearly rich and well-established, and it is still large and impressive although it suffered badly in the fires which devastated parts of the island in 2000, and it does not now support sixty monks as it did in the seventeenth century. The impressive paintings in the church are dated to 1596 and the rich ecclesiastical furnishings have survived although they are now mostly in the museum. The archbishop's failure to mention this grand monastery, except as an afterthought, may be explained, perhaps, by the fact that it was not subject to his jurisdiction, but only to that of the Patriarch of Constantinople.[17]

But Georgirenes in his *Description* travelled by the old winding road to Pagondas, a substantial village then, 'enrich'd by the Manufacture of Silks', and on by an even more circuitous route skirting the intervening hill to little Spatharei, 'famous for making Pitch, which they sell at *Megale Chore* [i.e. at Chora] for three quarters of a Doller, and sometimes a Doller the Kintal'.[18]

16 *Description of the Present State*, pp. 25–6; M. G. Barbousnes, *Oi Mones tēs Samou* (Athens, 2006), pp. 54–65.

17 *Description of the Present State*, p. 26. See also E. Hartig and K. Meyer, *The Monastery of the Great Mother of God on the Island of Samos* (Rodermark, 2004); Barbounes, *Oi Mones tēs Samou*, pp. 40–53.

18 Georgirenes was evidently intrigued by the process of manufacture, the same as that observed by the elder Pliny in the first century, for he describes it in great detail, *Description of the Present State*, pp. 14–15.

Just offshore is 'Little Samos', Samio Paulo, the source of *mouskoulia*, a plant much in demand at Constantinople, where 'The Grand Signior wears it ordinarily in his Turbant, and by his Example, makes it a Fashionable wear among the Grandees of his Court.' Its musk-like fragrance, says the archbishop, is enhanced as it dries.

Over the hill from Spatharei the road leads to Pyrgos: 'Here is the Choicest Honey.' The best honey in Samos still comes from Pyrgos: no doubt the flora is the same, and the bees also. From Pyrgos Georgirenes continues up the same road to Pandrosso, the latter in his day a village of 'Arnaouts' or Arvanitai, i.e. Orthodox Albanians.[19] Thence by one or other steep and difficult track to the oasis of Platanos, 'both the Men and Women being generally longer Liv'd there, than any where else in the Island'. Though the archbishop derives the name 'from abundance of Plain Trees there formerly', there are, in fact, still three ancient planes in the square, at least one of them old enough to have been there in the seventeenth century. The good health the place enjoyed no doubt came from its excellent water supply, which issues now into two fountain houses, that in the square renovated in 1837.[20] Moreover, 'Their Waters hereabouts abound with Champinions, a great relief to the Poor, when the word is given out for publick permission to Fish'.[21] Georgirenes mentions two churches there which served at least 300 families. One of them will have been that of the Dormition, a substantial building of the seventeenth century where the southern nave preserves under its cupola a worn slab bearing a double-headed eagle in relief, apparently of the thirteenth century.[22] The village still retains an air of prosperity with its copious water-supply and the extensive terracing of its surrounding slopes for vines.

19 For the identification, see for instance Tsakos, *Samos*, p. 100.

20 An inscription recalls: 'Lord, remember the wife of Anagnostos.' See N. I. Zapheiriou, *Archeion Samou* (Athens, 1946), pp. 146–7.

21 This is an apparently unique use of the word in English to denote a species of fish. Certainly it baffled Galland, who omitted the statement from his retranslation, Galland, *Voyages inédits*, p. 264.

22 Hetherington, *The Greek Islands*, p. 283, suggesting that the southern nave was for the Orthodox majority, the northern for the Catholic population.

The road down to the valley is steep and winding, but gentler from there westward to Marathocampos, the 'field of fennel'. In the archbishop's time, it made a useful starting-point for exploration of the remote and rugged western part of the island, skirting the great mass of Mt Kerketias or Kerkis (4,660 ft, 1,434 m). Georgirenes first followed the track which makes for the head of the deep second valley to the west of Marathocampos, descending to what was then a hermitage of St George, also given to Patmos as a *metochion* in 1602. The ruins on this site are now dedicated to St John, for the St George's foundation was transferred *c.*1695 to its present well-watered, neatly terraced site on the west slope of the next valley eastward, where it became the centre of spiritual life in that part of Samos and it remained a *metochion* of Patmos until it was sold in 1966.[23] Today the ruins of the original hermitage are of a relatively substantial establishment, a small monastery with its *katholikon* set in a miniature courtyard, at the west end of which is a two-storey refectory with hearth and chimney in the upper room. The remains of the monks' cells form the south range, but there seem to have been no buildings on the north and east sides of the courtyard, which is entered through a gatehouse in the north corner of its west wall. The complex is strongly fortified, with a second entrance through the east wall between two particularly massive buttresses. The *katholikon* is of a form familiar in Samian country churches since *c.*1300, triconch and domed with an additional 'bay' to the west; the original doorway is decorated with carved vine-leaves on the side-posts, incomplete on the north side. Though these monastic buildings are of a later period it is not hard to imagine their earlier purposeful occupants, Georgirenes' 'two or three Hermits of *Patmos*', living their quiet lives here in these western valleys, in holiness and some contentment. The archbishop's next goal, nearby, was the reputed cave of Pythagoras, set high up the precipitous western slope of the valley, where Hosios Paulos established himself in the early tenth century.[24] At the mouth of the grotto is the little church of the Panagia Phaneromene, 'making herself visible', but the Virgin is given the further title Sarandaskaliotissa, 'she of the forty steps', a figure which

23 See Barbounes, *Oi Mones tēs Samou*, p. 125.

24 See Tsakos, *Samos*, pp. 93–5.

greatly underestimates the climb which her visitors have to make to her church. The site is no longer scattered with the whitening bones of refugees, or of the hermits who followed Paulos to this wilderness.

The archbishop had perhaps forgone the satisfaction of seeing the 1,434m summit of Mount Kerketias for himself: at any rate it is hard to locate the 'Lake on the very top, well stor'd with Eels', and the chapel of the Prophet Elias is some three hundred metres below. Beyond it, on the west side of the mountain overlooking Ikaria, Georgirenes records another chapel in a grotto, of unknown dedication. This is perhaps the chapel of the Panagia Makrini above Kallithea, a tiny thirteenth-century nucleus which formed the sanctuary of a mid-eighteenth-century triconch, or it may be the church of St George at Drakaioi. Georgirenes' records:

> That which increaseth the Religious esteem of this latter Chapel, is, a Tradition, That Light has often appear'd in the Night time, which the People conceive to be a Warning of some Holy Reliques that lyes here yet undiscover'd, and so neglected.[25]

Overall the impression remains that the latter phrase could as well be applied to the archbishop's own account of the heights and remoter side of this inhospitable mountain, 'yet undiscover'd, and so neglected'.

In his account Georgirenes now turns north, in his memory exaggerating the distance, across the watershed and following a deep and inaccessible gorge to a place where

> Stands another Hermitage; besides which, in a spacious Grotto, stands a little Church, Dedicated to the Virgin *Mary*. It hath but one way of access, and that up a steep Precipice so extremely dangerous, that it is called Παναγία εις τὸ Κακοπέρατον, or St *Maries*, upon the bad passage.[26]

There is still a hermitage there, inhabited and lovingly pot-gardened by one old woman admitted a nun in 1990. Access to the grotto containing the small perhaps Byzantine chapel of Georgirenes' hermit is no longer *kakoperaton*, no longer a stiff climb up the side of the gorge. Instead, an

25 *Description of the Present State*, p. 19.
26 Ibid. p. 19.

easy track for vehicles has been bulldozed from Kosmadaioi through pine forest bright with anemones, doronicum and euphorbia. The hermitage now looks down upon a grassy glade among the pines, humming with beehives. Three tiny fields, pasture for goats, bounded by a plashing brook, complete the idyllic scene. Small wonder, then, that the Virgin has surrendered her uncomfortable title and adopted that of the Zoodochos Pege, the spring of life.[27]

It was no doubt with some relief that the archbishop turned his steps away from the mountain, from its precipitous gorges and impenetrable forests, to the high road that runs from Marathacampos to Karlovasi by way of Kastania and Leka, each remembered as having fifty houses and one church.[28] Between them, a little way up the road to Kosmadaioi, the site identified by a roadside spring and a copse of half a dozen plane trees, lay another *metochion* of Patmos, the home of two or three hermits. Like so many ecclesiastical establishments in Samos, this church of the Holy Trinity was to be elaborated in the eighteenth century with a spacious *narthēx*, a finely carved *templon* and at least one outstanding icon, of the 'Portaitissa', painted in 1719.[29] It was not only the monastery of St John on Patmos that owned *metochia* in Samos. Beyond Leka was a priory of St George, where Georgirenes found four or five priests of St Catherine's Monastery in Sinai superintending the production of wine as a source of income for the house they maintained there. Here again the church has undergone extensive remodelling in the eighteenth century, with finely carved woodwork and icons of some quality, a reminder of the prosperity

27 For this hermitage, see Barbounes, *Oi Mones tēs Samou*, p. 118 (with dramatic view of the gorge); idem, *Laikē latreia kai threskeutikē symperiphora tōn katoikōn tēs Samos* (Athens, 1992), p. 67, citing I. Papalas, *Ē Ekklēsia tēs Samou apo tēs idreuseōs autēs mechri sēmeron* (Samos, 1976), pp. 15, 284.

28 At Kastania the church in question is probably that of Ag. Eleutherios, long, low and barrel-vaulted, of a form more familiar in Ikaria.

29 In 1964, the former hermitage was sold to a priest-monk loyal to the Old Calendar, who began the construction of an incompatible modern concrete monastery, now deserted. A little way up the hill, beside a newly built church of Ag. Demetrios, the priest-monk lies buried under the usurped title of Germanos, archbishop and metropolitan, 1914–2003.

which lasted into the nineteenth century when St George's still enjoyed the income of twenty-seven subordinate churches.[30]

In contrast to the continuing prosperity of the monastery dedicated to St George, that further to the east 'upon the hillside' dedicated to the Prophet Elias is now deserted and overlooked by a disused military camp. Georgirenes noted that in his day the house was notable for its generous hospitality to travellers. At one time the monastery may have housed some sixty monks judging by the number of cells, but the last abbot died in 1966 and the house now turns a blind eye to the world and is guarded by a fierce watch dog.[31] It is clearly with enthusiasm that Georgirenes moves northwards to describe Karlovasi, 'the greatest town of this island' whose inhabitants were 'the richest of any in the isle'. It is still probably the largest town on the island, but not as prosperous as Vathy or Pythagorio because it lacks the tourist attractions. In the nineteenth century its prosperity depended on a flourishing tanning industry: but earlier in the seventeenth century it was an important port (for the export of onions and wine) in spite of its exposure to the north wind which may, however, explain why Vathy has now overtaken it as the main port of the island. But in Georgirenes' day it had 500 houses and five churches.[32] He then moves on further east to a town which he calls Furni but which is now known as Idrousa.[33] It was here that in classical times the vessels were made (in the furnaces) in which Samian wine was stored and exported. The town was, and is, well watered and there is still a public fountain house in the church square as in Georgirenes' day. And the spring which fed the fountain in the seventeenth century still produces an abundance of water. There are now three churches at the site, sheltered by large ancient plane trees, instead of the single church dedicated to the Virgin which Georgirenes knew. Between Furni/Idrousa and the village of Vourliote to the east lies the mountain range dominated by Mount Ambelos. The mountains were well wooded and supplied timber for houses and ships: although these wooden products

30 Cf. Barbounes, *Oi Mones tēs Samou*, p. 126.

31 *Description of the Present State*, p. 20; Barbounes, *Oi Mones tēs Samou*, pp. 66–75.

32 *Description of the Present State*, pp. 20–1.

33 Information from Mr Ch. Landros.

were taxed and so fed the coffers of the Turkish Aga, yet, as Georgirenes noted, the chestnuts could be gathered freely.[34] The woods, and the making of pitch, supplied the main livelihood for the people who lived in the small town of Vourliote, a colony of Vourla on the coast of Turkey near Smyrna. In the seventeenth century it had a hundred houses and one church: it now has two churches, one of three naves, which is dedicated to St John the Theologian.[35] Georgirenes then moves south east to note the monastery of Panagia Touphronta which was founded in 1566 in rich and beautiful countryside and, in spite of the fires of 2000, the charred house is still surrounded by vineyards and the burnt woods are full of daisies and anemones. In the seventeenth century the house was comparatively small with only a dozen monks and what attracted the attention of Georgirenes was the fact that horses brought from elsewhere which grazed in the fields around the monastery swelled and burst, whereas those bred in the area were immune to such a catastrophe.[36] Continuing eastwards along the coast Georgirenes reaches Vathy (now the capital of the island and known as Samos) which, by contrast with Karlovasi, was an excellent port 'affording a safe harbour in all winds but the south'.[37] The economy of the town was based on fishing and also the export of sweet wine (muscat), but, whereas the wine of Karlovasi turned sour within six months, that of Vathy would last a whole year. The town numbered 400 households and four churches, with a further hundred houses and a church in the old town of Palaeocastro, further up the hill, which was also notable for its wines, and especially for the muscat. Ignoring the north-eastern part of the island completely, Georgirenes then turned his attention to Vourcaria (now Posidonio) a small port on the south coast which lay near a salt marsh which the inhabitants were disinclined to exploit because the product would then be taxed by the Turks. Instead they imported salt from the islands of Melos, and Naxos which supplied

34 *Description of the Present State*, p. 22.

35 Ibid.; Barbounes, *Oi Mones tēs Samou*, pp. 34–5.

36 *Description of the Present State*, pp. 22–3; Barbounes, *Oi Mones tēs Samou*, pp. 24–39.

37 *Description of the Present State*, p. 23. Georgirenes also notes the three small islands lying to the north-east which provided shelter for ships in all weathers. He names them as 'the isles of dirt', now known as Nisi.

most of the other islands off the coast of Turkey. Turning westwards Georgirenes describes a great plain called Ho Pisos Campos (the back field) watered by a stream which powered two mills and was fruitful in producing wheat, cotton and maize (ble de Turquie).[38] In the plain, now set among olive trees, is the church dedicated to St John the Theologian established there because it was believed that St John (together with St Paul) came to Samos and as a result miracles were performed here. It would appear still to be a place of local pilgrimage perhaps for a festival on 27 December, the feast day of the saint.[39] Finally Georgirenes makes his way to the village of Mytilene, a colony of people from the island of that name, with 200 houses and two churches. He has nothing to say about the village except that it is a mile from Magale Chora, his operational base and 'the principal place of the island wherewith we begun'. It may have been with some relief that Georgirenes reported 'and so we have finished the circuit of the whole island'.[40] The account he provides is remarkable when it is considered that he wrote it from memory some six years after he had left the island. His sense of direction and distance are somewhat random, and his interests seem to have been focused less on the religious practices and customs of his see (some of which he describes with a degree of scepticism) than on the economy and the sources of Samian prosperity – and taxation.

Georgirenes' survey of his diocese and its economy may be compared with the account of the Frenchman Tournefort, who came to Samos from Kusadasi barely thirty years later, on 30 January 1702, lamenting his inability to secure a copy of the archbishop's book: an independent account, therefore, and the more valuable for that.[41] His topography is chaotic, though he appears to have undertaken a comprehensive tour of the island. But

38 Ibid. p. 24. The texts here add, unhelpfully, the Greek name *erysimon*, today identified as *Sisymbrium officinale* (L.) Scop, a low-growing yellow-flowered crucifer, unlikely to have been grown as a field crop. I am grateful to Ruth Stungo for help in understanding the text at this point.

39 The small church had been recently done up (2007) and there was seating for many people and evidence of bonfires.

40 *Description of the Present State*, p. 25.

41 Tournefort, *A Voyage into the Levant*, pp. 305–27.

he is as interested as Georgirenes in seeking the economic foundations of Samian society, in order to understand the system of taxation which fed upon it. The significance of Pagondas as a producer of silk, for instance, is thrown into much sharper perspective by Tournefort's comment that, 'The Silk of this Island is very fine; 'tis worth 4 livres 10 sols, or 100 sols a pound; this Traffick one year with another may be rated at twenty or twenty five thousand Crowns.'[42]

By contrast Ikaria was too poor to support a suffragan bishop, so Georgirenes would have needed to appoint one, or two, vicars general, to judge from the utter remoteness of north from south, on either side of the ridge which forms this twenty-five-mile island, where time stood still before the creation of the even now skeletal road-system as recently as the 1970s.[43] As to the total complement of clergy, we have the evidence of Tournefort that in 1700, when he explored these islands at the command of Louis XIV, Ikaria had one monastery and twenty-four priests.[44] To judge from surviving wills and conveyances, the priests were also the landowners and businessmen, since they were literate.[45]

From time to time the archbishop would expect to hold a visitation in person: certainly Georgirenes was there in July 1670, for a deed survives, drawn up by him on the fifteenth of that month before local witnesses, recording the endowment by a priest's son of a festival for a church of Aghios Kirykos:[46] Ikaria contains several churches of this dedication, not

42 Ibid. p. 310.

43 Georgirenes, *Description of the Present State*, pp. 32f. The most useful recent accounts of Ikaria are by A. J. Papalas, *Ancient Icaria* (Wauconda, IL, 1992; Greek trans. by A. Kalokairinos, *Archaia Ikaria* (Ikaria, 2002)) and A. J. Papalas, *Rebels and Radicals: Icaria 1600–2000* (Wauconda, IL, 2005); on a larger scale, I. Melas, *Istoria tēs Nēsou Ikarias*, 2 vols (Athens, 1953–8). Beyond these, I had the great advantage, and pleasure, of exploring the island with Professor Papalas in May 2006, when I was able also to discuss the surprisingly substantial oral tradition of Georgirenes' visit to Ikaria with local historians Angelos Kalokairinos and Christos Malachias.

44 Tournefort, *A Voyage into the Levant*, i. p. 302.

45 Papalas, *Rebels and Radicals*, pp. 20f. and nn. 41–3.

46 Melas, *Istoria tēs Nēsou Ikarias*, pp. 84–5, the year wrongly given as 1660. I am grateful to Mr Kalokairinos for his kindness in pursuing and checking the original document.

least in the modern capital of the island which is named after the saint. But the inclusion of Papas Leon Gardias among the witnesses, as well as an *oikonomos*, a married priest who acted as a steward, Papas Ioannes, and the localization of the property forming the endowment in the neighbourhood of Keros, close to ancient Oinoe, strongly suggests that the church in question is Aghios Kirykos in the village of Pegi, close to the monastery of Theoktiste. For Gardias was probably of the same family as Papas Gerasimos Gardias, *hēgoumenos* of that monastery in 1643;[47] and the house would have provided employment for an *oikonomos*. This monastery lies within the very limited area with which the archbishop claims familiarity – so limited, in fact (and in contrast with his full and detailed acquaintance with Samos), that it is possible even to doubt whether he visited his second island more than once or twice. Nonetheless his account of it is vivid, touched here and there with humour, and not without sympathy for the plight of its chronically poor people, among the most destitute of Greek islanders. His sympathy is not in itself surprising; but it is noteworthy that elsewhere in his *Account* – whether of Samos, Patmos or Mount Athos – he concentrates on buildings and topography, and only in Ikaria gives the inhabitants centre stage. This may be because Ikaria was then, as now, so much less visited than the other three places, and its people correspondingly less well known. For their part the islanders remembered their visitor, perhaps indicating that archiepiscopal visitations were a rare event.

To reach Ikaria in 1670 from Samos, the archbishop would have taken ship at the ancient harbour of Tigani (now Pythagorio), with its huge breakwater constructed in the sixth century BC by the tyrant Polycrates – the handle of the 'frying-pan', *tēganē*, which gave the port its name – and sailed west along the south coast, briefly crossing the open sea north of the Fournoi islands. The nearest point of Ikaria, Cape Phanari with its lighthouse, loomed close to the Hellenistic tower at Drakanon, once (he was assured) the prison of Ikaros and his son, and the hiding-place of buried treasure as yet unretrieved. The archbishop dismissed this tale and

For Georgirenes' account of Ikaria, see *Description of the Present State*, pp. 54–70; Papalas, *Rebels and Radicals*, pp. 7ff.

47 See Papalas, *Rebels and Radicals*, p. 18.

launched into a tirade against 'the Itch of talking on one side, and the great credulity of ignorant People on the other'.[48] Nor were the harbour facilities to his liking, the whole island having 'not one Port nor Road for great Ships, but only two small Creeks for little Boats', both on the north coast. Sailing past the first, at Aghios Phokas, between Cape Phanari and Kioni, he appears to have landed on the beach below Keramio, a little to the east of the modern harbour of Evdelos (see Map 4, p. 384). From there he made his way inland to what he regarded as the three 'principal Villages'.[49]

'Cachoria', the first of the three, though it then had no fewer than '100 houses, and two or three *Ches* (churches)', is not now the name of any settlement in Ikaria. Local tradition in fact identifies Cachoria with modern Akamatra, whose land is anything but bad. Akamatra is a substantial village, set in good agricultural land, hilly but well terraced. It is particularly well watered, even in summer, by streams running off the hill to the south, one of which gurgles and spits its way across the main street as if contemptuous of the channel that contains it. As the island's capital until 1826, Akamatra, again in local tradition, saw the *denouement* of a notorious act of fiscal mutiny of which the inhabitants did not fail to tell the archbishop, himself no doubt intent on assuring the collection of his own annual levy of three hundred 'crowns':

> They have a great Happiness, by reason of their poverty, in not being molested by the *Turks*, who think it not worth their while to come among them, nor if they should, were they likely to enjoy any quiet, without keeping a stronger Guard than the Revenues of the Isle would maintain. Once they slew a *Caddee*, being sent by the Grand Signior, and being Summon'd to Answer for their Crime, they by common consent own'd the Fact, but would name no particular Man. So that the *Turkish* Officers looking upon their beggarly Cloaths, thought there was neither gain nor glory in punishing such Miscreants, and that in Justice, they must punish all, or none, dismiss'd them untouch'd. From that time no *Turk* ever troubled them.[50]

48 *A Description of the Present State*, p. 57.

49 Ibid. p. 58.

50 *Description of the Present State*, pp. 67f.; cf. Papalas, *Rebels and Radicals*, pp. 12ff., who reports the tradition that the *cadi* was tipped from his sedan over a cliff at Kako Karavostasi, and the subsequent response of the Ikarians on trial, '*Ouloi ēmeis, Effendi*', 'It's all of us, Sir'. See also Randolph, *Present State of the Islands*, p. 53: 'The

Akamatra still has its two or three churches. Just below the square, on the main street, stands Aghioi Taxiarchai, a substantial building with some pretension to architecture, which must have been yet grander before the demolition of its *pronaos*. There is a small apse at the east end, and high over the west door a Roman funerary relief set into the wall. The church would readily hold a congregation of sixty. The second church, by contrast, is a smaller and more rustic affair, away on its own hillside to the east of the village, its distinguishing feature a bell-turret over the west door. It does not boast a *pronaos*, but the long nave is divided by a wooden screen in addition to the iconostasis. This is perhaps the church of St Basil in which oral tradition has it that Georgirenes celebrated the liturgy.[51]

The second of the three villages, Steli, 'famous for great abundance of Nut-Trees', still bears the name which Georgirenes knew. It is a small hamlet, set amid an abundance of walnut trees, no more than a mile from Akamatra. The third village listed by Georgirenes is Musara, now Mesarias, the area which lies between Akamatra and Steli and extends slightly to the west of them, and was soon to be made an Ottoman tax-division. Beyond 'Musara' the archbishop's memory flags, for it is not Mesarias but Pegi 'besides which is an Hermitage, and a Church, wherein are kept the Reliques of St *Theoctistes*, who was of *Lesbos*, and whom the People do think yet does Miracles at this day'.[52] The Hermitage is a remarkable site, on a hillside strewn with vast boulders amid woodland of evergreen and deciduous oaks and many pines. One huge boulder of granite has come to rest looming over another. Between them, as if to steady the upper stone by means of a retaining wall, some hermit has in-filled the gap with his exiguous cell, approached up a flight of steps, with a low door and a tiny window to light

---

Inhabitants are generally very poor, as the Privateers cannot get any thing out of them; nor can the *Turks* bring them to pay any considerable tribute.'

51 See Papalas, *Rebels and Radicals*, p. 39 n. 19. Down the hill to the west among fields is a third church, of St Paul, now derelict, its iconostasis and other interior fittings gone, but still showing traces of the paintings with which it was once decorated, and carrying the date 6612 (AD 1103), Papalas, *Archaia Ikaria.*, trans. Kalokairinos, p. 221; G. N. Kokkinos, *Ē Paradosiakē Katoikia tēs Ikarias, kai to idiomorpho ktisto petiballon tou nesiou* (Athens, 2005), p. 165 and figs 355–6.

52 *Description of the Present State*, p. 58.

the rough interior.[53] This hermitage, called locally Theoskepaste – 'covered by God' – is much as Georgirenes saw it, though a larger window was later added, and the interior has a quadrant-shaped iconostasis constructed (as its inscription says) with the help and at the expense of the *hēgoumenos* ('abbot' or 'prior') Gregori Ioacheim in 1849. The church of St Theoktiste, whose saintly life ended in Paros in 872 and whose bones were plundered for Ikaria when on a much later voyage home to Mytilene, stands some little way down the hill, set in a monastery garden of honeysuckle and roses, snapdragon and Madonna lilies.[54] Inside it is decorated with an unusually fine *ensemble* of frescoes, dominated on the north wall by a large-scale St George slaughtering an already captive dragon, its leash held by a fearless Alexandra. Modestly tucked away in the south-west corner, among the saints, are the founding *hieromonachos* and his mother. The completion of the decoration is commemorated by an inscription dated 6 October 1688, twenty years after Georgirenes' visit.[55] Between hermitage and church is a house, now derelict, a one-roomed *chyton* with single slope roof, of a form popular in Ikaria from the sixteenth century to the eighteenth, which is likely to have been the residence of the monks in Georgirenes' day.[56] From the monastery of Theoktiste, his thoughts turn to the ruins of ancient Oinoe, and perhaps his footsteps turned in that direction also, completing the circuit back to the sea. It is a small area, no more than two miles square as the gull flies, but with some scope for agriculture on either side of the broad but sometimes precipitous valley of the Voutside, by no means rich land but more than merely viable by the standards of Ikaria, of which overall only 5 per cent is arable today. It could, but rarely did, make a worthwhile contribution to tax, whether ecclesiastical or Turkish.

Though the places he names occupy a small part of the northern side of the island, Georgirenes noted that there were 'a great many little Villages scatter'd up and down through the whole Island', and that they were less

53 Kokkinos, *Ē Paradosiakē*, fig. 342.

54 On the monastery, see Papalas, *Rebels and Radicals*, pp. 20f. and n. 42.

55 For recent conservation work on these paintings, see P. Valakou, 'Mone Osias Theoktistes', *Archaiologikon Deltion*, liv (2006 for 1999), B' Chronika, p. 829.

56 See Kokkinos, *Ē Paradosiakē*, pp. 41–58.

compact than villages in Samos in that the individual houses were surrounded by their own gardens and orchards. This is still so, perhaps to be explained by the shortage of viable agricultural land. As the archbishop goes on to say, 'The whole Island is for the most part Mountainous, and Rocky. The Valleys are few, and little in compass; so that with great labour and difficulty, they force out of so barren a Soil' no more than half of the food they need. Hence, he says, they have had to develop a lively maritime trade, exporting sheep and goats and charcoal, and carrying Samian timber, to Chios in exchange for grain, and in the process acquired a reputation for shipbuilding, itself another source of overseas income. Otherwise cheese and pork, beeswax and honey, contribute to their precarious economy.[57] The archbishop may have been a rare visitor to this part of his diocese, but he clearly has taken the trouble to understand the economic resources which supported his annual levy.

He goes on to give a vivid account of life at subsistence level, as he has observed it.[58]

> They provide no more Apparel than what they wear all at once, when that is past wearing any longer, then think of a new Suit. ... Their Habit for the Men, is a Shirt, and over it a short Cassock, down to the Knees, to which, in Winter, they add only a short Vest, that reaches a little below the middle. Stockings they never wear. Their Shoes are only a piece of thin Copper, bow'd to the shape of their Feet, and every one is his own Shoe-maker. The Women have nothing but one Smock, but so large, that they wrap it double, or treble down to the Girdle, but below the Girdle single. The Priests, for greater reverence in the Church, ty two Towels about their Legs, the one is their usual Bonnet, and the other their Girdle: so that they perform sacred Offices unguirt, as well as uncover'd.[59]

57 *Description of the Present State*, p. 59ff. See also *Voyages de Mr de Thevenot en Europe, Asie & Afrique*, 3rd edn, rev., 5 vols (Amsterdam, 1727), i. p. 349: *c.*1655 exports were sponges [*sic*], honey, wax, and an extremely diuretic pale white wine.

58 *Description of the Present State*, pp. 61–6.

59 Ibid. pp. 61 and 65–6. The same poverty of dress was observed by Randolph, *Present State of the Islands*, pp. 53f., who was amazed to have 'seen several of the *Nicariotes* in their Boats that row all naked, for which they give two reasons; one that with their coats they cannot be so active at the oar, the other that they wear out their clothes

The picture of poverty becomes even sharper when food is considered:

> Betwixt their ordinary times of Eating, there is not a piece of Bread to be found in the Isle. A little before Dinner, they take as much Corn as will serve that Meal, grind it with a Hand-Mill, bake it upon a flat Stone; when 'tis Bak'd, the Master of the Family divides it equally among the Family; but a Woman with child has two shares. If any Stranger comes in, every one parts with a Piece of his own share to accommodate the Stranger. Their Wine is always made with a third part Water, and so very weak and small. When they drink it, so much as is thought sufficient is put into one large Bowl, and so passes round.

The furnishings were as frugal as the fare:

> Their Houses are so plain, that all the Furniture you can see is an Hand-Mill, besides this, there is nothing but bare Walls: That little they have besides is all hid under Ground; not so much for fear of the *Corsairs* (from whom their Poverty is a sure guard) as out of Custome ... There is not a Bed in the Island, the Ground is their Tick, and the cold Stone their Pillow, and the Cloaths they wear is all the Coverlet they use. ... When I went to visit them as Arch-Bishop, and ignorant of the custom of the Country, carry'd no Bed. At Night, where I first lodg'd, asking for a Chamber, they told me they had no other than that where I first came; then asking for a Bed, they told me it was not the Custom of the Country; then desiring to borrow some Bed Cloaths for Love or Money, all they brought me was one Smock made of course [*sic*] Dimity.

Local tradition in Ikaria places this bleak experience not in any of the villages already named but in the more remote wooded ridges of the north-west, Raches, at Christos. Here since 1820 at least, a one-roomed *chyton*, known as the Skirianos house, has been recognized as 'the house where the bishop stayed'.[60] A great evergreen oak by the roadside marks the site. The house stands on a flat and extensive fertile plot planted with olives

---

much; for every time that they tugg the oar they rise with their bodys, and fall back on the banks as is usual in the Gally's.' For the copper shoes, see below, p. 229.

60 Kokkinos, *Ē Paradosiakē*, pp. 52 and fig. 66, 55 and fig. 73, 56 no. 13; Papalas, *Rebels and Radicals*, p. 23 and n. 48. The house has been owned since *c.*1820 by the Spanos family who, with many in Christos, preserve vivid memories of the archbishop's visit. I owe my knowledge of it to Professor Papalas, and to Christos Malachias and Angelos Kalokairinos, see n. 43. It is now attached to a *pyrgos*, a two-storey addition, the different date of construction of which is clearly shown by the vertical straight

and vines – the garden and orchard with which Georgirenes found that 'here every House is environ'd' – and separated from the next plot and the next house by a terracing wall. The *chyton* itself is very similar to the house already described at the monastery of Theoktistes; solidly built with thick walls, it measures internally 6.2 by 3.6m, about 20 by 12ft. The entrance is at the extreme left of one long side, and the visitor comes immediately to a schist shelf resting on corbels and recessed into the short wall, on which stood the hand-mill. Beyond that, in the corner, is another shelf of schist, the 'flat stone' on which the bread was baked by the fire on the floor beneath. Next to it along part of the back wall is a rough platform of stone, perhaps for seating. Opposite, corbelled into the entrance wall, is the arch of the fireplace and behind it a short flue channelling the smoke to be dispersed among the schist slabs of the open single-pitched roof; there is no chimney, apparently in order to avoid a tell-tale column of smoke and so deny a landmark to distant marauders. There are recesses for lamps on either side of the fireplace, and other recesses to serve as cupboards, and there is one window in the short wall at the far end. The floor is of earth. And that is all: even at this distance in time, one may sympathize with the archbishop in his discomfort and lack of privacy, to say nothing of the choking atmosphere of captive smoke. Folk memory adds to the story of his miserable bedding. His request for a blanket brought him a rug of felted goat-hair, warm, indeed, but intolerably itchy: were there no sheets? At last someone remembered the scented lady who had spent some time in Egypt. Perhaps she might have sheets. She had – and the people of Christos still dispute whether it was the scented sheets or the scented lady that brought more pleasure to the archbishop.

Perhaps wryly recalling a sleepless night, Georgirenes notes that it was almost a point of honour among the Ikarians to go without a bed:

> Nor are they all so poor, as not to be able to buy Beds, but custom has brought them into a contempt of Beds, as merely superfluous; insomuch, that when they Travel into other Islands, they refuse the offer of a Bed. A priest of *Nicaria* coming into

---

joint in the masonry between the two. This *pyrgos* is almost certainly later than Georgirenes' visit.

> *Samos*, was courteously entertain'd by those of his Order, and at Night was offer'd a Bed to lye in; he thank'd them, but refus'd, nor could by any importunity be prevail'd upon, but told them the Earth was his Mother, from whence he would not keep a distance; besides he was afraid of being Sick, if he should lye in a Bed; and therefore if they had a kindness for him, they must give him the liberty of sleeping in his own Country way.[61]

The Ikarian way persisted for two centuries more. When Sir Charles Newton visited the island in the mid-nineteenth century, he witnessed the import of a four-poster bed by an Ikarian who had spent time in Smyrna; it was at once destroyed by a party of islanders with axes.[62]

Georgirenes paints the Ikarians of his day as essentially stand-offish, anti-social rather than merely private.[63] At the most basic level, 'They have no great communication one with another, any farther than the publick times of sacred Solemnities, or Civil Business doth cause them to come together.' In particular, 'Formal Visits, Treats, and Entertainments, are things unknown.' And if some pressing business leaves no escape from the need to communicate, they do not visit each other's homes but simply shout across the intervening country:

> And this way of discoursing at a distance they practice more in the Fields and Mountains; their Voices being so strong, that 'tis ordinary to talk at a Miles distance; sometimes at four or five, where the Valleys interpos'd between two hills, give advantage to the Voice. Sometimes they can discourse at that distance, that the carriage of the Sound through the Winding of the Valleys, shall require half a Quarter

61 *Description of the Present State*, p. 63.

62 C. T. Newton, *Travels and Discoveries in the Levant*, 2 vols (London, 1865), pp. 234f., cited by Papalas, *Ancient Icaria*, pp. 4, 188f.

63 *Description of the Present State*, pp. 64–7. Fifty years later, Dr Charles Perry, windbound on Ikaria for three days, remarks that the few inhabitants he encountered were 'almost naked and savage, seldom seeing or conversing with any of the human Species, except those of their own Isle': *A View of the Levant: Particularly of Constantinople, Syria, Egypt and Greece* (London, 1743), p. 485. Other visitors, however, both in the eighteenth and throughout the nineteenth centuries, give the Ikarians a reputation for especially generous hospitality, see Papalas, *Rebels and Radicals*, p. 11 and n. 21; it was still a feature of the island in 2006.

> of an Hours time; and yet they make distinct, and proper Answers, both audible and intelligible, without the help of a *Stentorophonical* Trumpet.

Here, of course, we are in the realm of caricature, which presents the isolationism which prevented marriages beyond the island as nothing more than simple snobbery. 'They being, as they pretend, all descended of the Imperial Blood of the *Porphyrogenneti*, must not stain their noble Blood with inferiour Matches, or mixtures with *Choriats*, or Peasants, for so they term all the other Islanders.'[64] The archbishop could afford to be humorous at the expense of the Ikarians – peasants, as he saw them – so long as he did not have to visit them too often. It comes, then, as something of a surprise when he ends his account of the island with a passage of sermonizing approval:

> Thus you have an account of a small Island, the Poorest, and yet the Happiest of the whole *Aegaean* Sea. The Soil is Barren, but the Air is Healthful; their Wealth is but small; but their Liberty and Security is great. … Their Ignorance is equal to their Poverty, and contributes much to their content. … Whence we may learn, that they approach the nearest to Contentedness in this Life; whose desires are contracted into the narrowest compass.[65]

Nevertheless, one senses that it must have been with some relief that the archbishop returned to Samos, and to a bed.

He was not allowed to rest for long. On 5 September 1669 the Venetian commander Francesco Morosini, his beleaguered garrison reduced to 4,000 men, at last surrendered Candia to the Turks. The war had lasted twenty-one

64 *Description of the Present State*, p. 65. A few years earlier, in 1655, the French traveller J. de Thevenot, who surprisingly found Ikaria the island of sponge-fishers *par excellence* (as Kalymnos was until lately), and observed a curious rite of betrothal. When a priest or one of the richer islanders wanted to marry off a daughter, he fixed a day on which she would be awarded to the best swimmer; then all the young men would strip naked, in public in the presence of the girl, and dive into the sea, and whoever stayed submerged the longest carried off the prize (*Voyages de Mr de Thevenot en Europe, Asie & Afrique*, i. 349, cited by Papalas, *Ancient Icaria*, p. 2): 'il semble que ce gens-la soient plus poissons qu'hommes.'

65 *Description of the Present State*, pp. 68–70.

years, the final siege almost two years and four months, with horrific casualties on both sides, to say nothing of the colossal expenditure of *matériel*.[66] Though commercial relations between the Venetians and the Ottomans were soon restored, the Aegean was never again a Venetian lake. The effect was felt throughout the Archipelago. In Samos the archbishop's position began to seem untenable:

> He resided there for five years until, after the taking of Candia, the Turks returned to the island in great numbers and as a result were very much in control. This made a great difference, and as I was one of those whom they had attacked first with injuries and with insults which my character did not deserve, I preferred private life to the great prestige of my position and retired to the grotto of the Apocalypse in the isle of Patmos, after having resigned my position into the hands of the patriarch of Constantinople who had invested me with it.[67]

The detail that Georgirenes' resignation was placed in the hands of the same patriarch who had appointed him narrows the chronology. The archbishop would have completed five years in October 1671. In fact Parthenios' third patriarchate lasted from early March only until 7 September that year; hence Georgirenes' tenure must have fallen a little short of the full five years. He has left a fuller, self-serving, account of his resignation in a statement he compiled three years later for the Bishop of Volterra in Tuscany.[68] He recounts there how he went to Constantinople and sought the patriarch's permission to resign his appointment and retire to the monastery of St John on Patmos: his temperament, he said, had made the weight of responsibility for his flock unendurable. Four times Parthenios refused to countenance his request; but at length he acceded to the determination of youth, and let him go.

66 See, for instance, M. Llewellyn Smith, *The Great Island* (London, 1965), pp. 63–73.

67 Galland, *Voyages inédits*, pp. 277–8; cf. the briefer account in *Description of the Present State*, p. 37.

68 See E. I. Stamatiades, *Epistolimaia Diatribē peri Ioseph Georgeirēnou, Archiepiskopou Samou 1666–1671* (Samos, 1892), pp. 13f. On this account, see discussion below, p. 122.

Even the Volterra account is distinctly economical with the truth. Georgirenes was not the only metropolitan in the Archipelago to resign that year, and disturbance by newly confident Turks was not the only reason. In the spring of 1671 an ambitious Greek priest who wished to see the union of the Eastern and Western Churches, Theophanes Mavrogordatos, at that time the Metropolitan of Paronaxia, conceived a plan, in alliance with the Congregation for the Propaganda of the Faith, to secure the election of a new patriarch at Constantinople who would be a Catholic. This new patriarch would allow Catholic missionaries to 'proclaim Catholic truth' throughout the Eastern Church. Theophanes listed eight Orthodox bishops who were, he claimed, supporters of this project and willing to meet together to elect from among themselves a Catholic sympathizer as the new patriarch. Among the eight Theophanes included 'Joseph of Samos'. The new patriarch would be subject to the authority of Christ's Vicar in Rome, the legitimate heir of St Peter, and to the authority of the Sacred Congregation. Theophanes travelled to Italy in the summer of 1671 to promote his plan, but he was viewed with some scepticism in Rome and the proposed 'putsch' failed, in part because the scheme was not supported by the foreign ambassadors in Constantinople. Whether the patriarch Parthenios knew of the plan, or was sympathetic to it, is not clear but his successor, Dionysios IV, who was elected in September 1671, denounced Theophanes as an accursed Latin and a second Antichrist who had come to entrap the bishops and convert them to the 'cunning dogmas of the papists'.[69] It seems likely that his involvement in this proposed 'putsch' may, in part, explain Joseph's decision in 1671 to resign (or was he pushed?) from the archbishopric of Samos, although for the rest of his life he retained the title.[70]

Whether under a cloud, or in fear of his life, Georgirenes left Samos for Patmos, accompanied by ten or a dozen members of his family who

69 For a full account of Theophanes Mavrogordatos and of the proposed 'putsch' see I. Baan, *Theophanes Mavrogordatos (1626–1688), Metropolitan of Paronaxia and Administrator of Munkacs* (Nyiregyhaza, 2012), esp. pp. 91–112, 173–6.

70 In his will drawn up in 1695 he signs himself as 'Joseph, Archbishop of Samos', see below p. 221.

evidently comprised the archiepiscopal household. Patmos, with its flourishing community of 150 monks, though much impoverished by the destruction and loss of its Cretan estates in the late war, was a particularly desirable retreat for a former archbishop, still young and needing to map out the future course of his life. For its charters had made the monastery virtually independent of both church and state and, of particular importance to Joseph, the patriarch's writ did not run there. Although the island was of course within the Ottoman dominions, successive sultans had honoured the commitment of their Byzantine predecessors to forego all intervention in its affairs. Here, if anywhere, was a place for escape, rest and reflection.

CHAPTER 5

Patmos, Tuscany and Rome (1671–1675)

Georgirenes appears to have spent at least four years on Patmos (1671–4), yet his account of the island in his *Description of the Present State of Samos, Nicaria, Patmos and Mount Athos* is extremely frugal. In all only thirteen pages are devoted to this great monastic island community, whereas even the small island of Ikaria has sixteen pages, Samos fifty-three and Mount Athos twenty-seven. He briefly describes the great fortified monastery founded by St Christodoulos in the eleventh century and then moves on to an account of the Holy Grotto some half mile away where St John is thought to have written down his Revelation. Although Georgirenes mentions a small monastery (one of four hermitages on the island) there under the jurisdiction of a *caloir* (monk) he does not say that he was himself in charge of the Holy Grotto although he makes this claim elsewhere.[1] He does, however, describe the special fig tree whose fruit when cut open bore the words 'apocalypse' written in seeds, rather in the manner of Brighton rock, and the stone font nearby where St John baptized converts. But the rest of his account of Patmos is entirely topographical, listing first the various ports, their food supplies and neighbouring crops (see Map 5, p. 385). His only excursus is to describe a great rock near the port of Diakopti said to be inhabited by a magician or devils. An even briefer description of five inland villages is followed by a detailed account of the activities of the pirates (mostly Christian) who prey upon the islanders. But there is one distinctive aspect of Georgirenes' account of Patmos: for the only time in his *Description* he describes a 'little nunnery containing 40 nuns', built comparatively recently and not endowed, so the nuns were obliged to live by their own labour. The great monastery provided them with a 'Reverend Ancient [so beyond

1 *Description of the Present State*, p. 37; Galland, *Voyages inédits*, pp. 302–3.

temptation?] Monk to do all sacred offices among them'.[2] It is possible that Georgirenes spent all his time in the Cave of the Apocalypse and so rarely ventured out into the rest of the island, whereas as archbishop he would have been expected to travel around Samos and Ikaria. But he certainly met visitors to the island.

Over the winter of 1673–4 the French ambassador to the Sublime Porte, the Marquis Charles-Marie François Olier, marquis de Nointel, made a leisurely voyage from Constantinople through the Aegean to Syria and Jerusalem, on the look-out for antiquities or manuscripts for his master Colbert, the chief financial minster of Louis XIV. For the ambassador himself, never the most modest of men, this Levantine journey was an almost royal progress, to celebrate the signing of a new trade agreement with the sultan.[3] The negotiations had been difficult. On his arrival at the Sublime Porte in 1671, Nointel had been received with studied disrespect, which he no doubt rightly attributed to Turkish resentment of the French king's military support for the struggles of Hungary and Candia. His brief had been to demand the exclusion of all newcomers from commerce in the sultan's dominions, and permission for the French to trade where and in what they wished. His instructions had allowed him discretion to make what other concessions he deemed necessary, but he was required to hold firm on one point, a reduction in customs dues from 5 per cent to 3 per cent. Even though the Turks themselves needed the French market, it had taken a threat to recall the ambassador, reinforced by the well-publicized dispatch of two warships to secure the hoped-for result, should the bluff be called.[4] New capitulations had finally been signed at Adrianople on 5 June 1673, giving France favoured nation status similar to that enjoyed by Venice and England, the right to import and export at will, customs dues

2 *Description of the Present State*, pp. 82–3.

3 See A. Vandal, *L'Odyssée d'un ambassadeur: les voyages du Marquis de Nointel (1670–1680)* (Paris, 1900), esp. pp. 113ff.

4 P. Clement, ed., *Lettres, instructions et mémoires de Colbert*, 7 vols (Paris, 1861–2), ii, pp. 628–30, in a note dated 20 Aug. 1671; cf. Nointel's formal instructions from the king, ibid. pp. 841–50. See also P. Clement, *Histoire de la vie et de l'administration de Colbert* (Paris, 1846), ch. x, pp. 256ff.

reduced to 3 per cent, and the privilege of maintaining a permanent mission to the Porte with full diplomatic immunity together with the right to represent other nations which had no diplomatic standing of their own.[5] It was indeed a triumph to celebrate.

But Nointel's interest was not confined to trade agreements. A devout Catholic, but of the Jansenist persuasion which Rome found unacceptable,[6] he shared with fellow Jansenists of the Port-Royal in Paris a keen interest in the doctrines and practices of the Orthodox Church, and nursed a longing to bring about an end to the Great Schism of 1054 and the reunion of Orthodox and Catholic within the papal fold. To this end he had been urged by Antoine Arnauld and Pierre Nicole, leading theologians of the Port-Royal, to find out whether the Orthodox Church believed in the real presence of Christ in the Eucharist, and in transubstantiation in the sense in which it was understood at Rome.[7] The question had been given a new and encouraging urgency by the publication of the decrees of the Orthodox Synod of Jerusalem (sometimes known as the Synod of Bethlehem) in 1672, which appeared to have brought the Eastern tantalizingly close to the Western Church. This Synod resoundingly rejected the 'calvinist' leanings of the earlier Patriarch Cyril Lucaris and reaffirmed the Orthodox doctrines such as free will, the seven sacraments and the veneration of images. The Acts of the Synod were published under the heading 'A Shield of the Orthodox Faith'. After this 'one hears no more of Protestantism within the Orthodox Church'.[8]

5 Clement, *Histoire*, p. 256.

6 The Jansenists emphasized the role played by Divine Grace in salvation, and their rigorous views had been condemned by Pope Innocent X in the bull 'Cum Occasione' in 1653.

7 On Nointel's theological interests, see Vandal, *L'Odyssée d'un ambassadeur*, pp. 47ff.

8 A. Fortescue, *The Orthodox Eastern Church* (London, 1920), pp. 267–8; S. Runciman, *The Great Church in Captivity* (Cambridge, 1968), p. 308. For a more nuanced interpretation, see Judith Pinnington, *Anglicans and Orthodox: Unity and Subdivision 1559–1725* (Leominster, 2003), pp. 144f. For the text, see G. Williams, *The Orthodox Church of the East in the Eighteenth Century, Being the Correspondence between the Eastern Patriarchs and the Nonjuring Bishops* (London, 1868), pp. 67–76.

A vivid picture of Nointel's compulsive preoccupation with the Eastern Church may be seen in the diary of the English ambassador's chaplain, John Covel, who was in Constantinople from 1670 to 1677 and had been commissioned by the bishops of Ely and Chester to pursue the same inquiries as Nointel as to the beliefs of the Orthodox Church, though in hope of a different, more Protestant, verdict.[9] Nointel befriended Covel, originally perhaps as a possible source of political and commercial intelligence in the course of his essentially anti-English mission, and made a point of including him on various forays into Orthodox territory.[10] The two evidently became such a familiar sight together that Greek clergy could even regard them as if singing from the same hymn-sheet. So it was that on 7 February 1673 a young priest who gave his name as 'Hilarione Bubuli' (i.e. Greek Bouboulis) visited Covel to inquire whether the embassy had any mail for Venice: Covel described how Bubuli had told him that he came from Venice, was a monk of the Order of St Basil which was Roman Catholic but followed the Eastern rite.[11] Bubuli thought that Covel, since he was so often in the company of Nointel, was also a Roman Catholic and so revealed to him a plot to remove the current patriarch (Dionysius IV) and replace him with a patriarch known to be sympathetic to the Roman Catholic Church. Covel was amused by Bubuli's misapprehension.[12] In August 1673 Dionysius was indeed replaced by another patriarch (Gerasimos II). Meanwhile, Nointel had in June been successful in securing the trading concessions which he sought, and on 20 September he embarked on his frigate at Tarapia on the Bosphoros for a journey around the Aegean.

Nointel's journey was the more remarkable in that foreign envoys were rarely allowed to travel beyond the Dardanelles, let alone on a warship. Pausing only to receive and return the salute of coastal batteries wherever

9 On Covel, see E. Leedham-Green, *ODNB*, xiii, pp. 726f., and see below, p. 143.

10 See, for instance, Covel's diary, BL, Add. MS 22912, fols 147–8.

11 BL, Add. MS 22912, fol. 148v; repeated in Covel's published account half a century later, *Some Account of the Present Greek Church* (Cambridge and London, 1722), preface, p. i. The date given is 1672; for 1673 as the true date, see the narrative in BL, Add. MS 22910, fol. 95.

12 BL, Add. MS 22912, fol. 148v.

he passed, the ambassador followed a reasonably direct route to Chios.[13] From there, bypassing Samos and Ikaria, he made for the Cyclades, collecting a rich haul of antiquities from Paros and Delos, and then sailed on to Patmos. Among Nointel's numerous retinue of writers and artists was the young French traveller and writer Antoine Galland, best known for his later introduction of *The Thousand and One Nights* to western readers but then recruited by Arnauld and Nicole from his post at the Collège Mazarin to serve as the ambassador's secretary and theological attaché.[14] It was in Patmos, as Galland later recalled in the introduction to his French translation of Georgirenes' *Description of The Present State of Samos, Nicaria, Patmos, and Mount Athos*, that he first made the acquaintance of the archbishop.[15] For Georgirenes, it was to prove a most significant encounter. It can be dated with some precision: the French party left Herakleia for Patmos on 9 January 1674 and sailed for Leros on 16 January, having therefore stayed in Patmos for exactly a week.[16] Georgirenes was still in Patmos, then, at the beginning of 1674. Ever the opportunist, he seized the opportunity not

13 For Nointel's touchiness on the matter of salutes, see also Comte de Laborde, *Athènes aux xve, xvie et xviie siècles* (Paris, 1854), pp. 91–3.

14 See *Journal d'Antoine Galland pendant son séjour à Constantinople, 1672–3*, ed. C. Schefer, 2 vols (Paris, 1881), ii, pp. 152ff.; cf. *Revue Retrospective*, 2nd series, xii, pp. 1–69, 226–91. Nointel's own account is contained in his letters to Colbert. Others of the party also wrote of their experiences: see A. des Barres, *L'estat present de l'Archipel* (Paris, 1678); Cornelio Magni, *Quanto di piu curioso, e vago ha potuto raccorre C. M. nel primo biennio da esso consumato in viaggi* (Parma, 1679). It was on the return journey that Jacques Carrey made his well-known drawings of the pediments and other sculptures of the Parthenon at Athens, essential evidence of their appearance before the Venetian bombardment of 1687: see H. Omont, *Athènes au XVIe siècle: dessins des sculptures du Parthenon attributes a J. Carrey et conservés a la Bibliothèque Nationale, Paris* (Paris, 1898); T. R. Bowie, *The Carrey Drawings of the Parthenon Sculptures* (Bloomington, 1971).

15 Galland, *Voyages inédits*, p. 250. Most unfortunately, Galland's diary does not survive beyond Chios. For the later relations of Galland and Georgirenes, see below, pp. 136–9; 225–30.

16 Des Barres, *L'estat present de l'Archipel*, pp. 172–6.

only to secure letters of introduction or 'passports' from the Marquis de Nointel but also to initiate a lasting relationship with Galland.[17]

No doubt Georgirenes played his part in showing the French visitors the main sights of the island. The visitors' chief interest will have been in the story of St John's sojourn in Patmos, and in the tradition of his composition of the Book of Revelation on the very spot where the archbishop dwelt, half-way up the hill from the harbour of Skala, in the convent of the Apocalypse. 'It is no small credit to a Place, otherwise very inconsiderable', he could tell them, 'that that great Apostle, once the peculiarly beloved Disciple; who of all the Apostles, did alone survive our Saviours judicial coming into his Kingdom of Power and Vengeance upon the *Jewish* Nation: that he should be for no small time an Inhabitant of this Island, and there Pen that Mysterious and Sublime Book, which to him indeed was *Apocalypse*, but to all others *Apocrypha*, to him a Revelation, but to us yet an hidden Mystery. ... The Tradition of this Island is very positive, that he writ his Gospel here likewise, and that upon the Request of the Islanders, who at his departure, after seven years abode in the Island, did importune him to leave them in writing what they ought to believe: Whereupon he stayed eight days longer, to dictate the Gospel to his Disciples that writ it. They add more, that as he was beginning the Work, there happened a great Thunder and Earthquake, whereupon, looking up to Heaven, he spoke those words: Εν ἀρχῇ ἦν ὁ λόγος: *In the beginning was the Word.* Besides, it is a most confirm'd Tradition, that the Cavern, which now goes by the name of the Holy *Grotto*, was made by the Rupture of the Earth, in that Earthquake.[18]

One can imagine the wave of the hand with which he would indicate the very grotto where they stood. And after that he will have accompanied them up the hill to the great fortified monastery itself, and the once prosperous town huddled about it for protection, and told them of its

17 Galland, *Voyages inédits*, p. 303.

18 *Description of the Present State*, pp. 73–5, 77. Nointel wrote drily to Colbert, 'Il ne faut pas oublier de visiter la grotte ou saint Jean a écrit les révélations de l'Apocalypse.' See Galland, *Journal*, ii. 210.

foundation by Christodoulos in the time of the Byzantine emperor, Alexios I Komnenos (1081–1118).[19]

Georgirenes might also have aroused their curiosity with his story of the origin of the offshore rock of Kynops. The archbishop writes,

> That the Island, at St *John*'s first coming were all Idolaters, had people possessed with Devils, and were mis-led with Magicians, is more than probable. That St *John*'s casting a Devil out of young *Apollonides*, had a great influence on the peoples Conversion, and rais'd him the Enmity of a Magician, and all that he could draw after him, is a thing reasonably credible. The Name of *Cynops* the Magitian, is known to all the People to this day; yea, not without some very improbable circumstances of the Story, that St *John* should cause him to jump twice into the Sea, and the second time to be turn'd into a Rock, which now bears his name. ...[20]

One of Nointel's party, Antoine des Barres, repeats this story which they may well have heard from Georgirenes, in a rather different version when he tells of their attempt to visit this threatening place:

> Below this town, and on the saddle of this hill, is the grotto where this beloved disciple wrote this gospel, reclining in the bosom of the Eternal Father and there is in this place a church served by monks. The inhabitants of this place are all Greeks, and therefore people to whom one should give little credence; but they maintained as the absolute truth that the devil, coming one day to tempt St John in a cave on the edge of the sea, was eager to persuade the saint to throw himself into the water. But the evangelist himself commanded the devil to throw himself down, and he could not disobey. He threw himself down and was at once changed into a rock, which is said still to be in the same place. We wanted to go and look for this rock, but were told that it was too difficult to approach. So I do not even know whether there is a rock; but for all that it has kept little of its original nature, this must be a dangerous reef.[21]

19 Ibid. pp. 75f., with error over the date, which is given as late tenth to early eleventh century, rather than, as correctly, eleventh to twelfth. The monastery was in fact founded in 1088.

20 *Description of the Present Sate*, p. 73.

21 Des Barres, *L'estat present de l'Archipel*, pp. 173ff.

Ambassador Nointel had not confined himself to his publicly avowed brief of negotiating new capitulations with the Porte to the advantage of French merchants. In his religious preoccupation he sought also to use the opportunity which the voyage offered to investigate such matters as belief in transubstantiation among the eastern Christians far from the theological hothouse of Constantinople, and so assess the likely durability of a closer bond between the Roman and Orthodox Churches. An encouraging answer in the affirmative appeared recently to have been given in the unmistakably pro-Roman decrees of the Synod of Jerusalem or Bethlehem, engineered by the patriarchs Dionysios of Constantinople and Dositheos of Jerusalem in 1672:[22] were they more widely acceptable among the adherents to the Orthodox Church? The presence of an under-employed Orthodox archbishop in the Cave of the Apocalypse on Patmos may have provided Nointel with an opportunity to carry his designs further. As will emerge, Georgirenes was nothing loath to engage in theological discussion, and he may have been encouraged, or even recruited by Nointel, to embark on what is otherwise a surprising turn in his adventurous career.

A word of caution at this point: unusually, we have a continuous narrative source for what follows. It is Georgirenes' own account, which we have already used for the episode of his resigning his archbishopric and taking up residence on Patmos. The narrative, however, should carry a double warning. In the first place, it was written in Italian later for the Roman Catholic authorities in Volterra, and Georgirenes' desire to be seen by them in a favourable light is likely to have dictated something of the content, or at least the emphasis or 'spin'. It was not intended to be read by Greeks, still less by Anglicans or other Protestants. Secondly, the original document has disappeared, and we are dependent on a Greek translation of it, made for the Samian historian Epameinondas Stamatiades at the end of the nineteenth century, who was frankly shocked by the whole course of events it disclosed.[23] That said, there is nothing inherently implausible

22 See above, p. 3; below, pp. 144–6.

23 For the Greek text, translated by P. Zerlentos, see E. I. Stamatiades, *Epistolimaia diatribē peri Ioseph Georgeirēnou, Archiepiskopou Samou 1666–1671* (Samos, 1892), pp. 13–18, who comments that it 'contains nothing but monstrous arrogance from

about Georgirenes' account, and (as will be seen) it is compatible with the considerable documentary evidence that survives: it should probably be taken as a reliable, if not necessarily complete, account.

Although Galland later reported that Georgirenes had left Patmos simply in order to see 'les parties occidentales de l'Europe', the archbishop in his own statement at Volterra told his Italian friends of his search for an opportunity to visit the Holy City (meaning Rome) and to secure remission of his sins – the latter a remarkable enough ambition for an archbishop of the Orthodox faith, but one no doubt calculated to appeal to his audience. He shared his plan with the Abbot of Patmos, who saw in it a means of alleviating the dire poverty to which the loss of its rich Cretan estates had lately consigned his monastery: if Georgirenes could appeal to the pope and other Christian rulers in the name of the holy grotto, perhaps some help might be forthcoming.[24] *Prima facie*, this might seem little more than a pipe-dream. But the archbishop could cite precedents: in time gone by 'the Islanders have procur'd Charters and Patents from the Pope; the King of *France*; from the State of *Venice*; from the Dukes of *Tuscany*; from the Grand Master of *Maltha*'.[25] It was certainly not absurd to attempt a fresh appeal to Rome, capitalizing on the favourable mood engendered by the Synod of Jerusalem.

His plans laid, around midsummer in 1674 the archbishop embarked for Italy, with two monks as well as family members among his entourage. Significantly he paused at Syros to help the Greek Catholics (who formed the larger element of the population) by ordaining fifteen priests, since their own bishop was unavailable and his deputy lacked the necessary

---

beginning to end'. In the view of E. Legrand, *Bibliographie hellénique du XVIIe siècle*, 5 vols (Paris, 1894–1903), v. pp. 299–301, Stamatiades' work 'contient, accommode à la sauce hellénique, a peu pres tout ce qui concerne Joseph Georgirenes, mais elle gagnerait beaucoup a être reduite de moitié' ('contains, prepared with the Hellenic sauce, nearly everything that concerns Joseph Georgirenes, but it would gain greatly by being reduced by a half').

24 Galland, *Voyages inédits*, p. 303; Stamatiades, *Epistolimaia*, p. 15. On the poverty of the once rich monastery, see *Description of the Present State*, pp. 76, 82–4: its annual income from Crete had fallen from 13,000 dollars to a mere 200.

25 Ibid. p. 81.

authority.[26] By this time word of his journey and its purpose had reached the new patriarch Gerasimos II (1673–75), who promptly excommunicated him as a covert Catholic, to Georgirenes' professed amusement at so ineffective a gesture. When he reached the sanctuary of Venetian territory at Zante (Zakynthos), he found that word had already come to alert the local Orthodox hierarchy of Zante, themselves tainted with what the archbishop chose to present as the patriarchal schism, 'denial of the authority of the Vicar of Christ'. His life threatened, as he believed, the archbishop managed to persuade a captain of his acquaintance to sail urgently for Venice. Once there, for greater security and to shorten his journey to Rome, he re-embarked for Ancona.

Although Ancona had had a local Greek community since 1524 it was riven by disputes between the Orthodox and the Uniates (i.e. those in the Eastern Churches who were in communion with Rome) and the settlement had fallen into rapid and precarious decline.[27] The lesson would not have been lost on Georgirenes. Arrived at Ancona, the archbishop at once sought out the papal representative, Mgr Barezzi. The latter advised him not to make straight for Rome in the stifling summer heat but instead to go to Bologna and stay in Tuscany till the end of October. Easily persuaded, he was received at Bologna and entertained most cordially by the archbishop, Cardinal Hieronimo Buoncampagni, who saw to it that his

26 For the whole narrative, see Stamatiades, *Epistolimaia*; cf. idem, *Samiaka, ētoi Historia tēs nēsou Samou*, 5 vols (Samos, 1881–7), iv. 212. P. P. Rodota, *Dell' origine, progresso, e stato presente del rito Greco in Italia, osservato dai Greci, monaci basiliani, e albanesi*, 3 vols (Rome, 1758–63), iii, pp. 231–2, implies a much earlier date for the voyage, making him already active in Italy by 3 May. This is an error, however, the result of attributing to Georgirenes an act which in fact preceded his arrival.

27 Z. Tsirpanlis, 'Eklogē mētropolitē Italias apo tous Ellēnes tēs Ankonas', *Dodone* ii (1973), pp. 61–76; idem, 'Gia tēn eklogē mētropolitē Italias sta mesa tou 16 aiōna (Prosthēkē kai diorthōseis)' iii (1974), pp. 143–50; M. I. Manousakas, 'Structure sociale de l'hellénisme postbyzantin', *Jahrbücher der österreichischen Byzantinistik*, xxxi (1981), pp. 791–821, esp. pp. 809f.; A. Fortescue, *The Uniate Eastern Churches: The Byzantine Rite in Italy, Sicily, Syria and Egypt*, ed. G. D. Smith (London, 1923), pp. 136f.

guest was re-equipped to befit his standing. In the frenetically extravagant and competitive society of Counter-Reformation Italy what mattered was outward display. One of the most telling status symbols was the number of carriages a prince or an ambassador could muster; and princes of the church were not immune to the demands of competition, indeed the cardinal legates of Bologna had often led the way in notorious excess.[28] So Buoncampagni hastened to equip Georgirenes with carriages and with servants: an archbishop could not be seen to go about on foot and unattended. He also provided him with a Greek priest, one Bubuli, as tutor and companion night and day, and encouraged him to officiate at divine service in convents of nuns.

The name of Bubuli is familiar. He it was, the Greek Catholic monk 'Hilarione Bubuli', who had visited John Covel, chaplain to the English ambassador at Constantinople in February 1673, when he was indiscreet enough to disclose the far-reaching plot in which the French and Venetian representatives were implicated, to seize the patriarchate for the Roman cause.[29] Not that Bubuli enjoyed an altogether favourable reputation in the Serene Republic. The papal nuncio in Venice was later to fill in some further details of this enigmatic figure. Bubuli's parents were 'schismatic' – that is, Orthodox – but he himself had been received into the Catholic Church in Rome, at the Sant' Ufficio, in December 1672. When he returned to Venice and sought to be ordained priest, the archbishop there refused, despite pressure from members of the Venetian Senate, regarding him as 'di cervello instabile' (of unbalanced mind). However, he managed eventually, perhaps after his visit to Covel in Constantinople, to secure ordination by the Catholic Bishop of Zante. He was, said the nuncio, no great scholar: he could, indeed, cope with ancient Greek, but he had little Latin. Still,

28 See L. Collison-Morley, *Italy after the Renaissance: Decadence and Display in the Seventeenth Century* (New York, 1930), p. 148, noting the many tales of Cardinal Bonaccorsi's rapacity in grinding the faces of the poor; ibid. p. 171. More recently, when the future Grand Duke Cosimo III married Marguerite d'Orléans, niece of Louis XIV and granddaughter of Henri IV, the bride was met at Leghorn by twenty coaches, while no fewer than 300 paraded at the wedding: ibid. pp. 289ff.

29 See above, p. 104.

he was reputed to be of good character.[30] That Bubuli was now attached to Georgirenes is unlikely to be mere coincidence, given the work that the archbishop was shortly to be called upon to do. On the contrary, it perhaps discloses an excellent network of communication between the voyaging Nointel and both Constantinople and Venice. It is possible that the recently ordained Bubuli was still at Zante in 1674 when Georgirenes arrived there. Whether Georgirenes was a willing accomplice or merely Nointel's puppet, the availability of Bubuli at Bologna may not have been a matter of chance, so much as evidence of a high level of determination and administrative competence on someone's part.

In Cardinal Buoncampagni's palace the Greek archbishop was fortunate enough to find himself dining with Cardinal Sigismondo Chigi, younger brother of Prince Agostino Chigi, and, more significantly, nephew of Fabio Chigi, the late Pope Alexander VII (d. 1667). Sienese in origin, the Chigi had for some time been settled in Rome, where Sigismondo (1649–77), a cardinal since he was eighteen, served as Ferrara's envoy to the papal court; more significantly, he was cardinal prefect of the Greek College in Rome. A cousin, Cardinal Flavio Chigi, had lately secured the unwilling election of the octogenarian Emilio Altieri as Pope Clement X (1670–6) and on the same day as the appointment of his own kinsman by adoption, Paluzzo Altieri, as a cardinal: Clement was, of course, the pope to whom Georgirenes intended to direct his appeal.[31] The Chigi were evidently a powerful team, and the Archbishop of Samos is likely to have recruited the influential Cardinal Sigismondo to his cause.[32] And so he passed on from Bologna to Florence, where he found himself equally generously received by Cardinal Francesco Nerli, secretary of state in plurality, hand

30 Vatican, *Acta*, xlv, 1675, fols. 84v–86v: Th. Papadopoulos, 'Maniates apoikoi stēn Italia tou 17° aiōna', *Lakonikai Spoudai*, xiv (1979), pp. 410f.

31 On Clement X and his relations with the Altieri and Chigi, see L. Osbat, in *Dizionario biografico italiano*, xxvi (1982), pp. 293–302, esp. p. 298, and bibliography. On Altieri, see A. Stella, ibid. ii (1960), pp. 561–4; on Flavio Chigi, E. Stampo, ibid. xxiv (1980), esp. pp. 749f.

32 On the Chigi, see U. Frittelli, *Albero genealogico della nobile famiglia Chigi patrizia senese* (Siena, 1922).

in glove with Altieri, who counted among his myriad responsibilities the prefecture of the Congregatio de Propaganda Fide.[33] Among the many gifts Georgirenes was given was a copy of a curiously apposite decree, issued by the late Grand Duke of Tuscany Ferdinand II (1628–70) out of his devotion to the holy grotto, assuring protection for the monks and others from Patmos and Melos, from attacks by pirates from Leghorn (Livorno).[34] Both islands were, of course, especially significant to Georgirenes; presumably the scope of the decree was wider. Most loyal to the pope of all the Italian states, and therefore given its head in church affairs, Tuscany had long had good relations with Greeks, to whom, however, the grand duke had only recently been persuaded to allow a church in Florence of their own.[35] Here, as at Bologna, Georgirenes was invited to conduct services in nunneries, monasteries and other institutions.

Georgirenes came to Florence as something of a *deus ex machina*. The papal nuncio and titular Archbishop of Edessa *in partibus*, Carlo Francesco Airoldi, had found himself faced with an influx of Orthodox refugees from the Mani, who had arrived in Tuscany at the invitation of the grand duke, and it was his responsibility to oversee their assimilation to the Church of Rome. As Orthodox, and subjects of the ecumenical patriarch, they were schismatic. Plurality of doctrine was inadmissible, plurality of discipline

33 For names and other details of Catholic prelates, see P. B. Gams, *Series Episcoporum Ecclesiae Catholicae* (Regensburg, 1873–86; repr. Graz, 1957). For a contemporary view of the pre-eminence of Chigi, Nerli, and above all Altieri, through the eyes of one well acquainted with Greece and the Greek church, see J. Spon, *Voyage d'Italie, de Dalmatie, de Grèce, et du Levant, fait des années 1675 & 1676 par Iacob Spon, Docteur Médécin Aggregé à Lyon, & George Wheler, Gentilhomme Anglois* (Lyon, 1678), pp. 390f.

34 In his account of Patmos, Georgirenes refers to charters from the dukes of Tuscany protecting the islanders from the attacks of Christian corsairs, *Description of the Present State of the Islands*, p. 81.

35 *Calendar of State Papers, Venetian, 1673–1675*, ed. Allen B. Hinds (London, 1940 [1943]), p. 160: see below, p. 114 and n. 36. For the interdependence of ecclesiastical relations between Tuscany and Rome, see Domenico Sella, *Italy in the Seventeenth Century* (London and New York, 1997), pp. 110, 164–5; F. Diaz, *Il Granducato di Toscana, i Medici* (Turin, 1976), pp. 186–97, 235–81.

unthinkable: although both had become established *de facto* in Venice under the sheer weight of numbers of Greek immigrants, and had been a constant irritant to the smooth running of the papal machine. The Maniates in Tuscany had to be made Uniates, that is, they had to be brought to accept the authority of Catholic doctrine, symbolized by the inclusion of the *filioque* clause in the creed, and they must recognize the authority of the throne of Peter. That said, Rome was always prepared to be accommodating over forms of worship. As Pope Benedict XIV (1740–58) later explained in his bull *Etsi pastoralis*, issued especially for the Italo-Greeks on 26 May 1742:

> They and their children are to keep studiously and carefully the habits, institutions, rites and customs which they have received from their Greek fathers, only to show to the Roman Church due obedience and reverence. ... Our predecessors, the Roman Pontiffs, considered it more proper to approve and permit these rites, which in no way are opposed to the Catholic faith, nor cause danger to souls, nor diminish the honour of the Church, rather than to bring them to the standard of the Roman Ceremonies. ... Nor do we allow any Latin Ordinary to molest or disturb these or any of them.[36]

The reference to the regulations made by Benedict's predecessors recalls the words of Clement VIII, confirmed by Urban VIII in 1627, that 'the Greeks are not to be dragged to the Latin rite, but that provision be made for a Greek Catholic priest, united with the Roman Church, to enable them in their own rite to keep the Catholic faith, in accordance with the decrees of the Council of Florence'.[37] These were the guiding principles which were to dictate the treatment of the Maniates in Tuscany, even though individual Latin bishops and others might be reluctant to practise such restraint.

Archbishop Airoldi, the papal nuncio in Florence, was an experienced diplomat. He had already served as nuncio in Flanders, where he made use of the proximity to visit England in 1670 and assess the religious climate, and had only recently been moved to Tuscany, in November 1673. He was clearly regarded in Rome as a 'safe pair of hands'. After barely two years in

36 *Benedicti p. XIV Bullarum*, 4 vols (Venice, 1778), i, pp. 75–83, as paraphrased by Fortescue, *Uniate Eastern Churches*, p. 33.

37 Papadopoulos, 'Maniates apoikoi stēn Italia tou 17° aiōna', p. 396.

Florence he was to be appointed to Venice, always a more substantial task in less compliant surroundings and currently even more of a challenge than usual. For the moment, however, the Maniate Greeks were enough of a challenge. At the best of times life in the Mani was hard, the soil as impoverished as the people, the latter beset by an endemic tendency to blood-feud. To this had been added a new level of persecution. The Turks, intoxicated by their increasingly successful campaign to take Candia from the Venetians, had lately moved into the Mani in strength. For the Maniates, it was the end of the road. They emigrated in great numbers in every direction, some even to attempt a new life in stony Ikaria, to such straits were they reduced.[38] The more ambitious looked overseas, beyond Ottoman reach, and particularly to Italy, since ancient times a haven for political refugees and for whole agricultural communities. To the Orthodox, the Papal States were perhaps not the most inviting destination, while Sicily was the disputed prey of Louis XIV and Spain. So their eyes turned rather to Tuscany and Savoy. On 25 January 1669, while Candia still held out though plainly doomed, Grand Duke Ferdinand II issued a decree inviting as many as 1,500 Maniates to make a new home in Tuscany. Two years later it was his successor Cosimo III who gave leave for them to settle at Bibbona and Casalapi in the diocese of Volterra (Bibbona is a small town near the sea close to Casale, Casalapi a village in the orbit of Piombino), and further afield at the inland hamlet of Sovana, east of Grosseto, and at other places in the same region.[39] Two more years passed, and then, late in 1673, the first

38 A. J. Papalas, *Rebels and Radicals: Ikaria 1600–2000* (Wauconda, IL, 2005), p. 19.

39 Z. N. Tsirpanles, 'Oi Maniotes tēs Toskanēs kai tēs Periochēs tou Taranta (b miso tou 17ou ai.)', *Lakonikai Spoudai*, iv (1979), pp. 105–59, esp. p. 109; P. P. Rodota, *Dell' Origine, Progresso, e Stato presente del Rito Greco in Italia, osservato dai Greci, monaci basiliani, e albanesi*, 3 vols (Rome, 1758–63), iii, pp. 231f; Fortescue, *Uniate Eastern Churches*, pp. 143f; Georgirenes' own account of his experiences at Bibbona, see. Stamatiades, *Epistolimaia*, pp. 16–17. The account which follows here is heavily dependent on the work of Tsirpanles, 'Oi Maniotes tēs Toskanēs' and on that of Papadopoulos, 'Maniates apoikoi stēn Italia', as well as on the indispensable guide to the records of the Congregatio de Propaganda Fide provided by P. S. Korolevskij, 'Italo-Greci ed Italo-Albanesi nell' archivio di Propaganda Fide: documenti esistenti nell' archivio', *Archivio Storico per la Calabria e la Lucania*, xvi (1947), pp. 113–53.

wave of immigrants arrived at Bibbona; their numbers are variously given as 120 persons, or 120 families, 320 individuals; others went to Casalapi, and by February 1674 still other settlers had reached Sovana also.[40]

It was all very well for the grand duke to see in the Maniates a welcome supply of labour. As schismatics, to the Catholic Church their transformation into Uniates represented a weighty task, to be undertaken under the supervision of the Congregatio de Propaganda Fide, which had been founded in 1622 for the very purpose of accommodating non-Latins to the papacy. There was a precedent established, however, and experience available in the settlement of the Greek merchant community at Leghorn.[41] At Bibbona the Maniates had arrived with three priests of their own, the hieromonk (a monk who was a priest) Ioacheim Tsiriklianos (Siciliano), and two secular priests Theodoros Melissenos and Georgios Sebastos, whose ordination was 'irregular' in Catholic eyes, having been performed by their bishop in the Mani: they were Orthodox and therefore schismatic.[42] However, on 19 January 1674 the Holy Office lifted the stigma of irregularity from those named, extending this conciliatory decision to any other Maniate priests provided that their names were reported. A letter to this effect was to be sent to the Bishop of Volterra. Hence on 16 February Bartolomeo Roggi, Catholic overseer of Bibbona and priest of the town's main church of Sant'Ilario, was able to assure the bishop, Orazio Albizzi, that he had indeed communicated the decision of Pope Clement X to the Greek priests; by this time they had been reinforced by the arrival of five more clerics, Daniel (younger brother of Georgios) and Makarios Sebastos, 'Ioannisio' Chrysaphes, Dionysios Mouzalos, and the priest Theodoros 'Tueni'. Roggi added that the settlement at Bibbona had now been augmented by the arrival of thirty more Maniates, all lay men, and that he had

40 Papadopoulos, 'Maniates apoikoi stēn Italia', esp. p. 402. It seems that these were not in fact the first refugees to reach Tuscany. As many as 800–1000 had arrived a decade earlier: see Tsirpanles, 'Oi Maniotes tēs Toskanēs', p. 133 and n. 1; M.-A. Comnene, *Cargese, une colonie grecque en Corse* (Paris, 1959), p. 85.

41 See Tsirpanles, 'Oi Maniotes tēs Toskanēs', p. 133 and n. 1.

42 Ioacheim Siciliano was to follow Georgirenes to England and to cause trouble by pretending to be the archbishop, see p. 213 and n. 18.

tried, and failed, to persuade any of the plethora of priests to join the somewhat remote community at Sovana, who had none. Finally, he asked for the bishop's written permission for two of the priests, Theodoros Melissenos and Georgios Sebastos, to go about locally in quest of charitable funds for 'the church' – that is, presumably, to establish a Greek church – and for other pressing needs, taking with them as interpreter a Catholic priest, one Francesco Scotti. If the bishop received the letter, he was in no hurry to reply. The initiative was seized by the Maniates and their ally Scotti, who applied to the Congregatio de Propaganda Fide on their behalf to be allowed a church of their own. On 3 May 1674 the Congregatio announced its decision in favour of the three Greek priests first named: they were to be allowed to establish a church of their own dedicated to San Rocco near to the town of Bibbona where they could use their own rite. It is clear that Francesco had been able to produce the necessary testimonials and to reassure the Congregatio that the Greeks were indeed of 'proven faith'.[43] The Greek church of San Rocco exists today in Bibbona only in the name of the street on which it stood, the road that leads eastwards out of town past the cemetery towards the wild and lovely Macchia della Magona and the open country beyond. Here, opposite the elementary school of 1929 and adjacent to the surviving neoclassical chapel of San Niccolò, from 1856 the oratory of the Niccolini family, stood the 'piccolo oratorio' of the Greeks. Redundant and derelict, it was demolished by the *comune* in 1956–7.[44]

As the spring of 1674 turned to summer, and summer to autumn, the presence of a substantial and increasing Maniate element in his diocese brought ever more anxiety to Bishop Albizzi of Volterra. If he could not forever put off urgent decisions, as he had over the Greek priests' request for

43 *SOCG*, 464, fol. 84; 451, fol. 60; cf. *Acta*, 45, 1675, fols 84v–86v. See Papadopoulos, 'Maniates apoikoi stēn Italia', pp. 402–3 and nn. As to 'the church', it would appear that Bishop Albizzi was less than enthusiastic, for the leave sought was not granted until a year later, on 10 February 1675. By then the application had in part been overtaken by events. Nevertheless, Roggi conveyed the bishop's permission to the Maniates on 10 March, and within the week the two priests were gone: ibid. p. 403 and n. 1.

44 Susanne Mordhorst, *Guida alla Val di Cecina* (Siena, 1996), pp. 61, 73.

leave to seek alms, he could at least attempt to fix responsibility elsewhere. On 12 October he wrote from San Gimignano to the nuncio in Florence to tell him what he knew already, that the grand duke had allowed asylum and a church of their own to 120 Maniates in Bibbona; they had been examined, he said, and had been found to be good Catholics.[45] It so happened that Georgirenes' deliberately slow progress on the road to Rome had brought him to Florence about this time, his presence apparently not yet known to the Bishop of Volterra. In forwarding Albizzi's letter to Rome three weeks later, the nuncio also reported the arrival of the Archbishop of Samos, to whom he had passed on the information that the priests from the Mani were eager to make their assent to the Catholic creed. The nuncio had urged Georgirenes to go to Bibbona and attend to the matter.[46] Though written from a different perspective, the nuncio's report to the Congregation in Rome agrees well with the very full account which the archbishop himself left afterwards at Volterra. He reported that when the Greeks of Bibbona heard that he was in Florence, they sent a priest with one companion, presumably a layman, to meet him and seek his intervention in their religious affairs because their community, like many left behind in Greece, was rent by schism between the Orthodox and Catholic elements. In discussion and by letter Georgirenes urged them to 'abandon and reject their schism and embrace holy Catholic doctrine absolutely and in everything', and their priests formally to make their assent to the Roman creed. The Greek priest and his companion conferred with the papal representative and were at one in persuading Georgirenes to postpone his journey to Rome and himself come to Bibbona. Once there, they hoped he would bring about agreement over the creed, within the Greek language, for the good of all their souls. For his part, the archbishop recognized that this was God's work. But first he knew he must have the formal consent of the diocesan, Albizzi the Bishop of Volterra, who he learned was then at

45 *SOCG* 451, fol. 54; Papadopoulos, 'Maniates apoikoi stēn Italia', p. 403.

46 *SOCG* 451, fol. 53, of 6 Nov. 1674; Papadopoulos, 'Maniates apoikoi stēn Italia', p. 403.

San Gimignano.[47] So there he went, and was received as warmly as he had been in Bologna and in Florence, again delighting the people by his conduct of services in monasteries and other churches. After a few days in that city of towers he was ready to proceed, with the bishop's commissary and other priests for escort – to say nothing of the Archbishop of Bologna's carriages. The cumbrous train will have trundled off up the valley of the Era, under the welcome shade of holm oaks, to the cliff-top citadel of Volterra. There, with his whole entourage, and his by now well-honed skill of landing on his social feet, Georgirenes was welcomed into the *palazzo* of Cav. Francesco Maffei, and even conducted the holy liturgy in the cathedral.

And so to Bibbona, in the nineteenth century still a carriage ride of more than seven hours over rough roads.[48] The Greek refugees whom Duke Cosimo installed had originally numbered between 120 and 320, enough for a village of their own. To put these figures in perspective, the Italians of Bibbona at that time numbered not many more than 200, so the Greeks formed a substantial part of the whole population, perhaps even the majority.[49] Of church buildings there was something of a superfluity. In the old town on the hill, in mediaeval times one of the strongest forts of the Pisan coast, the narrow streets contain several churches, the chief of which, then as now, is the twelfth-century Sant'Ilario, enlarged in the fourteenth century and given special importance from the sixteenth. In the lower town, outside the massive walls reinforced against pirates in 1615, the grandiose structure of Santa Maria della Pietà, Greek-cross in plan and domed, built by the Florentine architects Vittorio Ghiberto and Rainiero da Tripalle in the late fifteenth century, stands at the junction where Georgirenes would have turned off the main Volterra–Cecina road to make the steep ascent

47 It may be significant that an older kinsman of the bishop, Cardinal Francesco Albizzi (1593–1684), had been a close associate of the Chigi Pope Alexander VII, who made extensive use of his diplomatic skills.

48 See G. Dennis, *Cities and Cemeteries of Etruria*, 2 vols (rev. edn; London, 1879), ii, pp. 202–5.

49 Mordhorst, *Guida alla Val di Cecina*, p. 61.

to the old town.[50] A church of Greek form but Catholic dedication might have been thought appropriate for the newcomers. Instead, as we have seen, Duke Cosimo had assigned to them the little oratory of San Rocco, in the Via S. Rocco outside the walls.

It was to San Rocco that Georgirenes brought the Greeks of both traditions for Vespers.[51] They then made their way to the 'church on the hill', Sant'Ilario, where, for more than an hour, the archbishop preached a long and elegant sermon in Greek, urging his compatriots to believe, obey and read (the order is curiously confusing, but his own) the commands of the Catholic Church. The following morning he celebrated the liturgy in San Rocco, where significantly, he invited equal access to the church for women: hitherto they had been accustomed simply to stand at the entrance and their attendance was in any case rare, typically only once a year.[52] This marginalization of female worshippers was not specifically Maniote, but evidently a general Greek practice of the day. A quarter of a century later the French traveller Tournefort, wrote:

> They are too observant of the Laws of Nature in the *Greek* Church, not to forbid the Women entrance into their Churches at certain times: they are obliged to remain at the Door; and as if their breath was tainted, they are not suffer'd to communicate in that condition, nor to kiss any Image. They are not so scrupulous in those Monasteries where they keep Women to wash the Monks Linen. ...[53]

Georgirenes evidently entertained no such prejudice. From this time forward they were to come in and participate fully, the women on one side of the church, the men on the other (as, of course, has since been the traditional Orthodox practice, now beginning to give way to integration). No

50 According to the guidebook of the Touring Club Italiano, its siting at a particularly perilous blind corner gives unintended point to the inscription over one of the three entry doors, 'Terribilis est locus iste'. The building had Chigi connexions, according to A. Angelini, *Gian Lorenzo Bernini e i Chigi, tra Roma e Siena* (Siena, *c.*2000).

51 Stamatiades, *Epistolimaia*, pp. 16–17. From this point on, the account left at Volterra is supplemented by the report which Georgirenes wrote a few days later to the nuncio: see below, n. 56.

52 Cf. letter of Odorisio Pierio (see below, p. 127) to the secretary of the *Sacra Congregatio de Propaganda Fide* from Bibbona, 1 Nov. 1675, see Vatican, *SC*, fols 131v, 132v.

53 M. Tournefort, *A Voyage into the Levant*, 2 vols (London, 1718 ed.), i, p. 89.

doubt he judged that if he could win over the women by this simple act of inclusion, they would see to it that their menfolk followed along the path he indicated.

Then the archbishop made his way once more to Sant'Ilario where he presented the centrepiece of the process of reconciliation, a Catholic mass, at which the six Orthodox priests of the second wave of immigrants publicly made their new profession of faith. 'Then I began the service. I preached, after the gospel, on the Holy Spirit, the basic point of difference between us.' (The papal nuncio reported that it was a 'fine sermon', and urged the whole Greek community to unite in worship.) And so to the climax. First the *Veni Creator Spiritus* was sung in Greek, and then the five priests recited the Catholic creed together, also in Greek. It was important to have an interpreter present – perhaps Francesco Scotti again – in order that a reliable and unanswerable account should reach the Roman authorities. Finally Georgirenes distributed the remaining blessed bread (*antidōron*) to the people.

After dinner the archbishop called the Greeks back to their own church, of San Rocco, for Vespers, and for a kind of sacrament which he devised *ad hoc*. 'I told them to bring as a symbol holy water from the Catholic church, precisely in order that the union of the one and the other church might be impressed upon them' in the sprinkling of the Greeks with water from the Catholic church; and he continued to press upon them their new union by using the Catholic litany while in the Greek church. 'The following morning I conducted the service again in their church' (the Volterra account makes it clear that the church in question is Sant'Ilario) 'and I offered a prayer for their dead, buried in the cemetery there', and remitted sins, before making a final plea for all the Greeks, and not only their priests, to affirm the Catholic creed. A hundred of them did so.[54] Then, leaving orders, advice and encouragement, he returned to Volterra, to his own regret and to the distress of both parties, Catholic and Orthodox, clear indeed that their souls were saved but dismayed by the shortness of his stay, a matter of a few days. He stayed a short while in Volterra, ministering in nunneries, and distributing little crosses as souvenirs of the occasion, and pebbles brought from the holy cave of the Revelation at Patmos.

54 Georgirenes, memorandum written in Rome on 29 Jan. 1675: see below, n. 58.

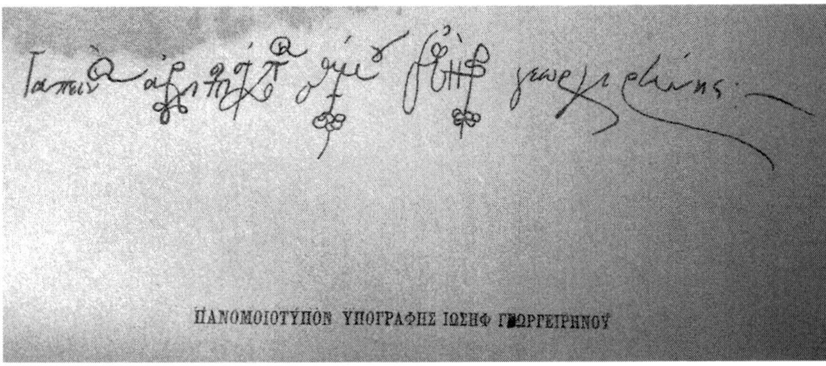

Figure 1: The signature of Georgirenes on the account of his activities which he gave to the Roman Catholic authorities in Volterra, 28 October 1674.

On 28 October 1674 Georgirenes signed the statement his Volterra hosts had taken down (see Figure 1). Headed 'An account of the arrival of a Greek archbishop at Volterra from the islands of the Archipelago', it was countersigned by Canon Antonio Maffei, Cav. Francesco Maffei and Alessandro Riccobaldi del Bava, all of them members of the prosperous and distinguished aristocracy of the city. It is not clear for whom or for what purpose the account was written – whether simply for Bishop Albizzi, or for onward transmission to the papal court; what is clear is that it is a highly slanted account, designed to show Georgirenes' actions and motives from the moment he left Patmos in the most favourable light in the eyes of his Catholic hosts. When he found the account in the archives of Volterra in the late nineteenth century, the loyally Orthodox Epameinondas Stamatiades was shocked by what he read; and Georgirenes' reputation with posterity has suffered accordingly, modern Greek historians labelling him simply *philokatholikos* and, in the light of his later activities in England, *philoprotestantēs.*[55]

55 Stamatiades, *Epistolimaia*; Tsirpanles, 'Oi Maniotes tēs Toskanēs', p. 133.

His business complete, the archbishop was free to resume his mission to the pope. By 2 November 1674 he had reached Siena, where he was made welcome in the convent of Sant'Agostino. He sat down to write a further account of his efforts at Bibbona, this time for the information of the papal nuncio in Florence; the Volterra and Siena narratives supplement one another at crucial points. Ten days later the nuncio forwarded the letter to Rome, together with one of his own, in which he reported the continuing unease of the Bishop of Volterra. Albizzi had written that the five priests whom Georgirenes had persuaded to say the Roman creed now sought permission to officiate at services including the mass. Albizzi himself hesitated to allow this, since their ordination by a schismatic bishop might still be invalid. The nuncio had confirmed that their ordination was indeed valid, since the irregularity had been lifted earlier in the year (as we have seen), but conceded that in canon law they were not authorized to conduct services.[56] After another month, on 18 December, the whole issue was considered by the Sacred Congregation, and their conclusion (we do not know what it was) sent to the Sant' Ufficio.[57]

From Siena Georgirenes pressed on to Rome, reaching the Holy City before the end of January 1675. On arrival he wrote yet another memorandum of his doings at Bibbona, this time for the Congregatio de Propaganda Fide, which considered it on 29 January.[58] His continuing commitment to 'his' Maniates is patent in the urgent appeal he makes for books and other equipment for their church, and above all for a permanent priest to be appointed who would pursue the instruction of the hundred he had himself received, to say nothing of a new contingent of no fewer than 500 refugees as well as any who might arrive in the future. The arrival of so substantial a number seems to have been news to the authorities in Rome, for it was not until 5 February that the nuncio Airoldi wrote from Florence to Cardinal Altieri at the Congregatio to notify him of the 'arrivo di 500

56 *SOCG*, 451, fol. 56, a copy, forwarded by the nuncio to Rome four days later; Firenze, Archivio: summarized by Papadopoulos, 'Maniates apoikoi stēn Italia', p. 404.

57 *Acta*, 44, 1674, fols 375v–376v.

58 *SOCG* 452, fols 135–6v; *Acta* 45, 1675, fol. 23; Papadopoulos, 'Maniates apoikoi stēn Italia', p. 408.

altri Mainotti sopragiunti cola [Bibbona] di nuovo'.[59] However that may be, the Congregatio was puzzled by the need for a priest: were there not five already, whose confession of Catholic faith Georgirenes had himself received and who were therefore no longer schismatic? Bishop Albizzi's continual raising of the question of the canonical effect of the priests' schismatic ordination was becoming tedious. Nonetheless a letter was sent to Florence, seeking further information on the needs of the Maniate church and on the priests who had submitted to Rome. The nuncio responded on 19 February, adding his weight to Georgirenes' appeal for the appointment of an unequivocally valid priest. As to the converts, he had, he said, referred the inquiry to the Bishop of Volterra, who had in turn passed it on to his parish priest in Bibbona, Bartolomeo Roggi.[60] The latter replied on 15 March giving the names of those priests received by Georgirenes at his special service, in addition to those regularized before he came, and adding one or two who had arrived since the archbishop's departure. Chief among them all, he added, was Georgios Sebastos, one of the three who came with the first wave of immigrants. At the same time he enclosed a memorandum of the church's needs, for books and a chalice and paten.[61]

By this time, on 4 March 1675, the Congregation had given serious attention to Georgirenes' plea for a Greek Catholic priest to be provided for Bibbona, and had made inquiries of three possible sources, in search not only of a priest for Bibbona but of another for Sovana also, where the need was even greater.[62] The most promising source was the Greek College

59 *SC*, fol. 59; cf. Tsirpanles, 'Oi Maniotes tēs Toskanēs', p. 110. These seem likely to have been those whom the Paronaxian Metropolitan Mavrogordatos encountered in the *lazaretto* at Leghorn in July 1674, and about whom he wrote to the Duke of Savoy without evoking any immediate response: Papadopoulos, 'Maniates apoikoi stēn Italia', pp. 405ff.

60 *SOCG* 452, fols 334–5v.

61 SC, fol. 65; the list of church service books and other desiderata, ibid. fol. 64, quoted by Tsirpanles, 'Oi Maniotes tēs Toskanēs', p. 134 n. 4, who gives the date of Roggi's letter to Albizzi as 17 March (cf. p. 117). The successive waves of immigrant priests, and their standing, are usefully summarized by Papadopoulos, 'Maniates apoikoi stēn Italia', p. 409 and n. 1.

62 *Acta*, 45, 1675, fol. 53; Papadopoulos, 'Maniates apoikoi stēn Italia', p. 410.

in Rome, the Collegio di Sant' Atanasio, founded a hundred years before by Pope Gregory XIII for the higher education of Aegean Greeks, both Catholic and Orthodox, with a view to their promoting the union of their churches when they returned home. To the prefect of the College, Cardinal Rasponi, went the first letter, asking for a list of students of the college, their studies, and personal details of each individual, in order to form a clear and precise view *an adsit alumnus habilis ad effectum de quo agitur* [whether there was an alumnus suitable to achieve what is proposed]. The cardinal responded as asked, with a list of students as of 15 March and a recommendation of two names in particular, both 'Italo-Greeks', that is to say Italian-born of Greek descent. One, Antonio Parrino from Palazzo Adriano in Sicily, was aged twenty-seven, in minor orders only; he had interrupted his studies for family reasons three years previously, after only a year's theology, but was in fact now eager to return and complete the course for ordination to the priesthood. The other, D. Fabrizio Cortese, aged fifty, was the parish priest of his home town, Lungro in Calabria, and eager to get away.[63] The second inquiry went to Cardinal Carlo Barberini, asking him to discover whether the Benedictine monk 'Peresius' might agree to be sent to Sovana. This 'Peresius' is almost certainly to be identified with the Chian Benedictine monk Odorisio Maria Pierio, who was soon to be given a central role in the Maniates' affairs. The third approach was to the nuncio at Venice: might he be able to discover there any priests, *regulares seu seculares*, who would be suitable for Sovana? The nuncio could think of none – apart from the ubiquitous Hilario Bubuli, who was currently to be found in Corfu. His attachment to Georgirenes had evidently proved as *instabile* as his *cervello*.[64] If the Congregation were interested, the nuncio would get Bishop Labbia of Corfu to sound out Bubuli, or, alternatively, to suggest some other candidate. On 1 April 1675 the Congregation considered the responses received. The secretary noted that Georgirenes was then in Rome, and that he himself might therefore be asked for further information about the Maniate priests. The decision was to ask Cardinal Rasponi to find out what Pietro [*sic*] Parrino might think about being

63 *SOCG*, 464, fols 85, 88.

64 Ibid. fol. 86. See p. 111.

sent to the Maniates, or, alternatively, to seek his view as to which of the college's two alumni he himself thought more suitable for the mission.[65]

Meanwhile at Bibbona the work of assimilation continued, and six weeks later, on 12 May, Bartolomeo Roggi, the local priest, on the instruction of his bishop received into the Church two further priests and ten laymen.[66] There was still no sign of the much-needed books, however, as Airoldi wrote to Rome.[67] Chalices and patens could no doubt be borrowed, but Greek service books were less easy to come by. By this time the Uniate community – no doubt a majority of the settlers and all of their priests – had gathered considerable strength, and would no longer fit into San Rocco's little oratory. Bishop Albizzi found more spacious accommodation for them within the walled town and across the main street from the church of Sant'Ilario, in the church of San Sebastiano.[68] He also took an interest in the training of the young, requiring the priests to teach them the Lord's Prayer, the *Ave Maria* and the creed every Sunday.[69] But there were problems. Converted but unreformed, the Maniates were felt to be drifting. Divorce was available on the usual *Orthodox* terms, and marriages had taken place within the prohibited degrees; Orthodox saints unknown to the pope were receiving illegitimate honour; and the people were inclined still to regard the ecumenical patriarch as 'for all practical purposes the head of the whole of Christendom', for all their local submission to the Roman pontiff. The Congregatio in Rome decided that the moment had come for the appointment of an apostolic visitor for the Uniates of Volterra and Sovana, whose brief would be to reform their abuses. Their choice for the task was Odorisio Maria Pierio, a Benedictine monk of Monte Cassino and therefore of the Latin rite, but born in Chios as Georgios Pieres-Spartales and therefore (it

65 *Acta*, 45, 1675, fols 84v–86v.

66 *SC*, fols 78, 79, all the converts named: K.K. Speliotakis, 'Neōtera Stoicheia peri tēs metoikeseōs tōn medikōn tēs Manēs eis Toskanēn', *Lakonikai. Spoudai*, i (1972), pp. 199–211; cf. Papadopoulos, 'Maniates apoikoi stēn Italia', p. 411 and n. 2; Tsirpanles, 'Oi Maniotes tēs Toskanēs', pp. 133f.

67 *SC*, fol. 77.

68 *SC*, fol. 146. This building, now converted to parish rooms, was formerly the church of Sant' Andrea: Mordhorst, *Guida alla Val di Cecina*, pp. 67f. Its *alias* of San Sebastiano comes from the name of the fraternity based there.

69 *SC*, fols 78–9v, cf. 71.

was hoped) likely to earn the trusting cooperation of the Greeks. Odorisio took up the reins in June.[70] He quickly became committed to the Maniates, identified with their concerns, and remained among them for three years until ill health drove him to take sanctuary in Rome. Even then, he left his younger brother to continue his work. From the vantage-point of Rome, Georgirenes may well have felt that the community he had built the previous autumn, however brief his stay there, had now achieved a measure of stability and, so far as he could tell, permanence.

It was not to be. As Odorisio reported in letter after letter to the secretary of the Congregatio, Urbano Cerri, 'Sono questi Mainotti per la maggior parte miserabilissimi e poverissimi, e tutti riccorron da me' (these Maniates, for the most part, are very poor and wretched, and they recoil from me), convinced that their dire circumstances were the punishment of God for their blood feuds and robberies. And poorest of all were the priests.[71] As well as poverty, leading in some cases to starvation, disease took its toll. The exodus to the other Maniate settlement at Sovana began in September, and by the end of 1675 fewer than half of the Maniates were still in Bibbona. Of eight priests, only five remained in mid-November, and at the end of the year two of these were on the point of leaving. The year 1676 saw the departure of most of those who remained; and it became Odorisio's policy to promote their concentration at Sovana, nearer to Rome and to the watchful eye of the Congregatio.[72] By 1678 only thirty-nine remained in Bibbona, and four years later all were gone and San Rocco's oratory deserted.[73]

The collapse of what Georgirenes believed he had left as a sound community with a promising future had been particularly rapid. But there was in fact nothing peculiar about the fate of Bibbona. Sooner or later, all the

70 *SC*, fol. 90, his letter to the Congregation from Florence, 15 June 1675; cf. three letters from the nuncio all sent in June, ibid. in order of date fols 88, 86, 92.

71 See, for instance, his letter of 1 November, *SC*, fols 130–2v. The pessimistic tone is already observable before the end of July, cf. ibid. fols 96–7, 98–9, two letters written on successive days.

72 For the details of the decline of Bibbona and the promotion of Sovana, see Tsirpanles, 'Maniates apoikoi stēn Italia', pp. 111–14.

73 Mordhorst, *Guida alla Val di Cecina*, p. 61.

Maniate settlements petered out, with the sole exception of that in Corsica. Lack of paid work, a poor road-system and a climate that favoured deadly diseases quickly reduced the settlers' numbers, in Tuscany as elsewhere. As for those hardy enough to survive, everywhere Catholic bishops pressed them to abandon Orthodoxy for the Uniate, Greek Catholic, rite; and when that had been achieved, willy-nilly, they were pressed further until they became fully assimilated as Roman Catholics, their distinctive origin extinguished or forgotten.[74] This was the process in which Georgirenes had found himself called to play a part. He had proved not merely willing but enthusiastic in his commitment. But he cannot have foreseen the outcome.

When the Archbishop of Samos sought the approval of the *hēgoumenos* (the leader of a monastic community) of the monastery of St John, his declared purpose in leaving Patmos had been to throw himself upon the generosity of the pope in Rome, and to solicit a contribution to the monastery sufficient to make up for at least some of the disastrous fall in revenue it had suffered as a result of the loss of its Cretan estates. His work of conciliation in Bibbona had been suggested, and accepted, simply as a diversion, a means of occupying the time until the aged pontiff returned from his summer quarters. In the event the diversion took longer than intended. But we have seen that Georgirenes had reached Rome by the end of January 1675, and that he was still there on 1 April.[75] He had therefore had two months in which to seek an interview with the pope and to present his case. It appears that he was successful because, many years later, Georgirenes recalled that Pope Clement X (1670–6) received him in fatherly manner and granted him several favours, which appear to have included permission to take services and ordain priests. Whether it was the pope who urged him, or Georgirenes who decided to look westwards, is not clear, but later that year he made his way to France.

74 M. I. Manoussacas, 'Structure sociale de l'hellénisme postbyzantin', *Jahrbucher der osterreichischen Byzantinistik*, xxxi (1981), pp. 791–821, esp. p. 810f.; Tsirpanles, 'Oi Maniotes tēs Toskanēs'; Papadopoulos, 'Maniates apoikoi stēn Italia'.

75 Above, p. 125 and n. 65.

CHAPTER 6

Marseilles and Paris (1675–1676)

Some time in the latter part of 1675, following his visit to Rome, Georgirenes concluded that what he could do for the Greeks in Italy, he had done. Reconciled or not, he would leave them in the care of the Benedictine monk, Pierio, from Chios[1] and set out on a new venture exchanging Tuscany for France. Whether this decision was taken on his own initiative or by invitation, we do not know; but it provided an opportunity to renew an important link forged in the previous year.

When Georgirenes had met the marquis de Nointel and his party of Frenchmen on Patmos in January 1674, he had made what was to prove a most useful acquaintance with the ambassador's secretary Antoine Galland. Nointel had just concluded a most satisfactory trading and diplomatic agreement with the sultan.[2] The real triumph, however, belonged to his far-sighted and determined master, the French king's chief minister Jean-Baptiste Colbert. For the latter, as he wrote in a note on possible tactics for Nointel's mission, 'Le seul commerce considerable qui se fasse en France est celuy du Levant'; and, as he wrote then and repeated in frequent letters to local officials, the sole viable base for this trade was the port of Marseilles.[3] For the most serious potential rivals in the western Mediterranean, Leghorn (Livorno) and Genoa, were in decline and Nice had preferred to become a

1 V. Skouvaras, in A. Martinos ed., *Threskeutikē kai ethikē enkyklopaidia*, 12 vols (Athens, 1965), vii, col. 125.

2 See above, p. 102; P. Clement, ed., *Lettres, instructions et memoires de Colbert*, 7 vols (Paris, 1861–82), ii, pp. 628–30, in a note dated 20 Aug. 1671; cf. Nointel's formal instructions from the king, ibid. pp. 841–50. See also P. Clement, *Histoire de la vie et de l'administration de Colbert* (Paris, 1846), ch. x, pp. 256ff.

3 Clement, *Lettres*, pp. 628–30 and note; cf. letters to M. Rouille de Meslay, *intendant* at Aix, dated 13 Jan., 27 Jan., 14 July 1673, ibid. pp. 268, 673.

haven for Savoyard corsairs from Villefranche. Hence, ever since 1660, Louis XIV and his ministers had worked to improve the security of Marseilles and increase its effectiveness. The Marseillais were not an easy people to help. Earlier in the century chronic indebtedness had driven the more energetic of them almost to the point of civil war and, in common with Provence in general, the only thing which united them was their shared resentment of interference from distant Paris.[4] So when the king came to the city in 1660, he was compelled to force an entry through a breach in the walls. During the following decade the harbour was re-fortified, with a new Fort S. Nicolas on the south side of its mouth, while on the north side the venerable crusader fortress of the knights of St John was refurbished and updated. These forts were to serve not only as a defence against Algerian pirates or marauding Turks, Savoyards and Spaniards, but as a deterrent to simmering local dissidence as well. Step by step, the necessary infrastructure was provided – new quays around the old rectangular harbour, a dry dock for the construction of galleys, and an Hôtel de Ville of some pretension.[5] Alongside the physical improvements new and less divisive arrangements for local government were decreed, power transferred from the aristocracy into the hands of the merchant middle class, with the creation of a Chambre de Commerce distinct from, and independent of, the civic authority.

Colbert gave due attention also to the establishment of a new regulatory framework. In March 1669 Marseilles was declared a free port – free of customs, that is, for the goods of French merchants carried on French ships, their interests protected by a 20 per cent tariff against foreign shipping. There was, however, explicit encouragement to foreigners to settle and become naturalized.[6] In the following year, Colbert was writing to M. Oppide, *premier président* at Aix, of the advantage to Marseilles of establishing a *chambre des assurances*;[7] and at the end of 1672, to the *intendant*,

4 On Marseilles in the seventeenth century, see for instance R. Pillorget, in E. Baratier, ed., *Histoire de Marseille* (Toulouse, 1973), pp. 171–97.

5 For the appearance of Marseilles not long afterwards, in the early eighteenth century, see ibid. pl. xii, opp. p. 193.

6 R. Paris, *De 1660 à 1789, le Levant*, in G. Rambert, ed., *Histoire du commerce de Marseille*, 7 vols (Paris, 1949–66), v, p. 85.

7 Clement, *Lettres*, ii, p. 532, 30 June 1670.

M. Arnoul, in support of the latter's project for a new banking-house.[8] Colbert well understood what was needed in the context of what he saw as a permanent trade war with the English and the Dutch, even if he could not always supply the need. But his dealings with the Marseillais brought him endless frustration, as echoes clearly through the instructions which he drafted in the king's name for Nointel on his departure for the Porte: 'Pour remedier a la mauvaise foy des Marseillois et a leur foiblesse, Sa Majeste a forme une compagnie puissante, laquelle elle assiste d'un fonds considerable'.[9] What he did not add was that the new *Compagnie du Levant* was not in fact to be based in Marseilles but in Paris, financial rather than mercantile, with sixteen of Colbert's banking friends behind it but only two Marseillais merchants.[10] Notwithstanding Colbert's devising, the company did not carry all before it. By 1679 Colbert was complaining to the *intendant*, M. Rouille Comte de Meslay, that, whereas the number of Marseilles-based merchant ships had increased sharply between 1660 and 1670, between the latter year and 1678 they had actually diminished in number from eighty-four to fifty-six, despite the advantage of free-port privileges granted by the decree of 1669.[11] They were, he believed, their own worst enemy, idly preferring to pay for goods from Turkey in cash or bullion, with consequently disruptive effects on exchange-rates, rather than carrying French manufactured goods as outward cargo on which they, and therefore the manufacturers, could make a profit.[12]

If the French community did not exploit their new opportunities to the full, the security and modern facilities of Marseilles, in contrast with

8 Ibid. p. 67 and n. 2, 23 Dec. 1672.

9 Ibid. p. 847, 12; cf. vi, p. 70.

10 F. Bluche, *Louis XIV*, trans. M. Greengrass (Oxford, 1990), pp. 149f., citing H. Blet, *Histoire de la colonisation française: naissance et déclin d'un empire* (Paris, 1946), p. 130.

11 Clement, *Lettres*, ii, pp. 711f., 28 Dec. 1679.

12 Ibid. pp. 695–8, 706, 720ff., repeated letters of 1679–81. On Colbert's mercantile policies, see Bluche, *Louis XIV*, pp. 145–52. By 1700 a visitor could gain a more favourable impression: see Joseph Pitton de Tournefort, *A Voyage into the Levant* (London, 1718), pp. 5–14; esp., on commerce, pp. 11ff. – noting that in Ottoman ports French merchants trade primarily with the Jews, and do well, 'So that if a Man is prudent, he need not doubt growing rich; especially if he avoids Commerce with the *Greek* Women, who are the most dangerous Traders in the World'.

the decline of old trading posts elsewhere, gave the port considerable attraction in the eyes of foreign traders; with the encouragement of Colbert's decree and to avoid the punitive 20 per cent tariff, they soon began to settle and establish their own businesses there. The archives of the Chambre de Commerce speak not only of Italians and Spaniards and traders from the islands of the western Mediterranean, and of Dutch, Scandinavian and 'American' adventurers, but men from the eastern Mediterranean – not poor men or debtors, like the Marseillais themselves, but men of substance, comfortably off or even rich, with the ambition to do even better – and among them, of course, the Greeks.[13] Greeks had, indeed, already provided an *entrepôt* for western commerce with the Levant for more than two millennia, ever since the Phokaians of Asia Minor, pioneers of long-distance trade carried in warships, established a settlement at Massalia in 600 BC.[14] The town had made a welcome landfall, with its secure harbour of Lakydon; the natives were friendly and willing to intermarry with the Greeks; and the site stood at the end of a well-worn trade route, up the Rhône and down the Seine, which gave access to such invaluable materials as Cornish tin without the need to risk the wrath of Biscay. Two millennia on, as Leghorn weakened and Marseilles rose in importance, the more enterprising of the Greeks overseas began to transfer their business to the old familiar site. And, like all Greeks of the *diaspora* at all periods, they sought to preserve their ethnic identity through the agency of their religion. In short, they needed a church.

So it was at an opportune moment that Georgirenes came on the scene. We do not know precisely why he decided to leave Italy for France, but it is certain that he did so and that his port of entry was Marseilles.[15]

13 Rambert, *Histoire du commerce de Marseille*, iv, p. 498. See, however, ibid. p. 532 and n. for the modest scale of the Greek community in the eighteenth century.

14 See T. J. Dunbabin, *The Western Greeks* (Oxford, 1948), p. 339; J. Boardman, *The Greeks Overseas*, 4th edn (London, 1999), pp. 214–15; F. Salviat, in E. Baratier, *Histoire de Marseille*, pp. 13ff.

15 Georgirenes' interest in Marseilles is known from a short statement in a letter of 1 Sept. 1676 from Thomas Smith to Henry Dodwell, Oxford, Bod. Lib., MS Smith lx, p. 48, see below p. 151. Georgirenes later recalled that when in Paris he

No doubt he made his way first to Leghorn with its community of Greek merchants under the protection of the Grand Duke of Tuscany, there to take ship for the French port, accompanied perhaps by his brother Lawrence and by at least some of his Italian entourage. Whether by the coastal route past Genoa, thence running the gauntlet of the pirates of Nice and Hyères, and so to Toulon, or by a direct course across the open sea, it is a voyage of no great length.[16] Before long the archbishop would have found himself in safe waters, sailing past François I's brooding castle of If, where the Marseillais leader of the independence party, Glandèves de Niozelles, served six years' imprisonment for refusing to remove his hat in the presence of Louis XIV – a telling illustration both of the disrespect which the French king encountered among the Marseillais and also of his own exasperation with them, and a significant contrast with the story of the Quaker William Penn's refusal to uncover in the presence of Charles II, who in his usual relaxed way ironically took off his own hat, remarking that it was the local custom for only one to remain covered. Turning east at the lighthouse, Georgirenes would have entered the port of Marseilles between the two great forts that Louis had set to guard it, and tied up at one of the new quays. He would have been impressed, as John Locke was when he came as a tourist some weeks later, by the recently completed Hôtel de Ville, 'exceedingly handsomely adorned with figures of graved stone', and would have watched the evening quayside promenade as Locke did.[17] From there he is likely to have sought shelter in one of the Catholic religious houses – S. Victor, perhaps, Charité, near the cathedral and the bishop's palace, in the overcrowded old town up the hill opposite, 'which is not soe safe ... nor sweet' since the buildings in multiple occupation 'have no houses of offices, but instead of that all is don in pots & thrown

---

had secured the liberty of many Greeks who had been condemned to the galleys in Marseilles.

16 The open sea route would have been comfortably far to the north of the current campaign of the French fleet against the Spanish off the coast of Sicily (Stromboli 1675, Lipari 1676), on which see Bluche, *Louis XIV*, pp. 256f.

17 For Locke's impressions of Marseilles in April 1676, see J. Lough, ed., *Locke's Travels in France, 1676–1679* (Cambridge, 1953), pp. 73–6.

out of the windows, which makes the streets very ill sented always & very inconvenient anights'.[18]

The next step was to make contact with the Greek settlers and assess their spiritual needs. Above all, they needed a church building to serve both as a centre of religious observance and as a focal point for the community to maintain its identity.[19] To satisfy this need, Georgirenes had learned in Italy, he would require the cooperation of the Catholic authorities, as well as the permission and perhaps even the active support of the king himself. He would have gone first to the Bishop of Marseilles, to whom Colbert gave generous credit for his role in promoting the growth of the city and its trade with the Levant.[20] Presumably the bishop proved accommodating, for Georgirenes felt encouraged to strike north for Paris. But many years later Georgirenes recalled, for the benefit of the Spanish king, that he had another purpose: in Marseilles he had encountered Greeks working as galley slaves in the ships harboured there and he determined to go to Paris to negotiate to secure their freedom.[21]

Travel by water was possible, but slow. By coach the first leg of the journey, as far as Lyon, could be covered in two and a half days. Unhappily he missed the opportunity of a meeting (or reunion) there with the local doctor and publisher Jacques Spon, an enthusiast for the topography and antiquities of the Archipelago well known in Parisian intellectual circles, who was even then travelling in Greece at the instance of Colbert and Vaillant, *Antiquaire du Roy*, on the lookout for 'medals' and other antiquities for their collections. With him was a young Englishman, George Wheler; over the next few years both men published accounts of that expedition.[22] Pressing

18 Ibid.

19 That Georgirenes hoped to establish a Greek church in Marseilles is attested by Thomas Smith in his letter to Henry Dodwell dated 1 Sept. 1676, Oxford, Bodl. Lib., MS Smith lx, p. 48.

20 Clement, *Lettres*, ii, p. 619, 1 May 1671.

21 See above, p. 132.

22 J. Spon, *Voyage d'Italie, de Dalmatie, de Grèce et du Levant, fait és années 1675 & 1676 par Iacob Spon, Docteur Médécin Aggregé à Lyon, & George Wheler, Gentilhomme Anglois* (Lyon, 1678), with a dedication dated 15 Nov. 1677 to the king's confessor Père de la Chaise; G. Wheler, *A Journey into Greece* (London, 1682).

on, the archbishop reached Paris, a journey which Tournefort accomplished in 1700 by 'Flying-Coach' in the opposite direction, from Paris to Lyon, in seven and a half days.[23] Arrived in Paris, Georgirenes made himself the guest of an abbot, not otherwise identified, but of course a Catholic;[24] and he resumed his acquaintance with Antoine Galland, whom he had last met in Patmos a couple of years before.

In March 1676 the immediate task was to gain the favour of Louis XIV, that is to say the favour of Colbert; without that, there could be no Greek church in Marseilles and no freedom for the galley slaves. That favour, Georgirenes will have expected, would be easily bought, for he knew well how to commend himself to the rich and powerful of western Europe. He had evidently taken the precaution of including in his baggage a number of gifts from Patmos: not only the little crosses and pebbles from the holy grotto which he had distributed at Volterra, but even books from the great monastic library which had so impressed Ambassador Nointel – 'kept in the sacristy, on the left as you approach the choir', as the ambassador wrote to Colbert. No one who had watched Nointel's embassy with any attention, and noted the atmosphere of barely controlled covetousness in which his party had viewed Patmos, could doubt that the way to Colbert's heart lay through gifts of antiquities and coins and, above all, manuscripts to swell the royal collection or his own. In the *Ancien Fonds Grec* of the Bibliothèque Nationale are two thirteenth-century gospel manuscripts, each of which bears in Greek an identical note:

> This book of the four Gospels was brought from the library at Patmos by me, Joseph Georgirenes, humble archbishop of Samos, and was presented to the Most Pious and Mighty King Louis the Great, in the year of Christ 1676, March 25.[25]

These are both very modest volumes, small, battered and showing signs of considerable use. But neither Colbert, nor the Royal Library is likely

23 Tournefort, *A Voyage into the Levant*, p. 3.

24 Oxford, Bodl. Lib., MS Smith lx, p. 48.

25 Paris, Bibliothèque Nationale, Anc. Fonds Gr., 86, fol. 12v; 118, fol. 238v: E. Legrand, *Bibliographie hellénique ou description raisonnée des ouvrages publiés par des Grecs au dix-septième siècle*, 5 vols (Paris, 1894–1903), v, p. 301.

at this date to have had many volumes produced by Greek monks during the medieval period. Their basic illustrations, simply the drawings of the four evangelists, and their unpretentious format, contrast markedly with the volumes produced for use in the western church in the thirteenth century. The gift to the 'Mighty King Louis' and his minister Colbert was not opulent, but it was telling.

It is not clear whether Georgirenes managed to secure an audience with the king himself at his court of Saint Germain, to make his gift and plead his cause. If he did, he will have received no more response than the king's notorious 'Je verrai'. What is clear is that Louis was preoccupied – with Versailles, with his favourite Françoise d'Aubigne whom he had not long installed at Maintenon, with his current mistress Mlle de Ludres, above all with preparations for war in Flanders. For this was the year of the brilliant campaign which Louis commanded in person, memorable for the lightning and successful sieges of Condé and Bouchain, each surrendered in only nine days. In the first week of April Louis was at his desk in Saint Germain, in correspondence with his war minister Louvois, and dispatching detailed instructions to Marechal de Créqui for the siege of Condé; and he was still there on 14 April.[26] Two days later, after a flying visit to Versailles, he was on his way to the front. He stayed with the army until 4 July, when he left Flanders to return to Versailles. If he had any thought at all for the needs of the Greeks of Marseilles, which is more than doubtful, it will have been to leave the matter in the capable hands of Colbert, *vir marmoreus*, who gave the archbishop no immediate encouragement. Georgirenes claimed that he had been able to secure freedom for the galley slaves of Marseilles, but the Greeks there had to wait for the Napoleonic era before they obtained leave to build themselves a church.

Baffled by his failure to obtain a straight yea or nay from royal authority, Georgirenes remained in Paris. It may perhaps have been his friend Antoine Galland who advised this patient course. Certainly it was Galland who devised a way to pass the time, as he himself was to describe three years

26 For closely detailed chronology, see for instance *Œuvres de Louis XIV*, ed. P. A. Grouvelle and P.-H. de Grimoard, 6 vols (Paris, 1806), iv, pp. 23–99.

later in the introduction to his translation of the archbishop's *Estat present des isles de Samos, Nicarie, Patmos, et du mont Athos*:[27]

> La passion toute particulière que j'ai de connaître les îles de l'Archipel, fit qu'à l'arrivée de Mr l'archevêque de Samos à Paris, je l'engageai à composer en grec vulgaire une relation de ces trois îles et du Mont Athos, où il a pris l'habit de caloyer et demeuré six années. Je la mis en même temps en notre langue à mesure qu'il m'en fournissait les cahiers.[28]

> [The special passion that I have to know about the islands of the Archipelago led me, on the arrival in Paris of Monsieur the Archbishop of Samos, to engage him to compose in vernacular Greek, an account of these three islands and Mount Athos, where he had taken the habit of a monk and lived for six years. At the same time, as he went along, I translated the pages into our language.]

The title of the book ties it firmly to a genre of handbooks equally popular in France and England.[29] It was not published in France at that time, although it was Galland's intention that it should form part of a larger study of the Archipelago.[30] In fact the book first saw the light of day in England. But that is to run ahead of the story.[31]

27 Galland, *Voyages inédits*, p. 249; F. Lyna, *Catalogue des manuscrits de la Bibliothèque Royale de Belgique*, xi (Brussels, 1927), pp. 269f: Galland's manuscript was acquired in 1912 from a bookshop in Leiden; in the early nineteenth century it was the property of the oriental scholar Louis-Mathieu Langles. See *Le Voyage à Smyrne: un manuscript d'Antoine Galland: contenant Smyrne ancienne et moderne et des extraits du Voyage fait en Levant*, ed. F. Bauden (Coll. Magellane: Paris, 2000), pp. 29–34. See also E. Legrand, *Bibliographie hellénique ... des ouvrages publies par des Grecs au dix-septieme siecle*, 5 vols (Paris, 1894–1903), ii, pp. 345ff.

28 Galland, *Voyages inédits*, p. 249.

29 Note, for instance, Sir Paul Rycaut, *The Present State of the Greek and Armenian Churches* (London, 1679).

30 The Brussels MS volume contains three works: *Smyrne ancienne et moderne*, by Galland (folios 3–137, autograph); Georgirenes' *Samos* (folios 138–83, in Galland's hand, but a second version made in 1679, as he tells us, and cf. Legrand, *Bibliographie hellénique*, p. 346 and n. 2); and a *Relation de l'Isle de Tines*, signed by the Jesuit Jacques-Paul Babin and dated 3 April 1679 (folios 185–96). All three works carry the signature of the censor Moreau; Claude Barbin was intended by Galland to be the publisher, but on his return from the east early in 1689 he found that nothing had happened, see Bauden, *Le Voyage a Smyrne* ..., ii, p. 345.

31 See below, pp. 225–7.

It was no doubt Galland also who introduced Georgirenes to the circle of Henri Justel as a source of useful contacts in the corridors of power.[32] Justel (1620–93) was a Protestant who had succeeded his father Christophe (a distinguished scholar of canon law)[33] in the office of Conseiller Secretaire du Roi, nominally from the age of sixteen and effectually from before his father's death in 1649, until his own forced resignation in 1664 when, in the increasingly intolerant religious climate of the day, his *protestantisme* had made his position untenable. His personal relations with the court seem to have remained cordial. When he resigned, his services were recognized by *lettres d'honneur*; for several years he received substantial sums from the king by way of pension as a distinguished *homme de lettres*, and in the end he was allowed to anticipate the revocation of the Edict of Nantes, being granted permission to depart for England in 1681 without suffering confiscation of his comfortable resources.[34] If Justel's official position, notwithstanding his resignation, still gave him access to court circles, from his background and by his own actions he enjoyed good relations also with Huguenots of the upper class. He was a scholar and lover of scholars, both French and foreign: his weekly *soirées* and well-stocked library attracted many of the leading intellectuals of the day. With those who could not come in person, he maintained a voluminous correspondence on matters both scholarly and ephemeral. His role was recognized in the pension he received, 'en considération de son application aux belles-lettres' and 'à

32 On Justel, see P. Dally, 'Les Justel: II. Henri Justel (1620–1693)', *Bulletin de la Société de l'Histoire du Protestantisme Français*, lxxix (1930), pp. 9–32; H. Brown, 'Un cosmopolite du grand siècle: Henri Justel', ibid. lxxxii (1933), pp. 187–201; G. Treasure, in *ODNB*, xxx, pp. 843–4.

33 Henri's first publication had been the completion and revision of his father's *Bibliotheca Juris Canonici Veteris*, in two folio volumes (Paris, 1661).

34 These consisted of the capital on which he had lived, together with the proceeds of the sale of his library of 7,000 books. His leaving France was said to have been the result of a request to Louis by Charles II. In fact, it seems to have been engineered by the Bishop of London at Justel's own request: see Brown, 'Un cosmopolite', pp. 198f. He was able to survive without a salaried post, for that of assistant keeper of manuscripts at St James's Palace to which he was appointed in 1681 appears to have been honorary; in 1689 he became keeper, at a salary of £200 p.a.

cause du commerce qu'il entretient avec la plupart des savants hommes de l'Europe':[35] a useful ally indeed for Georgirenes.

Omnivorous in his interests and catholic in his acquaintance, Justel was not immune from the preoccupations of his age; his own background gave him an urgent interest in the current controversies between the Roman and the reformed churches of Europe. In this pursuit he saw himself as undogmatic, seeking only the truth, which he expected to find in close study of the Bible. He laboured to publish a polyglot text, with apocrypha, concordance and commentary – eschewing the polemic of his contemporaries. At his table Romanists and Protestants could meet on equal terms to discuss ideas and arguments on either side in amiable surroundings.

Justel was in touch with Antoine Arnauld (1612–94) and Pierre Nicole (1625–95), two of the leading proponents of the defining Catholic doctrine of the centrality of the eucharist as Christ's sacrifice *re-enacted* in every celebration of the mass (and not simply a *commemoration* of His 'sacrifice of Himself, once offered', as the Protestants held), together with rigid acceptance of the literal truth of transubstantiation.[36] An expanded edition of their joint great work on *La perpetuité de la foi de l'église catholique touchant la eucharistie* had lately appeared in three volumes, 1669–74. Though Arnauld's and Nicole's earlier study of Augustine had left them tainted with an almost Calvinist belief in predestination, it was their formulation of eucharistic doctrine upon which controversy was focused, both in France and abroad. Protestant as he was, with a wide acquaintance among Protestants overseas, it is no surprise that Justel's circle included the leading antagonist of Arnauld and Nicole, Jean Claude (1619–87), Protestant minister of Charenton – so much the leader, in fact, that on the revocation of the Edict of Nantes in 1685, under which Huguenot pastors were allowed a fortnight to leave the country, Claude was given only twenty-four hours and then personally escorted to the frontier.[37] That lay in the future: in 1676 his notoriety centred on his publications against Arnauld and Nicole. These began in 1665 with a *Réponse* to the original edition of

35 Quoted by Dally, 'Henri Justel', p. 10.

36 For Arnauld and Nicole, see *Nouv.Biogr.Gén.*, iii, cols 282–9, and xxxvii, cols 1018–26.

37 *Nouv. Biogr.Gen.*, x, col. 694.

their *La perpetuité de la foi*, commonly known as '*la petite perpetuité*', which had been published the previous year. The *Réponse* was explicitly refuted in the three-volume '*grande perpetuité*' of 1669–74, ... *contre le livre du ministre Claude*, who defended his view against theirs in two volumes of a new *Réponse* in 1671. In that year Arnauld issued a *Réponse générale à M. Claude*, while Nicole launched his *Préjugés legitimes contre les calvinistes.* Unbowed, Claude followed in 1673 with a *Défence de la reformation contre le livre intitule: Préjugés légitimes contre les calvinistes.* Not since dancing angels jostled for room on the head of a pin had theological controversy aroused more urgent excitement. The Greek archbishop must have been utterly bemused to find himself in such company, and, of course, expected to adjudicate on matters fundamental to western belief and to the Greek church of supreme indifference.

As the historic Catholic Church *par excellence*, Rome claimed for its eucharistic doctrine a *perpetuité* extending unbroken back to Peter and to Christ himself. It was this continuity that the reformed churches denied. In this war of the books, both sides hoped to find support in the authority of the early Church, and therefore engaged in intensive study and interpretation of the Fathers, particularly the Greek Fathers. It was clear, however, that there was no unambiguous answer to be found. The matter could be settled by appeal neither to the decrees of the seven ecumenical councils, which had been concerned with the greater issue of the nature of Christ himself, nor yet to the Fathers, who held different views of the nature of His presence in the eucharist verging variously on both the later Roman and later Protestant positions, with little attempt at precise definition and no hint that the issue might be controversial.[38] It soon emerged that the nature of Christ's presence had first become a matter of serious dispute among the logic-choppers of the Western Church, but not before the ninth century. The first formal definition of the doctrine of transubstantiation was Roman, at the Fourth Lateran Council in 1215, the decrees of which were, of course, in no way binding on the Eastern Churches. Rightly sensing, nevertheless, that the Orthodox Church had enjoyed a greater degree

38 See, for a useful summary, *Oxford Dictionary of the Christian Church*, 3rd edn, by E. A. Livingstone after F. L. Cross (Oxford, 1997), pp. 468–9.

of *perpetuité* than the Roman, both sides thought it relevant to adduce the *contemporary* belief and practice of the Greeks. But what was that?

In February 1670 Justel wrote to the Oxford astronomer and theologian Edward Bernard, apologizing for this approach from a stranger, but confident that

> your love of the truth will not allow you to refuse the request I make on behalf of M. Claude, whose name is perhaps known to you, who is working on a response to the book of M. Arnauld, which is so *célèbre* in the Church of Rome: *il aurait besoin de quelques témoignages des grecs modernes ... pour faire voir qu'ils n'ont point cru la transsubstantiation.*[39]

He asked Bernard to search Oxford's library catalogues for the purpose. Bernard did more: he evidently consulted one of the leading Anglican theologians of the day, Henry Dodwell of Trinity College Dublin, from whom in June 1670 he received a six-page reply to his inquiry after the beliefs of the modern Greeks.[40] It was not altogether reassuring. It was, said Dodwell, important to make a distinction between the official doctrines of the church and what individuals within it have in fact believed; and he went on to analyse the writings of Greeks ever since the patriarchate of Photios in the ninth century, leading to particular emphasis on the *Confessio* of Cyril Lucaris, patriarch as recently as 1620–38, whose Calvinist views, welcomed by Protestants in the west, were said to have prompted the Jesuits in Constantinople to intrigue for his execution by the Turks.[41]

39 Oxford, Bodl. Lib., MS Smith viii, p. 25.

40 MS Smith xlv, pp. 1–6. In her very interesting account of Dodwell's part in the controversy, Dr Judith Pinnington writes that the identity of the recipient is unknown: *Anglicans and Orthodox: Unity and Subversion 1559–1725* (Leominster, 2003), pp. 87–95 and nn. 60, 66. Certainly the letter was not written to Smith (on whom see below), since the latter is referred to as a 'third party' on p. 2 (as in a further letter from Dodwell, p. 13). On a tipped-in page of contents in a later hand, the whole volume is headed 'English letters to Dr B'; and many items are explicitly addressed to Bernard. In one of those from Dodwell (p. 13, of 1673) the recipient is congratulated on his appointment as Savilian Professor of Astronomy; this was Bernard.

41 For Lucaris see in general S. Runciman, *The Great Church in Captivity* (Cambridge, 1968), pp. 259–88.

Dodwell was clear that, in the history of Orthodoxy, Lucaris' beliefs were an aberration and did not represent the views of the 'considerable persons' of the 'Orientall Church'.[42]

The practical question was: which of the opposing views of the eucharist now prevailed among the Greeks? On this, said Dodwell, 'I hope we may be better informed at the return of our friend Mr Smith.' This great authority on current Greek belief was Dr Thomas Smith, a graduate of The Queen's College and fellow of Magdalen College, Oxford, where he was later to be a controversial vice-president and bursar before his unwilling removal as a non-juror to the less sensitive post of librarian of the Cotton Library. As chaplain to the English ambassador in Constantinople from 1668 to 1671, Smith had developed a keen interest in the Orthodox Church amounting to something of an obsession over certain of its dogmas and practices, and had seized the opportunity to get to know the current Greek hierarchy and seek enlightenment from them. Clearly Dodwell was right to regard him as the best possible witness to the current beliefs of that church. In concluding his response to Bernard, and notwithstanding the admiration he expresses for Claude as a polemicist, Dodwell notes with regret that: 'I had not been thus confident in the delivery of my own thoughts concerning a controversy so differently maintained by such learned persons if there had been any probable equallity in their proofs.' But he was still willing to listen, and to keep an open mind. All this Bernard will no doubt have passed on to Justel and Claude.

This was in 1670, while Georgirenes was still in Samos. Since then the French publications had continued. Meanwhile Dr Smith had returned to Magdalen in 1671, leaving the chaplaincy at Constantinople in the hands

42 'For as for Cyrill, besides the great exceptions lying against him already mentioned, and that he has in some things most notoriously misrepraesented the present sentiments and practices of his countrymen, as particularly in the Quaestion of Images and the invocation of Saints, and, I doubt, in the article concerning reprobation [i.e. the opposite of election in Calvinist predestination]; and that he did not as much as consult the sense of the generality in any fair and equall way, but without the privity or approbation of any considerable persons of their Church, praetended to set forth a confession of faith in the name of all the Orientall Churches', Oxford, Bodl. Lib., MS Smith xlv, fol. 5.

of an equally curious but less sympathetic student of the Greek Church, Dr John Covel of Christ's College, Cambridge.[43] On his return, Smith had turned to writing up the material he had gathered in Turkey, and in 1672 (with a second edition in 1678) he published in Latin the work he later entitled *Remarks upon the Manners, Religion and Government of the Turks, together with a Survey of the Seven Churches of Asia as they now lie in their Ruins.* Dodwell saw a more urgent need, however, and pressed Smith to use his unrivalled first-hand knowledge to write an authoritative account of Greek beliefs and practices, noting in particular those which separated the Orthodox from Rome and those which they shared with the Church of England. As he wrote on 23 April 1673:

> My present earnest desire is to be acquainted with the present state of the Greek church, how they are affected to the Protestants, and particularly how the actions of their late famous Patriarch Cyrill [Lukaris] are resented, whether his party be at present considerable ... I think your labours in this kind would be ... very seasonable at this juncture wherein men are somewhat more than usually intent on the Popish controversyes.[44]

The suggestion fell on fertile ground. Smith was always ready to write of such things. Two months later, writing to Dodwell, he discussed the phenomenon of Lucaris, and the assault on his doctrines in a Greek book published in 1662 on the Orthodox Apostolic church,

> wherein contrary to the belief of their Predecessors they seem to comply with the Romanists in the belief of their famed transubstantiation ... But they have not, I am sure, studied that controversy; for when they are urged in disputation with the ill consequences and absurdity of such an opinion they stand amazed, and are gravelled, and know not what to say for themselves. I found the Patriarch of Constantinople & the Patriarch of Jerusalem ... and several Metropolitans very obliging, when I went to make them visits, and some of them very inquisitive about the State of our Church. They ... have a great opinion of themselves; and certainly it must be allowed, that

43 See above p. 104. His voluminous diaries and discussions formed the basis of his much later book, *Some Account of the Present Greek Church, with Reflections on their present Doctrine and Discipline, Particularly in the Eucharist and the Rest of their Seven Pretended Sacraments* (Cambridge, 1722).

44 Oxford, Bodl. Lib., MS Smith xlix, p. 49.

> however afflicted & oppressed they be, notwithstanding some superstitious customs that by degrees have crept in among them, they are a considerable part of the Catholic church, and who deserve to be more respected, than they are.[45]

Dodwell, in reply, expressed delight that Smith had agreed to write on the Greek Church and Smith evidently set about his task with some energy, for by 4 October he could write to Dodwell that he was looking forward to the publication of his book.[46] He would not need to discuss doctrine, he said, because the Orthodox had lately issued their own statement of doctrine, signed by the four patriarchs and several metropolitans. A copy of this statement, the decrees of the Synod of Jerusalem of January 1672, had been obtained by Smith's successor, Covel, at the request of two English bishops, Pearson of Chester and Gunning of Chichester, together with the Dean of St Paul's, Sancroft, later to become archbishop of Canterbury. Though couched in moderate terms, it left no doubt that the signatories accepted belief in transubstantiation in the full Roman sense, in the efficacy of prayers to saints, and in all seven of the sacraments.[47] Dodwell's judgement of three years before was thus entirely confirmed. But that did not mean that Smith gave up hope of an accommodation. Transubstantiation, after all, had only lately 'crept in among them', and he did not doubt that he would have been admitted to communion in the patriarchal church, had he so wished.

> They are scarce at leisure, oppressed and harassed as they are, to inquire into our articles of doctrine. I could never hear otherwise but that our liturgy ... is highly approved of among them. They seem to be in a profound ignorance of all things done at so great a distance in these parts of the world, and the information they have of the state of the Britannick churchs, or indeed of the reformation in generall, from the errours and corruptions of the Church of Rome, they derive from a priest or two of their own church.

45 Oxford, Bodl. Lib., MS Smith lx, pp. 32–3.

46 Oxford, Bodl. Lib., MS Smith xlix, p. 111, 12 July 1673. Dodwell kept up the pressure, ibid. p. 113 (12 June 1674), cf. p. 119 (22 June 1675), and p. 134.

47 See above p. 108.

Smith derived this opinion from his discussions at Constantinople with the Patriarch of Alexandria, 'who was as ignorant of the state of our church as I am of some Country or Island in the South Sea'.[48]

Smith's book, written in Latin as Dodwell had suggested, was unexpectedly long delayed, and it was not until early in 1676 that the volume *De Graecae Ecclesiae Hodierno Statu Epistola* at last appeared, from the Sheldonian Theatre in Oxford. The reason for this delay, initially at least, was that Smith had simply tired of the task; he may also have been discouraged by the fact that Sir Paul Rycaut, consul in Smyrna while Smith was in Constantinople, was himself engaged on what appeared to be an identical task.[49] It took the encouragement of the Earl of Anglesey, Lord Privy Seal, and Sir Joseph Williamson, secretary of state, to get Smith back to work.[50] Once again he set to with a will, and the preface is dated from Magdalen College, Oxford, 1675. By the time that Georgirenes was in Paris in March 1676 presenting his two gospel books from the Patmos library to Louis XIV, Smith's book had begun to circulate: by the end of the month a copy was on its way to Claude.[51]

Meanwhile the ground had shifted dramatically in Arnauld's favour. The virtual alignment of the Greek Church with that of Rome was already suspected as news of the decisions of the Synod of Jerusalem in 1672 reached Europe, but it was important to obtain an authoritative account of its decrees.[52] Smith must have wished he had delayed a little longer, for the

48 Oxford, Bodl. Lib., MS Smith lx, p. 35 (4 Oct. 1673).

49 P. Rycaut, *The Present State of the Greek and Armenian Churches in 1678* (London, 1679), published at the instance of the king himself. Rycaut had, however, already told Smith of his projected book in a letter of 17 May 1669, Oxford, Bodl. Lib., MS Smith liii, p. 153.

50 See Anglesey's letter of 1 July 1675, Oxford, Bodl. Lib., MS Smith xlvii, p. 31.

51 Oxford, Bodl. Lib., MS Smith lv, p. 119, 20 March (old style). Dodwell had read the book by 21 April, Oxford, Bodl. Lib., MS Smith xlix, pp. 125–6.

52 Note also Bernard's letter to Smith of 7 Dec. 1676, reporting Galland's assurance that the Synod had indeed taken place, Bodley, MS Smith xlvii, ff. 37 (as noted above, Galland was in a position to declare this with authority).

first published account in fact appeared later in the same year as his own, the work of the Maurist Benedictine Antoine-Michel Fouquère. In this, however, the translations from Greek into Latin were so inaccurate as to be indefensible even in the Roman camp, and would inevitably call into question the good faith of the translator. The book was withdrawn, though not before Bernard and no doubt others of Justel's friends had acquired copies; and it was not until 1678 that the accepted version appeared, revised with the assistance of Arnauld and the Dominican François Combelis.[53] Antoine Galland seems to have known all about the Synod long before the publication of its decrees, to judge from the many entries in his diary for the early months of 1672, which leave no room to doubt that the Synod itself had been much influenced by the French ambassador Nointel on behalf of Port Royal, at the very time when its doctrines were being formulated. Though the Synod had dealt with many areas of doctrine – the nature of God, the authority of the Church, predestination and justification, the reality of Purgatory, the seven sacraments – and had explicitly renewed the condemnation of Patriarch Lucaris, the eventual inclusion of the phrase *pro reali praesentia* in the title of both editions makes it clear that for the Catholic sponsors of the publication the most important issue was that of transubstantiation. Once the publication appeared, this would be seen as a powerful fillip to Arnauld and Nicole and potentially devastating to Claude. With Georgirenes in Paris and a close associate of Galland, himself a considerable expert in the field, the availability of a Greek archbishop who travelled with books – one on Greek canon law, and his own *Anthologion* in search of a printer,[54] as well as the manuscripts from Patmos – offered

53 A.-M. Fouquère, *Synodus Jerosolymitana: Adversus Calvinistas haereticos, orientalem ecclesiam de Deo rebusque divinis haeretice cum ipsis sentire mentientes, pro reali potissimum praesentia, anno MDCLXXII sub patriarcha Jerosolymorum Dositheo celebrata: Interprete domno Michaele Fouquère e congregatione Sancti Mauri, ordinis Sancti Benedicti* (Paris, 1676). In the 1678 edition, as well as correcting the translation, the opportunity was taken to recast an inelegant phrase in the title: ... *haeretice, ut sentiunt ipsi, sentire mentientes*, ... For Bernard's purchase, see Oxford, Bodl. Lib., MS Smith xlvii, fol. 37.

54 See, respectively, Oxford, Bodl. Lib., MS Smith xlvi, p. 255, and Georgirenes, *An Account of his Building the Greek Church in So-Hoe Fields*. See below, p. 146.

an opportunity for an independent and authoritative review of the alleged beliefs of the Orthodox in Greece.

Smith soon became aware of Georgirenes' presence in Paris. He may well have been informed by Claude, who would have received Smith's book by the middle of April, or perhaps by Justel, who had visited Oxford the previous summer to receive the degree of DCL from the University in recognition of his gift to the Bodleian Library of three seventh-century manuscripts of particular importance for the study of the beliefs of the early Church.[55] Or he may have heard from Galland, with whom he conducted a desultory correspondence and with whom he had coincided briefly in the Turkish capital in 1670–1 when they were in the service of their respective ambassadors. Whoever it was who told him of Georgirenes' arrival, Smith will have recognized an opportunity not to be missed, and he lost no time in arranging an urgent visit to Paris. As good luck would have it, his older friend Dr Edward Chamberlayne, a seasoned traveller well connected in court circles, and an associate of Lord Treasurer Danby, was also planning to travel to Paris at that time. Currently tutor to the Marquess of Worcester's uncommonly precocious son Charles, Chamberlayne accompanied the young milord on the last of a series of European grand tours before his entering Christ Church in 1677. They welcomed Smith to join them. The party set off on or about 11 May (old style), and, 'having met with a quick and no very uneasy passage at sea betwixt Dover and Calais', reached the latter in time to attend a Whitsun service in the Protestant church at nearby Guines on 24 May (new style).[56] It seemed best not to delay further, for fear of attracting the attention of the Spanish garrison at St Omer, 'the soldiers of which oftentimes advance so farr, and pillage the neighbouring villages, and make prisoners all they meet with. … We

55 The three volumes are now, Oxford, Bodl. Lib., MS e Mus. 100–2, including the Acts of the Council of Ephesos: see article by Geoffrey Treasure on Henri Justel, *ODNB*, xxx, pp. 843–4.

56 For the journey, Oxford, Bodl. Lib., MS Smith lvi, fol. 24. For Chamberlayne and Lord Herbert, M. McClain, *Beaufort, the Duke and his Duchess, 1657/1715* (New Haven and London, 2001), p. 111; Oxford, Bodl. Lib., MS Smith xlviii, p. 223.

applaud our good fortune, that we escaped so well, and are very apprehensive of the great hazard we run in going thither.'

After eight days on the way they reached Paris, whence Smith sent an account of their adventures to his Magdalen colleague Thomas Bayley. Writing on 6 June, he was still full of his repugnance at what he had witnessed two days previously:

> On Thursday last being Corpus Christi day, which they call here *the great feast of God*, there was a most solemn and a most glorious Procession according to outward appearance. Thousands of people bare-headed with tapers and candles in their hands, besides the vast number of Priests attending on the Host, carried under a rich and stately canopy; the streets through which they past being all hung with rich Arras hangings, and altars dressed up in several places, where they stopped, with most glorious furniture. The whole glory of Paris seemed to be summed up in this days solemnity. How I was affected at this shew, you may easily imagine. If anyone has a Mind to quit his religion, there cannot be a more effectual cure, than to get to Paris just before Corpus Christi day. But I remember I am in a Catholic country, and have been too free already.[57]

If Smith needed any further incentive to seek the authority of the Greek Church against Rome, this vivid demonstration of a Catholic country's popular support for the hated doctrine of transubstantiation would have provided it.

In the first few days since his arrival Smith had already been in touch with Claude and Justel, as well as Bernard, who was now in Paris; and Justel had provided him with a 'Memoire de c^e^ qu' il faut voir a Paris'.[58] But he does not yet appear to have made contact with Georgirenes. That soon changed. Smith has left two accounts of discussions with the archbishop on a point of eucharistic doctrine, in letters written to Henry Dodwell after his return from Paris, which give a lively impression of Georgirenes' debating style.[59] Dodwell was, if that were possible, even more obsessed than Smith with the evil of belief in transubstantiation. For both of them this was apt to focus on the practice of infant communion (not in fact followed either by Roman

57 Ibid.

58 Oxford, Bodl. Lib., MS Smith xxxiii, pp. 35–8, cf. pp. 27–34.

59 Oxford, Bodl. Lib., MS Smith lx, pp. 43, 47.

Catholics or by Protestants), which seemed highly relevant to the search for established Orthodox belief, since it implied that to receive communion was beneficial in itself, the ingestion of a sacrificial substance whose spiritual nourishment did not depend on the understanding or even the consciousness of the recipient. In the Anglican view, on the contrary, in which the eucharist was merely commemorative, the taking of communion in both kinds as Christ himself directed was designed rather to help focus the mind in a deeper level of concentration and understanding, an activity beyond the wit of infants. Infant communion served therefore as a kind of litmus test of Orthodox *congregational* belief, a practical demonstration independent of what their theologians might decree.

In the first of the letters, dated 15 July 1675, Smith addressed the issue of infant communion in one kind, namely in wine:

> Having been lately in Paris, I met there with the Archb. of Samos, a Greek by nation I add, that you may not think him to be a mere Titular, & made so at Rome, with whom I had a long discourse about this custom now used in the Greek church: against which when I urged the words of our B. Saviour, St John ch.6. which imply an equal necessity for the bread as well as wine, his evasion was, that flesh was not a proper food for infants new born or of one or two years; & this he thought sufficient to justify their Practise.[60]

In the 1678 edition of his book Smith recorded this conversation with a Bishop of the Greek Church, learned but anonymous, and described the explanation as ludicrous.[61]

In the second letter, dated 1 September, he returned to the theme of infant communion, which he (wrongly) declares to be a 'Romish practise lately come in, against the express assertions of Patriarch Ieremias' as recently as the late sixteenth century, 'notwithstanding the poor shift &

60 Oxford, Bodl. Lib., MS Smith lx, p. 43.

61 Thomas Smith, *De Graecae Ecclesiae Hodierno Statu Epistola* (London, 1678), pp. 128–9. Evidently he nonetheless wished to preserve Georgirenes' reputation among Anglican readers of his book. Some years later, disappointed and estranged, Smith was to reveal that this *egregius cavillator* was indeed none other than the Archbishop of Samos, see T. Smith, *Miscellanea, in quibus continentur Praemonitio ad Lectorem de infractum Communione apud Graecos* etc. (London, 1686), prelims fol. 4.

evasion of the Archbishop of Samos, which I formerly mentioned to you'. When he was in Constantinople and Smyrna, with an opportunity to observe Greek Church practice at first hand, he had not had the interest to watch how it was done,

> but to satisfy me about the manner of it, the Archbishop of Samos, when I was discoursing with him at Paris about this Subject, bid his Servant then waiting upon him, fetch a glass of water and a spoon; which He dipped in the glass and presently took out several drops, or some moisture at least sticking to the hollow of it: in like manner, said he, the [tongs] is dipped in the Chalice, & given to the infant to suck: and by no means would he allow any of the [crumbs], that were in the Chalice to be given at the same time.[62]

Georgirenes' readiness to turn to visual illustration by way of argument is a trait we have already encountered, in his attempt to reconcile Orthodox and Catholic at Bibbona, when he asked priests from both sides to consecrate holy water which he then mixed: as the waters were not different, nor were they. Smith the scholar was unimpressed. 'The only way of ending this controversy,' he told Dodwell, 'is to send into Greece, and get it under the hands of the several Bishops, whether this be practise or no'; otherwise they just tell you what they think you want to hear. In fact, he went on, Pappas Daniel (Vulgaris), a Greek priest in London known to both Smith and Dodwell, had told him that the Greek Church did not give communion to children under the age of seven; whereas the Archbishop of Tiberias on the river Strymon, Patriarch of Bulgaria, who had lately been in Oxford and had discussed transubstantiation and infant communion, had managed to avoid any mention of the sacrament of chrism, about which there was a precisely parallel controversy. In short, Smith was quite dissatisfied by his conversations, and inclined to be suspicious of what looked only too much like a tendency towards Rome.

> You suspect the same in your letter of the Archbishop of Samos, lest He be one of οἱ Λατινιζοντες [the Latinizers, that is, sympathizers with Rome]; and possibly your suspicion, such I acknowledge to be very just, may increase when I tell you he lay in

62 Oxford, Bodl. Lib., MS Smith lx, p. 47.

> an Abbots house, and the discourse which I had with him, was before some Roman Catholicks, who had lived several years in Turkey.[63]

In the course of his conversations with Georgirenes and others, Smith learned the purpose of the archbishop's presence in Paris, 'to solicit in the French Court for leave to erect a Greek Church in Marseilles'. He heard, too, that this solicitation had not met with success.[64] Notwithstanding the unfavourable view he had formed of Georgirenes' theology, amounting even to suspicion of a Romish tendency, when he heard that the archbishop's purpose in Marseilles had made little headway, but that he nonetheless intended to make his home in France 'by favour of the Most Christian King',[65] and that he might therefore be at a loose end and in need of a further venture, Smith conceived a bold plan, which he pursued with some urgency. This demanded his early return to London, contrary to the expectation of his Oxford colleagues, and contrary too to his own inclination.[66] In fact, though he had only reached Paris at the beginning of June, before the month was out he had been to the English ambassador (and envoy to the peace negotiations between France, Holland and Spain at Nijmegen), the septuagenarian and apoplectic Lord Berkeley of Stratton, to obtain a passport for the return journey. Berkeley was, like Smith himself, a graduate of The Queen's College, Oxford, but of an earlier vintage: his career in public service extended back to the time of Charles I, for whom he had been briefly ambassador to Queen Christina of Sweden forty years before.[67] Lord Berkeley signed the necessary document on 29 June.[68] Shortly afterwards, Smith was on his way home. This time he had to run the gauntlet of the Spanish garrison at St Omer without the reassuring company of Dr Chamberlayne.

63 Oxford, Bodl. Lib., MS Smith lx, p. 48.

64 Ibid.

65 Smith, *Miscellanea*, prelims fol. 4r.

66 Oxford, Bodl. Lib., MS Smith lix, p. 331.

67 On Berkeley, see D. W. Hayton, *ODNB* v, pp. 380–2.

68 Oxford, Bodl. Lib., MS Smith xxix, pp. 80–3.

CHAPTER 7

London and the Greek Church (1676–1678)

Smith's project was to bring the Archbishop of Samos to England, to give weight to an attempt, already begun but moving slowly, to found an Orthodox church in London. In Paris, the two will surely have talked of a matter of such obvious mutual concern, and though it is no more than a conjecture that it was Smith who urged Georgirenes to take a practical interest in the project, he is by far the most likely source of the suggestion. Moreover his own premature return to England and the archbishop's immediate and well-informed intervention (as we shall see) leave little room for doubt. That Smith's return was indeed for a particular purpose is tolerably clear from a letter which he sent from Paris to a Magdalen colleague on 30 June 1676, the day after he had obtained Lord Berkeley's passport for his return to England. It is full of the enjoyment of his stay, and of the glories of the king's library and the fine collection of Greek manuscripts which Colbert had amassed – but not 'so pleasing and stately to the eye as the Bodleyan' – 'the king being as ambitious to render himself glorious to posterity by his advancing & encouraging learning as by his arms and buildings'. As to his own plans, Smith writes, 'I am so charmed with the civility of the French both Gentlemen and Scholars of our own & the Roman communion here, that I could willingly spend all the Summer here in Paris, but for very good reasons I intend to be with you at or before Magdalen tide [22 July].'[1]

* * *

1 Oxford, Bodl. Lib., MS Smith lix, p. 331, to Thomas Cradock (elected public orator as the anti-establishment candidate in 1677, but died shortly afterwards).

Greeks were not unknown in England and there was considerable interest in Greek Orthodoxy. There had long been a community of Greeks in the capital, intent, as at Bibbona, on preserving their identity as well as their solidarity by means of their religion. We know little of them, apart from one or two individuals such as the egregious Constantine Rhodocanaces, a 'Grecian of the Isle of Chios', who composed a poem in his native Greek to celebrate the restoration of Charles II, published a bestseller on the virtues of spirit of salt as a panacea for internal and external application alike (his own preparation of it was advertised under the royal arms), and followed it with a treatise on the medicinal uses of antimony.[2] Then there were the proprietors of coffee houses – following in the footsteps of Nathaniel Konopios who introduced coffee to Oxford in the 1640s – among them George Constantine of The Grecian, in Threadneedle Street before the Great Fire and later in Devereux Court near Temple Bar, who numbered

2 *Carmina Graeca rhythmica gratulatoria de reditu serenissimi, sacratissimi & principis Caroli II Magnae Britanniae, Galliae & Hiberniae Regis* (Oxford, A. & L. Lichfield, 1660), reproduced by E. Legrand, ed., *Le retour de Charles II, roi d'Angleterre: poème grec du prince Constantin Rodocanacis, publie d'après l'édition de 1660* (Paris, 1873); *Alexicacus, spirit of salt of the world, which vulgarly prepar'd is call'd the spirit of salt, or, The transcendent virtue of the true spirit of salt ...* (London, 1662; repr. St Peter Port, 1977), seven editions by 1670; *A discourse in the praise of antimonie, and the virtues thereof* (London, 1664); 'The great Preserver of *Mankind*, which is ALEXICACUS, SPIRIT of SALT of the WORLD, now Philosophically prepared and purged from all hurtfull or corroding qualities; far beyond any thing yet known to the World; being both safe and pleasant for the use of all Men, Women and Children. *By* CONSTANTINE RHODOCANACES *Grecian of the Isle of* Chios, *and one of His* Majesties *Chymists*. In London, next door to the *Three Kings* Inne, in Southampton Buildings near the King's Gate in Holborn. By His Majesties special Directions and Allowance', broadside advertisement, London, *c.*1664. [These advertisements may be seen at the Houghton Library, Harvard University, Marquess of Bute broadsides, A 193, 195: see J. P. Crichton-Stuart, 3rd Marquess of Bute, *A List of Broadsides and Satires, ... illustrative of English History and Social Life* (London, 1892); H. Amory, *Bute Broadsides in the Houghton Library, Harvard University: Guide and Index to Microfilm Coll.* (Woodbridge, Conn., 1981).] For a less than favourable view of Rhodocanaces, see R. Browning, 'Some Early Greek Visitors to England', in *Essays in Memory of Basil Laourdas* (Thessaloniki, 1975), pp. 387–95, esp. p. 394. (I owe this reference to Dr Penelope Bulloch.)

Isaac Newton among his clients, or 'Nicholas the Grecian' of The Rainbow near Temple Bar, or the proprietor of another Grecian Coffee House, in King Street, Covent Garden.[3] These were but a few individuals in a booming local industry, catering to the English taste for coffee and politics; and those who sold Rhodocanaces' panacea at eight shillings a pint, as listed in his advertisements, all bear English names. Unlike the communities of Greeks in cities such as Venice, Leghorn, Amsterdam or Marseilles, the London Greeks were birds of passage, often sailors working on ships of many different nations which put into the port of London. Few of them were wealthy merchants.[4] But the fall of Crete on 5 September 1669, after a siege of Candia lasting more than two and a half years, had occasioned a massive outpouring of whole towns and villages of refugees not only to the Ionian islands and Italy but to many countries with which Cretan merchants had enjoyed trading contacts in happier times, England among them. Such an influx revived the enthusiasm among those in England to provide a Greek church in London.

But there was also a theological, or intellectual, drive backing the establishment of a Greek church in London. Orthodoxy in particular seemed to offer the young Church of England a most desirable partner, a church which spoke still the authentic language of the fathers, episcopal and apostolic, above all anti-papalist. The Church of England, of course, sat on the western side of the Great Schism over the nature of the Holy Trinity, believing that the Holy Spirit derived, or 'proceeded', from both the Father and the Son, not simply from the Father. But it joined the Orthodox in its rejection of Purgatory and in more practical matters such as the administration of communion in both kinds, using ordinary (that is, not unleavened) bread; and it could live with the Eastern Church's lack of

3 See B. Lillywhite, *London Coffee Houses* (London, 1963), pp. 172f., no. 294 (1651–81), 243 no. 494 (perhaps a later phase of the same), 243, no. 493 (1673); cf. Jonathan Harris, 'The Grecian Coffee House and Political Debate in London 1688–1714', *London Journal*, xxv (2000), pp. 1–13.

4 See Jonathan Harris, 'Silent Minority: The Greek Community of Eighteenth-Century London', in D. Tziovas, ed., *Greek Diaspora and Migration since 1700* (Aldershot, 2009), pp. 31–43.

precision or even equivocation over the issue of transubstantiation: hence the great interest in Orthodoxy which arose among Anglicans, lay as well as clerical, in the early years of the seventeenth century, and was sustained and enhanced in the generations which followed.[5]

The first practical move, however, seems to have come from the Orthodox side, with an approach to Archbishop George Abbot *c.*1615 by Patriarch Cyril Lucaris, who had himself studied in Venice and Padua, and had observed the threat to Orthodoxy posed there by the vigorous endeavours of the Jesuits, only to find the same endeavours pursued with the same relentless vigour in Constantinople itself.[6] Faced by such well-drilled opponents, Lucaris asked Abbot to provide access for promising young Greek clergy to educational opportunities of a quality that they could no longer find in their homeland: in Oxford, at Abbot's Balliol, they would not only be trained in theology but be taught to think and to argue – in a word, to fight the Jesuits on their own ground. This will have led to much preening of Anglican feathers, with what results will be seen later. Certainly it had the effect of encouraging a number of Anglican divines to think in terms of unity, perhaps even union, with the Eastern Church. It was an interest further nourished and reinforced by contact with the Orthodox in their own territory enjoyed by a succession of English travellers, embassy chaplains, diplomats and merchants of the Levant Company in its trading posts in Constantinople, Smyrna and Aleppo. One of the most significant of these was Isaac Basire de Preaumont, a Huguenot of the petty nobility from Rouen, who settled in England before the Civil War and was briefly Archdeacon of Northumberland before he was overwhelmed by that upheaval. Basire travelled in the Near East in the years 1650 to 1654, where his enthusiasm for the Anglican Church – according to Evelyn he regarded

5 See S. Runciman, *The Great Church in Captivity* (Cambridge, 1968), pp. 235, 276 ff., and esp. ch. vii. See also Hugh Trevor-Roper, 'The Church of England and the Greek Church in the Time of Charles I', in D. Baker, ed., *Religious Motivation: Biographical and Sociological Problems for the Church Historian* (Oxford, 1978), pp. 213–40.

6 See W. B. Patterson, 'Cyril Lukaris, George Abbot, James VI and I, and the Beginning of Orthodox–Anglican Relations', in P. M. Doll, ed., *Anglicanism and Orthodoxy 300 Years after the 'Greek College' in Oxford* (Oxford and Berne, 2006), pp. 39–55.

it as 'for purity of doctrine, substance, decency and beauty, the most perfect under heaven' – made him a virtual missionary 'planting the Church of England in divers parts of the Levant and Asia', while at the same time he made himself familiar with the beliefs and practices of the Orthodox.[7] Basire served as chaplain to the embassy in Constantinople for a year. Better known are Thomas Smith and his successor in the role of embassy chaplain, John Covel, as well as Sir Paul Rycaut, consul in Smyrna, who each wrote an account of the beliefs and practices of the Greek Church (and Smith in addition collected material for a detailed treatment of Lucaris).[8] Their books were eagerly devoured in the lay world. But the growth of interest and sympathy had begun much earlier. It is not irrelevant that Archbishop Abbot's own brother Maurice was a merchant of the Levant Company.[9] Such people were invaluable caterers to the insatiable appetite for patristic manuscripts from the great libraries of Mount Athos and elsewhere, to be devoured in English libraries.

A more 'official' perspective was provided by the interest of successive Anglican prelates: Archbishop Abbot was not alone in this. Indeed the instinctive sympathy of Anglican for Orthodox is already palpable, though not yet explicit, in the writings of his contemporary Lancelot Andrewes, Bishop of Winchester, under James I.[10] It can be followed implicitly or explicitly in the writings of several learned bishops of the seventeenth

7 C. Brennan, in *ODNB*, iv, pp. 232–4, quoting E. S. de Bere, ed., *The Diary of John Evelyn*, 6 vols (London, 1955), iii, p. 303. For an excellent and sympathetic account of the impact of Orthodoxy on Anglican theologians, see J. Pinnington, *Anglicans and Orthodox, Unity and Subversion 1559–1725* (Leominster, 2003); for Basire, ibid. pp. 51–6.

8 T. Smith, *De Graecae Ecclesiae Hodierno Statu Epistola* (Oxford, 1676; London, 1678), cf. *An Account of the Greek Church* (London, 1680), with an appendix on 'The State of the Greek Church under Cyrillus Lucaris', later republished as *Collectanea de Cyrillo Lucario* (London, 1707), and based on Bodley, MS Smith xxvi, pp. 1–6; J. Covel, *Some Account of the Present Greek Church* (Cambridge, 1722); Paul Rycaut, *The Present State of the Greek and Armenian Churches* (London, 1679). See Pinnington, *Anglicans and Orthodox*, pp. 57–155.

9 Patterson, 'Cyril Lucaris, George Abbot', p. 44.

10 Pinnington, *Anglicans and Orthodox*, p. 19.

century. Moreover, as we have seen in the case of Isaac Basire, the enforced diaspora of the Civil War brought contacts which would not otherwise have been made. In April 1657, for instance, John Cosin, ejected from the mastership of Peterhouse and the deanery of Peterborough and now in exile as chaplain to the Anglican element of Henrietta Maria's court in Paris, there fell in with Metropolitan Kyrillos of Trebizond, a follower of Lucaris whose anti-papalist stance he shared, whom Cosin observed celebrating the Greek liturgy of St Chrysostom before the widowed queen.[11] He found the opportunity for a series of deep and reassuring discussions with the metropolitan, covering all those nagging issues which so exercised the Anglican Protestant mind – transubstantiation, the invocation of saints, Purgatory and prayers for the dead. Kyrillos flattered him by asking to see and then declaring approval of the Book of Common Prayer. Cosin concluded that in all material areas, Anglicans and Orthodox were at one. When three years later, at the Restoration, he was appointed to the influential see of Durham, where he at once took Basire as a close colleague, his view of the Greeks achieved even greater significance.

By the later years of the century, however, as we have already noted, such sympathetic prelates as John Pearson of Chester and Peter Gunning of Chichester were becoming reluctantly concerned at the swing of the Orthodox pendulum:[12] the Synod of Jerusalem in 1672 would have become an insuperable barrier to closer union, even if the Orthodox themselves, on closer inspection, had not found themselves repelled by certain aspects of the Anglican stance. But for the moment, in the 1670s, the cry was for first-hand knowledge. Smith and Rycaut were in demand, their books on the 'present state' of the Greek Church eagerly reprinted and devoured. Better still was a captive archbishop. On all these grounds, and in this context, the Archbishop of Samos and his English friends could expect a favourable hearing for their plans to provide a Greek church for the expatriates in London.

It is necessary to trace the story back a little way. On 8 January 1675, while Georgirenes was still in Italy, the Privy Council in London considered

11 For Cosin, see A. Milton in *ODNB*, xiii, pp. 531–38; Pinnington, *Anglicans and Orthodox*, pp. 20ff.; Oxford, Bodl. Lib., MS Smith xlvii, fol. 21, cf. 18r.

12 Cf. above p. 144.

a petition by three Greeks, 'Daniel Bulgaris, Lewis Orbinaty, & Demetry of Constantinople, in behalfe of themselves and other Grecians ... with their Familyes having setled here'.[13] Bulgaris (henceforth 'Vulgaris') was a priest, a Cretan, perhaps a refugee.[14] Demetry was a merchant with connexions in both London and Amsterdam.[15] Orbinaty seems otherwise unknown, though his Christian name suggests a western European origin and the surname is not plausibly Greek.[16] They had heard of the king's generosity to strangers, they said, and reminded him of their countrymen's service in his navy and merchant marine. They hoped that his 'glorious and Christian Care and protection' might be extended to them, 'to the encouragement of others in Foreign parts to resort to the same Royal Fountain, & the increase of his Majestie's Subjects, & augmentation of his revenue'. They therefore asked 'Liberty to Build a Church in any part of the City of London or Liberties thereof, where they may freely exercise their Religion according to the Greek Church'. It was a good moment to make such a request. After Candia, the suffering of contemporary Greeks at the hands of the Turks kindled new and powerful waves of sympathy among the customers of the fashionable Greek coffee houses, where easy conversation of ancient Greece, its history and its literature, was disturbed by horror and concern at the plight of a civilization brought so low.[17] No doubt the king shared these

13 TNA, PC 2/64, p. 341; cf. Georgirenes, *From the Arch-Bishop of the Isle of Samos in Greece, An Account of his building the Grecian Church in So-hoe Feilds, and the disposal thereof by the Masters of the Parish of St Martins in the Feilds*, broadsheet (London, 1682), copies in Oxford, Bodl. Lib. MS. Wood 417, no. 103, and MS. Ashmole F.1 no. 74; London, BL, 816, m. 9/118.

14 Unless, that is, he is identical with the *hieromonachos* and *kastrisios* Daniel, *oikonomos* of the monastery of Patmos, who petitioned for the favour of William Sancroft, then Dean of St Paul's: Oxford, Bodl. Lib., MS Tanner 33, fols 48–9, endorsed in Sancroft's hand and therefore read by him. Dean since the Restoration, Sancroft left St Paul's for Canterbury at the end of December 1677. For Vulgaris as Cretan, 'pappas Daniel a greeke priest of Candia', Oxford, Bodl. Lib., MS Smith lx, p. 47.

15 See below p. 161.

16 *Urbinate*, perhaps, i.e. 'From Urbino' (cf. the painter Raphael). Luigi Urbinate, if that is the true interpretation, will have been a second-generation immigrant, perhaps the child of a mixed marriage.

17 See Harris, 'The Grecian Coffee House', pp. 5–6.

feelings. Vulgaris and his colleagues received the permission they sought, but were left in no doubt that the raising of the necessary funds would be their own responsibility:

> His Majestie taking into Consideration the petitioners request, was graciously pleased to grant the same, they making themselves capable to enjoy this his Majesty's[s] grant and favour to them.

A month later, on 16 February 1675, Vulgaris received a warrant 'to be made a free denizen of England', that is, to become naturalized.[18] Neither Orbinaty nor Demetry is mentioned in this context.

It seems likely that Vulgaris and his congregation began their search for funds right away, but although it appears that nothing practical had been done by the middle of 1676. Georgirenes was evidently persuaded to intervene. Within two or three weeks of Smith's return to England, the archbishop had mastered his brief sufficiently to feel encouraged to visit King Charles' ambassador in Paris, Lord Berkeley of Stratton. Significantly for Georgirenes, the ambassador was a crony of the Duke of York. On 18 July Berkeley wrote to his master, Secretary of State Coventry, that Georgirenes had sought to enlist him to the cause:

> There hath been with me twice this week a person of a very reverent aspect, that says he is a Grecian, and Archbishop of Samos in Greece, he hath desired my intercession to his Majesty in the behalf of his nation, and the last night sent me this memorial by one of his Aumoniers, The matter seems not to me to be of any great difficulty, for the present, he desiring only that the money may be detained in Amsterdam in the hands of those that have it in possession, until the truth of the pretended procuration can be discovered, which upon the least intimation I suppose will easily be obtained, For their building of a church I can say nothing to it, unless it be that at the first view it seems to be no imprudent Charity if it should be thought fit to allow them that liberty, He requested me that this whole affaire might be as little public as might be.[19]

18 TNA, Home Office Warrant Book I, p. 47; *CSPD, 1673–1675*, p. 591.

19 Longleat, Coventry Papers, vol. xxxiii, fol. 313 (wrongly calendared in HMC, *Fourth Report*, Pt. i (London, 1874), App. p. 245, as stating that Georgirenes' approach was to the confidential agent John Brisbane, rather than to Berkeley himself).

The memorial, which explains a somewhat complex situation, itself is carefully drawn, and written in a secretarial hand, in French. In translation it runs as follows:

> To His Excellency the ambassador of England: Sir, Joseph Georgerin, Greek archbishop of the island of Samos, sheweth very humbly to Your Excellency that there died a little while ago a merchant of Greek nationality named Demetrj in Greece, and Augustin in Amsterdam, who left at his death the sum of approximately ten thousand *ecus* to certain other Greeks who are in London, and in Amsterdam have pretended a PROCURATION on behalf of the brother of the deceased, and an order by the brother of the deceased addressed to Mons. Moulorbec, merchant of Amsterdam, in whose hands the said sum was deposited, to remit it into the hands of a Greek named Father Daniel Vulgari, who is at present in London, and of certain others. The grace, Sir, which is sought from Your Excellency is to be so kind as to order (in England) that if Fr Daniel Vulgari, in London, has received the money he be required to deposit it at once in the hands of whomever it shall please you to nominate for this purpose; [but] that if the money is still in the hands of Mons. Mourlorbec, merchant of Amsterdam, he be instructed on no account to give up possession of it pending a new order, in order that there may be time to discover from Constantinople whether the PROCURATION is real or pretended; and that in the event that the deceased had no relatives, as is believed, this sum be employed to build in London the Greek church which His Majesty has given permission to build there: and in the meantime the said archbishop of Samos will pray God, Sir, for Your Excellency, whose very Humble and very Obedient Servant he is.[20]

The series of events as rehearsed in this account submitted by Georgirenes to Lord Berkeley seems to be that a Greek merchant in Amsterdam named Demetry or Augustine had left ten thousand ecus (approximately £4,000)[21] to some London Greeks. It was not clear whether the money was still in the hands of Monsieur Mourlorbec, a merchant of Amsterdam who was, presumably Demetry's executor, or whether it had already passed to Daniel Vulgaris, one of the London Greeks who had petitioned Charles II in the previous year to be allowed to set up a Greek church in London. Meanwhile,

20 Longleat, Coventry Papers, vol. lxix, fol. 294.

21 See Grace Lee Nute, *Caesars of the Wilderness: Medart Choucert, Sieur des Groseilliers and Pierre Esprit Radisson, 1618–1710* (American Historical Association, 1943, reprint 1978), p. 145 n. 15.

a claim on the money had been lodged by a 'pretended' brother of the deceased who appears to have been living in Constantinople. Georgirenes is asking Lord Berkeley to ensure that the money, whether in the hands of Vulgaris or Mourlorbec, is frozen until news of the 'brother's' claim is received from Constantinople.

Clearly Georgirenes did not trust Vulgaris. This unfavourable view of Father Daniel's honesty can only have come from Smith who, it will be recalled, already knew Vulgaris in London and had been less than impressed by what he took to be his dishonest attempt to explain away the Greek practice of infant communion.[22]

Three weeks later, and perhaps impatient for a response to his memorial, the archbishop resolved to seize the initiative himself and to travel to London. A second visit to Lord Berkeley duly secured for him a letter of introduction to Coventry, in which the ambassador recalled his earlier letter and noted that he had since been approached 'by some learned men of this kingdome' on Georgirenes' behalf. Who they may have been, we can only guess: Justel is the obvious answer, or one of his *salon*, perhaps Galland; but the reference may simply be to new friends lately made since the archbishop's arrival in Paris. At any rate, Berkeley wrote that Georgirenes 'hath a very venerable aspect and seems to have a great desire to settle a Greek Church in London and with little or no charge to his Majesty'. The ambassador is confident that 'none ... takes more delight than you do to do all the good you can in relieving the distressed which I take [to be] all Christians that are subject to the Turk'.[23] At the same time, to judge from subsequent events, it seems not improbable that Berkeley added a second letter of introduction, to his friend the Duke of York.

So, with Berkeley's letter of 7 August 1676 to Coventry as his passport, the Archbishop of Samos prepared to set out for England; and on 10 August his friend Galland wrote to notify Smith of his imminent departure.[24] He perhaps left Paris in some haste, and certainly to the confusion of Galland, for the latter was at that moment making arrangements for the publication

22 Oxford, Bodl. Lib., MS Smith lx, p. 47, 1 Sept. 1676 to Dodwell: see above p. 150.
23 Longleat, Coventry Papers, vol. xxxiii, fol. 329.
24 Bodley, MS Smith xlvi, p. 207.

of his French translation of Georgirenes' book. Unexpectedly, the archbishop took the French version with him, leaving the original Greek in Paris, and exacting from Galland a promise that the book would not appear in French until it had been first published in English.[25] The obvious but conjectural explanation of his hasty departure is concern over the security of Demetry's bequest. It is possible, indeed, that he did not travel directly to London, which would have meant taking the coach to Calais and crossing to Dover; for it was not until 26 October that Smith, normally a most assiduous correspondent, wrote to Galland to thank him for a gift of books and a letter, which Georgirenes had brought from France and forwarded to Smith in Oxford.[26] A plausible explanation of this interval of two months is that the archbishop had thought it prudent to visit Amsterdam and M. Moulorbec on the way. Whenever he did reach London, he could be sure of a welcome from the secretary of state. Henry Coventry, like both Smith and Berkeley, was another of the graduates of The Queen's College who had a part to play in the English scene of Georgirenes' unfolding drama – a decade younger than Berkeley, older than Smith, a trusted public servant since the Restoration and secretary of state since 1672, first for the northern and now for the southern department.[27] A contemporary noted that in the House of Commons Coventry 'managed for the court', and that he 'was an ancient member and had the nice step of the house, and withal was wonderfully witty and a man of great veracity':[28] a desirable patron indeed – but already troubled, though not yet crippled, by the gout which was soon to become a distraction from affairs of state.

Georgirenes himself left an account of his part in the project for a Greek church, written after it had failed, which passes rapidly over this early phase, and has no mention of the intervention of Smith or indeed

25 See p. 225.

26 Bodley, MS Smith lv, p. 138.

27 See S. Handley, in *ODNB*, xiii, pp. 730f.

28 R. North, *The Lives of The Right Hon. Francis North ... The Hon. Sir Dudley North ... and The Hon. and Rev. John North*, ed. A. Jessop, 3 vols (London, 1890), i, p. 119.

of his own visit to Paris. Somewhat disingenuously, in view of the undeniable fact of his approach to Berkeley in Paris and his concern to secure the fortune of the dead Demetry for the project, he avers an altogether unrelated motive for his coming to London and makes his own part in the affair simply an accident of timing:

> In the Year 1676 I came into *England* with the intention to publish a Book in print called *Anthologion*, for the use of the Eastern Greek Church, but finding they had no place allotted for the Exercise of our Religion, but some Persons of our Country, *Daniel Bulgaris* a Preist, and others, who had earnestly indeavoured to get one builded, and in order thereunto had obtained his Majesties Gracious Grant for the same, two years before my arrival; but wanting means, methods, and interest to proceed to the accomplishing this their purpose, they desired me to take the business upon me; in which, though some difficulties appeared unsuitable to my Function; yet in Piety to the Church, and to promote the exercise of the Divine Service thereof, I undertook the charge, and proceeded therein, as followeth ...[29]

As he goes on to say, once in London Georgirenes lost no time in making contact with the new Bishop of the diocese, Dr Henry Compton.[30] Yet another graduate of The Queen's College, Compton had been lately but briefly Bishop of Oxford, from December 1674 to November 1675. No one was more heartily, even fanatically, anti-papalist than he. His hostility to Rome and all her works brought him the implacable hostility of the Romish Duke of York, and was to frustrate his otherwise well-grounded aspiration to the see of Canterbury. But he never wavered. Moreover, the bishops of London had long held particular responsibility for alien churches.[31] For Compton, this became sharply focused in two directions, support of anti-papalist churches abroad and provision for immigrant and refugee Protestant congregations in England – provided that their doctrines and practices were compatible with the tenets of the Church of England as by

29 Georgirenes, *An Account of his Building the Grecian Church.*

30 See the excellent biography by Edward Carpenter, *The Protestant Bishop* (London, 1956), esp. pp. 357–63; see also A. M. Coleby, in *ODNB*, xii, pp. 883–9.

31 Andrew Pettegree, *Foreign Protestant Communities in Sixteenth-Century London* (Oxford, 1986), p. 137, the Bishop of London was appointed superintendent of the foreign churches in London in 1559.

law established. At the same time, the civil government seems to have been pursuing a parallel policy. For in October 1673 the king's former minister to the Grand Duke of Tuscany, Sir John Finch (lately promoted to be ambassador in Constantinople), had pressed the grand duke to grant permission for a place of worship for Greeks (and places also for Armenians, 'semitics' and Jews) in Florence, as had already been conceded in Leghorn.[32]

The success of the project for a Greek church in London would depend on three main factors: support from Bishop Compton, availability of a site, and provision of funds. None of this was to be taken for granted, as Smith wrote to his friend Bernard in Paris at the end of November.

> The Archb. of Samos endeavours to get leave to build a Church for the exercise of the religion of his Countrymen. The Bp. of London at first liked the design mightily, but I think of late is grown cool and makes several demurres. But if leave were granted, where is the money to build it? For I perceive he is poor, & little encouragement, God knows, he finds at present, and what can 2 or 3 poor Greeks, who sell coffee, contribute toward it? I believe the poor man would willingly stay here if he could subsist, as having no mind to return into Turkey.[33]

Meanwhile the archbishop's friends in Paris were impatient for word of his doings, and between late November and mid-January there was a flurry of correspondence between Galland and Bernard in France and Smith in England, seeking or giving the latest news; at the same time Georgirenes himself exchanged letters with Galland, though these seem not to have survived.[34] Apart from a general plea for news (in Galland's case expressed in lively demotic Greek), there is much expression of interest in the progress of the archbishop's book.

Georgirenes' arrival in London from Paris in the autumn of 1676 had already added considerable weight to the initiative of Daniel Vulgaris and

32 *Calendar of State Papers, Venetian, 1673–1675* (London, 1940 [1943]), p. 160: dispatch of Giovanni Giacomo Corniani, Venetian resident at Florence, to the doge and senate, 28 Oct. 1673.

33 Oxford, Bodl. Lib., MS Smith lvii, pp. 7–9, 28 Nov. 1676.

34 Oxford, Bodl. Lib., MS Smith xlvi, pp. 209, 213–15, Galland to Smith, 23 Nov. and 12 Jan; ibid. 47, pp. 37, 34, Bernard to Smith, 7 and 27 Dec.; ibid. 57, p. 7, Smith to Bernard, 28 Nov.

his friends. In his search for the means, methods and interest which had so far been wanting, his archiepiscopal status gave him entrance to circles previously closed – and it is significant that in England, as previously in Italy and France, he never advertised himself as the *former Archbishop of Samos*.[35] He made an early approach to Bishop Compton, whose support was of course essential, who undertook 'to speak to the other Bishops, and other Gentlemen to bestow their benevolent Contributions'. Not all of these gentlemen had a clear understanding of either the archbishop's identity or his purpose. Or, at least, they did not always pass an ungarbled account to their wives. Lady Chaworth, for instance, wrote in a gossipy letter from London to her brother Lord Roos at Belvoir Castle on 10 March 1677, 'here is an Archbishop and Bishop of Samos & Paphos of the Greek Church & will be allowed a church here'.[36] A month later, on 10 April, the recusant Catholic dilettante Thomas Blount wrote from Shoreditch to his friend Anthony Wood, the antiquary of Merton College in Oxford, 'I suppose you have heard, that the Archbp of Samos has got leave to build a Greek Church here, our Bps promoting it, because he disacknowledging the Pope's supremacy.'[37] With the assurance of Compton's active support, Georgirenes was ready for a new approach to the king. Permission the Greeks already had: this time the request would be for some financial assistance.

But first he needed a site. His friends directed him to the newly developing suburb of Soho, in the northern part of what was then the parish of St Martin's in the Fields.[38] During the early part of the seventeenth century, Soho – the name is said to have been a hunting cry, like 'tally-ho',

35 Not, for instance, on the title-page of his book, 'By *Joseph Georgirenes*, Arch-Bishop of SAMOS. Now living in *London*.' Only in his catalogue of the holders of this office is the true position made explicit, *A Description of the Present State*, p. 37

36 Belvoir Castle, Archives, Add. 7, 'Letters from Grace Lady Chaworth to her Brother John Lord Roos ... 1663–98', no. 60; cf. Papers of the Duke of Rutland, HMC, *Twelfth Report*, App., Pt. v, ed. H. C. Maxwell Lyte (London, 1889), p. 41. For Lord Roos' contribution to the building fund, see below, p. 211.

37 Oxford, Bodl. Lib., MS Wood F.40, fol. 225.

38 For the development of Soho, see the *Survey of London*, vols xxxiii–xxxiv, *The Parish of St Anne, Soho*, ed. F. H. W. Sheppard (London, 1966).

later adopted by the Duke of Monmouth, a Soho resident, as a battle-cry at Sedgemoor – was exploited as a source of brick-clay, and in that capacity makes its appearance in the St Martin's rate-books from 1636. As recently as 1671 a royal proclamation had forbidden further development in 'the fields adjoining So Hoe', as a threat to the water supply and general amenity of Whitehall Palace. But pressure for expansion westward from the City proved too strong to be denied. By 1676 the inevitable had been accepted, and entrepreneurs were urgently at work within an overall plan for Soho drawn up by Sir Christopher Wren. The crown of Wren's characteristically grandiose scheme was to be a fine King's Square at the northern end (later Soho Square), with a palatial house for the Duke of Monmouth in the centre of its southern side, flanked by two straight roads running south, later named Frith Street and Greek Street. Among the men of energy and vision drawn to take part in the development was Dr Nicholas Barbon, a restless soul who had shelved medical practice in favour of property speculation, who invented fire insurance in the wake of the Great Fire, crossed swords with John Locke over monetary theory, and ultimately achieved respectability as member of parliament for Bramber in Sussex, fortified by the possession of a fortune reputedly of the colossal order of £2 million.

Barbon, a pioneer of the Tory Land Bank, was then providing himself with ample territory in Soho, particularly in the area of the former Military Ground, between Leicester Square and King Street (Shaftesbury Avenue), which he began to develop in 1677;[39] and it was with him that Georgirenes was put in touch. 'As soon as he was acquainted with my design,' the archbishop recalled,

> he promised to give me a piece of ground, and to build the Foundation at his own charge; thereupon I went again to his said Lordship [Compton], and telling him thereof, he promised to give me a piece of ground himself, and sent one *Mr Thrift* with me, and marked out the ground.[40]

39 See S. Bradley and N. Pevsner, *London 6, Westminster*, *The Buildings of England*, founding ed. N. Pevsner, rev. edn (New Haven and London, 2003), pp. 388, 407.

40 Georgirenes, *An Account of his Building the Grecian Church*. The history of the Greek church in Soho is comprehensively reconstructed by P. A. Bezodis in the *Survey of*

'Mr Thrift' was in fact Richard Frith, a builder and member of the Tylers' and Bricklayers' Company, whose significance as a developer of Soho is to this day commemorated in the street named after him.[41] The new site which Compton 'gave' Georgirenes formed part of a complicated property deal, brokered by the bishop, between Frith and the parish authorities of St Martin's in the Fields.[42] Georgirenes depended on Compton, and Compton apparently himself bore the additional costs of the transaction. The site, rather more than a third of an acre in extent and in shape a triangle shorn of its apex, fronted on to Hog or Hoggen Lane (later Crown Street, now Charing Cross Road). Crucially, however – and this the archbishop, with his poor English and less law, did not understand – it was not freehold but held under sub-lease from St Martin's. Before Compton's deal, Frith had held it on a sub-lease from the brewer Joseph Girle. Girle's interest, too, took the form of a sub-lease: the head-lessee was Henry Jermyn, Earl of St Albans, the freeholder the Crown.[43] It was a hugely complex arrangement, and only too likely to go wrong at one level or another. It is no surprise to find that the lease was not finally prepared for signature until 8 August 1677. Perhaps by this time this was regarded as a mere formality: the archbishop was encouraged to go ahead.

'Hereupon I went to his Majesty, the Duke of York, and most of the nobility and Clergy, who were pleased to contribute freely to the Building.'

London, vol. xxxiii, pp. 278–84 and pls 16–19. For Barbon, see R. D. Sheldon, in *ODNB*, iii, pp. 352–4.

41 For Richard Frith (d. 1695) see Penelope Hunting, *They Built London: History of the Tylers and Bricklayers' Company* (London, 2016), pp. 116–19.

42 *Survey of London*, xxxiii, pp. 283–4.

43 Georgirenes, *Account of his Building the Grecian Church*; Westminster Archives Centre, Churchwardens' Accounts of St Martin in the Fields, F 404, f. 204, no. 8, Inventory of writings etc., belonging to the church, dated 31 January 1681/2 includes attested copies of two indentures dated 8 Aug. 1677 recording the exchange of sites for St Anne's Church and the Greek church. The Vestry of St Martin's agreed to the exchange on 22 August 1677, see ibid. F 2004, Vestry Minutes St Martin in the Fields, f. 197 and inserted folio. TNA, KB 27/2040, no. 1186, of 26 Dec. 1684, rehearses the complex history of fifty-year building leases in the area; see esp. folios 4v–6r; cf. *Survey of London*, xxxiii, pp. 278f.

On 19 March 1677 the register of the Privy Council records that the king, noting that Georgirenes and his friends had 'procured a convenient place or piece of ground for that purpose, & [had] obtained subscriptions of the Right Reverend the Archbishops & other the Bishops towards the building a little Church', was 'pleased that the sum of one hundred pounds be subscribed as of his Royall bounty'.[44] The Duke of York made a generous donation also, recognized in due course in the foundation inscription over the door of the church;[45] and it was, in consequence, to him that the archbishop dedicated his *Description of the Present State of Samos etc.* in fulsome terms the following year – 'not as a thing of any merit, but as a manifestation of my devoir and gratitude, for those great Obligations, which I, and in me all the Greek Nation has received'. In the register, the entry of the king's contribution is made in the name of Coventry's colleague, secretary of state for the northern department, Sir Joseph Williamson. It is not surprising to learn that he too was a graduate of Queen's, and indeed the College's greatest benefactor.[46]

It may indeed be that Williamson had himself been deliberately recruited to the cause by Smith, who was very conveniently placed for the purpose, at that time serving as his chaplain. The two had corresponded from time to time since 1661 and when Smith in 1668 went to Constantinople with the College's blessing,[47] Williamson is his 'most affectionate Servant', and sends him 'a paper left with me long since by Dr Basire, by which you may be intermitted into a very useful acquaintance at Constple. A paper

44 TNA, SP 44/46, p. 164; cf. *CSPD, 1677–78*, p. 38. For Compton's intervention, see HMC, *Report on the Manuscripts of the late Allan George Finch Esq., of Burley-on-the-Hill, Rutland*, ii London, 1922), p. 148.

45 See below, pp. 177–8.

46 A. Marshall, in *ODNB* 59, pp. 352–6. His monument is the north-east corner-block in Queen's Lane, opposite St Peter's in the East. This was the first stage of redevelopment of the mediaeval Queen's, in 1671–2, to make the remarkable range of buildings which eventually fronted on to the High Street and gave Queen's one of Oxford's finest and most dramatic facades. See J. R. Magrath, *The Queen's College*, 2 vols (Oxford, 1921), ii, pp. 43–50.

47 Oxford, Bodl. Lib., MS Smith l, p. 219, 8 June 1668, from Thomas Hyde, 'your very affectionate friend to serve you'.

that may be as serviceable to My Lord Ambassador in his business, as to you in your studies'. On Smith's return to England in 1671, the ambassador in turn wrote a warm testimonial to Williamson, urging him to recommend Smith to the former secretary of state, Henry Bennet, Lord Arlington. In July 1675 the Earl of Anglesey, delighted to think that Smith's book on the Greek church would 'contribute to those who may, by the providence and blessing of God repair the breaches of Syon and build up the walls of our decayed Jerusalem', reported a recent conversation:

> For these ends I shall be your sure remembrancer for such encouragement from our great patron of learning as may make your studies easy and free from distracting cares, Mr Secretary Williamson, and I had lately discourse of you which I shall take occasion to renew until some fruit arise to your advantage, as I shall not be forgetful of others of our College [Queen's] who now seem to want a helping hand.[48]

Now, in 1676, Williamson offered Smith the post of chaplain. Smith, however, at first had no wish to accept the offer. On 7 October he wrote from Williamson's to his Magdalen colleague Thomas Cradock to tell him of the offer and of his own reluctance,

> but truly tho I have lived in the family of an Ambassador, I am sensible already that I am not cut out for it, wanting perchance those arts of compliance and courtship, to which I was never bred, which, I see, a man must be guilty of, if he would please, and which I am now too old to learn; and therefore shall never part with my liberty, and live under continual restraint, it may be for 2 or 3 years, in hopes of a Prebend or a Living, when I can live happily all my life long in a College, and enjoy myself, as well as the great man at Lambeth.[49]

Yet less than three weeks later Smith was indeed Williamson's chaplain, installed in Stanhope House, Charing Cross. On 26 October he wrote to Bernard from that address, to say that the latter's recent letters had been forwarded from Oxford to London, 'where I think I shall reside for some while in the house of a very good friend of yours, Sir Joseph Williamson'.[50]

48 Oxford, Bodl. Lib., MS Smith xlvii, fol. 31rv.
49 Oxford, Bodl. Lib., MS Smith lix, p. 333.
50 Oxford, Bodl. Lib., MS Smith lvii, pp. 32–1 (sic), draft of 26 Oct. 1676, Williamson's name deleted and obliterated; on Dr Isaac Basire (1607–76), French Protestant

It must have been a powerful reason, to move him from the delights of college life, and opportunities for foreign travel,[51] to the 'continual restraint' of the chaplaincy: the opportunity to influence the secretary of state on behalf of the Greek church may have been that reason.

However that may be, by the spring of 1677 Georgirenes had received royal support, financial as well as moral, he had won the favour of the Bishop of London and other bishops and archbishops as well as prosperous and influential laymen, and he had a site for the building. By this time the dead Demetry's 10,000 ecus had perhaps been retrieved. On 26 June Smith was able to send Galland an optimistic report, summarizing this success: if there was no interruption to the work, he said, it was likely that the building would be finished before winter.[52] Writing from Oxford – no doubt he was there to attend the annual commemoration celebrations known as 'Encaenia' – he mentioned that the day before leaving London he had run into Georgirenes at Court, but that they had had no time for more than a word of greeting. In fact the archbishop was still fund-raising; and it was no doubt Smith who arranged for him to come to Oxford for 'some weeks' at the beginning of July. As Anthony Wood reports: 'He came to get money towards the finishing of the Greek church at London.' The university gave him £10.[53] It may be significant that the next payment listed in the

---

turned Anglo-Catholic priest and missionary to Greece and the Levant, see above pp. 156–8; Oxford, Bodl. Lib., MS Smith liv, p. 141, and MS Smith lix, p. 333.

51 Cf. the letter from his friend James Younger in Venice, 12 March 1677, who had expected news of Smith's coming to France and Italy, 'Till you inform'd me of your being fix'd at Stanhop House', where he would certainly find the 'Advantage, which certainly you will gain by so noble a Patron, & one so able as Sir Joseph Williamson to prefer you': Oxford, Bodl. Lib., MS Smith liv, p. 171.

52 Oxford, Bodl. Lib., MS Smith lv, pp. 145–8; probably in reply to Galland's letter to him dated 23 June (new style), mentioning that he had written to Georgirenes but did not know whether the letter had reached him, and asking for news of the archbishop, ibid. 46, pp. 223–6.

53 *Life and Times of Anthony Wood, antiquary of Oxford, 1632–1695, described by himself*, ed. A. Clark, 4 vols (Oxford Historical Society, 1891–5), ii, p. 379; A. Wood, *Fasti Oxonienses*, ed. P. Bliss, 4 vols (London, 1813–30), ii, col. 219; Oxford, Bodl. Lib., University Archives, WPB/21/5, Vice-Chancellor's Accounts 1666–97, fol. 45v, cf. Wood, *Life and Times*, iv, p. 76.

vice-chancellor's accounts for that year is 'to Mr Rhodocanaces, the Grecian, by the same consent [i.e. of the delegates of the University Chest], 5 *li*.' Rhodocanaces, a considerable self-publicist, appears to have been settled in Oxford at this time through the good offices of Smith, whom he had asked to approach the vice-chancellor on his behalf to obtain employment with the university.[54] (The London market for spirit of salt was perhaps already saturated.) It is at least possible that he now sought a seat on the archbishop's bandwagon; he might even have been useful in the role of interpreter, for Georgirenes knew no English.[55]

An equally important motive for the archbishop's visit, and one reason for its significant duration, will have been the need to visit the translator of his book, Henry Denton – a graduate and fellow of Queen's, of course – to make final arrangements for its publication. For it was at this very time, on 14 July 1677, that Dr William Jane, a close colleague and favourite of Bishop Compton, who had recruited him to his staff while Bishop of Oxford but had not yet secured him a new post in London, issued his licence to publish.[56]

When Smith was surprised to encounter Georgirenes at Court, it is more than likely that the archbishop was there to seek a further subvention: as any modern fund-raiser knows, the most likely contributors to one's cause are those who have already given to it. This is perhaps the context of a draft letter from Smith to Justel, dated only '1677', in which he says that the archbishop is labouring afresh, mightily, to build the church for his people; for work had stopped for some time while he toured the home counties in search of funds.[57] The appeal for funds was complemented by a degree of self-help. On 14 December 1677 'Laurence Georgerini, late of

54 Oxford, Bodl. Lib., MS Smith, xlvi, p. 585. See above p. 154.

55 Cf. Oxford, Bodl. Lib., MS Tanner 33, p. 58.

56 *A Description of the Present State*, title page. On Jane ('Janus' to some!), see R. A. P. J. Beddard, in *ODNB*, xxix, pp. 779–81: 'a clerical politician of a low type', appointed by Compton as his chaplain and later advanced from a canonry of Christ Church, Oxford, to one of St Paul's and to the archdeaconry of Middlesex, and a successful trimmer to the varying ecclesiastical and political winds until his death in Queen Anne's reign. Cf. Carpenter, *The Protestant Bishop*, pp. 24, 67f. Jane's role as censor seems not to have been noticed hitherto.

57 Oxford, Bodl. Lib., MS Smith lv, pp. 153, 'circum vicinas regiones'.

Milo [Melos], an island in the Archipelago, now belonging to the Grecian Church planted in this kingdom', was granted a warrant addressed to the attorney general, entitling him for fourteen years to a patent under the great seal of his 'art to pickle mackerel so as they shall continue for two years without decaying or perishing ... towards the better support and maintenance of the said Grecian church', which otherwise had 'as yet no maintenance settled upon it'. Lawrence was the archbishop's brother, one among an array of family members who accompanied him to London.[58]

During the summer of 1677, work began on the Church of the *Koimēsis*, the Dormition of the Mother of God. The archbishop no doubt hoped that it might still be possible to finish before winter. After all – as the king had been told – it was to be 'a little Church': set in the middle of its curtilage, and rectangular in plan, its overall measurements were to be no more than roughly seventy feet by fifty. The building was to be much altered over the years, serving first the Greeks, then the Huguenots, and finally the Anglicans as St Mary's Soho, a chapel of ease to St Anne's parish church, before it was at length removed in 1934 to make room for St Martin's School of Art. However, its appearance can be reconstructed with the aid of a late eighteenth-century watercolour drawing of the exterior by Jacob Schnebbelie, an anonymous interior of 1819, a group of drawings of the exterior and interior made by J. P. Emslie in 1898 when the church had been partly demolished for reconstruction on a larger scale, and an undated (post-1874) engraving reproduced in a later book (see Figure 2).[59]

58 TNA, SP 44/40A, fol. 223; cf. *CSPD, 1677–78*, p. 508. For references to his family, see, *CSPD, 1680–81*, pp. 691f.; for Lawrence as his brother, Longleat, Coventry Papers, vol. xi, fol. 333. For the four brothers mentioned in his will see below p. 221.

59 *Survey of London*, xxxiv, pls 17–18: London Metropolitan Archives, Corporation of London, SC/PZ/WE/01/0288 (Schnebbelie, 1819); SC/PZ/WE/01/0276, 0294–5 (Emslie), 1898); T. E. Dowling and E. W. Fletcher, *Hellenism in England* (London, 1915), plate p. 83. Cf. Hogarth's somewhat free engraving of *Noon*, 1738, by which time the building had become a church for Huguenot refugees: *Survey of London*, xxxiv, pl. 16a.

THE ORIGINAL GREEK CHURCH (NOW ST. MARY'S), SOHO

Figure 2: The Greek Church in Soho.

Although the church was built in brick with a bare minimum of stone or stucco dressing, it is clear that its architecture was undistinguished, perhaps best characterized as sub-Wren. Along the north and south sides, of six bays (the westernmost blocked in the nineteenth century), the windows were in two storeys. Two storeys of windows commonly imply provision for a gallery inside, and a tiered gallery with wood-panelled front resting on columns is indeed to be seen in the drawing of 1819;[60] no trace of it remained in 1898. The detailed form of the east end is unknown, for in 1872 it was removed in the course of construction of an immensely tall

60 It must, however, have been to some extent remodelled, since it is shown extending along the east wall, as well as the south and west.

chancel, added as part of the reconstruction then in progress.[61] All that can be said is that the original east end must have been more or less flat. The west end is a little better known, thanks to the engraved illustration made between 1874 and 1915 and to Emslie's exterior and interior views of it in its partly demolished state. In the centre of the gable the engraving shows an elliptical oculus, but this is incompatible with the flat ceiling as seen inside in 1819, and may simply be imaginative reconstruction.[62] The same engraving shows, at the peak of the gable, a small bell-turret. At ground level the *ensemble* was organized asymmetrically for some reason which can no longer be discerned. The entrance was placed in the second bay from the south, given emphasis by a heavy classical surround in which was incorporated the dedicatory inscription (on which, see below). As to the internal fittings, we know almost nothing, except that, for theological reasons to be noted later, they cannot have been elaborate: there will, for instance, have been no iconostasis, since Bishop Compton permitted no icons, though its place may, of course, been taken by a simple screen.[63] There is perhaps little point in speculation about the identity of the architect. Clearly, the building has nothing of the flair of Wren himself. Some features of the Greek church may recall the more pedestrian genius of Wren's partner Robert Hooke, the city surveyor, as evinced in his few surviving churches of the period such as St Edmund the King, Lombard Street, or St Benet, Paul's Wharf, both rectangular with flat east ends and flat ceilings rather than vaults; but there the resemblance ends.[64]

61 See Emslie's external view. For the nineteenth-century history of the building, see G. Hennessy, *Novum Repertorium Ecclesiasticum Parochiale Londinense* (London, 1898), pp. 400–1, clviii.

62 Emslie, however, does show the loose, presumably wooden, frame of a circular window standing loose against the north wall at its western end, perhaps removed by the demolition workers; this frame is elaborately 'gothick' (cf. the tracery of the side windows in Emslie's drawing, as noted above) and must surely be a later addition, perhaps within an originally plain window, but account must be taken of it.

63 See below, p. 180.

64 On Hooke, see P. J. Pugliese, in *ODNB*, xxvii, pp. 951–8, esp. 954. See also L. Jardine, *The Curious Life of Robert Hooke* (London, 2003), esp. ch. iv, a companion to her *On a Grander Scale: The Outstanding Career of Sir Christopher Wren* (London, 2002), in which the buildings of both are discussed. See also S. Inwood, *The Man Who*

Of surviving buildings of the period in and around London, none can be found with enough in common with the Greek church to suggest an identity for the architect.

If the architect remains unknown, we can at least identify the builder. The church was built by Frith himself ('Mr Thrift' not only to Georgirenes) who evidently had not waited for the transfer of his lease to St Martin's on 8 August. In July of that year two brickmakers were fined ten shillings for supplying a thousand bricks to Mr Thrift (Frith) for his works 'at the Grecian church in Sohoe-feilds' and a Mr Rice Williams was also fined ten shillings for supplying bad mortar.[65] So work, if not good work, was in progress. The building was not in fact finished before winter, and a hint of the exasperation felt even beyond Greek circles surfaces in a remark in the Verney papers dated 15 November 1677 to the effect that 'A Greek Church has been long a building in St Giles' Fields; it goes on slowly.'[66] By early December it had risen no more than a few courses of brickwork above the height of the door. At this point, however, Georgirenes allowed himself a pardonable show of triumph, inserting a baroque moulding over the door with an inscription in neo-Byzantine lettering which recorded the foundation of the church (see Figure 3):[67]

Knew Too Much (London, 2002), esp. ch. 10. If Hooke had himself been involved in the Greek church, the fact would certainly have emerged from his voluminous diary: H. W. Robinson and W. Adams eds., *The Diary of Robert Hooke MA MD FRS 1672–1680* (London, 1935; repr. 1968).

65 London, Guildhall Library, MS. 3047/2, Tylers' and Bricklayers' Company, Search Book 1650–80, under date 31 July 1677. It should perhaps be recorded that elsewhere, in St James's, Hooke supervised work by Frith, on behalf of John Hervey, treasurer of the queen's household: see Inwood, *The Man Who Knew Too Much*, pp. 250–1.

66 MS at Claydon, HMC, *Seventh Report* (1874), p. 494b.

67 See two letters from Smith to Bernard, dated 4 and 18 Dec., Oxford, Bodl. Lib., MS Smith lvii, pp. 17, 19. When the church was finally demolished in 1934, the inscribed stone was acquired from the Bishop of London by the Chian philanthropist Philip Argenti, who installed it in the present Greek cathedral of Hagia Sophia in Bayswater, London, in memory of his parents Pandelis and Fanny Argenti.

Figure 3: Inscription placed over the door of the Greek Church in Soho, now at the Greek Orthodox Cathedral in Moscow Road, London.

> In the year of Salvation 1677, this Church was erected on behalf of the Greek nation, the Most Serene Charles II being King, Lord James, Prince of Royal Birth, Duke; and the Right Reverend Lord Henry Compton, Bishop, at the expense of the above and the other bishops and nobles, and with the support of our lowliness, Bishop of Samos, Joseph Georgeirines, from the island of Melos.

The inscription annoyed Smith, but why? There is in fact reason to believe that he and the archbishop had been drifting further and further apart during the autumn. In his draft letter to the Protestant Justel dated simply 1677, already mentioned, in which he spoke of the interruption caused to the work by shortage of money, Smith went on to say that people took different views of the project. To some it not only made good sense: it was a work of religious duty to support a people in such extremity, and to adopt them into communion with the Church of England. Others regarded the Greek Church as desperately corrupt, particularly since the Synod of Jerusalem (Bethlehem) in 1672, and charged that the opportunity given to the Greeks would turn out disastrously for the established Church: it made little difference, they said, whether the mass was allowed to be said in Latin or in Greek. Only time would tell, said Smith, which view would be proved correct.[68] In allowing that the opposition might be proved right, Smith advertises the decline of his own commitment. He evidently wrote again in more disparaging terms, for on 17 November Justel replied agreeing with his judgement of Georgirenes' situation (*establissement*): Smith knew the contemporary Greeks and their ways all too well, he said. If there were any prospect of being able to buttress the Greek church with the Protestant, it would be worth taking any risk; as it was, one would do better to give one's fortune to the poor.[69] By December Smith had become seriously disillusioned. On 4 December he wrote to Bernard, 'The Greek

68 Oxford, Bodl. Lib., MS Smith lv, p. 153: *De proposito hoc varia sunt hominum judicia. Aliis non solum prudentiae sed pietatis esse videtur, hoc modo afflictissimae genti succurrere, et quasi in communionem nostram adsciscere: alii autem qui corruptissimum Graecae ecclesiae statum e Synodo Bethleemitica et appendice Constantinopolitana norunt, hanc facilitatem Religioni nostro detrimento ac fraudi fore criminantur, causati parum discriminis interesse utrum missa lingua Latina an Graeca celebrari permittatur. Cum vero res ad exitum pervenerit, utra conjecturarum meliori innitatur fundamento, dies et eventus docebunt.*

69 Oxford, Bodl. Ms., MS Smith xlvi, pp. 259–61.

church is not yet finished, the Greek Bishop has put a very silly Inscription over the gate, which I will send you in my next.' He sent Bernard the text two weeks later, dismissing it as 'barbarous Greek'.[70] But the most plausible reason why he thought the inscription was 'silly' is not the quality of the Greek. It is the content. It gave considerable prominence to the Catholic Duke of York. This letter to Bernard is the last mention of the Archbishop of Samos in Smith's surviving correspondence; the breakdown in relations between them was irrevocable. It is hard to think that this would have happened had a peacemaker been available still in the person of Antoine Galland. For the Frenchman was on close terms with both, maintaining a light-hearted correspondence with Smith in Latin and colloquial Greek and sending and receiving letters to and from the archbishop.[71] But by this time, Galland was out of reach, on his second voyage to the Levant.[72]

Notwithstanding the cooling of Smith's enthusiasm for Georgirenes and his Greek church, as 1678 began it must have seemed to the archbishop that his project was assured of success. The building was perhaps completed soon after Easter and what remained to be settled was the nature of the worship which the Bishop of London was willing to permit within his jurisdiction.[73] In general, as is clear from his better-documented relations with the French Protestants, the Compton's concern was for compatibility with the Church of England, if possible leading to intercommunion.[74] How was this requirement to be interpreted in relation to an Eastern Orthodox Church? The answer is contained in a declaration of conformity to the doctrines of the Church of England, a copy of which, dated 2 April 1678,

70 Oxford, Bodl. Lib., MS Smith lvii, pp. 17, 19.

71 Galland to Georgirenes, cf. Oxford, Bodl. Lib., MS Smith xlvi, pp. 223, 228; the archbishop to Galland, cf. ibid. p. 209.

72 Oxford, Bodl. Lib., MS Smith xlvi, p. 228, Galland to Smith, 18 Sept., on the point of departure; ibid. p. 255, Justel to Smith, 13 Oct., Galland has left; for Aleppo, ibid. 57, p. 17, Smith to Bernard, 4 Dec.

73 Guildhall Library, MS 3047/2, at date 13 April 1678, the Tylers' and Bricklayers' Search Book records an inspection of 'Mr Frith's works in Sohoe Feilds', which resulted in the breaking of 300 of 'Mr Pitcher's Tyles of Deptford'. If this relates to the Greek church, which is not of course certain, the ordering of tiles implies that work had reached the roof, or perhaps the flooring.

74 Carpenter, *Protestant Bishop*, pp. 70ff., 322ff.

was obtained by Thomas Smith and is preserved among his papers.[75] The declaration, endorsed by Smith and bearing the title 'The Archbishop of Samos his renouncing the superstition of the Romish and Greek Church, and his promise to give no scandal in the publick exercise of his Religion', runs as follows:

> We renounce transubstantiation of the Holy Mystery as a superstition recently established by the Romans; we renounce also the Synod of Bethlehem [Jerusalem, 1672] with all its false teaching which the Romans have introduced into the Eastern Church. We promise not to place icons in our church in London, nor to worship, revere or serve anyone but God alone; nor to pray for the dead, as the Romans pray, nor to hold any service which would be contrary to that of the Anglican Church or would give scandal to it. Thus we renounce, thus we promise in the name of God, Amen.

It is significant that Smith had obtained a copy of this declaration; he may of course have himself procured it to be made. The archbishop's promise appears to reflect a far harsher attitude than that expressed in the king's grant to Daniel Vulgaris and his colleagues in 1675 of 'liberty to build a Church ... where they may freely exercise their Religion according to the Greek church'.[76] No doubt it reflects the almost paranoid preoccupation with the peril of popery, which increasingly gripped England throughout the year 1678. In particular it reflects a growing sense of disillusion on the part of Smith himself. In that year, Bishop Compton's own obsession with matters of the kind renounced in this declaration evidently influenced his choice of issues to be debated at his diocesan conferences in 1679: Half

75 Oxford, Bodl. Lib., MS. Smith lxcviii, pp. 47–50; two leaves or one folded (the binding conceals the edge), then folded again (apparently as a letter), text on p. 47 only, 48–9 blank, endorsed by Smith on 50. For the Greek text see M. E. Martin, 'Some Western Images of Athos in Early Modern Times, *c.*1554–1678', *Byzantine and Modern Greek Studies*, xxii (1998), pp. 51–74, App. II, pp. 72–4. See also Georgirenes, *Description of the Present State*, epistle to the reader, where it is said that 'they', the Greek Church, 'accord with us', the Church of England – itself a curious perspective – on a number of details of eucharistic practice. It is possible that this epistle was, in fact, written by Denton (see p. 228).

76 TNA, PC 2/64, p. 341.

Communion (that is, communion in one kind), Prayers in an Unknown Tongue, and Prayers to the Saints.[77] That Orthodox doctrines and practices were topical is suggested by the doggerel response of the vicar of All Saints, Colchester, forwarded to the bishop by the rural dean. The second stanza cites the authority of Greek against Roman practice:[78]

> Christ & St Paul gave bread & wine;
> To these the Greek-church does incline,
> and we with them therein Combine:
> (But that they water mix with Wine).

Stanza 12, moreover, takes the Greek side on an issue which, as we have seen, much disturbed English theologians, the permissibility of infant communion:[79]

> More then, that moderns disavow
> The Eucharist to Infants now,
> Which Holy Church did once allow.

The vicar's cynical conclusion follows:

> Then Henceforth Let us never grieve
> To Pin our Faith o' the churches sleeve
> Or, as the Church believes, believe.

But for his bishop the answers to questions of belief were absolute, not relative, and Compton must have felt he had no choice but to require Georgirenes' declaration of conformity as a condition of the new church's licence.

As if the harder tone were not enough, there was the silence of Constantinople. For Bishop Compton had written the previous year to Patriarch Dionysios IV – Georgirenes' old enemy – presumably to secure some kind of approval, or at least acquiescence, for the establishment of the Greek church in London. When Smith wrote the earlier of his two

77 Carpenter, *Protestant Bishop*, pp. 62–6, 208f.

78 Oxford, Bodl. Lib., MS. Rawl. C983, fol. 15, dated 22 May 1679.

79 Cf. the preoccupation of Thomas Smith, above, pp. 149–50.

letters to Bernard in December 1678, he noted, 'No answer yet from the Patriarch of C[onstantinople] to the Bp of Londons letter, whom all who wish well to Religion & Learning wish Patriarch of our Church.'[80] (This was barely a month after the death of Archbishop Sheldon, before Dean Sancroft was appointed to the vacancy.) For Georgirenes, the silence from Constantinople was ominous.

80 Oxford, Bodl. Lib., MS Smith lvii, p. 18.

CHAPTER 8

The Popish Plot (1678–1679)

Georgirenes had come to England in 1676 intending to publish his *Anthologion* for the use of the Eastern Greek Church. In the event the *Anthologion* never appeared but, instead, in 1677 he published an English translation (provided by Henry Denton) of his *Description of the Present State of Samos, Nicaria, Patmos and Mount Athos* with a fulsome dedication in Greek and English to Georgirenes' benefactor the Duke of York. For a foreign suitor dependent on the goodwill of the Bishop of London to choose to dedicate his book to James might be thought an indiscretion at any time, for duke and bishop entertained a cordial dislike of one another that stemmed partly from the *odium theologicum* of a professed Catholic for the doughtiest champion not only of the Anglican establishment but of Protestant dissenters also, and partly from more personal slights. Though the Comptons had been in the front line of loyal supporters in the Civil War, and though the bishop himself had trailed a pike for James in Flanders, the duke did not hesitate to turn that service to a reproach and to disparage Compton as 'talking more like a colonel than a bishop'.[1] In early November 1678 the French ambassador reported to Paris that the Duke of York had

1 E. Carpenter, *The Protestant Bishop* (London, 1956), p. 12. For what follows, see in general J. P. Kenyon, *The Popish Plot* (London, 1972; 2nd edn, 1983). Kenyon's is one of the most vivid and chronologically precise modern accounts of the alleged Plot, and I have used it extensively. I have also profited greatly from three magisterial works by John Miller: *Popery and Politics in England, 1660–1688* (Cambridge, 1973); *James II* (Hove, 1978); *Charles II* (London, 1991). I am most grateful to Professor Miller for guiding me to, and through, important archival sources. See also now, Peter Hinds, *'The Horrid Popish Plot': Roger L'Estrange and the Circulation of Political Discourse in late Seventeenth Century London* (Oxford, 2010).

told him 'Que l' Evesque de Londres estoit son ennemy declare'.[2] James resented the king's intrusion of Compton into his household to ensure and oversee the Protestant education of the princesses Mary and Anne, culminating in the confirmation of both in 1676 and the marriage of Mary to William of Orange in November 1677, a match pressed also by Thomas Osborne, Earl of Danby, the avidly Protestant Lord Treasurer.[3] In that same month Compton as bishop had pressed the duke, not for the first time, to dismiss his wife's private secretary Edward Coleman on the ground of his proselytizing for the Catholic faith;[4] and in December James had retaliated by frustrating Compton's well-grounded aspiration to the see of Canterbury on the death of Archbishop Sheldon.[5] The wounds were recent, and open.

More potentially devastating to Georgirenes, however, in the over-heated political climate of 1678, was his brief entanglement at Bristol in the turmoil of the 'Popish Plot', an alleged conspiracy to kill the king and set the Duke of York upon the throne. Indeed, a malevolent reader might have suspected a certain covert sympathy for the Plot in the Horatian tag with which the archbishop decorated the title-page of his book:

> *Dum licet, & vultum servat fortuna benignum,*
> Romae *laudetur* Samos, & Chios, & Rhodos *absens.*[6]

2 TNA, 31/3/141, fol. 52, dated 17 Nov. (new style).

3 *CSPD 1673–75*, pp. 136f., 150f.; *CJ*, vol. ix, p. 303; Kenyon, *Popish Plot*, p. 16; Carpenter, *The Protestant Bishop*, pp. 33–7.

4 Carpenter, *The Protestant Bishop*, p. 42. Coleman was an enthusiastic Catholic convert, the son of an Anglican clergyman in Suffolk. He had at first been secretary to James himself, but appears to have been transferred formally to the duchess' service in 1674–5, though he in fact continued to serve both. James had already declined to secure his dismissal in 1676–7: Longleat, Coventry Papers, xi, fol. 245–6. See, in general, Kenyon, *Popish Plot*, pp. 34–8.

5 Cf. Carpenter, *The Protestant Bishop*, pp. 37–42, citing *Diary of Dr Edward Lake*, ed. G. P. Elliott, Camden Soc. xxxix (*Camden Miscellany* i), 1847, pp. 18–19.

6 Horace, *Epistles*, Book, 1, ch. XI. Translated by A. S. Kline 'While fate proves benign, and while you can, from Rome | Praise the far-distant, Samos, and Chios and Rhodes'. It seems likely that this Horatian tag was supplied by Henry Denton.

Fear of the Church of Rome and its supposed machinations to bring England back to the papal fold was a continuous source of anxiety, especially in the hothouse of political London. The persecutions of Queen Mary's reign were only a generation from living memory, vividly preserved through Foxe's highly coloured and highly popular *Book of Martyrs*, and many of those then living will have known older people who recalled that age. Such were the vivid reminiscences which could prompt the Earl of Essex, for instance, to declare to the Privy Council in 1679 'that the apprehension of popery made him imagine he saw his children frying in Smithfield'.[7] Catholicism meant subordination to the France of Louis XIV, and that in turn meant arbitrary government.[8] Happily, no word had got out of the succession of secret treaties between Louis and the king: in the Treaty of Dover promoted by the king's sister 'Madame', Duchess of Orleans, in 1670, and in the treaty of 1673, Charles agreed to declare himself a Catholic and restore England's allegiance to the pope. In two further treaties in 1676 and 1677 Louis gave Charles money so that he would not have to recall Parliament, which, at this time, was clamouring for war against France. Nor was it widely known that Charles had declared his own Catholic persuasion to his brother and three lords, sympathetic to Catholicism, early in 1669.

By 1678, however, the open adherence of the Duke of York to Rome had been a matter of common knowledge and a source of widespread mistrust for some five or six years. If anyone had missed the significance of his omission to receive Anglican communion at Easter 1672, his repetition of the same failure in 1673 would have put the matter beyond doubt.[9] The king's Declaration of Indulgence towards non-Anglicans on 15 March 1672, only two days before his declaration of war on Protestant Holland, had been supported by his whole Cabal – by Thomas Clifford and Henry Bennet, Earl of Arlington from the Catholic viewpoint, and by the others from

7 Viscount Halifax's Notebook, Chatsworth MSS, sub 'E', quoted by Kenyon, *Popish Plot*, p. 4.

8 Cf. A. Marvell, *Account of the Growth of Popery, and Arbitrary Government, in England* (London, 1677).

9 See, for instance, *The Diary of John Evelyn*, ed. E. S. de Bere, 6 vols (Oxford, 1955), iv, p. 7.

the standpoint of the Protestant dissenters. The Proclamation was stopped by the Commons in February 1673, and replaced by a Test Act requiring anyone holding office under Charles or James to take that summer the oaths of supremacy and allegiance, to receive the sacrament according to the rites of the Church of England, and to affirm on oath that 'I do declare that I believe that there is not any Transubstantiation in the sacrament of the Lord's Supper, or in the elements of Bread and Wine at or after the consecration thereof by any person whatsoever'. To refuse meant forfeiture of public office and a bar to the holding of any further office. The act was urged from the Cabal by Anthony Ashley Cooper, now promoted Earl of Shaftesbury, with quiet support even of the Catholic Arlington in face of the general fear of popery. Less than a year later, in January 1674, Shaftesbury articulated that fear: there were 16,000 papists around London, he said, and they might do something desperate.[10] Clifford withdrew from public office and died almost at once; the Duke of York was forced to give up the basis of his enormous power as lord high admiral.

Unabashed and unyielding as ever, James proceeded with the Catholic second marriage arranged for him by Louis XIV, to the princess Mary Beatrice of Modena, barely two years after the death of his first wife Anne Hyde, English and Protestant (though she had probably died a Catholic) and the mother of the two Protestant princesses.[11] On 3 November 1673 Thomas Player wrote to Secretary Williamson, then engaged on diplomatic duty in Cologne, 'the Duke of Yorke goes within a day or two to Dover to meet his new Dutchesse: shee will come very unwellcome to the people'. Indeed, they were already calling her 'daughter of the Pope'.[12] In the five years

10 See R. Paley, ed., *History of Parliament: the Lords 1660–1715*, 5 vols (Cambridge, 2016), ii, p. 694. It appears, however, that Catholic numbers were not rising but falling: Kenyon, *Popish Plot*, p. 25.

11 See Miller, *James II*, pp. 71–5; M. Hopkirk, *Queen over the Water* (London, 1953), pp. 5–22.

12 W. D. Christie, ed., *Letters addressed from London to Sir J. Williamson while Plenipotentiary at the Congress of Cologne in the years 1673 and 1674*, 2 vols (Camden Soc., n.s. viii–ix, 1894), ii, p. 56. It was fortunate for James that no one in England saw his and Mary's regular correspondence with the pope, for example the letter of 19 Sept. 1677 in which the pope's 'Ubbedientissimo Servitore e figlio Giacomo' ('Most Obedient Servant and son James') assures His Holiness that Princess Mary's marriage to William

since then, the duke had done nothing to alleviate the anxiety of which he was the focus. On the contrary, his refusal of Easter communion in 1676 had provoked a member of the City of London's Common Council to ask, 'If the presumptive heir of the Crown be a Roman Catholic, what security can be given that the King shall live eight or nine months?'[13] Meanwhile Lord Treasurer Danby, now the King's chief minister, joined with Parliament to pursue a positively Protestant policy.

The greatest anxiety related not so much to the present as to the succession. To be sure, the king was but forty-eight years old. But he had been married for sixteen years, and Queen Catherine was now almost forty, and childless. Nor was the king willing to consider divorce in the interest of a Protestant marriage and heir, as Shaftesbury advocated. Charles was untroubled by the Catholic threat, and perfectly happy to regard his brother as his heir.[14] It was not unreasonable to assume that the Duke of York would inherit the throne, nor indeed to doubt that this might occur at any time. In the 300 years since the death of Edward III, Elizabeth had been the only sovereign to reach the age of sixty. The king's health had already begun to give concern: in August 1673, Henry Ball wrote to Secretary Williamson that, 'He has lately had 3 sad fitts of an apoplexy'. The first of which had so disconcerted the duchess of Portsmouth that she besought him to forego his nightly visits, and his doctors urged him to 'refrain from company'.[15] But fatal illness was not the only risk. There were other means whereby the Catholic duke might find himself upon the throne. There were plots to kill the king and the most notorious of these was the famous Popish Plot from 1678 to 1679. It was Georgirenes' misfortune to be caught up in the extensive tentacles of this plot.

---

of Orange had been at the order of his brother and lord, not his own plan, and that 'mai omettero alcun diligenza e cura in preservazione e augmento della Religione Cattolica Apostolica Romana in questi regni' ('but I shall show all diligence and care in preserving and furthering the Apostolic Catholic Religion in these realms'): copy in 'Letters of Princes', TNA, 31/9/100A, fol. 298 (blue numbering).

13 *CSPD 1676–7*, p. 295, quoted by Kenyon, *Popish Plot*, p. 19.

14 See Kenyon, *Popish Plot*, pp. 8–9, 15, who notes that Charles made a distinction between born (i.e. involuntary) Catholics and converts.

15 Christie, *Letters ... to Sir J. Williamson*, ii, p. 35.

On 13 August 1678 the king's regular walk in St James's Park – taken normally at a brisk pace, with a hasty 'Good morning, good morning' to all he passed – was interrupted by one Christopher Kirkby, warning him of a plot against his life. Instinctively brushing off the threat, that night the king was induced to listen as Kirkby produced his informant Dr Israel Tonge, a clergyman attached to St Michael's Wood Street and scourge of the Jesuits, to unfold the details of the plot, concocted, he said, by English Catholics (and especially the Jesuits) with Pope Innocent XI and the King of France.[16] Tonge in turn named as his source Titus Oates, a clever and well-educated, but ugly and unstable clergyman, an Anglican from Westminster and Cambridge, who claimed that he had feigned conversion to the Jesuits in 1677 and had received a doctorate from Salamanca (which was not true), only to return to England the following year with a Jesuit commission to murder Tonge.[17] The plot centred, Oates alleged, on the household of the Catholic queen whose physician Sir George Wakeman was to prepare poison for the king. Failing poison, there were Jesuits to shoot the king or Irish ruffians to stab him. The Duchess of York's secretary, Edward Coleman, whom both the king and Bishop Compton had already attempted to have dismissed, was the channel for communication with the King of France via the latter's confessor Père de la Chaise. The king, in embarrassed disbelief of such charges which involved the queen's household, referred the matter to Lord Treasurer Danby, who questioned Tonge on the forty-three articles of his and Oates' allegations. Over the next few months, as Danby's

16 Israel Tonge had been appointed to the Rectory of St Mary Staining in June 1666 only three months before the Great Fire of London destroyed his church. It was not rebuilt but the parish was annexed to St Michael Wood Street where Tonge was not the Rector. He may, therefore, have been somewhat at a loose end and ready to meddle in religious plots.

17 The primary account of the alleged Plot and of the earliest phase of the investigation is the record of the proceedings of the Privy Council on 28–30 Sept., prepared by the clerk, Sir Robert Southwell: TNA, PC 2/66 (Privy Council Register, Charles II, vol. xiii), pp. 392ff.; cf. BL, Add. MS. 38847, fol. 201–22, together with Southwell's diary for 8 October, ibid. fol. 224ff. Bishop Compton attended regularly from 29 September. For a surprisingly balanced contemporary view of Tonge, see A. Wood, *Athenae Oxonienses*, ed. P. Bliss, 4 vols (London, 1813–20), iii, cols 1260–4.

investigation proceeded, the plot grew an abundant crop of circumstantial detail in fertile soil. It had reached seventy-one articles by 18 October.[18]

Tonge and Oates now approached Secretary Williamson, but he declined to discuss the matter; they also tried to enlist Bishop Compton, known to be fanatically anti-papalist, but with equal lack of success. Then, on 5 September, they went to a senior magistrate with powerful connections, Sir Edmund Berrie Godfrey, a prosperous Kentish fuel merchant, well read and well travelled, and asked him to take their depositions on oath that the contents of papers they carried were true. On 27 September Godfrey was appalled to learn what the papers contained, and agreed to take Oates' deposition on oath. Godfrey also informed Edward Coleman of the allegations against him; but the latter, no doubt from contempt of what he believed to be unprovable, failed to take the hint and did not destroy his own correspondence with Père de la Chaise, which was destined to appear plainly incriminating, and to provide clear confirmation of Oates' story.

On the following morning, Saturday 28 September, the Privy Council met for its first discussion of the affair.[19] The king and the duke attended. Secretary Williamson produced the bundle of letters he had received from Tonge. The latter was summoned, but nervously declared that all his information was from Oates: he knew nothing himself. The king did not trouble to attend the afternoon session. The Duke of York, of course, when questioned that afternoon expressed himself equally at a loss.[20] At this the royal brothers, plainly believing nothing of what was alleged, took themselves off to Newmarket, and were therefore not present later in the afternoon session when Oates came before the Council, brimming with confidence, to tell his tale. So plausible, so circumstantial was it that the Council swallowed every detail, and at once ordered the arrest of all those named as conspirators. Charles came back on Sunday afternoon, himself cross-questioned Oates and showed him unreliable.[21] It is clear enough that

18 BL, Add. MS.38847, fol. 232.

19 TNA, PC 2/66, p. 392.

20 BL, Add. MS.38847, fol. 202v–203.

21 Ibid. fol. 205; TNA, PC 2/66, pp. 396–7. See also HMC, *Calendar of the MSS of the Marquess of Ormonde, KP*, n.s. iv (London, 1906), pp. 457–60.

the king did not believe a word of Oates' story. Indeed, as late as the end of January 1679 he was still telling the French ambassador he did not credit it.[22] But the Council did, and the damage was done. Sir George Wakeman was ordered to attend to give an account of himself, and Coleman was to be arrested and his correspondence seized.

Coleman's letters comprised copies of his correspondence with various people abroad, and above all with Père de la Chaise, in which the enthusiasm of a convert to Catholicism led him sometimes to indiscretion. The letters no doubt expressed a hankering after restoration of the Catholic religion; and they spoke of the 'great design' of replacing Protestants with Catholics through the medium of trade, and of frustrating the will of Parliament. Sometimes they even alluded to one of the very purposes of the two kings' secret treaties – money for Charles from France rather than from the doubtful support of Parliament – although the existence of the treaties was not of course known to the parliamentary investigators who read the letters.[23] Reading and deciphering of the letters began on 4 October, and in a summary of their import prepared for the House of Commons

22 TNA, 31/3/141 (copies of the ambassador's reports to Paris), fol. 7–8, 10 Oct., 'un veritable fondement'; cf. ibid. fol. 32r, 31 Oct. – but with hostile comment on Coleman; 31/3/142, fol. 24r–v, 26 Jan., Oates and Bedloe are 'des parjures et des imposteurs' – but there may be an underlying germ of truth. Six days earlier, however, the king had told the Privy Council that he 'was not convinced of the Plot till now': Oxford, Bodl. Lib., MS Rawlinson A 136, p. 106. Others, too, doubted Oates' story: BL, Add. MS. 38847, fol. 235v (18 Oct.). Among them, and highly relevant to the attempt to incriminate Georgirenes (as we shall see) was the Marquis of Worcester: Miller, *Popery and Politics*, pp. 13, 61, 176. Against these honest doubts, however, was ranged the cynical wisdom of such as the king's confidant Lord Halifax, who counselled that 'the Plot must be handled as if it were true, whether it were so or not' (quoted by Kenyon, *Popish Plot*, p. 190). For comment on the general readiness to believe Oates in the political climate of 1678, see the remarks of the Earl of Huntingdon at Oates' trial for perjury in 1685: *State Trials*, ed. W. Cobbett and T. C. Howell, 34 vols (London, 1809–28), x, p. 1168; cf. Oxford, Bodl. Lib., MS Carte 130, fol. 223 (orig. no. 293).

23 *Collection of Letters ... from the Originals in the Hands of George Treby*, 2 pts (London, 1681), esp. i, p. 111, letter dated 29 ix, 1675, and i, p. 117, another letter probably of similar date. See also the letters included in full in *CJ*, ix, pp. 5255–9.

Sir Robert Southwell wrote, 'The general scope of all these letters which were either writ or received by Mr Coleman tend to bring the Roman Catholic religion here into England.'[24] In a parallel report to the Privy Council, Lord Chancellor Finch wrote that the letters were indubitable evidence of treason, carefully adding that 'in the chief part of this wicked & dangerous correspondence he [Coleman] hath presumed to make use of the Name of his Royal Highness without having any ground or authority so to do ….'[25] Inevitably, the letters were taken to be the smoking gun which proved the truth of Oates' allegations. By 31 October, ten days after their re-assembly following a brief prorogation, the Commons had resolved 'that there has been and still is a damnable and hellish plot, contrived and carried on by popish recusants for the assassinating and murdering the king, and for the subverting the government and rooting out and destroying the Protestant religion.'[26] Coleman was tried for treason at the King's Bench. Oates gave evidence against him on 27 November, but was mauled in the witness-box by Lord Chief Justice Scroggs. Coleman was convicted, and executed on 3 December, and with Coleman removed from the scene, the Duke of York could afford to relax. The ice had been very thin.[27]

Any lingering doubt of the truth of Oates' story, whether in the Council and both Houses of Parliament or among the public at large, had been by now dispelled by the news of the murder of Sir Edmund Berrie Godfrey. It appears that Godfrey was last seen alive on the morning of Saturday 12 October, when he walked from his lodgings near the Strand northwards up St Martin's Lane; he may have asked the way to Primrose Hill, and may have been seen at Marylebone.[28] Mysterious as his death was (and still is), at the time there was no doubt that Godfrey had been murdered by Catholics on account of his knowledge of the matters alleged by

24 BL, Add. MS 38142, fols 3–3v. See also his diary account, BL, Add. MS. 38847, fols 224–9.

25 TNA, PC 2/67, p. 421, 16 Oct.

26 *CJ*, ix, p. 530.

27 See Kenyon's excellent account, *Popish Plot*, pp. 118–25.

28 For a detailed account of this affair, see A. Marshall, *The Strange Death of Edmund Godfrey: Plots and Politics in Restoration London* (London, 1999).

Oates and Tonge. A reward of £500 was offered for information leading to the conviction of the murderers; and by 23 October, two days after their re-assembly following a series of prorogations since 15 July, both Houses established Examinations Committees to investigate the Plot in general and Godfrey's murder in particular.[29]

All this served to inflame parliamentary and public opinion to yet further extremes. On 4 November the Commons pressed for a demand that the king require the Duke of York to withdraw from his presence and his Council; and the Lords on 20 November carried a bill for the dismissal of papists from both Houses, their solitary exception of the Duke of York passing the Commons by the merest whisker of 158 to 156 votes.[30] Courts and Commons might occupy the foreground, but behind them was the pressure of an almost hysterical degree of public anxiety. Pope-burnings, always a feature of the Guy Fawkes season, were mounted with unprecedented fervour in November 1678. The reward for information about Godfrey's murder was claimed by one 'Captain' William Bedloe, a *poseur* from Bristol who had represented himself as a milord on the Grand Tour, when he happened to meet Oates in the latter's Jesuit phase at Valladolid in Spain in 1677; he was also a convicted perjurer.[31] It was from Bristol

29 The Commons reacted at once to the king's speech at the opening of the session on 21 Oct., *CJ*, ix, p. 516. The Lords that day asked the king for papers, and on 23 Oct. set up a very strong committee of fifty-five, including the Duke of York, *LJ*, xiii, p. 297. The record of the Lords' investigation, with which this account is primarily concerned, survives in the three volumes of the 'Examinations Committee Booke', HL/PO/JT/1/1; I am grateful to the staff of the House of Lords Records Office, and particularly to the former keeper, Mr Harry Cobb, for kindly making this material available. Much of it, interwoven with entries in the Journals, is printed in *Manuscripts of the House of Lords, 1678–1688*, ed. E. Fairfax Taylor and F. Skene, HMC, 11th Report, Appendix, Pt ii (London, 1887). For the Commons' investigation we depend chiefly on reports to the House recorded in the Journals.

30 *CJ*, ix, p. 543, cf. pp. 545, 547–8; incorporating matters continually adjourned, ibid. pp. 533, 536, 540, 542; *LJ*, xiii, pp. 365–6.

31 See Kenyon, *Popish Plot*, p. 57. It may be noted that on 15 Jan. 1679 the Privy Council agreed to defer payment of the reward to Bedloe until after the trial of those accused by him, 'when it will most clearly appear, who is best intituled to the said Reward' (TNA, PC 2/67, p. 21).

that Bedloe first wrote to Secretary Coventry, who received his letter on 2 November. Coventry at the same time received a letter from the Mayor of Bristol, John Lloyd, a voluble Welshman of eager credulity, who had taken it upon himself to discern treason on every side.

Bristol was not a particular stronghold of the Church of England: dissidence of any colour might be expected there. The bishop, William Galston, however, was a vindictive persecutor of Dissenters and was thought by some to be more concerned with his own precedence in relation to the mayor and corporation than with his mission to the people.[32] Late in 1677 one Richard Ellsworth wrote from Bristol to Secretary Williamson, in a determined attempt to upset a forthcoming parliamentary by-election, that the candidate he sought to block would have the support of the 'Presbyterian, Independent, Anabaptisticall and Quaker' elements among the voters, 'which are two thirds of this city'.[33] Small wonder, then, that the vicar of St Mary Redcliffe could declare in a sermon on 30 January 1679 that 'There was a great noise of a Popish Plot; but ... there is nothing in it but a Presbyterian Plot'; and 'that the devil blusht at the Presbyterians', or that he regularly spoke with apparent warmth of the Catholic element in the city.[34] The lord lieutenant himself, the almost princely Marquis of Worcester, was regarded as (at best) not unsympathetic to the Catholic gentry in his region.[35] But in the local government of Bristol, Dissenters

32 *CSPD, 1677–8*, p. 320, a soothing letter from Coventry to the bishop, 23 Aug. 1677, who had complained that in Corporation services prayers were said first for the civic dignitaries, ahead of bishop, dean and canons. Contrast ibid. p. 382f, Sir John Knight writing from Bristol to Williamson on 29 November that year, complaining of the arrogance of the bishop, who would 'put the mitre above the crown'.

33 *CSPD 1677–8*, pp. 423–7, esp. 426. He believed that the queen had been treated with disrespect on her recent visit to the city.

34 Cf. J. F. Nicholls and J. Taylor, *Bristol Past and Present*, 3 vols (Bristol, 1882), iii, p. 73. Rector of St Thomas's in plurality with St Mary Redcliffe, Richard Thompson was in the end impeached by the Commons for his Catholic sympathies (*CJ*, ix, pp. 693–5, 24 Dec. 1680; ibid. pp. 671, 673); he became Dean of Bristol under James II.

35 See Molly McClain, *Beaufort: The Duke and his Duchess, 1657–1715* (New Haven and London, 2001), pp. 80f., 161f. It was this great regional power that ensured that Worcester would not be attacked directly by Bedloe, who contented himself with

and Catholics were held in equally fearful suspicion. As mayor in 1678–9 John Lloyd pursued Catholics with determination, and thereby earned himself a knighthood – and the notice of Roger North, who wrote that he 'never saw nor heard any human thing speak so lofty as he did, and all in humour and tags of Latin'.[36] Made mayor on 15 September, on the very next day (and even before he was sworn in), he wrote to the Marquis of Worcester about one Turwell, a Catholic passenger on a ship from Ireland, who had 'spoken dangerous words', daring to question whether the Popish Plot had any reality outside the 'talke and report of some idle and fantasticall people'. The mayor had had him arrested and would keep him, together with Mr Daniel Arthur, a well-known Irish Catholic merchant who was said to be privy to the plot, until Worcester could obtain further orders for him from the Privy Council.[37] With Lloyd in charge, every allegation of popery would find a ready ear.

To his letter about Bedloe at the beginning of November Lloyd received a reply from Secretary Coventry instructing him to send the witness to London. He wrote again on 6 November to say he had now done so, and added news of a party of fourteen Irish Catholic soldiers who had been fighting the French in the Low Countries and were now passing through Bristol on their way home. There were, they had said, three hundred more behind them on the road: what was Lloyd to do about this imminent invasion? Coventry replied three days later to say that if the three hundred were genuinely bound for Ireland there was no problem – but that Lloyd should keep an eye on them, and report any suspicious behaviour to the secretary of state. On the same day, letters having no doubt crossed in the post, Lloyd wrote to the other secretary, Sir Joseph Williamson, who must have taken

---

imputing guilt by association, which he could later disavow: ibid. pp. 139f. In this context it is interesting to note the impatience expressed by the Privy Council, who on 29 Jan. 1679 instructed the marquis as lord lieutenant to investigate the failure of his magistrates to require adequate oaths from recusants (TNA, PC 2/67, pp. 55, 58).

36 R. North, *The Lives of The Right Hon. Francis North …, The Hon. Sir Dudley North … and The Hon. and Rev. John North*, ed. A. Jessop, 3 vols (London, 1887–90), i, p. 157.

37 Ibid. p. 71.

an interest in Bedloe's testimony, to say that he had already sent Bedloe to London, and that he must by now have arrived there.[38]

He had. On the previous day, 8 November, Bedloe made his first appearance before the Examinations Committee of the Lords to begin his damning tale. He provided detailed evidence about the supposed murderers of Sir Edmund Berrie Godfrey and elaborated upon these when he appeared before a closed session of the Commons on 28 December to describe a Jesuit gathering in a room close to the chapel in Somerset House (while he observed from the chapel itself), at which the Catholic Lords Belasyse and Powis were present along with Coleman, two French *abbés*, and two others whom Bedloe was persuaded to say he recognized from behind as the dukes of York and Norfolk. The queen had joined them, he said, and had tearfully consented to the 'taking off' of the king. Bedloe was followed by Oates, who, consummate actor as he was and fresh from giving evidence against Coleman in court the previous day, inflamed the Commons by his own account of the queen's duplicity to the point that they demanded of the king that he banish her and her household from his presence.[39] Charles took no notice of their demand; he and his brother alone kept their heads throughout the crisis, no doubt because neither of them believed a word of Oates' story.

Such was the hysteria into which the capital had fallen when further allegations arrived from Bristol, centred this time not upon a Catholic but upon the former Archbishop of Samos, who was said to have made certain manifestly treasonable remarks to a servant on 3 August, ten days earlier, even, than the king's encounter with Kirkby in St James's Park.[40] The background to the accusation against Georgirenes is explained in a petition which the archbishop later addressed to the king and his Council. He claimed that he had been in the course of prosecuting his servant Dominico Gratiano for having stolen money which they had been collecting for building the Greek church. The case against Gratiano was to be tried at Bristol

38 Nicholls and Taylor, *Bristol Past and Present*, iii, p. 72.

39 *CJ*, ix, pp. 549–50. Cf. A. Grey, *Debates of the House of Commons, 1667–94*, 10 vols (London, 1769), vi, pp. 287, 295–6.

40 For the date, see p. 200 and n. 48.

where he was in prison. But Georgirenes claimed that 'being a stranger and unacquainted with the language and also with the right method of prosecuting such offenders' he was having difficulty in prosecuting the case and in getting his witnesses to attend the court in Bristol. Meanwhile Gratiano, in prison, had accused the archbishop falsely 'out of mere malice and revenge' of 'matters of very great consequence of which your petitioner is not guilty in the least'.[41] The petition is preserved among the papers of Archbishop Sancroft, to whom the surviving copy must have been forwarded. It is undated. By his name clearly an Italian, Gratiano may have been with Georgirenes ever since his adventures in that country. If so, he knew all too much of the archbishop's dalliance with the Catholic Church, enough to make him a considerable embarrassment in the present circumstances and to lend an air of verisimilitude to his accusations.

By 30 November a deposition by Gratiano had arrived from Bristol, sworn on 26 November, 'concerning words uttered by the said Josephus Georgerine', 'who stiles himself a Grecian bishop'. Coventry had evidently regarded the information as of some serious urgency, for the Lords' Journals

41 Oxford, Bodl. Lib., MS Tanner 33, fol. 58. Petition of 'Joseph Giorgoreene, Archbishop of Psalmos': 'That your peticioner having lately prosecuted one Dominico Gratiana sometime his servant for running away with a considerable summe of money which he was instructed by your peticioner to receive & gather towards ye building of ye Greek church, your peticioner being a stranger and unacquainted with ye language and also with ye right method of prosecuting such offenders and ye said Dominico being prisoner to be tryed att Bristoll where your peticioner could not have his most materiall witnesses, to prove both his guilt and Confession of it ye said Dominico tooke advantage thereof to avoyd your peticioners just accusation And out of meere malice and Revenge hath accused your peticioner most falsely with matters of very great consequence of which your peticioner is not guilty in ye least your Peticioner being able to prove ye premisses at [*sc.* and] yt ye said Dominico is guilty of other and greater Crimes and being ready to cleare and Justify his owne Innocency as to anything hee is charged with Most humbly prayeth your Majestyes most Royal favour and Order yt your peticioners accuser may appeare before your Majestys most honourable privy Council face to face to make out the cause of his false and malitious accusation and yt for so doing he make satisfaction to your peticioner for so infamous a scandall and yt your peticioner may be admitted to make his iust Defence and to vindicate his Innocence.'

record action that same Saturday. Their meeting that day was an occasion of considerable emotional tension. In their midst sat the king, arrayed in his robes of state with the great crown of St Edward on his head, as the royal assent was pronounced to the 'Act ... for disabling Papists from sitting in either House of Parliament'. In a speech from the throne the king made clear his own disapprobation of the act, 'which is of very great Importance, of which there may be ill Consequences hereafter'; but he had nevertheless been willing to give his assent, he said, 'to oblige them who have thought it fitting at this Time'. His concern arose from the consequent loss of some score or so of pro-government members. The remainder of the sitting was occupied by the farewell speeches of the Catholic peers, beginning with the Duke of Norfolk, recalling their good and loyal service now cut short; they did not fail to wring their hearers' hearts, and Norfolk received a special vote of thanks. It was in the aftermath, in the presence of both the king and the duke, and of the Bishop of London as well as Dr Barlow of Lincoln and Dr Fell of Oxford, that Gratiano's deposition was at last read to the House. For all the urgency of proceeding, the 'words uttered' do not appear in the printed *Journal* or in the fair copy from which it was made: the drama of the main business of the day no doubt led to a more perfunctory record of this item. But the clerk's rough minutes from which the official version was written up record that Georgirenes' words were 'of one who hoped to heare masse in Bristoll Cathedrall'. Received on such a day it is not hard to imagine the dramatic effect of Gratiano's deposition, nor the seriousness with which it was viewed. The Lords were shocked – many of them, no doubt, had joined the king and the duke in supporting the archbishop's scheme for a Greek church when it was launched in the previous year – and they at once issued an order for the sheriffs of Bristol 'to take especial Care ... that the said *Dominico Gratiano* may be forthwith sent up ... in safety, to attend the House of Peers'.[42] Secretary Coventry, however, foresaw a problem in securing the sheriffs' compliance. On the

42 *LJ*, xiii, p. 395; House of Lords Record Office, MS Journal of the House, lvii, 30 Carol. 2nd, 23 May–30 Dec. 1678, p. 531; MS minute book ('Journall'), 17 May–30 Dec. 1678, under 30 November. It was the last business of the day.

same day, 30 November, he wrote formally from Whitehall to seek the opinion of the attorney general, Sir William Jones:

> I have received an information from Bristoll that one Dominico a Prisoner in their Newgate upon an action of debt from the Greek bishop that gathereth money for the building the Greek Church, accuseth the said Bishop of divers dangerous words & some of them relating to this Plott. Quaere whether my Letter to the Major of Bristoll be a legal authority to the Major to send both the accuser & accused up hither; the first being a Prisoner for debt; or if not I pray advise what course is to be taken.[43]

Since Dominico Gratiano was imprisoned for debt, the problem was whether, if he was released and sent to London, the authorities in Bristol would become liable to his creditor (in this case Georgirenes). Meanwhile the excitement and urgency of inquiries into the Plot had led to the establishment of yet another special investigating committee, this time of the Privy Council. The latter began to take an interest in Georgirenes' alleged indiscretion in their session of 5 December, the very first day of their commission.[44] The committee ordered both Gratiano and the archbishop to 'Attend uppon some complaints from Bristoll against him relating to words for hopeing for and encouraging Popery'. But since Georgirenes was not in London, he was ordered to 'attend their Lordships at his Retorne'.

As Secretary Coventry had anticipated, when the Lords' order reached Bristol on 7 December, it produced a degree of consternation among the city fathers. They were indeed concerned that compliance would entail releasing from the Bristol Newgate one imprisoned for debt, and that they might thereby themselves become liable to his creditor. By return a reply to the secretary was drafted by the town clerk, Jonathan Romsey. Couched in suitably obsequious terms, it mentions a covering letter sent earlier the same day with a copy of the examination of Gratiano already held locally – a further copy had been entrusted to the mayor to be delivered by hand to the Marquis of Worcester – and goes on to inform Coventry that Gratiano had not yet been sent to London since 'theyre obedience of that order had Exposed the Sherriffes to Contest the Jurisdiction of the Lords against that

43 TNA, SP 44/51, p. 94.
44 Oxford, Bodl. Lib., MS. Rawl. A 136, pp. 439–40.

of the Kinges bench in case an escape had bene brought against them': they would of course comply once they had received a further order covering this issue.[45] It is not clear whether Romsey's letter had reached the Lords by 11 December; but on that day, evidently fortified by an opinion from the attorney general in answer to Coventry's inquiry of 30 November, the Bristol fathers found the means to overcome their anxieties by making use of the Habeas Corpus procedure. At a meeting of the House attended by the king and the duke, as well as Archbishop Sancroft and Bishops Compton and Fell (but not Barlow), it was ordered that 'His Majesty's Writ of *Habeas Corpus ad Testificandum* be directed to the Sheriff of *Bristol*, for bringing *Dominico Gratiano* ... to testify against *Josephus Georgerine*, concerning dangerous Words uttered by the said *Josephus Georgerine*.'[46] Obedience to a writ of Habeas Corpus would be a sufficient defence before the King's Bench, if any action were brought against the sheriff for permitting the 'escape' of a debtor. It may be thought that the phrasing of the order implies a view of the burden of proof: it is not so much for Gratiano to prove the archbishop guilty as for the latter to establish his innocence. And it must be borne in mind that the archbishop, by his own account, spoke no English. The disputed conversation, if it took place, will have been in Italian – and Gratiano was the sole possible witness to what would certainly have been regarded as evidence of treasonable intent were he to be believed.

Meanwhile Romsey had written yet again to Secretary Coventry, on 9 December, enclosing a copy of a second deposition by Gratiano taken that day before the mayor; who, he said, had also sent a copy to the Marquis of Worcester. Most powerful of the local magnates, and deeply sceptical of the existence of the Plot, Worcester was already closely involved in the Lords' investigation as a result of the intervention from Bristol of Bedloe, who was to provide the most plausible and circumstantial corroboration of Oates' tale. Romsey added that he had tried to discover where 'the Graecian Bppe' was to be found, but could only suggest an approach to the latter's brother Lawrence, who lived in a house of his own near the Greek church in Soho.

45 Longleat, Wilts., Coventry Papers from the archives of the Marquess of Bath at Longleat, vol. 5, fol. 378: letter dated 7 December [1678].

46 *LJ*, xiii, p. 412.

The copy of Gratiano's deposition which was enclosed with Romsey's letter is preserved among Coventry's papers. Worcester handed in his copy to the Lords' Examinations Committee on 12 December;[47] and a further copy, forwarded to the Examinations Committee of the Commons, is preserved among the papers of the chairman of that committee, Sir George Treby.[48] The Coventry and Treby copies are identical, and run as follows:

> Bristoll. The further Information of Dominico Gratiano taken the ninth day of December 1678
>
> Who says upon his Oath that upon the third day of August last past Josephus Georgerini a Graecian Bishopp (as he styles himselfe) being then in this Citty did in his discourse say unto the Deponent that he did not question but that the Duke of Yorke would be King of England in a short tyme & that then he the said Georgerine should be preferr'd to a Bishoppricke under him in this Kingdome.

Having seen Gratiano's second deposition the House (including, of interested parties, the king, the duke, the Archbishop of Canterbury, and the three bishops of London, Lincoln and Oxford) directed a further order, at once more detailed and more reassuring, to the sheriffs of the county

47 HL/PO/JT/1/1, p. 88, of Thurs.12 Dec. 1678. The date of the deposition is here given as '9° 7bris 78' presumably a slip rather than a reference to yet another, earlier, deposition.

48 48 Derbyshire County Record Office, Matlock, D 239 M/O 1604 (among the Fitzherbert papers, see HMC, *Thirteenth Report*, Appendix, pt vi, *Manuscripts of Sir William Fitzherbert, Bart.* (London, 1893), p. 141). This deposition is the first evidence for the date of the archbishop's alleged remarks. Newly elected MP for Plympton Erne, at a by-election in 1677, and a future Lord Chief Justice, Treby took seriously the responsibilities of the chairmanship of this 'secret committee'. He was careful to keep its deliberations secret, and free from interference. When he was criticized for the omission of Sir George Wakeman from the list of accused plotters in his report, he retorted, 'If the House does command me to inform them of any transactions of my committee, then I am discharged of secrecy. Persons named in the impeachment are not there for names' sake; but for that, several kinds of men of all professions, cardinals not excepted, had a hand in the plot.' Quoted in B. D. Henning, *History of Parliament: The House of Commons, 1660–1690*, 3 vols (London, 1983), iii, pp. 580–3.

and city of Bristol, the keeper of Newgate Prison in Bristol and other concerned officers. The Lords insisted that Gratiano must indeed be delivered to them, but in whatever custody the sheriffs considered adequate to assure his safe return to their jurisdiction once his evidence had been given; and they made it clear that they would pay the expenses of the journey in both directions.[49]

On the same day that the Lords made this new order, they wound up their committee and handed their papers and the whole enquiry over to the existing committee of the Privy Council which had hitherto chiefly concentrated on the narrower question of the murder of Sir Edmund Berrie Godfrey. The membership of this committee included, Secretary Williamson, Lord Treasurer Danby, Lord Chamberlain Arlington, Secretary Coventry and at least six other senior peers.[50] This was the forum in which the inquiry into the allegations against Georgirenes would continue.

Although the investigation had now been entrusted to the Privy Council Committee, nevertheless, when Gratiano at last reached London, it was the full House of Lords, sitting on the afternoon of Saturday 21 December which ordered that Gratiano should appear before the Lord Chief Justice and meanwhile be committed to the Marshalsea Prison to remain in 'readiness to be sent for, as this House shall see cause'.[51] And it was the same day, at its morning session, that the Lords' Committee had heard the evidence concerning the disposal of Godfrey's body, which had been carried in a sedan from Somerset House 'as far as the new Grecian Church in *the Soho*'.[52] The statement cannot have failed to startle the attention of those privy councillors who heard it, and then again when the same

49 11 Dec. 1678, *LJ*, xiii, p. 414; cf. MS Journal (see n. 48), lvii, p. 584.

50 Oxford, Bodl. Lib., MS. Rawl. A 136, p. 1, 12 Dec. 1678. The attendance of Essex, indeed, or of the Lord Privy Seal or the Earl of Bridgwater, was required in order for any session to be recognized as quorate.

51 *LJ*, xiii, p. 430; cf. MS Journal of the House, lvii, p. 630 – to which a second hand has added in the margin, 'German bishop comitted to ye Marshalsea'! Among those present: the king, Duke of York, Archbishop of Canterbury, Bishop of London; but not the bishops of Lincoln or Oxford.

52 HL/PO/JT/1/1, vol. ii, pp. 19f.; *LJ*, xiii, pp. 436ff., esp. 438; MS Journal of the House, lvii, p. 654.

members found Gratiano on the afternoon agenda of the Lords; it will not have helped Georgirenes that the precincts of his new church could be thus stigmatized as a safe haven for murderous villainy.

These investigations continued amid immense political convulsions. Ralph Montagu, former ambassador in Paris, had recently revealed secret negotiations in which Lord Treasurer Danby had taken part. On 23 December Danby was impeached, though four days later, on 27 December, the Lords refused to commit him to prison.[53] He had been a leading investigator of the Plot since the beginning. Three days later still, on 30 December, in the wake of this crisis the long-serving Restoration Parliament was prorogued, and shortly afterwards it was dissolved, with elections called for a new Parliament to assemble on 6 March. The Privy Council's work was not, however, interrupted and its investigations continued daily.[54] The archbishop himself had evidently now been found, perhaps at the home of his brother Lawrence in Soho, as the Bristolians had suggested. The story resumes on 2 January 1679, when the committee considered Gratiano's deposition and agreed to send a copy of it to Georgirenes, 'who is to retorne Answer thereunto with all Convenient Speed and then their Lordships will report the whole matter to his Majesty in Councell'.[55] By the end of another week Georgirenes had responded, and at a well-attended session the committee resolved to submit Gratiano's deposition and the archbishop's answer to magistrates, who would also interview the parties. Sir James Butler, KC, was chosen to head the investigation. He was instructed to summon the archbishop to answer the accusation in the presence of Gratiano. When he

53 See Kenyon, *Popish Plot*, pp. 148–9. A. Browning, *Thomas Osborne Earl of Danby*, 3 vols (Glasgow, 1944–51), i, ch. 13.

54 TNA, 2/66 (Privy Council Reg., Chas II, vol. xiii), p. 503; further reinforced three times in early January, PC 2/67 (vol. xiv), pp. 6, 8, 16.

55 Oxford, Bodl. Lib., MS Rawl. A 136, fol. 5. Two days later, 4 January, the committee received through the Marquis of Worcester a letter from the ever-vigilant Mayor of Bristol, warning of a fire to be 'effected by Mr Bedlow', that crucial witness in the Godfrey affair. In response, they asked Worcester to encourage the mayor to be careful – 'but know not how to make any thing of the advice', ibid. fol. 15. On 6 Jan. the committee wrote to the mayor commending his good work: TNA, PC2/67, p. 5, the letter received on 3 Jan., and referred to the committee.

had done this, Butler was to send a report back to the Lords, who would lay the whole matter before the king.[56]

As chief investigator, Sir James Butler was an interesting choice. Born *c.*1642 into an obscure branch of the rambling Anglo-Irish family headed by the twelfth Earl (later first Duke) of Ormonde, Butler held, among other perquisites, the post of attorney general to the Catholic Queen Catherine, for whom he would have held a watching brief as a succession of 'witnesses', and whom the House of Commons came ever closer to accusing of direct complicity in the Plot. He must have been as well acquainted as anyone with every brick of the huge and creaking, though not yet crumbling, edifice built on Oates' shifting foundations. It must be remembered that the king, who was present at the Council on 9 January when Butler was selected, was by this time himself beginning to believe that some germ of truth lay behind the story of the Plot; it should also be remembered that Charles had given Georgirenes substantial support for his Greek church, and that the archbishop's patron was the Duke of York. In these circumstances Butler may not have been inclined to be over-zealous in the search for incriminating evidence. So it is probably significant that he chose as his colleague an elderly courtier, Member of Parliament for Bridgwater until the recent dissolution. Sir Edmund Windham, of the Somerset family of that name, was now seventy-eight years old. Born c.1600, he had entered Parliament in the year of King James I's death, and had been a member, on

56 Oxford, Bodl Lib., MS. Rawl. A 136, fol. 31. 'There was this day read before the Lords of the Committee an answer from the ArchBishop of Samos to a deposition made against him by Dominico Gratiano in November last, He being then a prissoner in Bristoll at the suite of the said Arch Bishop. But whereas he is now removed to Kings Bench, where this matter well Ley faire for Examination, The Lords have comanded me to send you the said Deposition, and the said Answer and that you would take to your assistance some Other Justice of the peace [and] summon the Arch Bishop to Attend you there and in the presente of Gratiano to answer what is Objected and when you have considered the Nature of the Objection and the defence their Lordships dessier you would send them a report of the matter together with your Opinions thereupon that so their Lordships may lay the whole matter before his Majestie in Councell and receive his finall pleasure therein. I am &c –'. As usual, the Marquis of Worcester was among those present.

and off, since then, with the notable exception of the Cromwellian years when (unlike so many) he did not stay to trim but took himself abroad.[57] His wife, Christabella Pyne, had been governess to the young Prince Charles. The Windhams remained close to Charles in exile and as king;[58] Sir Edmund was regarded as a dependent of the court, mouthpiece of government. He had been appointed to take some of the depositions against Coleman; and the Commons had made him a member of the committee entrusted with the examination of Coleman's letters.[59] Had they been still in session, even the more excitable members would have found it hard to cavil at Butler's choice of Windham as his colleague. Yet neither the king nor the duke will have felt cause for any apprehension.

The story ends on Monday 18 January 1679, when Sir Edmund Windham and Sir James Butler reported on their examination under oath of both Dominico Gratiano and the Archbishop of Samos. They judged that 'the Enformer [was] unlikely to have been trusted so far in matters of that weight and secresy by one that persued him with the severity of the Law'. In consequence their Lordships were of the opinion that the archbishop should be discharged on giving security of £200 to appear when required.[60]

The demand for security in the form of a very large sum of £200 – twice as much as the king's very generous donation towards the Greek church, perhaps equal to the contributions of both the king and the Duke of York together – may indicate that the Lords of the Council were not altogether satisfied of Georgirenes' innocence, or perhaps simply that they wished him to be more prompt in his attendance should they ever have need to require

57 See the very full account by Irene Cassidy in Henning, *History of Parliament … 1660–1690*, iii, pp. 773–5.

58 Cf. his signed letter from Paris, Oxford, Bodl. Lib., MS Carte 130, fol. 151 (old fol. 131).

59 *CJ*, ix, pp. 524 (31 Oct.), 539 (14 Nov.).

60 Oxford, Bodl. Lib., MS Rawl. A 136, fol. 91; the Archbishop of Canterbury was among those present. The judgment delivered by Windham and Butler was not quite the last word. It was not until 24 Oct. 1679 that the Bristol sheriffs, William Jackson and William Clutterbuck, Esqs, succeeded in obtaining an order for the repayment of the expenses of their sending Gratiano to London to be questioned: TNA, PC 2/68 (Privy Council Reg., Chas II, vol. xv), p. 247.

it in future. But there is no evidence of any further action, or that the security was ever called upon. And by May 1679 the archbishop had resumed his peregrinations in search of support for his church. Amid the hysteria of that autumn and winter, which even forced the king to banish his brother, by the time the new Parliament assembled on 6 March, Georgirenes had had a fortunate escape; others before and after were executed for no greater crime than that alleged against him, and on no better evidence. Certainly it was well for him that no one appears to have known of his venture of collaboration with the Church of Rome, still less of Cardinal Altieri's support of his initiative at Bibbona. Even more surprisingly, no play was made with the circumstances of his arrival in England from Paris only two years previously, when his gift of manuscripts to Louis XIV may well have been rewarded with an introduction to his royal patrons in London. Certainly he was lucky not to have been named in Coleman's correspondence with Père de la Chaise. And was he innocent in fact? The argument which persuaded the Council was very English, very characteristically class-conscious: Gratiano was, after all, not only an embezzler but the archbishop's former *servant*.[61] It is hardly conclusive. But we shall never know.

61 It is intriguing to notice that the Marquis of Worcester, who, however, was not present at this sitting, had himself used an almost identical argument to refute an allegation that he was involved, alongside his Badminton servants, in the royalist Gloucestershire Plot of 1659: he would never, he had said, 'entrust common porters with what so highly concerned his life and his estate'. In those days the argument cut less ice, for he found himself imprisoned for two months in the Tower: see McClain, *Beaufort*, p. 31.

CHAPTER 9

Exclusion from England (1679–1682)

The Greek archbishop owed his discharge on 18 January 1679 to a very English assumption about class, and he may well have been fortunate at that. The conviction of others on no better information than that laid against him continued throughout 1679, the smoke of suspicion and the flames of accusations made by Oates and others continually fanned by politicians of both Lords and Commons, whose overriding concern was to preserve the Protestant succession and therefore to exclude the Catholic Duke of York. The 'exclusion crisis' was indeed the dominant theme in politics from 1679 to 1681. It became the obstacle to all progress on any other front.[1] For the king, determined that his brother should eventually succeed him, and no doubt more prepared to accept his assurance that his own personal religion would not induce him to subvert the Protestant settlement, this political ferment created a severe dilemma. On the one hand Charles needed Parliament from time to time to grant him the substantial funds required to conduct his government and especially to maintain the armed forces; on the other, he sought to restrain it from seizing every opportunity to promote legislation whose purpose was to isolate or even to remove the duke. When James refused to resume conformity with the Church of England the king wrote with anguished spelling to 'my Dearest freend the Ducke of Yorck', instructing him to leave the court and go abroad:

> you may bee shoore, I shall never desier it longer then it will bee absolutly nessecairy, boht for your good & my service, ... and desire it may bee as soone, as conveniently

1 See, for instance, J. Miller, *Popery and Politics in England, 1660–1688* (Cambridge, 1973), pp. 169–88; idem, *James II: A Study in Kingship*, rev. ed. (London, 1989), pp. 92ff.; J. P. Kenyon, *The Popish Plot*, 2nd edn (London, 1983), pp. 132–76; A. Fraser, *Charles II* (London, 1979), pp. 354–75, 392–8.

> you cane, you may nicely be leve, wiht waht troubel I write this to you, there beeing nothing I am moer sensibel of then your constant kindnes, ... and I hope you are so just to mee, as to be assured, that no absens, nor any thing ells, cane ever change me from being trouely and kindly yours C.R.[2]

On 3 March 1679 the Duke and Duchess of York sailed for Holland. Three days later a new Parliament duly met, and quickly showed itself no more biddable than the old, even though in his speech from the throne the king, undertaking to exercise both existing and new laws against Papists, included a very specific and conciliatory passage:

> And, above all, I have commanded My Brother to absent himself from Me, because I would not leave the most Malicious Men Room to say, I had not removed all Causes which could be pretended to influence Me towards Popish Counsels.[3]

Amid these relentless manoeuvres against his now banished patron the Duke of York, and following his own narrow escape from mortal suspicion of popish aspirations, it is small wonder that Georgirenes' first instinct was to quit this dangerous field and return to the more familiar (if no less hazardous) world of Orthodoxy in the Archipelago.

His friend Antoine Galland, who spent the first nine months of 1679 at Marseilles, awaiting the moment to embark for a third and more prolonged journey to the East – his second, it will be recalled, had occupied something less than a year, while the archbishop was engaged in building the London church – recalls that while there he received a copy of the 1677 English translation which Denton had made and published from Galland's own French translation of Georgirenes' book, written originally in Greek. It will no doubt have been a letter enclosed with Denton's translation that told Galland of Georgirenes' plans: 'J'apprends qu' après avoir vu l'Italie, la France et l'Angleterre, il doit bientôt se rendre en cette ville de Marseille pour retourner dans l'Archipel' [I think that having seen Italy, France and England, he must soon present himself in this town of Marseilles to return to the Archipelago]. Galland was delighted by the news of the archbishop's

2 BL, Add. MS 32095, fol. 164. For this episode, see Miller, *James II*, pp. 88–91.

3 6 March 1679, *LJ*, xiii, p. 449.

impending arrival. It raised the hope that he might at last have the opportunity to persuade Georgirenes to share his knowledge of a wider range of islands than his book described, and so contribute 'au dessein que j'ai sur une description générale de tout l'Archipel' [the plan which I have for a general account of the whole archipelago].[4] In the event the archbishop did not come, and the *Description générale* was never written. But at least the arrival of the English edition released Galland from an undertaking he had made when Georgirenes first left Paris for England that he would not publish his French version of Georgirenes' book until it had appeared first in English. Galland now occupied himself in preparing a new edition of Georgirenes' book, retranslating Denton's English back into French (since he no longer had access to his own earlier translation), supplemented here and there from his own memory of Georgirenes' original Greek. This he completed; and when at last he sailed, in September 1679, he left it to be published in Paris as part of a volume which would also contain his own substantial book *Smyrne ancienne et moderne* together with a slighter *Relation de l'île de Tine* by Jacques-Paul Babin, a Jesuit.[5]

Meanwhile the archbishop's resolve to stay in England had somehow been stiffened. There was no more talk of flight to Marseilles. Instead, there was the duty to find maintenance for the church he had founded. It was to this that he now turned his attention, and it is probably to this phase that we should ascribe an undated petition of 'Joseph Gogorino, Archbishop of Samos, to the King', to be found among the State Papers:

> Petition for a brief throughout England for the benevolence of people whereby he may be enabled to maintain the Greek church and himself, and to relieve his countrymen who came to England in distress. The money given him was laid out in building the church, in supporting himself and family and in assisting his countrymen that have been slaves and fled hither, so that now he has nothing left.[6]

4 Galland, *Voyages inédits*, pp. 250–1.

5 On his return from a decade travelling in the East, Galland was to find that the book had not progressed beyond manuscript. Galland's manuscript is now in the Cabinet des Manuscrits of the Royal Library in Brussels, Bibliothèque Royale de Belgique, MS II 5359.

6 *CSPD, 1680–81*, pp. 691–2.

It would appear that his petition was granted. By the latter part of May 1679 the archbishop was back on the road for the first time since the debacle at Bristol. On 21 May, an entry in the account book of Haddon Hall, the Derbyshire residence of the Earl of Rutland, records that £5 was paid to the earl 'which hee gave to the grecion Church in London'.[7] The decision to approach the Earl of Rutland may have been significant, for it was the earl's daughter, Lady Chaworth, who had been the first identifiable member of the aristocracy to notice the presence of the archbishop, in a letter written to her brother Lord Roos, to Belvoir Castle, on 10 March 1677.[8] At any rate, the approach was successful, and £5 a not negligible amount.

It was no doubt on the same journey that Georgirenes met the Presbyterian divine Samuel Ogden, whom in Cromwellian days the Earl of Rutland, himself a Covenanter, had presented to the benefice of Fairfield in Derbyshire, on the edge of Buxton. Ogden was a scholar and a brilliant teacher, who in the 1670s was running a school in Derby. Writing of him in 1713, Edmund Calamy is full of his praises and noted that he was indeed 'a very ingenious Man, and a Polite and excellent scholar'.[9]

> He valu'd no Notions that were mean or trivial, but was ever taken up with the more Curious and Manly Parts of Learning. … He was a good Languist, he wrote pure *Latin*. He would take *Eusebius* or any other such *Greek* Author, and read it. Currently in *English* at first sight. When the pretended Archbishop of *Samos* Travel'd through *England*, he visited Mr *Ogden*, who entertain'd him in the *Greek* Tongue.[10]

7 Belvoir Castle, Leicestershire, volume headed 'Haddon | Mr Edwd Sympson^{s} Act: pro | Anno 1678–1679': pp. 1–9 list income and rents, then new numbering from p. 1 lists expenses for Lord Rutland; the donation for the 'grecion [*sic*] Church' is to be found on p. 11.

8 Belvoir Castle, MS Add. 7, 'Letters from Grace Lady Chaworth to her Brother John Lord Roos, … 1663–98', no. 60: see above, p. 166.

9 E. Calamy, *An Account of the Ministers, Lecturers, Lecturers, Masters and Fellows of Colleges and Schoolmasters, who were Ejected or Silenced after the Restoration in 1660* (London, 1713), as vol. ii of the second edition of his *Abridgement of Mr Baxter's History of his Life and Times*, 1st edn (London, 1702), p. 192.

10 Ibid. By the time Calamy wrote, Georgirenes' reputation was at a low ebb. 'Pretended' could as well be a reference to the archbishop's continuing use of the title he had resigned, now held by a successor. See below, p. 214 and n. 19.

Sadly, neither party to this conversation has left an account of it. It is probable that Georgirenes will not have been altogether happy to undergo another cross-examination of the kind he had had to parry in his days with Thomas Smith. He was ready to move on.

A week after leaving Haddon Hall, on 28 May, the archbishop next appears at the other great residence of the Rutlands, Belvoir Castle. There too he received £5, from Rutland's son and heir Lord Roos, who already knew of him from his sister Lady Chaworth.[11] On the following day – Oak Apple Day – the minutes of the corporation of Lincoln record the decision by a large majority to make the archbishop a donation. Again it is for the by now standard amount of £5.[12] Who else may have been approached, we can only guess: there were many stately seats and many corporations on the road from London to Derby, Derby to Lincoln, and many more on the route back to Soho.

While Georgirenes toured the northern midlands for funds, the political situation in London had gone from bad to worse, if that were possible. On 27 May 1679 Parliament was prorogued to 14 August, but on 12 July it was dissolved and elections called for a new Parliament to assemble on 7 October. Meanwhile, an unprecedented degree of genuine anxiety was aroused when on 22 August the king fell suddenly and dangerously ill, apparently of malaria.[13] The duke was summoned to his bedside. He reached England on 2 September; and although he returned to the Continent three weeks later, he took with him the assurance of the Lord Mayor of London that he would have been proclaimed king had the occasion arisen. It is possible that in those three weeks Georgirenes had managed to see the duke, or at least to find in the lord mayor's assurance reason for new confidence

11 HMC, *Manuscripts of the Duke of Rutland at Belvoir Castle*, 4 vols (London, 1888–1905), iv, p. 553. I have not been able to see the original, and there is a temptation to consider the HMC's reference a confusion with that in the Haddon account book, which is housed at Belvoir. But the date given is different, and time and place are entirely plausible, since (unlike Haddon) Belvoir is an easy day's journey from Lincoln.

12 HMC, *Fourteenth Report*, Appendix, pt viii, *Manuscripts of Lincoln ... Lichfield ... etc* (London, 1895), p. 107.

13 Fraser, *Charles II*, pp. 381ff.

in the long-term stability of his own position. To other eyes, the new risk of the sudden death of the hitherto formidably healthy king gave increased urgency to the need for legislation in Parliament to exclude the Duke of York from the succession. Against this Charles was adamant. Parliament, called for 7 October, did not in fact meet until 17 October, and was immediately prorogued to 26 January 1680.[14]

The frustration and resentment which the king's characteristically robust response provoked, especially among the Commons whose behaviour he was less able to control than that of the more deferential Lords, erupted into further public demonstrations and even more enthusiastic pope-burnings than usual, and into a flurry of petition-signing designed to press the king into allowing Parliament its head.[15]

It was against this background of continuing anxiety amounting to hysteria over the Popish Plot itself, and frustration at the king's steadfast determination not to give the Commons their head, keenly felt in London and particularly so in the new Middlesex suburbs such as Soho, that Georgirenes had resumed his struggle to maintain the church that he had built and to retain the congregation which he led. For him the absence of the Duke of York was a mixed blessing. On the one hand he had suffered the loss of his patron who, though never actually excluded from the succession, despite more than one positive majority vote in the Commons, discreetly kept away from England and was appointed to manage the affairs of Scotland, where he remained until 1682.[16] On the positive side, if his close association with the duke had served to fuel the suspicion of Catholic sympathies which had so nearly brought him down, the removal of this

14 *LJ*, xiii (1675–81), pp. 595–7.

15 Petitions, cf. William Harbord's exclamation to the House of Commons in 1680 that 'next to Popery the matter of petitioning is the greatest point': A Grey ed., *Debates of the House of Commons 1667–94*, 10 vols (London, 1769), vii, p. 387. The complex detail of this petitioning is well summarized by M. Knights, 'London's "Monster" Petition of 1680', *Historical Journal*, xxxvi (1993), pp. 39–67.

16 For this part of James' career, see Miller, *James II*, pp. 92–110.

link perhaps enabled him to make a fresh start on the difficult task of raising support for his church.

But there were more serious obstacles to be overcome. During the winter of 1679–80 the archbishop became aware that he was not the only beggar on the road, soliciting support for the Greek church. The *London Gazette* for 9–12 February 1680 has the story.

> Whereas a Grecian Minister of a high Stature, with black bushy hair and a long black beard, whose name is Joachim Cicileano, of the Isle of *Ceffalonia*, has gone up and down the Country under the name of the Bishop of *Samos* in *Greece*, and hath been assisted with Christian Contributions towards building the Grecian Church, which he hath lewdly spent, to the prejudice of the said Church and the scandal of the said Bishop. Now to prevent any farther abuse to the Countrey, these are to give notice that the said Bishop of *Samos* is an indifferent tall man and slender, with long black hair, having a wart on the right side of his nose just against his eye, a Cut under his right eye, and black whiskers with very little Beard; which said Bishop writ the History of *Samos*, and with the Assistance of good Christians hath built and almost finished the Grecian Church in *Sohoe* Fields, by Licence from His Majesty.[17]

It is quite possible that it was in fact Cicileano, and not Georgirenes, who was the 'pretended Archbishop of *Samos*' entertained by Samuel Ogden 'in the *Greek* Tongue' in Derbyshire, as recalled in Edmund Calamy's later account published in 1713.[18] If so, then the Earl of Rutland and his son, as well as the city of Lincoln, will have been among his victims. But since it is indubitably Georgirenes himself, and not an impostor, who was to be stigmatized already in the 1690s, several years before Calamy wrote, as 'the false titular Archbishop of Samos', presumably on the ground that he continued to use the title though he had resigned the see, it seems likely

17 *London Gazette*, No. 1485v, dated '1679'.

18 Cf. p. 210 and n. 10. Georgirenes had encountered Cicileano before at Bibbona (see Chapter 5, n. 42) and Cicileano evidently suffered no great harm by this exposure, for he was surely the Ciciliano 'of Caffalonia' who was still in England in 1685, when his departure for Greece is recorded in *CSPD, 1685*, ed. F. Bickley (London, 1960), p. 434, as noticed by P. A. Bezodis, in *Survey of London*, xxxiii, p. 281.

that the Derbyshire traveller was in fact Georgirenes himself.[19] What is clear, however, is that in February 1680 the genuine archbishop was still concerned to secure support for his church: whatever he may have told Galland in his despair of the previous year, he was now determined to continue, and to see the project through.

Meanwhile in far-off Constantinople much greater trouble was brewing, and it would be astonishing if no rumble of distant thunder from it had reached the archbishop. It will be recalled that in early December 1677 Thomas Smith had noted in a letter to his friend Edward Bernard that the Bishop of London had not yet had a response from Patriarch Dionysios IV to a letter he had sent him concerning the Greek church.[20] The increasingly ominous silence had continued through 1678, and was at last broken in February 1679 when the patriarch approached the English ambassador, Sir John Finch, and opened a discussion of the theological and ecclesiological issues involved.

To the subtle Byzantine mind, they were anything but as simple and straightforward as 'colonel' Bishop Compton no doubt supposed. The ambassador, though by inclination and training more of a professor of Anatomy than a diplomat, and disquietingly aware of his inadequacy in his current post, was at least keenly interested in matters theological which he was not at all unwilling to discuss. On 17 February 1679 Sir John in Constantinople received a commission of five Orthodox archbishops, led by the Archbishop of Herakleia and sent by Patriarch Dionysios IV.[21] They reported that the patriarch was concerned to learn more about the foundation of the Greek church in London. Finch replied that the church had been established with support from the king and the Duke of York

19 The damaging phrase is Benjamin Woodroffe's, a marginal note in the manuscript of his *Draught or Model of a Colledge*, London, BL, Additional MS, 70263, Portland MS, Harley Papers, File 11, Letters W-Z; see E. D. Tappe, 'The Greek College in Oxford', in P. M. Doll, ed., *Anglicanism and Orthodoxy* (Oxford, 2006), pp. 153–74 and pp. 415–20.

20 Oxford, Bodl. Lib., MS Smith lvii, p. 18.

21 HMC, *Report on the Manuscripts of the Late Allan George Finch, Esq., of Burley-on-the-Hill, Rutland*, ii, pp. 148–50.

(there was no mention of the Archbishop of Samos) and that the Bishop of London had set out the conditions under which the church might operate in conformity with the laws of the English church and state. Finch went on to name the four conditions, which were exactly the same as those listed by Georgirenes in the declaration that he had sent to Thomas Smith in April the previous year: no icons in the church, no adherence to the doctrine of transubstantiation, no prayers to saints and no conformity to the Council of Bethlehem/Jerusalem (1672).[22] The prelates' response was unanimous and unambiguous. To the first condition they objected that

> they could not without pictures in their church officiate, and that they could upon no conditions be stript of them. To the second they gave an answer with much heat and exclamation, saying that they differ'd not from the Church of Rome as to the point of transubstantiation, and then with one voice thundred out that the very Body of Christ that was crucify'd on Mount Calvery, was after consecration there present and that they would never alter this doctrine.

To the third condition they retorted that 'all their Liturgys were composed of prayers to saints and to the Blessed Virgin'. As to the Synod of Bethlehem (otherwise known as the Synod of Jerusalem), they claimed rather implausibly to know nothing of its import and so had nothing to say of it.

Finch now warmed to the theme: in England popery was against the law, 'and t'wer the same thing to the government of his Majesty, and scandal to the Church and people of England, that these "tenents" should be published and practised in Greek as in Latin'. Icons and prayers to saints were unknown to the early Church; and the doctrine of transubstantiation was as much at odds with the circumstances of the Last Supper as it was with common sense. 'But I added that I should acquaint my Lord of London with their resolution'. The Greek archbishops did not yield an inch on those three topics and now invoked the authority of the patriarch and the Holy Synod to add three further demands: that leavened bread might be allowed to be used for the sacrament, that in the Creed the Holy Ghost be said to proceed from the Father only, and – most provocatively – that the Greek church in London be removed from the jurisdiction of the Bishop

22 See above p. 180.

of London and, like that in Venice, be placed instead under the jurisdiction of the patriarch himself. Finch replied that the use of leavened bread raised no difficulty: it was indeed the practice of the Church of England, against that of Rome. But the eastern view of the procession of the Holy Ghost was 'directly repugnant to the articles of our Church', and therefore quite inadmissible. As for their 'extravagant and unreasonable demand' for the Greek church in London to be removed from the authority of the diocesan and transferred to that of the patriarch, Finch allowed that the patriarch might be given the right to appoint ministers of the church but left the commission in no doubt that, as to jurisdiction, 'my Lord Bishop of London would never be deprived of his right in his own diocese, of governing ecclesiastical affayrs under his Majesty, and that I could not give them the least hopes of such an ill-grounded demand'. At this the meeting broke up, Finch undertaking to acquaint the Bishop of London with what had been said, and to bring the patriarch 'his Lordship's sense of the whole conference' in due course. Compton's reaction is not recorded, but is not hard to guess.[23]

Discussions were evidently drawn out for one year more. Finally, on 27 January 1680 Finch sent a further letter from Constantinople to the Bishop of London, 'being a fundamentall account of what relates to the Greeke church designed to be settled in England'.[24] Of course the patriarch could not trim and compromise as Georgirenes had been prepared to do. But his refusal to give way at any point was the death knell for the hope of a Greek church in London. Although Georgerines continued to seek royal support it seems clear that his project was doomed.[25] The archbishop claimed in a broadsheet published in 1682 that he had raised £1,500 for the building of the church; £800 had been spent on the building itself and the remainder on 'servants' wages and those lines (?) in going about the country and in my maintenance for these six years last past'.[26] Georgirenes

23 See n. 21.

24 HMC, *Finch*, ii, p. 65.

25 *CSPD 1680–81*, pp. 691f.

26 London printed for A. F. There are two copies of this broadsheet in the Bodleian Library: MS Wood 417, no. 103, in a volume mainly of broadsheets and folios

claimed that the church in Soho Fields was 'too remote from the abodes of most of the Grecians (dwelling in the furthermost part of the city)'.[27] In these circumstances he was forced to try to sell the building back to the parish of St Martin in the Fields who held the head lease, but since the archbishop would not accept their derisory offer for the church, the men of the parish broke in and then sold the building to the Huguenots – who were favoured by the Bishop of London – and they continued to use it for worship until 1822.[28]

So the first Greek church in London had lasted for only four or five years. In spite of Georgirenes' intention to found a new Greek church in a more favourable part of London, circumstances were against him. Henry Compton, the Bishop of London who had originally favoured the project, had cooled; Thomas Smith had grown impatient of Georgirenes' opaque Orthodox theology; the Duke of York, who had been a particular supporter, was currently excluded from the kingdom; and the patriarch in Constantinople had implacably refused to accept the accommodating terms on which the archbishop had been allowed to establish his church in London. On a personal level Georgirenes had narrowly escaped being tried for treasonable Catholic sympathies: he was dogged by imposters and deceitful servants and abandoned by the intellectual theologians who had at first enthusiastically courted him. Clearly it was time for the archbishop to leave England and to move on: was it to be back to Italy and the Archipelago, or on to pastures new?

---

containing anti-papalist songs; and MS Ashmole F.1 (74), in a collection of tracts favourable to the French Protestant cause and hostile alike to papists and Quakers. See John P. Barron, 'Archbishop Joseph Georgirenes and the Prehistory of the Greek College', in P. M. Doll, ed., *Anglicanism and Orthodoxy 300 Years after the 'Greek College' in Oxford* (Oxford, 2006), pp. 79–112, at p. 84 n. 17.

27 See Jonathan Harris, 'Silent Minority: The Greek Community of Eighteenth-Century London', in D. Tziovas, ed., *Greek Diaspora and Migration since 1750: Society, Politics and Culture* (Aldershot, 2009), pp. 31–43, esp. pp. 34–5.

28 On 7 December 1681, The Vestry agreed to pay 'the Greeks' £168 for the church and no more, Westminster Archives Ccentre, F2004, Vestry Minutes St Martin in the Fields, f. 326. See P. A. Bezodis, in *Survey of London*, vol. xxxiii: *The Parish of St Anne Soho*, ed. F. H. Sheppard (London, 1966), p. 281.

EPILOGUE

The New World (1682–c.1700)

John-Paul A. Ghobrial

On 1 March 1694, a small fishing boat called the *San Sebastían* ran aground somewhere near Buenos Aires. When local residents gathered to the site, they came face to face with an eclectic and somewhat curious group of people. For among the survivors on board the *San Sebastían* that day were two friars of the Order of St Augustine, their servants – described as lesser clerics ('de menores ordenes') – and two African slaves. What was perhaps most striking about this motley crew of passengers were their diverse origins: of the two friars, Fr Juan de la Seca came from Spain and the other, Fr Francisco Guarino, was from Naples. As for the servants, one was English and the other Portuguese. And at the head of this ragtag assemblage was the captain and owner of the vessel, a Greek man with a distinctive beard whose name was Joseph. He called himself the Archbishop of Samos.

As he told it, they had been travelling southwards along the coast of Brazil in an attempt to reach the Colonia del Sacramento, a Portuguese settlement established in 1680 directly across the water from Buenos Aires. What Georgirenes could not explain, however, was what exactly he and his companions were doing there in the first place. Migration to the New World was heavily regulated by Spanish officials, and the Atlantic crossing required an individual to have obtained a special document (or 'licencia') issued by the king. None of them carried the appropriate paperwork. As for proof of the archbishop's identity, he claimed to have lost his papers in Brazil, somewhere in the region of Bahia where he had been travelling. Even so, he was able to present a copy of a curious document written in the Arabic script, which he insisted was the letter of appointment ('berat') to the archbishopric of Samos, which had been issued to him years earlier by the Ottoman sultan. Faced with such a strange story, Don Agustín de Robles, the governor of Río de la Plata since 1690, decided, quite sensibly, to encourage the archbishop and his companions to make haste and continue their efforts to reach Sacramento. Better the Portuguese than he when it came to the mess of paperwork that was likely to result from such mysterious and, almost certainly, illegal wayfarers.

The governor did not have his way in the end. For when the crew of the *San Sebastían* set out for a second time to reach Sacramento, they were caught in a sudden storm and the ship was cast back on land. This time, the boat was so badly damaged – and the archbishop himself had nearly drowned – that the governor decided to allow the group to remain in Buenos Aires, at least until he could obtain further guidance from Spain about what to do with them. It was in this way that Joseph Georgirenes once again found himself at the mercy of suspicious locals, setting off a flurry of paperwork between imperial officials anxious to figure out who this man was, how he got there, and what was his story.

It took Robles six weeks before he finally wrote back to Spain with news of the affair, and his letter set the stage for a long, detailed investigation of Georgirenes and his adventures in the New World. The result of this enquiry is preserved today in the Archive of the Indies in Seville, scattered across correspondence records, Inquisition files, and even a massive casebook containing interviews of ship captains, clerics, and others who had encountered Georgirenes in the New World. While a full study of this period of his life is now under preparation, a few important details suffice here to describe what happened to him after his departure from England. Georgirenes appears to have spent some time in Portugal before travelling onwards to Spain where, in November 1682, he obtained a royal licence allowing him to collect alms for a specific period of one year. In itself, this was unexceptional: there are countless examples of other Eastern Christians who, like Georgirenes, managed to obtain permission to collect alms in the Spanish empire. Indeed, the phenomenon was so regular that it warranted comment in a chapter on alms-collecting found in the book of laws of the Spanish empire published in 1681 where specific mention was made of 'Greeks, Armenians, and monks of mount Sinai'.[1] What is certain is that by

1 The full text of the law can be found in volume 1 of *Recopilación de Leyes de los Reynos de las Indias* (Madrid, 1681), book 1, chapter 21, law 10. For the story of one of Georgirenes's contemporaries in the New World, a Christian priest from Mosul,

the time of his shipwreck in March 1694 Georgirenes had long overstayed his welcome in the New World. In itself, that would have made him a target of suspicion on the part of royal authorities in Spain. Not surprisingly, when they read Robles's account of his appearance in Buenos Aires at a meeting of the Council of the Indies in November 1694, they immediately ordered that the archbishop and his companions be transferred back to Spain for further investigation and, most likely, punishment.[2]

It is unclear when news of the Council's decision first arrived to Buenos Aires. But as the order made its way across the Atlantic, Georgirenes's health must have been in decline because he appears to have prepared two wills in August and September 1695, which are preserved today in the Archivo General de la Nacion in Buenos Aires.[3] If he had preserved any sympathies for Anglicanism from his earlier adventures in England, they are entirely absent from the wills, both of which speak of his firm belief ('crehemos firmemente') in the mysteries of the Holy Trinity and his desire to 'live and die' as a Catholic. At the same time, the wills are a poignant testament to his memories of the Mediterranean world he left behind. He left his goods to his four brothers, named as Lawrence, Martin, Nicholas and Peter, although there is no evidence at all that any of them was ever with their brother in Buenos Aires.[4] He appointed his servant, perhaps secretary, Don Joseph Rendon as his executor, in appreciation for his fidelity to him throughout the period that he had served him.

It would have been months after Georgirenes had drawn up his wills (see Figure 4) that an order dated 12 December 1695 arrived from Madrid instructing Robles to send the archbishop, the two mendicants and their

---

see John-Paul Ghobrial, 'The Secret Life of Elias of Babylon and the Uses of Global Microhistory', *Past and Present* 222.1 (2014), 51–93.

2 The note of the Council's decision on 17 November 1694 was scribbled on to the margin of Robles's original letter.

3 The wills are dated 18 August and 26 September 1695, and they are now in the Archivo General de la Nacion (Buenos Aires, Argentina), Sala IX, Legajo 48-8-2, ff. 175r–176v, ff. 267v–272r. I am very grateful to Juan Pablo Artinian and Ariel Morrone from the University of Buenos Aires for their help in locating and transcribing these wills.

4 Of the four brothers mentioned, Lawrence is the only one who appears to have accompanied Joseph to England, see above pp. 172–3.

Figure 4: Georgirenes' signature on his will, 18 August 1695.

servants first to a convent for safe-keeping and then back to Spain on the first available ship. At the same time, the Inquisition in Lima had also begun an official inquiry into Georgirenes, armed with the suspicion that he had reverted to the Orthodox confession.[5] Eighteen months later, in May 1697, further orders were sent from Madrid requesting again the dispatch of Georgirenes and his companions; this time, the letters were sent not only to Robles but also to the Viceroy of Peru. In spite of further letters, this seems not to have happened. In part, this might have had something to do with the machinations of de La Seca and Guarino, the two friars, who had concocted a plot to fool the authorities in Buenos Aires. The two men claimed that they had in fact secured permission to remain in the New World from none other than the Viceroy of Peru, and they provided official letters purported to have been issued by the Viceroy's scribe. When Robles wrote to Lima to check the authenticity of the letters, he learned that they were forgeries. The two men were arrested and imprisoned for a short time before they managed to escape and flee, in spite of the governor's

5 This was a common enough occurrence. See Stuart Schwartz, 'The Greek Gunners and the Spanish Conquest', in Anthony N. Zahareas and Yangos Andreadis, eds., *Grecia en España, España en Grecia: Hacia una historia de la cultura mediterránea* (Madrid, 1999), 337–41.

efforts to locate them. In the latest dispatches from Spain, dated July 1699, no further mention is made of the friars but only of the Archbishop of Samos who was to be returned to Spain by the quickest means possible so that he could be held to task for 'the confusion he had caused' ('… por la confusión que ha causado').

For his part, Georgirenes managed successfully to dissociate himself in Buenos Aires from his disreputable companions. Evidence from local sources indicates that he was permitted to celebrate mass and carry out baptisms: on 8 April 1700, as one chronicler described it, a baptism was performed in the cathedral in Buenos Aires by the 'Arzobispo de Padmos' [sic.], certainly a reference to Georgerines. We do not know when, or where, he died. In his will he asked to be buried in the crypt of the cathedral in Buenos Aires where other bishops were buried. Perhaps he is lying there although it is doubtful whether such a roving spirit ever came truly to rest. Whatever the case may be, his presence in Buenos Aires lived on in the memory of locals well into the eighteenth century and beyond. In 1949, a short article in the journal *Criterio* by the Jesuit priest and scholar Guillermo Furlong, resurrected Georgerines for local historians and readers.[6] A year later, the Argentine storyteller Manuel Mujica Láinez published a collection of forty-two short stories recounting the history of Buenos Aires from its founding in 1536 until 1904. Among the stories was a story entitled simply 'El Arzobispo de Samos (1694)', which told the fantastical tale of a Greek bishop imprisoned in Buenos Aires and awaiting trial by the Inquisition. That Georgirenes should end up a character in the pages of such a tale are a fitting end to a man who lived his life navigating the precarious boundary between fact and fiction.

6 Guillermo Furlong, S. J., 'El arzobispo de Samos y su extrana comitiva en la Buenos aires de fines del siglo 17', *Criterio* (22 May 1947), 505–8. A more developed version of this article was published by Furlong as an introduction to his edition, *Manuel Querini S. J. y sus "Informes al Rey" 147–1750* (Buenos Aires, 1967), 7–15. For a brief obituary of Furlong by his student, Magnus Morner, see *The Hispanic American Historical Review* 55 (1975), 91–4.

Introduction to the *Description of the Present State of Samos, Nicaria, Patmos and Mount Athos*

Georgirenes' text *A Description of the Present State of Samos, Nicaria, Patmos and Mount Athos*, first published in English in 1677, has a complicated textual history. When Georgirenes arrived in Paris in 1676, the traveller and scholar Antoine Galland encouraged him to write an account of the places which he knew well in the Eastern Mediterranean: Mount Athos where he had become a monk, the two islands of Samos and Ikaria where he had been the Greek Orthodox archbishop, and Patmos where he was the guardian of the Holy Cave of the Apocalypse, and where he had first met Antoine Galland, who came there in the company of the French ambassador, the marquis de Nointel in January 1674.

Georgirenes wrote his *Description* in 'grec vulgaire' while he was in Paris and Galland then translated this text into French and intended to have it printed. But while this work was in progress, Georgirenes was persuaded to travel to England. He left behind with Galland his Greek text of the *Description*, but took with him to England Galland's French translation. Before he left, Georgirenes extracted from Galland a promise not to publish the text in France until he had been able to have it translated into English and printed in England. Because of his friendship for Georgirenes, Galland agreed to this, and gave Georgirenes the freedom to dispose of his French translation as he wished.

With considerable speed an English version of the *Description* was licensed for publication in July 1677 and printed by Moses Pitt in 1678. The title page records that it is the work of Joseph Georgirenes 'now living in London' and that it was 'Translated by one that knew the Author in Constantinople'. We know that this translator was Henry Denton, who had, indeed, met Georgirenes in Constantinople early in the 1660s when Denton was the chaplain to the English ambassador to the sultan, Heneage

Finch, Earl of Winchilsea.[1] The wording of the title page suggests (perhaps deliberately?) that the work was translated from the original Greek of Georgirenes when, in fact, what Denton did was to translate Galland's French text.

In 1678 Galland, without knowing how Georgirenes had got on in London, made his second voyage of some ten or eleven months to the Levant. When he returned he still had no news, but while he was waiting at Marseilles, in 1679, to return for a third time to Turkey, he finally received a copy of the printed English version of the *Description*. Since Galland did not have to hand Georgirenes' original Greek text (presumably because this was in Paris) he embarked on a new French translation, this time using Denton's English text. However, as he tells us in his Preface, he fortified his shaky knowledge of English by employing his own memories of the original Greek text. On the title page he writes 'traduit du grec vulgaire en français par Antoine Galland, Antiquaire de sa Majeste Tres Chretienne'. It was Galland's intention that this work, together with his own substantial account of Smyrna, should be published by his friend, the scholar and antiquary Jacob Spon.[2] The surviving manuscript of these two works written out in a fine hand, together with an account of the island of Tinos by Jacques-Paul Babin, all corrected and marked up for printing (presumably by Spon), is now in the Royal Library in Brussels.[3] But the work was never, in fact, printed. It was not until 2001 that Galland's second French version of Georgirenes' text was finally published by Manuel Couvreur and Didier Viviers in the series *Voyages inédits*.[4]

Although Galland was able to acquire a copy of the English version of the *Description*, it appears not to have been widely available. Joseph

1 A. Wood, *Athenae Oxonienses, to which are added the Fasti*, ed. P. Bliss, 4 vols (London, 1813–20), iv, p. 219. Wood, evidently misled by the title page, writes that Denton translated the work 'from Greek', which was not the case.

2 In December 1678 Spon had written to Covel, who was about to depart for the Levant, to tell him that he had received 'une relation angloise de Samos, Patmos, Icaria et du Mont Athos'; see H. Omont, *Missions archéologiques françaises en Orient aux XVIIe et XVIIIe siècles*, 2 vols (Paris, 1902), ii, pp. 1202–3.

3 Brussels, Bibliothèque Albert Ier, MS II 5359.

4 A. Galland, *Voyages inédits*, ed. M. Couvreur and D. Viviers (Paris, 2001).

Tournefort wrote in 1717, 'Joseph Georgirene, Bishop of Samos, was no doubt a very diligent enquirer into all these things, but the Description he has given of Samos, NIkaria and Patmos, is so scarce, tho' translated out of vulgar Greek into English, that I have not been able to procure it'.[5] Clearly Tournefort was misled (as may have been the intention) into believing that the English translation was from Georgirenes' original Greek. But although Galland's French version of the *Description* was not published until 2001, Georgirenes' text was known in France and used by French authors, but their knowledge of the work was probably derived from the printed English version.[6] There was, however, a German edition of the text, probably published without permission, since the wording on the title page carefully obscured its origins and omits (as does Galland) both the Greek and English Prefaces. This pirated German version was printed in 1689 and then republished by Heinrich Paulus in 1799.[7]

Neither Georgirenes' original Greek text nor Galland's first French translation is now extant, although they may one day come to light. It would be particularly enlightening to have Georgirenes' original Greek text since we have very few Greek texts known to have been written by him: the account of the circumstances of his leaving Patmos which he gave to the authorities in Volterra in October 1674 was written down in Italian.[8] There remain the two inscriptions in the copies of the Greek Gospels which Georgirenes presented to Louis XIV,[9] and his 'Epistle Dedicatory' to James, Duke of York, with which he prefaces the English translation of the *Description*.[10] Although Denton provides an English version of this

5 Joseph Tournefort, *A Voyage into the Levant: performed by Command of the late French King*, 2 vols, trans. John Ozell (London, 1718), i, p. 325.

6 For example, V. Guerin, *Description de l'Ile de Patmos et de L'Ile de Samos* (Paris, 1856).

7 H. E. G. Paulus, *Sammlung der merkwürdigsten Reisen in den Orient* (Jena, 1799), pp. 264–328. Oddly Paulus altered the order of the texts, beginning with Patmos, followed by Samos and Nicaria and ending with Mount Athos.

8 See above p. 122.

9 See above p. 135 and E. Legrand, *Bibliographie hellénique ... des ouvrages publiés par des Grecs au dix-septième siècle*, 5 vols (Paris, 1894–1903), ii, p. 301.

10 *Description of the Present State*, pp. 231–4. This Greek dedication may have been included to encourage the reader to believe that the English translation came directly from the Greek.

dedication, it seemed helpful to provide a more literal translation here since it offers a unique insight into Georgirenes' overblown style of writing. It is true that those who write dedicatory prefaces tend towards hyperbole and Georgirenes is no exception. But the dedication provokes a consideration of the kind of Greek text it was that Antoine Galland had to translate. It could be that Georgirenes wrote down sections of text and otherwise dictated material to Galland, so that what he left behind in Paris with Galland was not a single text in 'grec vulgaire' but jottings and separate passages which Galland then moulded into a coherent whole. The shifts of tone and style in the *Description* tend to suggest that several hands have been at work, pruning and expanding on occasion as they saw fit.

We can compare Henry Denton's version of Georgirenes' *Description* with that which Antoine Galland produced using Denton's text.[11] On the whole Galland sticks closely to Denton's translation but he makes frequent, usually minor, editorial changes. Some of these are explanatory and others are corrections where Denton has clearly misunderstood or mistranslated. Where Denton interprets or glosses Georgirenes' work he usually refers to classical texts, and he situates the *Description* in the world of ancient Greek and Latin authors, as might be expected from a classical scholar of Oxford University. Moreover Denton's knowledge of the Eastern Mediterranean was confined to Constantinople. Galland, on the other hand, situates Georgirenes' text within his own first-hand experience of extensive travels in the Levant. This is particularly apparent where he adds quite a number of explanations and details to Georgirenes' account of Patmos, which we know he visited with Nointel in January 1674 (and where he first met Georgirenes).

Apart from his cumbersome Epistle to the Reader, Denton also supplies side notes (more numerous at the beginning of the text) which refer to Pliny or Horace, and he offers a couplet from Horace for the title page[12]

11 I am grateful to Ruth Stungo for carefully reading and comparing the English and French translations and for providing welcome editorial advice.

12 See p. 184.

and lines from Ovid inspired by the mention of the Ikarian sea.[13] It seems likely, also, that it was Denton who inserted such passages as those about the origins of the name Porphyrios, and the origins of monasticism omitted by Galland.[14] Whereas Denton assisted the English reader by explaining that the first abbot of the monastery at Patmos was St Christodoulus at the time of the Emperor Alexius Comnenus who was contemporary with William the Conqueror and Godfrey of Bouillon, one of the leaders of the First Crusade, Galland omits these references in favour of simply 'lorsque l'on entreprit la premiere croisade'.[15] On occasion Galland corrects what were probably misunderstandings on the part of Denton: the inhabitants of Ikaria wore shoes made, not of copper, but of leather, and the gown which a monk of Athos puts on when he is professed is probably 'l'habit de pauvreté' which Galland describes rather than Denton's 'garment of gladness'.[16] In an interesting shift of emphasis, where Denton describes how the Blessed Virgin assisted St Athanasius in founding the Great Lavra by seizing his staff with which she struck a rock to produce a spring of water before planting it in the ground where it became a tree, in Galland's version the Virgin uses her own staff to achieve these miracles. Both men can be sceptical of some of the more superstitious aspects of the beliefs of the inhabitants of these islands and Galland adds a vehement criticism of those Greeks (of Samos) who pay more attention to serving the local Aga than Jesus Christ.[17]

It is Galland who recounts that it was only his desire to see the countries of Western Europe which induced Georgirenes to leave his duties at the Cave of St John at Patmos, supplied with letters of introduction from the Marquis de Nointel (himself en route for Jerusalem) which 'contribue beaucoup a me faire recevoir avec honneur dans toutes less villes ou je me suis presenter'.[18] The re-embarkation of the marquis in the shelter of the

13 *Description of the Present State*, p. 55.
14 Ibid. pp. 67, 101–4.
15 Ibid. p. 75; Galland, *Voyages inédits*, p. 301.
16 *Description of the Present State*, pp. 65, 107; Galland, *Voyages inédits*, pp. 295, 322.
17 Ibid. pp. 291, 273; *Description of the Present State*, p. 58.
18 Galland, *Voyages inédits*, pp. 302–3.

island of Tragonisi is again referred to by Galland, but ignored by Denton.[19] Galland's knowledge of Patmos can also be inferred from his added reference to a manuscript giving the history of Prochorus to be found in the monastery library there and in his description of the church of the Great Lavra 'qui n'est point considérable pour sa grandeur, mais pour les peintures à la mosaïque et pour le marbre attaché contre les murailles dont elle est embellie, avec un petit dome qui la rend très agréable'.[20] These details must derive either from earlier remembered conversations with Georgirenes or from his own recollections of that visit in 1674 in the entourage of the Marquis de Nointel.

The final paragraph reflects a difference perhaps between Georgirenes' two translators: Galland writes how remarkable it was that the monks of Mount Athos, numbering more than 6,000 and living in an area of only 160 miles circumference, far from the business of the world, should have been able, over the centuries, not only to perpetuate themselves but to multiply, without having any contact with women.[21] Denton merely remarks that it is a thing remarkable that 'there should not be seen a woman'.[22] He may have thought that this emphasis on monasticism and chastity would not have been acceptable to an English audience.

The text of *A Description of The Present State of Samos, Nicaria, Patmos and Mount Athos* reproduced here, is photographed from a copy now in the Cambridge University Library, Classmark: Dd*4 26(F).

CMB

19 Ibid. p. 304
20 Ibid. pp. 301, 302.
21 Ibid. p. 325.
22 *Description of the Present State*, p. 112.

Translation of the Dedication

Nicholas Richardson

To the most highly esteemed and royal [lit. born in the purple] Prince Lord, Lord James Duke of the great city of York, I, least of archbishops, Joseph Georgeirenes, of the see of Samos, offer my humble reverence.

Those who search for wisdom, most highly esteemed Prince, not only are accustomed to give their attention accurately to the sublime aspects of things, but also do not disdain to have a full understanding of matters of lesser importance. In like manner also the renowned people of Britain do not stop at things familiar and near, as many do who engage in research, but steadfastly and with full attention continue examining in addition the state of each single matter, and the regular course of life, the opinions of those who act, and the causes, even in the case of people who are far away. For which reason among those men who are here lovers of learning and renowned for noble birth, no few, being by nature curious, have earnestly entreated me to describe as needed the condition of the Ionian region and of the Cyclades islands, as far as I am able to do so, declaring in addition to these matters in what manner our people, who are now subject to the impious and barbarous Hagarenes, and are deserving of kindliness and protection, conduct the government of their life, and are evidently suffering countless troubles at their hands. And so, taking very much to heart the curiosity of these men, and considering it useful, I have decided to present a comprehensive description of some of the Cyclades islands, namely Samos, Icaria, Patmos and the holy mountain of Athos.

But since this enterprise appears to be uncultured and wanting in learning, it is bound to be in need of some protection and assistance, so that it should not appear ignoble and unseemly to the more learned. For these reasons I have undertaken to have recourse to the splendour of the all-glorious name of your Highness, and with all respect and discretion, I consecrate it to your most august Highness, not judging it worthy of this, since it is of little worth, but as evidence of my humble [lit. servile] reverence towards it [i.e. your Highness], and of the benefits which I have clearly received from it [your Highness], and through me the whole people of Greece. I therefore beg of your Highness that, as you have considered me worthy of many benefactions, so too you should also give me a share in your present favour, and with good will, as you are wont to do, to accept this gift of your servant. And in addition to these things, as our most kindly protector, to preserve it and ourselves under your most highly esteemed shelter, free from censure by those who are accustomed not so much to imitate (*mimēsasthai*), but rather to criticize (*mōmēsasthai*). And we shall, by way of return, continually pray to the all-best and most mighty God that your Highness may be happy for endless years, living your life with strength, peace and joy. Amen.

Notes

The language of this Greek Dedication is predominantly classical. It is written in a very florid and elaborate style. A small number of words are not found in ancient Greek. Of these some occur in Byzantine Greek, whilst others do not seem to have parallels elsewhere.

Byzantine

(1) πορφυρογεννητός: literally 'purple-born', commonly used of members of the Byzantine imperial family.
(2) πανεύδοξος ('all-glorious'): a compound form of classical εὔδοξος ('glorious', 'famous'). Stephanus gives two Byzantine examples.
(3) συνεπιμετρεῖν ('give a share also to'): another compound form of classical ἐπιμετρεῖν ('measure out to'), attested in Stephanus' *Thesaurus* and in the *Lexikon zur byzantinischen Gräzität.*

Not found elsewhere

(1) παναριστομέγιστος ('all-best and mightiest'): a compound form of classical πανάριστος ('all-best') and μέγιστος ('mightiest'). This is presumably the equivalent of the classical and Christian Latin formula *Deus Optimus Maximus* ('best and mightiest God').
(2) συμπεριεξετάζειν ('examine in addition'): another elaborate compound form of classical ἐξετάζειν ('examine well', 'scrutinize') and the pronominal prefix συμπερι- ('together with' or 'altogether').
(3) ὑψηλοπρεπής ('highly esteemed') and ὑψηλοπρέπεια ('Highness'): modelled presumably on classical μεγαλοπρεπής, μεγαλοπρέπεια ('magnificent', 'magnificence') and σεμνοπρεπής, -εια ('dignified', 'dignity'). Georgirenes also uses the superlative σεμνοπρεπέστατος in this passage, in the phrase translated as 'your most august Highness'.

From this survey one can see that, apart from the purely Byzantine πορφυρογεννητός, all the others are elaborations of common classical words. One might say that Georgirenes is reluctant to use a simple expression whenever he can find something more complex to replace it.

The translation by Henry Denton adapts the original to some extent, to make it more accessible for English readers. The version I have provided is purely literal.

For Byzantine or post-classical Greek cf.:

E. Kriaras, *Λεξικο της μεσαιωνικης Ελληνικης δημωδους γραμματειας* (*Lexicon of Medieval Greek Demotic Literature*): *1100–1669* (Thessaloniki, 1968–).

E. A. Sophocles, J. H. Thayer, and V. Drisler, *Greek Lexicon of the Roman and Byzantine Periods (from B.C. 146 to A.D. 1100)* (Cambridge, MA, 1914).

H. E. Stephanus, et al., *Thesaurus Graecae Linguae*, new edn (Paris, 1831–65).

E. Trapp, and others, *Lexikon zur byzantinischen Gräzität* (Vienna, 2001–).

For modern Greek cf. G. D. Babiniote, *Λεξικο της Νεας Ελληνικης Γλωσσας*, 2nd edn (Athens, 2002).

Nicholas Richardson

A

DESCRIPTION

OF

The Present State

OF

SAMOS, NICARIA, PATMOS, and Mount ATHOS.

By *Joseph Georgirenes*,
Arch-Bishop of SAMOS.
Now living in *London*.

Translated by one that knew the Author in Constantinople.

Dum licet, & vultum servat fortuna benignum,
Romæ *laudetur* Samos, & Chios, & Rhodos *absens.*
Hor. l. 1. Epist. 11.

July 14. 1677.

Licensed,

W. Jane.

LONDON,
Printed by *W. G.* and sold by *Moses Pitt*, at the *Angel* in St. *Paul's* Church-yard. 1678.

Τῷ ὑψηλοπρεπεστάτῳ τε καὶ πορφυρογεννήτῳ ἄρχοντι κυρίῳ, κυρίῳ Ἰακώβῳ τῷ ἡγεμόνι τοῦ μεγαλοπόλεως Ἐβοράκου, ὁ τῶν ἀρχιερέων ἐλάχιστος Σάμου Ἰωσὴφ ὁ Γεωργειρήνης ταπεινὴν προσκύνησιν ἀπονέμω.

ΟΙ τῆς σοφίας ἀντιποιούμενοι, ὑψηλοπρεπέστατε ἄρχων, οὐ μόνον τοῖς μετεώροις τῶν ὄντων ἀκριβῶς προσέχειν πεφύκασιν, ἀλλὰ καὶ τὰ τούτων ἐλάττονα οὐκ ἀπαξιοῦσιν ἐξεπίστασθαι. τούτοις μὲν δὴ καὶ τὸ περίβλεπτον τῆς Βρετανίας γένος ἑπόμενον, οὐ μέντοι παντελῶς πως τὰ συνήθη καὶ ἐγ-

γὸς, ὡς οἱ πολλοὶ περιεργαζόμενοι, ἀλλ' ἑνὸς ἑκάστου πράγματος κατάστασιν καὶ ἐνιαύσιον διαγωγὴν καὶ τὰς γνώμας τῶν πραξάντων καὶ τὰς αἰτίας διατελεῖ συντόνως ἅμα καὶ προσεχῶς καὶ μακρὰν ὄντων συμπεριεξετάζον· ἀνθ' ὅτου τῶν ἐνταῦθα φιλομαθῶν καὶ εὐγενείᾳ περιφήμων ἀνδρῶν οὐκ ὀλίγοι, φύσει φιλοπράγμονες ὄντες, ἐξελιπάρησάν με τὴν τοῦ Ἰωνικοῦ μέρους στάσιν τε καὶ τῶν Κυκλάδων νήσων, ὅσον ἐμοὶ ἐφικτόν ἐστιν, εἰς δέον περιγράψαι· συνεπιδεικνύων πρὸς τοῖς ὃν τρόπον τὸ νῦν ἔχον ὑπὸ τῶν ἀσεβῶν καὶ βαρβάρων Ἀγαρηνῶν τὸ φιλανθρωπίας ἄξιον καὶ ὑπερασπισμοῦ γένος ἡμῶν τὸν βίον διεξάγον πολειτεύεται, καὶ μυρία δεινὰ παρ' ἐκείνων πάσχον φαίνεται· ἐγὼ μὲν οὖν τὴν ἐκείνων φιλοπραγμοσύνην περὶ πλείστου ποιησάμενος, καὶ χρησίμην οὖσαν ἡγησάμενος, καταληπτικήν τινα περιγραφὴν τῶν, Κυκλάδων νήσων, τῆς μὲν Σάμου, Ἰκα-

ρίας

είας, Πάτμου καὶ ἁγίου ὄρους τοῦ Ἄθωνος, τούτῳ παραδοῦναι προῄρημαι. ἀλλ᾽ ἐπειδὴ τουτὶ τὸ ἐγχείρημα ἄμουσόν τε καὶ σοφίας ἄμοιρον εἶναι δοκεῖ, σκέπης τινὸς καὶ ἐπικουρείας ἐξ ἀνάγκης προσδεῖται· ὡς ἂν δήπουθεν μὴ τοῖς σοφωτέροις ἄδοξον φανείη καὶ ἀειδές· διὰ δὴ ταῦτά γε πρὸς τὸ ἔκλαμπρον τοῦ πανευδόξου τῆς σῆς ὑψηλότητος ὀνόματος προστρέχειν ὑπείληφα, καὶ μετὰ πάσης αἰδοῦς καὶ εὐλαβείας αὐτὸ τῇ σῇ σεμνοπρεπεστάτῃ καθιερῶ ὑψηλότητι, οὐχ ἄξιόν κρίνας αὐτῆς, εὐτελὲς ὑπάρχον, ἀλλ᾽ ὡς τῆς ἐμῆς πρὸς αὐτὴν δουλικῆς προσκυνήσεως τεκμήριον, καὶ ὧν παρ᾽ αὐτῆς εὖ ἐγὼ πεπονθὼς, καὶ δι᾽ ἐμοῦ ξύμπαν τὸ τῆς Ἑλλάδος γένος φαινόμεθα· δέομαι τοίνυν τῆς ὑψηλοπρεπείας σου ὡς πολλῶν εὐεργεσιῶν ἐμὲ ἄξιον ἡγήσαο, οὕτω καὶ τὴν παροῦσαν συνεπιμετρῆσαι χάριν, καὶ εὐνοϊκῶς, ὡς εἴωθας, τοῦ σοῦ οἰκέτου τουτὶ ἀποδέξασθαι τὸ δώρημα. Ἐπι

δὲ

δὲ πρὸς τοῖς καὶ ὡς φιλανθρωπότατος
ἡμῶν ὑπερασπιστὴς αὐτό τε καὶ ἡμᾶς
τῇ ὑψηλοπρεπεστάτῃ σκέπῃ σου ἀμώ-
μους διατηρῆσαι ἀπὸ τῶν οἰωθότων
οὐ μέντοιγε μιμήσασθαι, ἀλλὰ μωμή-
σασθαι· ἡμεῖς δὲ δίκην ἀμοιβῆς τῷ
παναριστομεγίστῳ Θεῷ διατελοῦμεν εὐ-
χόμενοι τὴν ὑμετέραν εὐδαιμονεῖν ὑψη-
λοπρέπειαν εἰς ἀπεράντους ἐνιαυτοὺς
ἐρρωμένας, εἰρηνικῶς καὶ περιχαρῶς τὸν βίον
διάγουσαν. Ἀμήν.

TO THE
Most High PRINCE
Of Royal Birth,
JAMES,
DUKE of York, &c.

JOSEPH GEORGIRENES
Of SAMOS,
The least of Arch-Bishops, offers his most Humble Reverence.

Most High Born Prince,

THey that aspire to the Attainment of Wisdom, do not content themselves with the Accurate Search of sublime objects, but also condescend to enquire into lower matters. In like manner, the renowned *Britains* do not confine their contemplations to their own homes, or to their neighbour Nations; but enlarge their prospect unto the most remote Countries, and with a piercing Eye, diligently pursue the exact discovery of their state and condition. To which purpose, many persons of honour, and of curiosity, have importun'd me to give some description of the Coasts of *Ionia*, and the *Ægean* Islands; and to declare the present Condition of those great objects of Pity and Protection, the *Greeks*, now under the cruel Tyranny of the Wicked and Barbarous *Hagarens.* The desire I had to gratifie their learned curiosity, whose Judgements I had reason highly to esteem, prevail'd with me to undertake a Description of some Isles of the *Archipelago*, namely, *Samos*, *Nicaria*, *Patmos*, and Mount *Athos*, now called *The Holy Mount.* But because this Work may seem to want that Elegance, or depth of learning, requisite for a Book that must appear upon the Stage of *England*, it stands in need of shelter and protection.

Which

Which put me upon the bold neces-
sity of flying to the Shadow of your
Royal Highness's Patronage, to
escape the scorchings of Contempt,
and with all humble Reverence, to
shelter it under the umbrage of your
Royal Highness's propitious Name.
And I most humbly offer it, not as a
thing of any merit; but as a mani-
festation of my *devvir* and gratitude,
for those great Obligations, which I,
and in me all the *Greek* Nation has
received. I therefore most humbly
beseech your Highness, that as you
have thought me worthy of your
Bounty, so to continue the same fa-
vourable aspect, in accepting this
small demonstration of my Grati-
tude, and by your gracious Patro-
nage, to secure it from their censure,
who are not so forward to imitate
our well intended pains, as to ex-
pose our defects. For which unde-
served Favour, we can make Retri-
bution only in our daily Prayers to
Almighty God for your Highness's
Health and Prosperity in this
World, and Eternal Happiness in
the World to come.

THE EPISTLE TO THE READER.

The habitable Earth, by Divine disposal, bestow'd upon the Children of Men, is but one great Island. And those Four eminent Parts of it which divide the whole among them, not by equal portions, but by the casual intervention of Seas, are not totally separated one from another; but make one perpetual Continent. Africa *is joyn'd to* Asia, *by no very small neck of Land betwixt the Mediterranean and the Red Sea: And is no more an Island properly so call'd, than* Peloponnesus. Europe *and* Asia *are joyn'd above the Lake of* Mæotis *with a large space of ground betwixt the* Hyperborean *Ocean, and that Lake. And* Asia *is joyned to* America, *by the Streights of*

Anian

Anian *in all probability. There has nothing yet been discover'd to the contrary, and the great Absurdities that attend the peopling of it are no way so easily solv'd. Besides this Main Continent which is mounted above the Face of the Waters in one entire continuation of parts, there are many lesser Islands, entirely surrounded by the Sea, and divided from all other ground. And all these are but smaller Sisters to that great product of Nature, the Main Continent, not differing from it in kind, but in bulk and size. Whether they owe their birth to the general Deluge, or date their antiquity from the day of the Creation, the Scripture is silent, and so am I. The Opinion of several Islands being rent from the Main Continent, by the violent Incursion of Seas, has been more forwardly embrac'd, than convincingly prov'd, and owes more to Poetical Fancy, than to any solid Foundations of Philosophy. However, certain it is, that many Islands are of later Antiquity than either the Creation, or the Flood, as on the contrary, many have either subsided, or been over-whelm'd.*

The same Earthquake does sometimes produce both effects; and the same time brings Birth to one, and Burial to another. But these are the irregular miscarriages of nature, labouring under a Convulsion Fit, and teach us what may be, not what must be; what nature may sometimes suffer, not what she always doth. As for the whole Globe of Earth and Water, the admirable intermixture of them both for use and beauty, doth highly bespeak the Wisdome of the Maker, and doth no less merit our contemplation, than the Canopy of Heaven. And that the rather, because the inferiour World doth more neerly approach our Senses, and affords us clearer notice of their state and condition. Among all the associate Collection of Islands, that by reason of their mutual vicinity, pass under one common name, there are none more remarkable than those of the Ægean *Sea, or the* Archipelago. *These were so eminent in the days of the Prophets of the Old Testament, that from them all the Western parts of*

the

the then known World that was planted principally by the Sons of Japhet*, went under the common name of the Isles of the* Gentiles*, and the Islands of* Chittim. *The* Phœnicians*, the first eminent Navigators since the Flood, and the first Planters of Learning and Civility, as well as Colonies, along the shores of the* Mediterranean *and* Atlantick *Seas, began their discoveries in these Islands: And there they have left such visible Footsteps of their first Plantation, that the names they bear to this day are most of them of* Phœnician *Extraction. The Colonies planted in these Islands by the* Phœnicians*, gave beginning to all those Arts and Sciences for which the* Greeks *were afterwards so famous, and their Language been held in such admiration to this day. The* Æthiopick *Islands are known all by* Greek *names; but they are as far inferiour to the* Cyclades *in renown, as they are in number, having neither been the Scene of Actions recorded by such Immortal pens, nor the native Soil of persons so eminent for Arts and Arms.*

The conceit of Elysium, *or such a future happiness as the* Heathens *dream't of, was thought fit by their Poets to be fix'd upon some remote Islands; therefore call'd the* Blessed, *or* Fortunate Islands. *The* Hesperides *and* Canaries *have been Competitors for the Title, and our modern searchers into* Brittish *Antiquity do strain hard to make the* Cassiterides, *or the* Scilly *and* Man, *and* Anglesey, *put in for a claim. But the Poets have been more accurate in maintaining the Character of an earthly Paradise, and describing a felicity of state beyond that of a* Platonick, *or* Utopian *Commonwealth, than in directing us by any rules of Geography, where it is to be found. And as they have left it indifferent to the Reader to fix the Local Situation of such Islands where they will, so they have left it impossible to any Reader to find such a place in the whole World. Indeed it is the high prerogative of great and lasting Wits to affix an esteem and veneration upon those places they make the Stage of their Stories, be they true or false.*

But

But in this point of credit, the Islands of the Archipelago *do far surpass any other in the World. And this is true, not only of the licentious and extravagant Fables of their Romantick* Mythologie; *but also in the graver and more creditable Records of sober History. They did heretofore in a manner engross the Monopoly of all the Wit and Fancy both of* Greece *and* Rome: *Insomuch, that 'tis hardly possible for a man well vers'd in the* Greek *and* Latin *Tongues, to be a stranger to the antient Geography of these Places: And* Pliny, *who was in nothing less erroneous, than in this part of his natural History of these Islands, does honour the Bay wherein they are situate, with the Title of* Sinus claritatis literarum. *A large* Encomium, *and such as no other aggregate body of Islands had equal right to. The* Japan, Philippine, *and* Molucco *Islands in the* Oriental Ocean, *are far beyond these for number; but the only thing they are sought for is some natural products peculiar to their Soil and Climate, in which commendation, they do not exceed*

ceed the late discoveries in the Ame-rican *Ocean; but we find not that the World was ever beholding to the one, or the other, for the Propagation of Learning or Civility. Nor is it only famous for the early rise of Humane Learning and civil Culture, in the days of* Gentilism, *but also for the early appearance of the more glorious Sun-shine of the Heavenly Doctrin of the Gospel. St.* John *the Divine, honoured in the Oracles of God, with the peculiar Title of* the Disciple whom Jesus loved, *was once an Inhabitant of these Islands; where he founded the* Christian *Religion, and writ that Divine and Mysterious Book, which was indeed to him* Apocalypse, *but to all future ages* Apocrypha. *St.* Paul, *that great Apostle of the* Gentiles, *did often cross this Sea, to plant the Doctrin of Salvation in all the neighbouring Shores of* Europe *and* Asia. *And in future ages, when the Divine Providence raised up a* Christian *Emperour to protect his Church from persecution, these Islands were the very centre of once the most Orthodox and learned Church in the*

the World. To whom we owe not only the transmitting the Holy Scriptures to our knowledge; but also the digesting the Doctrin of them into Articles of Faith, the defence of Truth against all invasion of Errour, the faithful Records of most pure and primitive Tradition, the clear Exposition of many obscure passages, which without their direction, might have been at this day unintelligible, and the great advantage of many learned and elaborate Volumes of Orthodox Divinity, both Polemical and Practick. And of all those many different Sects of Christianity *in the East, they have to this day most firmly retain'd the ancient Truths, and made the least Deviation into Errour. If that ignorance which those barbarous extinguishers of learning, the* Turks, *keep them in, renders that afflicted Nation obnoxious to be impos'd upon, and incapable of knowing better, it deserves rather our pity, than our contempt and scorn. It is rather a Miracle of Gods gracious Providence, that under such tyrannous Masters, and such proud and contemptuous enemies of*

the

the common name of Christianity, *the light of Evangelical Truth is not only dim'd, but utterly extinct, as it has hapned in the* Latin *Church in* Africa, *once inferiour to none for purity of Doctrin, and piety and learning in their Professours. Yet this cannot be deny'd them, but that they accord with us in many things wherein we differ from the* Romish *Church. I may add this more, that in the Sacrament of the Eucharist, the* Greek *Church doth not bear that conformity or similitude with the* Romish *Church, as the great Champions for* Popery *would affix upon them. And that will easily appear in these particulars.* 1. *They use not the Elevation of the Host.* 2. *No carrying it in Procession.* 3. *The People stand when they receive it.* 4. *They give it in both kinds to all.* 5. *The bread is of a common sort before Consecration. It is besides, the business of this Preface, to enlarge upon the present State of the* Greek *Church, which the reverend Author hath in some measure done in his account of* Samos, *and Mount* Athos: *And that subject is more largely handl'd by a late*

learned

learned Author * *in the* Latin *and* English *Tongues. All that I shall add is, that scarce any part of* Greece *has less intermixture with the* Turks *than these Isles, where the* Greek *Language and Religion is less intrench'd upon. There are no less than twenty Bishops in the* Archipelago, *some with the Title of* Metropolite, *as* Metelyn *and* Methymia; *others with the Title of Arch-Bishop, as* Samos, *and* Andros, *and some with the bare Title of Bishop, as* Sciathus. *Yet neither of the two first differ from the last in any thing, but in Title, or priority of place. Their jurisdiction is alike, it being ordinary here for a* Metropolite, *and an Arch-Bishop to be without a* Suffragan. *The reason is, because of the great Revolutions, many of the old Bishopricks are lost, and the ancient frame of Ecclesiastical Polity much alter'd. The Patriarch continues the Title of* Metropolite *upon all the places that formerly were so, and the Title of Arch-Bishop, upon those that depend immediately upon the Patriarch, without any subjection to a* Metropolite, *al-*

* Smith's *remarks upon the* Turks.

although they have no Bishop under their jurisdiction. The following Treatise giveth an account of three Islands of the Archipelago, *and Mount* Athos, *the Great* Academy *for the* Greek *Clergy. In all these places, he liv'd, and writes nothing, but what he saw, or what he receiv'd from the constant Tradition of the places: So that as to matters of fact, he may be better rely'd upon than those that write of places to which they are great strangers. For the Truth of what is related, is the main* Postulatum *of an History.*

A

DESCRIPTION Of the ISLE of SAMOS:

AND

Of its present State at this Day.

SAmos, is one of the greatest, and most remarkable Islands of the *Archipelago*, situate near the Continent of *Asia*. It is well known that this was the Country of *Pythagoras*, and once was Govern'd by Kings of her own, and has made stout resistance against *Athens*, what time they both liv'd under a Democratical Government. The ruins which yet are to be seen there

there are a Teſtimony of her former greatneſs and wealth. But this Iſland hath been ſubject to great changes and revolutions, even to utter deſertion of Inhabitants for many Years. Yet it being my main intent to give an account of its preſent State, I ſhall wave the former Tranſactions of Ancient times, whereof there is frequent mention amongſt Hiſtorians, and proceed to a ſurvey of its condition in theſe Modern Times, under the *Turkiſh* Empire; how it is now Govern'd; what Revenues it yields, with a Geographical Deſcription of the Country.

It is certain, that what time it pleas'd God for our ſins to permit the *Turks* to ſubdue *Conſtantinople*, and the *Archipelago*, the Iſland of *Samos* was totally diſpeopl'd. Afterwards one *Kilitch Aly Baſha* arrived here, and Landing with a ſmall Company to Hunt, was ſo taken with the place, that he was reſolv'd to ask leave of the Grand Signior, to re-people the Iſland: Which

Which having done, he transported several Families from all the Voisinage especially from *Metelyne*, so that by degrees, it became full of Inhabitants, and now counts to the number of 18 Towns and Villages, which I shall now describe according to their Situation.

The Isle of *Samos* is 26, or 27 *French* Leagues in compass, and lies in length East and West. At the West end it has the Isle of *Nicaria*, some twelve Miles distant: The East end is so near the Continent of *Asia*, that in some places men can Discourse one with another from the two Shores. This nearness of the East end of *Samos* to the Continent of *Asia*, causes a narrow Frith about six Miles in length, no where above 3 Miles in breadth, which by reason of little Islands in it, is a great Nest of Pirats, whom no Ships that come into this Strait can escape, but by putting to Shore on each side, where they are in equal danger of being made a Prey. These Pirats for the most part are either from *Malta*, *Legorn*, *Savoy*, or *Sardinia*.

At the entrance into this Streight, which the *Turks* call *Dardbogazy*, *i. e.* The Mouth of the Streight, lies all along the Mountain for the ſpace of a Mile, the place where the Old City of *Samos* ſtood, remarkable yet for ſome remainders of the Walls and ruins of old Churches, and large Stones, ſome 3, ſome 4, ſome 5 yards long, beſides many Marbles and Pillars, notwithſtanding the many choice pieces carried away by the *Venetians*, when they were Lords of the *Archipelago*. But the *Greeks* at this day dare not touch a Stone, ſo much as to Build with, for fear of Impriſonment by the *Turks*, under colour of having found a Treaſure in thoſe old Ruins.

Old Samos

And being once Impriſon'd upon ſuch a pretence, they are ſure to lye faſt till all they have be ſeiz'd.

Theſe Ruins are no leſs than ſix miles in compaſs. Upon the ſame Mountain in the middle of a deep and large Grotto, ſtands a Church Dedi-

Dedicated to the Virgin *Mary*; known there by the name of Γαναγία Σπιλιάνι * *Panagia Spiliani*, or The most Holy Virgin of the Grotto. All the *Samians* pay great Devotion to this place, not only in honour of the Virgin *Mary*, but for the belief of many Miracles there done. Here is also an artificial Channel, six Miles long, drawn from a River of a perpetual stream, which besides the Mills it drives, does water the Country in times of greatest drought. This water arising near the Village of the *Arnhauts* (of whom we shall speak more hereafter) becomes large enough by new supplies of other Currents, to deserve the name of a River, and is that which the Ancients call'd *Imbrasus*.

* *Panagia Spiliani*, St. *Maries of the Cave Spiliani*, from Σπηλαιον

At the bottom of the aforesaid Mountain, where Old *Samos* stood, towards *Scirus*, lye the Ruins of an old Haven for Galleys; the *Samians* call it *Tegani*, i. e. *Bason*, from its roundness. Near to which Port stands a little Church Dedicated

* *St.* Nicholas.

to * St. *Nicholas*, but now become a Refuge for the Mariners, who come privately to fetch Water from a Well hard by, that has a moſt excellent Spring: Yet here is always a ſtrict Watch kept, one by Day, and two by Night, to carry Intelligence to the next *Aga*, or the next *Caddee*, what Ships come in, whence they are, and whither bound; And if the *Aga*, or *Caddee*, happen to hear of any Ships coming by ſome other Meſſenger, before he that is to Watch, brings the News, he is ſure to receive 500 Baſtinadoes upon the Soles of his Feet for his neglect.

* *Megale Chora*, or *New Samos*.

Over-againſt the Old City, about a Mile diſtant to the Weſt, ſtands the New, now known by the name of Μεγάλη χωρα, *Megale Chora*, or the great Town, becauſe it is bigger than the reſt of the Iſle. Here the principal Men of the Iſle have their reſidence, *i. e.* the Arch-biſhop, the *Caddee*, with three or four *Turkiſh* Families, the *Aga*, with ten or a dozen other *Turks* to aſſiſt

him

him in the Execution of his Charge.

The *Caddees* Office is to pronounce Law, and the *Aga*'s to put it into Execution, and to Levy all Taxes whatsoever. There are many who submit themselves to the Jurisdiction of the Arch-bishop, especially the Ecclesiasticks. But if any Man rest unsatisfied with the Arch-bishops Judgment, he may appeal to the *Caddee*. There are very few *Turks* in this Isle, besides the forementioned. They had a Mosque, but the *Venetians* batter'd it down the first time they came with their Fleet to subdue the Island to their obedience, and to oblige them to contribution. But the *Samians* at first refus'd to pay Contribution, or to appear before the General, but made their escape into the Mountains, fearing the *Venetians* would soon be repuls'd by the *Turks*, and they be chastis'd for so quick a Revolt. But when the great Town was taken, and plunder'd, and the Mosque in it quite batter'd down, the *Aga* and *Caddee*, gave permission to the Islanders to pay a yearly tribute of 80000 Dollers or Crowns to the *Venetians*. Yet after the Peace made, when the *Turks* were re-establish'd, they would neither repair their batter'd Mosque, nor build a new one, for fear of some such casualty. Out of a Superstition they have, not to build a Mosque, but only where they are confident it shall never be profan'd by *Christian* violence.

Upon the coming of a new *Caddee*, or a new *Aga*, the Chief of the Villages assemble at the great Town, or upon any publick Affair which concerns the whole Island, especially upon the coming of the Officer appointed to gather the Poll-Money, called *Haratch*; Which is the only Revenue the Grand Signior receives out of this Island, all other the Revenues of the place, are as they call it, *(a) Vacouf*, that is

(a) *Vacouf* amongst the *Turks*, are all such Lands as we in *England* call Church Lands, especially Collegiate Churches, to which the Great Mosques in *Turkey* bear a great resemblance; for they have alwayes a Nursery of Men train'd up only to Sacred Employments; and a Governour, who is called

called *Sheich*, and under him other principal Men, that are well maintain'd, and out of whose number a *Sheich* is chosen upon any vacancy. These Colleges they call *Medrasa*, and they are always close by the great Mosque.

---

to say, Consecrated to Religious use, and they belong wholly to the great Mosque at (a) *Tophana*, by *Galata*, over against the Grand Signiors *Seraglio* at *Constantinople*.

(a) *Tophana*, is the House of Guns, and it has its name from the use it is put to, being the great Store-house for the Grand Signior's Ordnance, and Artillery, and the place of Residence for the *Topgy-Basha*, or Master of the Ordnance to the Grand Signior.

In other parts of the Empire, all Males that are not *Turks*, from 14 years and upwards, do pay yearly three Dollers a Head, but in *Samos* only Married Men are oblig'd. Yet if a Married Man dies leaving a Male Child, the *Haratch* shall be demanded for the Child, though he be but a sucking Infant. Strangers that come, pay this *Haratch*, Married or un-married. In like manner, the *Samians* that quit their Country to exercise any Trade or Traffick elsewhere in the Empire, do pay this *Haratch*, though un-married. When the

the Collector of this Poll-Money (whom they call *Haratchgy*) comes, he first goes to the *Caddee*, and shews him the Imperial Mandat. Whereupon the *Caddee* summons the chief Men of every Village, whom they call *Proesti*, to come before him at the great Town, where having read to them the Imperial Mandat, he charges them to take all possible care for the speedy Levying of the Tribute, which they promising, are dismiss'd. Then the *Haratchgy* goes to every Village, demanding of the *Papas*, or the Minister of the place an exact Catalogue of the names of those that are oblig'd to pay, which if the *Papas* fail to do, or omit any names that should have been put in, he is sure to be laid down, and drub'd. There is no excuse for any person, and he that cannot pay, is clapt into Chains, and led about as a Prisoner, till he has either sold his Goods, or beg'd Money to defray the charge of this Poll-Money.

The *Caddee* is sent hither by one of

of the *Caddileskers*, whereof there are two, the one for *Europe*, call'd the *Romily Caddilesker*, the other for *Asia*, called the *Anodal Caddilesker*. These two are next to the *Mufty* for Dignity and Power, and take place next to him. By one of these are all the *Caddees* sent to their respective charges. The Perquisits of the *Caddee* of *Samos* arise from the Courts of Judicature, where he is President: And upon the Death of any Person, he takes an Inventory of all his Goods, which being priz'd, he takes three *per Cent*, according to their value. But he meddles not with the Lands, being all appropriated to the aforesaid Mosque of *Tophana*: But if any Man dye without Issue Male, the *Aga* has power to seise his Lands, and to sell them to whom he pleases. Neither Male nor Female can inherit the Lands of their Mother, but they fall to the *Aga*, who has power to sell or dispose of them as he thinks fit. If a Man leave his Lands uncultivated for seven Years, the

the *Aga* has power to sell them, and to demand satisfaction for those dues that might have accru'd to him, if the Lands had been cultivated those seven Years. We will return to the remaining part of the Description of *Megale Chore*, and other remarkable places of the Isle.

The whole Town, and all the Gardens about it, are supply'd with Water from two (*a*) Fountains, that of the two, whose Water is sweeter to the tast, is called *Platanos*, the other *Messaki*. There are but six Churches, and those small ones. Nor is it expedient in that Country, that any thing which concerns the Christian Religion should make any outward appearance of Magnificence, or costliness, least it should provoke the envy aud avarice of their proud Masters to Sacrilegious rapine. On the South side of the City lyes a large plain, by a word mixt with *Greek* and *Latin*, call'd (*b*) *Megalocampos*, being the greatest Plain in the Isle; which by reason of abundance of standing Water

(a) *Plin. l.* 5. *c.* 31. *Fontes Eucarto, Leucothea.*

(b) *Megalocampos.*

Water wherewith it perpetually ſtagnates, yields no benefit, but great nuiſance to the neighbouring Inhabitants: Yet is it like to continue ſtill a Fenny Marſh, ſo long as the Tyrannous Government of the Country gives ſo ſmall Encouragement to the improvement of Lands. The Mariners that ſail by that Coaſt are the better for't, to whom it affords freſh Water enough to furniſh a whole Fleet, in four ſtreams that iſſuing from this Fen, diſembogue themſelves into the Sea, ſome ſix Miles diſtant from the Fen: Yet the Coaſt is ſo open, that no Veſſel can ride there but when the Wind is in the North.

Beyond this plain a large ſpace of fruitful Lands, water'd with the foremention'd *Imbraſus*, belongs to *Imbraſus.* a Monaſtry in *Patmos*, giv'n by a *Greek* Architect, one of the firſt Planters, who dying without Iſſue, left all he had to the ſaid Monaſtry. Beyond theſe Lands which belong to the Monaſtry of *Patmos*, upon the ſame River ſtands a village of ſome

200 Houses, with one Church; It's called (a) *Mily*, or the Mills, from that abundance of Water Mills, which *Imbrasus* drives there. Here Lemmons and Oranges are so plentiful, that 500 may be bought for one Doller. Westward of this Village lies (b) *Pagontas*, Situate on a Hill bedeck'd with Trees, the most healthful and pleasant Village of the Island. It hath no less than 300 Houses, and two Churches,, and is enrich'd by the Manufacture of Silks. Some three Miles distant from this Town, towards the Mountain, lies (c) *Spatharei*, a small Village consisting of about 50 Houses, and one Church, but famous for making Pitch, which they sell at *Megale Chore* for three quarters of a Doller, and sometimes a Doller the *Kintal*. (d) Their way of making is like *Pliny*'s description of it, *l.* 16.*c.*11.

(a) *Mily.*

(b) *Pagontas.*

(c) *Spatharei.*

(d) Their way of making Pitch is thus. They take *Sapines*, that is to say, that part of Firs, or other unctuous Trees as is betwixt the Root and the Boughs, so far as it hath no Knots; and shaving away the extreme parts, they leave only that which is nearest to the middle, and the Pith: That which remains they call *Dadi*, (from the old *Greek* word Δαδες, whence comes the Latin *Tæda*) These *Dadi*, or Torches, they cleave into small pieces, and laying them on a Furnace,

nace, put fire to the upper part, till they are all burnt, the Liquor in the mean time running from the Wood, and let out from the bottom of the Furnace into a hole made in the Ground, where it continues like Oyl; Then they put Fire to't, and stir it about till it thicken, and has a consistence; Then putting out the Fire, they cast Chalk upon it, and draw it out with a Vessel, and lay it in little places cut out of the Ground, where it receives both its form, and a firmer consistence for easie Transportation.

Over-against the Village of *Spatharei*, about a quarter of a Mile distant from Shore lies a little Island a Mile in compass, called (*a*) *Samio paulo*, or Little *Samos*; furnish'd with a safe Harbour against all Winds towards great *Samos*. This Island abounds with a peculiar sort of Flower, which from a Fragrance it hath, like unto *Musk*, the People call (*b*) *Muskoulia*, others call them *Coree*. This Flower has that esteem in *Turky*, that they are sent for as far as to *Constantinople*, whither they are transplanted with much care into their choicest Gardens. The Grand Signior wears it ordinarily in his Turbant, and by his Example, makes it a Fashionable wear among the Grandees of his Court. It hath this

(a) *Samio Paulo*, or *little Samos*, formerly *Narthecus*.

(b) *Mouskoulia*.

this quality, that time doth not decay, but augment the Fragrance of its Smell.

Three Miles distant from *Spatharei*, on the Hill side, stands the Village of (*a*) *Pyrgos*, consisting of about an 100 Houses, and 2 Churches: Here is the Choicest Honey.

(a) *Pyrgos.*

Above this Village stands a small Village and Colony of the (*b*) *Arnaouts*, or *Albanians*; for so is that Nation at this day called by the *Greeks* and *Turks*: And they have many Colonies in the Empire, being encourag'd with special priviledges and immunities from the Grand Signior: yet they lose not their Language (which in all likelihood is the old *Illyrian*) for it is not understood by any of their Neighbour Nations; nor is it an Of-spring of the *Slavonick*. Their Religion is the same with the *Greek*.

(b) *Arnaouts* Village.

Six Miles from *Pyrgos*, towards the South, lies (*d*) *Platanos*, so call'd, from abundance of Plain Trees there formerly. This Town hath

(c) *Platanos.*

hath at least 300 Houses, and two Churches, and is remarkable for its good Air. Both the Men and Women being generally longer Liv'd here, than any where else in the Island. Their Waters hereabouts abound with Champinions, a great relief to the Poor, when the word is given out for publick permission to Fish. Which word with them is *Anoixe to libarintous*.

Six Miles from hence, towards the West, lies a Village of some 200 Houses, and two Churches, call'd (a) *Maratha-campos*, from the abundance of (b) Fennel thereabouts, which the *Greeks* call *Maratha*. This Village looks toward *Patmos*, from whence it is distant some Forty Miles

(a) *Maratha-campos.*
(b) *Gal. Fenouil.* Μάραθρον

Three Miles from this Village lies a small Hermitage, by the Name of (c) St. *George*'s Hermitage, where two or three Hermits of *Patmos*, commonly reside. Not far from this Hermitage is a Grotto upon the top of a Mountain of most difficult access, which the People, by Tra-

(c) Saint *George's* Hermitage.

dition do believe was *Pythagoras's* retiring place; it hath now a little Church, call'd Παναγία Φανερομένη, Or the Blessed Virgin appearing; Because of a Tradition that the Blessed Virgin *Mary* has here appeared, and done Miracles. The Bones of Dead Men that lie scatter'd hereabouts, give occasion to believe, that those that remained when the Island was deserted, made their escape hither; it being a Retreat of most difficult access: And the inner Parts of this Mountain are not well discover'd, in asmuch as people are seen to appear, and observ'd to gather Chesnuts, none of the Inhabitants of the Valley knowing any thing more of them.

This (*a*) Mountain is called *Kerkis*, the highest of the whole Island, from whose top may be seen the greatest part of the Isles of the *Archipelago*: It is cover'd with Snow almost all the Year, and hath a Lake on the very top, well stor'd with Eels. Here is a Chappel Consecrated to the Prophet

(*a*) *Mons. Cercetius.* Plin. *l.* 5. *c.* 31.

Elias

(a) *Elias*, whither many resort for Devotion: Here is likewise a Grotto, with another Chappel, which hath no Tradition of its Name or Dedication; yet many go thither to say their Prayers, and at *Easter* time it is much frequented. This chappel, and Grotto stand directly over against the Isle of *Nicaria*, some 12 Miles from hence.

(a) Elias's *Chappel.*

That which increaseth the Religious esteem of this latter Chappel, is, a Tradition, That Light has often appear'd in the Night time, which the People conceive to be a Warning of some Holy Reliques that lyes here yet undiscover'd, and so neglected.

Upon the same Mountain, some six Miles distant, towards the North, stands another Hermitage; besides which, in a spacious Grotto, stands a little Church, Dedicated to the Virgin *Mary*. It hath but one way of access, and that up a steep Precipice so extremely dangerous, that it is called (*b*) Παναγία εἰς τὸ κακοπέρατον, or St. *Maries*, upon the bad passage.

(b) *Pandagia eis to Cacoperaton.*

Five Miles from *Maratha-campos*; towards the North, is the Village of (a) *Castanees*, so call'd, from abundance of Chesnut-Trees about it. It has about 50 Houses, and one Church. Not far from hence is the Hermitage of the Holy Trinity, where always two or three Hermits of the Monastry of *Patmos* do reside.

(a) *Castany*

Two Miles from *Castany*, stands (b) *Leca*, a Village of 50 Houses, and one Church.

(b) *Leca*.

Not far from *Leca* is the Monastry of (c) St. *George*, an Hospital for the (d) Monks of Mount *Sina*; it hath always four or five Priests, who look after the Revenues of the Hospital, which consists chiefly in Wine.

(c) *Saint* George's *Monastry*.
(d) *Monks of Mount* Sina.

Higher upon the Hill-side, over against *Leca*, is a Covent of Monks of *Elias*; Men abstracted from all secular employment, and they entertain all Passengers with what they have upon free cost.

Six Miles from hence, towards *Megalocampos*, lyes (e) *Carlovasy*, the

(d) *Carlovasy*.

the greatest Town of this Island, next to *Megale Chore*. It is situate by the Sea-side, over against *Sio*, and the Castle of *Siatsky*, upon the Continent of *Asia*. It hath no less than 500 Houses, and 5 Churches. The Inhabitants are the Richest of any in the Isle, by reason of their Traffick by Sea to *Sio*, *Smyrna*, Chios, and other places. Their principal Merchandise are Onions, and Muscat Wine. Yet their Port is so expos'd to the North Wind, and unsafe a Road for any Vessels, that they are forc'd to load their Vessels a Shore, and so to thrust them off: And at their return, without any delay they draw up their Vessels to Land.

Three Miles Eastward, from *Carlovasi* is the Town of (*a*) *Furni*, re- (a) Furni. markable for those Earthen Jars, and Pitchers, and other Vessels, which formerly were so much in esteem by the *Greeks*, and *Romans*, and were peculiarly call'd *Samian* Vessels. The Town hath at least 200 Houses, and two Churches, and has its name from the Furnaces where these Vessels are made. Besides this Town is a Fountain, whose stream is sufficient to make a Mill go; at the Spring-head is a Church, Consecrated to the Blessed Virgin, to which the Inhabitants of the Town pay great Devotion. From hence begins a row of Mountains, cover'd with Woods for the space of twenty Miles. It is furnish'd with all manner of Wood, fit for Architecture, as well for Vessels at Sea, as for Houses at Land, a great encrease to the *Aga's* Revenue; But the Chesnuts wherewith it abounds, are free for all Comers.

(a) *Vourlioté.*

Upon the top of this Mountain is a Village call'd (*a*) *Vourlioté*, a Colony of *Vourla*, a small Town by *Smyrna*. It hath about an 100 Houses, and one Church. The greatest Employment of the Inhabitants, is to cut Wood, and make Pitch.

(b) *Panagia Touphronta*,

Within half a Mile of this Town is a Monastry of a douzen *Caloirs*, by the name of (*b*) *Panagia Touphronta*.

The

The Grass about this Monastry in the Spring time is Venomous to all strange Cattle; so that if an Horse brought from a strange place be put into the Grounds, in a short time he shall swell and burst: But the Horses bred up about the Monastry, and the next Village, find no such inconvenience at all.

Ten Miles from this Monastry Eastward, stands (a) *Vathy*, a Village of 400 Houses, and four Churches, enriched with a Port, affording a safe Habour in all Winds but the South. But four Miles toward the North East lies another so well sheltred with three little Islands, (call'd τȣ πηλȣ νησία, or the Isles of Dirt,) that Vessels may ride safely in all Winds. These Islands are 20 Miles from *Scala nova*, a remarkable Port, and much frequented upon the Continent of *Asia*. The great Traffick of this Town is in Wine, especially Muscat, which will hold good a whole Year, whereas that of *Carlovasy* turns sower after six months age. It is

(a) *Vathy*.

likewise remarkable for Fishing.

(a) *Palaio-Castro.*

Near to this stands (*a*) *Palaio-Castro*, or the *Old Castle*; a Village of an 100 Houses and one Church: Here also are good Wines, especially Muscat.

(b) *Vourcaria.*

Four Miles from hence is the Port (*b*) *Vourcaria*, near to which is a convenient place for making Salt. But the Inhabitants fearing a great Imposition from the *Turks*, will not be at the pains to make any, being content with what is brought them from *Mylos*, and *Naxos*, from which two Islands all the *Archipelago* is supply'd.

(c) ὁ Πισσὸς κάμπος.

Two Miles from hence lies a great Plain, call'd (*c*) ὁ Πισσὸς κάμπος, *Ho pisos campos*, wherein rises a Fountain, whose only stream causes two Mills to go. This Plain is fruitful in Wheat, in Cotton, and the Grain of *Turky*, which the *Greeks* call Ἐρύσιμον, the *Latins Irio*, and the *French* peculiarly *Le bled de Turquie*, or the *Grain of Turky*. Here is a Church Dedicated to St. *John* the Divine; the Church is is called (*a*) τῦ θεολόγυ. The Inhabitants have an opinion of Miracles here done, and have a Tradition, that St. *John*, as well as (*b*) St. *Paul* has been in *Samos*, which causes great resort to this place for Devotion.

(a) Εκκλησία Ιωάννυ τῦ Θεολόγυ.

(b) *Acts* 20. 15. Τῇ δὲ ἑτέρᾳ παρεβάλομεν εἰς Σάμον.

Four Miles hence, towards the North, stands *Mytelene*, a Village of some 200 Houses, and 2 Churches. It is a Colony of the Island *Mytelene*. This Village is but a Mile from *Megale Chore*, the principal place of the Island wherewith we begun, and so we have finish'd the Circuit of the whole Island, and the Geographical Description of the Villages in it. It remains, that we speak of some Monastrys yet untouch'd.

The Monastrys hitherto omitted, are but two, Σταῦρος and Παναγία ϛα πέντε σπιτία.

1. Two Miles from the great Village is *Stauros*, or the Monastry of the *Cross*, wherein are 30 *Caloirs*. It is well endow'd with Lands, and a Farm House for Lay Fryers,

Fryers to Till their Ground. Besides it hath another Monastry depending upon it, where the Fryers chief Employment is to make Cloth, to do all other necessary work for the Service and Maintenance of the great Covent.

(a) Spete, *and* Spition, *in vulgar Greek signifies an house, from* Hospitium. *The first corruption of that Tongue came from the mixture of Latin words.*

2. (a) *Panagia sta Pente Spitia*, which in Vulgar Greek signifies the *Blessed Virgin of the five Houses*. This maintains 60 *Caloirs*, and has a smaller Monastry at *Pagondas*, subservient to it, in like manner as the former. This Monastry is not subject to the Arch-Bishop, but only to the Patriarch of *Constantinople*.

The Island is well stor'd with Sheep and Goats; But every Sheep is redeem'd with two Aspers, and every Goat with one, payable to the *Vacouf* or great Mosque at *Tophana* in *Galata*. Yet were this Law literally put in execution, it were well for the People; but the *Agas* take the boldness to levy more, as they think fit. Nor can the People help themselves, the charge of Appeal being greater than the

Pay-

payment injuriously exacted. And such is the Corruption of the *Turkish* Court, that the event of an Appeal would be as uncertain as the attempt unsafe.

Besides the *Aga* demands as his due, all the Butter he finds among the Inhabitants, what day soever he pitches upon to number their Flocks, in order to the gathering this *Vacouf* Money; which grievance arose by the inconsiderate bounty of a rich *Samian*, who to ingratiate with the *Aga*, presented him with a great quantity of Butter, since which time, the *Aga* has ever claim'd it as his due from all others.

The *Aga* is likewise presented by every man of stock with a Lamb and a Kid; which by a Charter obtain'd from the Grand Signior, the *Samians* have power to redeem with two Aspers and an half by the head, but the *Aga* exacts no less than five or six.

And now it is no wonder if this oppression by the *Turkish* Officers keep

keep the Inhabitants poor, ignorant and low spirited. *Kilitch-Aly-Bassa*, at his first coming to re-people the Island, brought none with him but men of low Fortunes, and the Tyranny they live under doth still keep them so. And the Malice of many slothful, but servile people among them, doth render it impossible for any person well affected to the Publick good, to effect any thing toward their Liberty, or redress of Grievances. For there wants not among the *Greeks* perpetual spies, that for their private ends, bring intelligence to the *Aga*'s Ministers of any motion made, or any word freely spoken towards the redress of Grievances. The *Aga*'s principal Engins are either those of his Family, (call'd *Musifarides*) or such creatures as lie dispers'd throughout the Island. Those of his Family, are his Secretaries and Interpreters: The latter sort are alwayes *Greeks*; for a *Turk* counts it a great dishonour to learn any *Christian* Language.

His Creatures abroad are the *Proesti*,

(a) *Proesti*, or Chief of the Villages, whom he alwayes makes his Creatures, and they for private ends are very forward to acquaint him any thing that may please him. They are more zealous and forward to pay their Homage to a Turkish *Aga's* House, than to serve Almighty God in his publick Worship; and as if Interest and Gain were their Godliness, they are more punctually careful to devote their time to a servile attendance in the outmost Gate of the *Aga*, among his Porters and meaner Servants, than in the solemn assembly of their fellow *Christians* in the Church of God. In so much, that though they are *Christians* by profession, yet on the most solemn days of publick Devotion, their greatest Religion is to wait at the *Aga's* House, to bid him good morrow, when he goes out to attend his pleasure, to drink Coffee, and smoak Tobacco among his Servants, and to speak nothing but what may flatter his Pride, or serve his Avarice. There is no Village

(a) Πρεστωτες.

Village in the Island so small, that wants such pestilent Spirits as these.

Samos is not inferiour to any Island of the *Archipelago* for good Soil. They are not beholden to other Countrys for any thing but Iron and Salt; and this latter they might have, did not the oppression of the *Turks* discourage their Industry. They are well stor'd with Trees of all sorts, with Pitch, Cottons, Corn, Oyl, Honey, and Wine, of whose Lees they make abundance of *Aqua vitæ* in the Month of *October*, by them call'd *Asynchoretos*, ἀσυγχώρητος: For when they make their *Aqua vitæ*, all Passengers are invited to tast of it, which he that refuses, is branded with the name of Ἀσυγχώρητος, in these words, Ἐὰν θὲν ἤρθες να ἔσαι ἀσυγχώρητος; *If you will take none, you shall never obtain pardon.*

Ἀσυγχώρητος, *unforgiven.*

All the People of the Country are Labourers, excepting the *Musafarides*, who farm out their Lands, and make it their business to attend

the

the *Aga*. Every Maſter of a Family is oblig'd to attend the *Aga* at ſuch time as he puts all his Corn in a readineſs to be meaſur'd. And then is one of the *Muſafarides* ſent, who is to be entertain'd at the charge of the Maſter of the Family, but inſtead of taking a Tenth of the Corn, which is ſtrictly his due; he takes Money according to his own valuation of the price of Corn.

All Wines, *Aquævitæ*, and Oyl, are Tith'd according to an ancient rate ſet down in the Court Rolls.

Heretofore there was no Impoſition taken upon Silks, becauſe it was a Manufacture exercis'd only by the hands of Women, 'till a certain *Aga* came, that deſir'd a little to make him a Girdle; and being preſented with a good handſome Basket full: The next year he demanded the like quantity every where as his due.

The Habit of the *Samians* is like the *Turks*: A long Veſt, like our Caſſock, down to the Heels with a Girdle about the Loins, and over

it

it a looſe Garment, like a Batche-lour of Arts Gown. The Women likewiſe imitate the *Turkiſh* Women in their Apparel, girded about the Loins, a white Vail over their Heads. The young Women let their hair hang down behind, in a long Lock plaited, and ty'd at the end with a Silver or Guilt Chain.

In former times, the greateſt part of the Iſles of the *Archipelago* were under the Juriſdiction of the Arch-Biſhop of *Rhodes*; and this Iſle had a Biſhop that was Suffragan to that Arch-Biſhop. But ſince the laſt re-peopling of the Iſle, it has been under the Patriarch of *Conſtantino-ple*, who beſtow'd it upon the great Church of *Conſtantinople*, and ſent a Vicar to collect all the Eccleſiaſti-cal Revenues. And in this condi-tion it continu'd for an hundred years, 'till the People of the Iſle did petition the Patriarch to let them have an Arch-Biſhop, which accordingly he did, and appointed them the Biſhop of *Nicaria* for their Suffragan; but that Iſland being too poor to maintain a Bishop at this day the Arch-Bishop of *Samos* has now no Suffragan at all.

When a new Arch-Bishop comes, he shews his Patent from the Grand Signior to the *Caddee*; then summons all the *Proesti* of the Villages, to whom having read his Patent, he has it Register'd in the publick Records of the Island. This done, they all accompany him to the Cathedral Church, where after the Reading of his Institutions, given by the Patriarch, he is plac'd in the Archiepiscopal Throne, where every one comes to kiss his Hand, and he bestows upon them his Benediction; and then makes them a Speech (if he find himself of sufficient capacity to do't.) This is the way of his Investiture into the Arch-Bishoprick of *Samos* and *Nicaria*.

At his first coming, the *Papas*, or Parish Priest of the Church of his Residence presents him 15, or 20 Dollers; they of the other Churches according to their Abilities.

The first year of his coming, every Parish Priest pays him 4 Dollers, and the following years 2. Every Lay-man pays him 48 Aspers, and the following years 24. The rest of his Revenues comes in by Ordinations and Marriages. One part of the Island come to *Megalo Chore*, where he Resides, for Licenses to Marry, the other part to his Vicar General at *Carlovasi*. The *Samians* pay one Doller for a License; all Strangers two: But he that comes after first Marriage for a License for a second, or third, pays three or four. Since *Samos* has been an Arch-Bishoprick, there has been hitherto but eight; 1. *Athanasius*; 2. *Anthimus*; 3. *Parthenius*; 4. *Cornelius*; 5. *Christophorus*; 6. *Neophytus*; 7. *Joseph* (who writ this History in vulgar *Greek*) and *Philaretus* that now succeeds him. Of whom here is a short account.

Athanasius, a Native of the Isle, and a Marry'd Priest, but his Wife dying about the time of his promotion, took upon him the Habit

bit of a *Caloir*, he was Arch-Bishop 20 years,

Anthimus, surnam'd *Judas*, because at the Ceremony of the Patriarch's washing the Feet of twelve Priests on *Maunday Thursday*, he being one, had the name of *Judas*. The Patriarch of *Constantinople*, in imitation of our Saviour, doth every year, on *Maunday Thursday*, Wash the Feet of twelve Men in Holy Orders, who are at that time called the twelve Apostles; and every Priest hath at that time the name of some particular Apostle. After he had been Arch-Bishop 15 years, upon a Complaint made against him by the Islanders to the *Capitan Basha*, or Admiral of the *Turkish* Fleet, he was clapt into prison, whence being releas'd by a sum of Money, he became afterwards Arch-Bishop of *Cæsarea* in *Cappadocia*.

Parthenius a *Theban*, was Translated from the Arch-Bishoprick of *Patras* to *Samos*, where he presided 12 years, only under the Title of προέδρως, or President; but after he had passed 12 years under this meaner and unusual Title, he was admitted to the full Rights and Dignity of an Arch-Bishop.

Cornelius of *Metelyne* was deposed by the Patriarch of *Constantinople*, after he had sat six years.

Christophorus a *Samian*, was clapt into the Galleys by the *Venetian* Admiral, for not paying Contribution to the *Venetians*, at the appointed time; for hapning to be Arch-Bishop in the beginning of that War between the *Turks* and *Venetians* (so calamitous to all the *Greek* Isles) the *Venetians* then Masters at Sea, forc'd all the *Archipelago* to contribution. He to secure his poor flock, the *Samians*, from immediate Plunder, Rapine, Captivity, and other Insolencies, did engage for raising the demanded Contribution, which was an high sum for that place, but was not able to make good his promise within the appointed time; because of the Peoples poverty: Whereupon the *Venetian* Admiral, without any

respect

respect to his Religion as a *Christian*, or to his place and quality as an Arch-Bishop, did most Barbarously put him into the Gallies, a punishment commonly imposed upon *Turkish* Captives, or such *Christians* only as were gross and notorious Malefactours, and judicially condemn'd for capital Crimes.

Neophytus of *Siphanto* sat 6 years, and deceased in the Island.

After him came *Joseph Georgirene*, of the Island of *Milos*, who was Consecrated, *October* 7. 1666. He sat here five years, till after the taking of *Candie*, the *Turks* grew more populous, and consequently more abusive: So that wearied with their injuries, he retired to the Holy *Grotto* of the *Apocalypse*, in the Isle of *Patmos*.

After he had voluntarily retir'd from his Arch-Bishoprick, the Patriarch of *Constantinople* did presently substitute in his place *Philaretus* of the Isle of *Siphanto*.

And thus much concerning the Arch-Bishop of *Samos*, his Inveſtiture, his Juriſdiction, and his Revenue. Proceed we to the Clergy, that under him have the Cure of Souls. And theſe not only in *Samos*, but throughout the whole extent of the whole *Greek* Church, are always dignifi'd and diſtinguiſh'd by the peculiar title of Παπᾶς, *Papas* which ſignifies a Father, becauſe in ſpiritual matters within the bounds of their Cure, they are Fathers, as well to Feed as to Govern.

(a) *Of thoſe whom the* Greeks *call* Papas, *or Parochial Prieſts.*

The *Papas* in the bounds of his Pariſh is oblig'd to perform all thoſe ſacred Offices which the *Greek* Ritual requires. They are not only allow'd to Marry, but oblig'd to do't, before they enter into the Order of Prieſt-hood. And not only thoſe *Greek* Prieſts that live under the Patriarch of *Conſtantinople*, but alſo thoſe *Greeks* that in *Sicily*, *Calabria*, and in the Iſlands under the State of *Venice* do embrace the *Romiſh* Religion, are by allowance of the Pope permitted to Marry. And ſuch Men (though Marry'd)

Marry'd) are commonly Ordained Priests at *Rome* it self, by some *Greek* Bishop of the *Romish* Religion in the College of *Greeks* at *Rome*, and in that of *Spain*, and in that called *Madonna del Populo*: Yet the *Greek* Church, for that esteem they have of a Monastick Life, do never advance a Parish Priest to a Bishoprick, except his Wife be Dead, or Divorc'd from him, and he take upon him the Habit and Profession of a *Caloir*.

A Marry'd Man, that would take Orders, is required to declare, that he has been but once Marry'd, and that his Wife was neither a Widow, nor a Slave, nor the Daughter of a Slave, or under the reproach of an Harlot: This done, he comes to a Confessour, who among other Sins, doth particularly put him upon the Confession of those Sins that by the Canon would exclude him from entring into Orders. And though his Confessour give him a good Testimony, yet a Week before the Ordination, the Bishop doth openly in the Church charge all the Assembly under the Peril of Excommunication, if they know him guilty of any Crime that may render him unworthy of Holy Orders, to reveal it before the next Sunday: Which if any Man do, and make good his Accusation, he is denied Holy Orders; if the Accuser be found to Impeach him falsely, he is Excommunicated for his false Accusation, and the other Ordain'd. After the *Candidate* for Holy Orders has thus made his way, the day before he enters into Priests Orders, he comes to the Metropolite, who having try'd whether he Read and Write without false Pronuntiation, or mis-spelling; and being satisfied in that point, doth presently Ordain him Sub-deacon and Deacon, and the next day Priest, if he be of sufficient Age. The Age for a Reader is 18; For a Sub-Deacon, 20; For a Deacon, 25. For a Priest, 30; Neverthelefs it is left to the Discretion of the Metropolite, to dispense with the Canon, as as he ſhall ſee occaſion, according to the example of *Anicetus*, who Ordained St. *Eleutherius* a Prieſt at 18, and Biſhop of *Illyrium* at 20. If a *Papas* Marry a ſecond time, he is deprived of his Orders, and called ever after *Apopapas*. But nothing hinders the Widow of a Prieſt to Marry again.

The *Papas* is obliged to Read Prayers, and Adminiſter the Sacrament every Sunday and Holy-day. The day before a Sacrament, he is to ſing the Veſpers, and after Supper, to rehearſe a Prayer call'd the Ἀπόδειπνον; if after that Prayer ſaid, he chance to Eat or Drink that Night, he is oblig'd to go to Church, and ſay that Prayer again: Likewiſe that Night he is not allow'd to lye with his Wife.

Every Pariſhioner is obliged to bring to Church a Loaf to the Weight of ſeven or eight pounds, which is mark'd with theſe three words; Ἰησοῦς Χριστὸς νικᾷ: *Jeſus Chriſt overcomes*. Of this Bread the Prieſt diſtributes to every one a Mor-

Morſel, and the reſt goes to himſelf.

If any man deſire the Sacrament upon other days than Sundays or Holidays, he ſends to the Prieſt the day before, to prepare himſelf according to the Canon. The next Morning the Prieſt ſends to him to bring with him what is neceſſary for Celebration, *viz.* a Loaf, marked as before, a Wax Taper of two Aſpers, and Incenſe of one Aſper, (for they never Celebrate without a lighted Taper, and Incenſe) and a Quart of Wine, and three Aſpers in Money: What is left of the Bread and Wine, goes to the Prieſt with three Aſpers. He that leaves it to the Prieſt to provide neceſſaries, brings with him 15 Aſpers.

The Pariſh Prieſts, excepting thoſe that are very ancient, or Widowers, never confeſs any. That employment is left ordinarily to the *Caloirs* of the Order of St. *Baſil*, whereof there wants not ſome every where diſperſed throughout the

the whole *Greek* Church, to beg Almes for the Monks of *Athos*, from whence they are ſent. Yet neither they, nor any Pariſh Prieſt confeſs any without a particular Licenſe from the Metropolite, who doth enjoyn them under a Mortal Sin, not to exact any Money for Abſolution. But if after Abſolution, the Penitent offer any thing, they receive it. If the Penitent deſires any Prayers to be ſaid for him in ſome Monaſtry of Mount *Athos*, he gives Money in conſideration of the Prayers to be ſaid for him.

If the Pariſh Prieſt have any Lands, he thinks it no ſhame to Till them himſelf. But he reſides conſtantly in the Pariſh, to be ready upon all occaſions for the Sick, to whom he ſays the Prayers appointed by the Church for Sick people.

If a Woman be in Child-birth, he is ſent for to ſay ſome Prayers appointed for that occaſion; nor can the company that come to aſſiſt the Woman in her Travail leave the Houſe, 'till the Prieſt come and perform

perform the Sacred Ceremonies appointed by the Church, for Women in Child-bed; accounting it a great contempt of God, and a thing ominous and of ill foreboding to the success of the person in Labour, to neglect their solemn address to God in the prayers appointed by publick Authority for that Emergency.

(a) *Of their Women in Child-bed.*

A Woman (*a*) after Child-birth stirs not abroad, neither to Church, nor to other Houses, till 40 days be expir'd. Then she is brought to the Church Door, where the Priest having said the Prayers appointed for that occasion, she is permitted to go to Church, or to other Houses.

(b) *Paedobaptism.*

The Children ordinarily are not (*b*) Baptiz'd till 40 days after Birth, sometimes, under pretence of the Parents or Gossips absence, not till half a Year, a whole Year, or more. But this is alwayes in case the Child be healthy and strong; for upon the least suspition of the Childs being weak, or likely to dye, the Priest

Priest is sent for by the Parents, and without any further Ceremony, the Child is Baptized in this manner.

N. N. **The servant of God doth Baptize thee, in the Name of the Father**, Amen. **Of the Son**, Amen. **And of the Holy Ghost, from henceforth and for evermore**, Amen.

In private Baptism they use only Water, Oyl, and a Lamp burning before the Picture of the Virgin *Mary*. For there is no House so poor, which has not the Picture of the Blessed Virgin, or some other Saint, before which they pray, Morning and Night, after they have lighted a Lamp.

In publick Baptism, the Child is brought to the Church Porch, where after the Priest has said an Exorcism, the Child is brought to the Font, and being interrogated by the Priest, the God-father makes answer, and rehearseth the Creed thrice. Then the Priest Consecrates the Water, which being hot

be

he pours into't Oil Olive, and Anoints the Child on ſeveral parts of the Body. The Child is Anointed on the Forehead, Mouth, Ears, Breaſt, Hands, Knees, and Feet with theſe words at every place; *The Seal of the Gift of the Holy Spirit.* Then the God-father claps a Croſs to the Childs Breaſt: This done, the Prieſt takes the Child ſtark naked, and baths him all over thrice in the Water, ſaying the ſame words as you had in private Baptiſm. After the third Bathing, he pours ſome of the Water upon the Child's Head: Then delivering the Child into the hands of the God-Fathers, he puts a Shirt on the Child, with theſe words; *Jeſus Chriſt our merciful God, cloathed with Light, give thee a bright Garment.*

Marriage. All the *Greeks* of the Iſland that (*b*) Marry, firſt obtain a Licenſe of the Arch-Biſhop, or his Grand Vicar: Then the Prieſt having examined if they have any Legal prohibition of affinity, or otherwiſe; either at the Church, or their own Houſes,

Houses, Marrys them in this manner. After the Reading of that part of the Liturgy which concerns Marriage, and the parties enterchanging a Ring, the Priest takes two Garlands made like Crowns, and signing them with the sign of the Cross, he puts one on the Bridegrooms Head, with these words:

The Servant of God N. N. is Crown'd to the Servant of God A. A. in the name of the Father, the Son, and the Holy Ghost, henceforth and for ever.

The like is done to the Bride, and then the Epistle and Gospel appointed for the Occasion is Read. Then he that gives them in Marriage, first Kisses the Garlands, and all the Company, in Testimony of their wishing Joy to the Married Parties.

On *Maunday Thursday*, which is an high day with the *Greeks*, * they Consecrate Bread, and pour upon it consecrated Wine, with these words:

* *Sacrament for the Sick.*

The

The Union and Conformation of the Holy Body, and Precious Blood, Amen.

This Bread is laid up till the first Sunday after *Easter*, and then the Priest in all his Formalities, lighting all the Lamps of the Altar, perfumes the Bread with Incense, and cuts it into pieces as small as a Grain of Wheat. Then being put up in a certain Vessel, it is laid up for all occasions of the Sick for that year. When any is Sick, he takes one of these Grains of Bread, and putting it into the Chalice, he carries it in his hand to the Sick Man's House: All that meet him by the way, go back with him to the sick Man's House: But at *Constantinople*, and other Cities where the *Turks* are numerous, the Priest carries it secretly under his Arm, for fear of some affront.

The Priest is oblig'd to carry this Sacrament to those that have the Plague, in which case, he puts the Grain of Bread into a Raison, and gives it him at the end of a long Cane.

When

When any person (*a*) dyes, a Lamp is lighted over the Corps, and the House is persum'd with Incense. Then the Corps being stript, they dip a Sponge or Lint in warm Water, and draw it over the Face, Knees, and Feet, in form of a Cross: Then taking a white Linnen Cloth, they make a Hole in the middle, large enough for the Head to come out, and sewing it up close at the Feet, they cloath him again with the best Garments the Party Deceased had. When the Corps are ready to go to Church, the Priest goes before the Corps with a Cross and a Taper in his hand, singing certain Prayers. At the Church, the Office for the Dead being ended, the Friends and Kindred of the Party Deceased, come and kiss the Corps. The Corps being brought to the Grave, the Priest takes some of the Earth, and sprinkling upon the Head, and the Feet, and the two Sides, in form of a Cross, saying these words:

(a) *Burial of the dead.*

The Earth is the Lords, and the fulness thereof; Take O Earth, that which is form'd of thee by the hand of God, who hath received that which was made according to his likeness, and do thou take the Body which belongs to thee.

Then the Priest throws upon the Corps some Water, or Oyl, out of one of the Church-Lamps, and a piece of flaming Incense, and so the Corps are covered. In *Samos* they give Bread and Wine at the Church, to those that accompany the Corps to Church.

Three days after Interment, the Friends of the (*a*) Deceased have a solemn Office at the Church for the Dead. After the Office is ended, they have a sort of small Junket, which they distribute, and Eat in the Church, with Wine, or Strong Water, to wash it down. This sort of Junket they call Κολυβα, *Colyba*, and they derive its first Institution from the time of *Julian* the Apostate, who to spite

(a) *Commemoration for the Dead.*

ſpite the *Chriſtians*, commanded all the Bakers to raiſe their Paſte with the Blood of Beaſts that were Sacrific'd to Idols. The *Chriſtians*, ignorant of the command, were about to buy the Bread, till St. *Theron*, that was a Martyr under *Maximin*, appearing to the Patriarch *Eudoxius*, admoniſh'd him to forbid the *Greeks* to Eat any Bread of the Bakers making, becauſe it was mix'd with the Blood of Beaſts offer'd to Idols. The Patriarch then ask'd the Saint what the People ſhould Eat. He told them *Colyba*, and ſo ſhew'd him the way how to make it. But now the *Greeks* uſe it at theſe Funeral Commemorations, and on a *Shrove-Sunday*; and the Sunday before *Pentecoſt*.

Moreover they have another Commemoration for the Dead, nine dayes after Burial, at the Houſe where the Party dy'd. Then again forty days; then at the end of three Months; then of ſix Months; then of nine Months,

 and

Publisher Note

This is to replace the incorrect printing of the bound page.

ſpite the *Chriſtians*, commanded all the Bakers to raiſe their Paſte with the Blood of Beaſts that were Sacrific'd to Idols. The *Chriſtians*, ignorant of the command, were about to buy the Bread, till St. *Theron*, that was a Martyr under *Maximin*, appearing to the Patriarch *Eudoxius*, admoniſh'd him to forbid the *Greeks* to Eat any Bread of the Bakers making, becauſe it was mix'd with the Blood of Beaſts offer'd to Idols.

and at last of twelve Months. The first Year of the party Deceased being expired, the Commemoration is only Annual.

Every Parish hath an anniversary Feast, in Commemoration of that peculiar Saint or Patron, to whose memory that Church is Dedicated, and by whose name it is called. All they of the Parish, and others that have a particular devotion for the Saint, carry with them a present of Bread, of a Wax-Taper and Frankincense. The Bread goes to the Arch-Bishops Vicar General; the Tapers and Incense to the service of the Church.

And now we have finished the Description of *Samos*, and the story of its present State and Condition, by which one place being one of the largest of the *Archipelago* for Circumference, and one of the Fruitfullest for Soil, We may guess at the condition of all the rest that are rich enough to maintain a Turkish Governour.

Besides

Besides it acquaints us in great part with the Religion of the whole *Greek* Church, which throughout the whole extent of the Patriarch of *Constantinoples* Jurisdiction, is very uniform, without any variation of Rites or Ceremonies.

A

A

DESCRIPTION

Of the ISLE of

Nicaria, olim *Icarus.*

THe Isle of *Nicaria* being under the Jurisdiction of the Arch-Bishop of *Samos*, I thought it expedient to add this Relation of it, as a Supplement to that of *Samos.*

Nicaria lies in length East and West; its prospect on the North is to *Scio*, on the South to *Paros* and *Naxos*, on the East to *Patmos*, and the West to *Mycone.* Three Miles distant from the Island, on the South-side towards *Patmos*, lye some small Islands unhabited; but known by the name of *Furny*, and furnish'd with good Harbours, capacious enough for all sorts of Vef-

Vessels. Here the *Corsairs* of *Malta*, and other *Christians*, us'd to lay in wait for Ships that trade from *Scio* to *Rhodes*. It lies twelve Miles distant from *Samos*. The Sea about it was formerly call'd the *Icarian* Sea, from *Icarus*, so Famous among the Ancient Poets.

Quid fuit ut tutas agitaret Dædalus alas,
Icarus *immensas nomine signet aquas?*
Tot premor adversis, ut si comprendere coner
Icariæ *numerum dicere coner aquæ.*
Ov. l. 4. El. tr. 5.

Icarus Icariis *nomina fecit aquis.*
Transit & Icarium, *lapsas ubi perdidit alas*
Icarus, *& vastæ nomina fecit aquæ.*
Ovid. l. 4. Fast.

It is upwards of fourscore Miles in compass, and yet has not one Port nor Road for great Ships, but only two small Creeks for little Boats. The one called τὸν ἅγιον

 φῶκα,

Φῶκα, *Ton Hagion Phoca*, from a Church here dedicated to St. *Phocas*: The other is called *Keramy*, so extremely bad, that they that come a shore here are forc'd to draw up their Boats after them. A Mile of *Keramy* is a little Island call'd Καραβοςάσι, *Karavostasi*, or the Rode for small Vessels, call'd *Karavia*. This affords a good retreat for Vessels in Tempestuous Weather. And when 'tis fair, they lade and unlade their Vessels with all possible speed, at the Shore of *Icarus*, and so retire, for fear of a Storm.

All the (*a*) Island is very Mountainous and full of Rocks, which causes but few Villages, and those very small, none of them exceeding an 100 Houses. The Promontory towards *Samos* is call'd *Phanari*, or the *Lanthorn*; because of a Watch Tower here built, to give light to Marriners in the Night. The Tower is yet standing, and the common People are so far mistaken in the common Fable, as to pretend that *Icarus* and his Son were

(a) Hor. *od.7. l.3. Scopulis surdior Icari.*

were here kept Prisoners. But they are given to a Credulity of new reports more inconvenient than that of old Fables, and that the belief of Treasures hid in all old Ruins ever since the taking of *Constantinople*, where so much was found long after it was burn'd. This conceit blown up by various reports, and the Itch of talking on one side, and the great credulity of ignorant People on the other, hath encreased into a vulgar Tradition, very incommodious to the *Greeks*, and whereat the *Turks* take great advantage against them, in case they meddle with any Ruins, either for Curiosity or Use. And these Islanders have a common Tradition, that about this old Tower of *Icarus* lyes a great treasure, whereof part, though not all, they say, was carri'd away some 40 years ago, by some *Asiaticks*, that came over by stealth, and in the Night, dug up all the ground; And an old Man, whom I spoke with, that saw them at work, but durst not come neer

till

till they had all gone aboard, and ſet Sail, upon his approach, found the dead Carkaſe of a Man newly ſlain; whom they ſuppoſe was ſacrific'd to the Genius of the place, or the Guardian Angel of the Treaſure. They add beſides, that before this adventure of the *Aſiaticks*, the place was haunted with a Spirit, which alwaies appear'd in black, and deſtroy'd their Oxen, at leaſt one in a year. But ſince that time, the place was no more haunted, nor did the Labourers ever complain of the loſs of an Ox.

About this Shore are the beſt Cockles of all the *Archipelago.* The principal Villages are 1. *Cachoria*, of 100 Houſes, and two or three *Ches.* 2. *Steli*, famous for great abundance of Nut-Trees. 3. *Muſara*, beſides which is an Hermitage, and a Church, wherein are kept the Reliques of St. *Theoctiſtes*, who was of *Lesbos*, and whom the People do think yet does Miracles at this day. Here are in the Iſle, the Ruins of a greater

Town

Town than any now is. The Church is yet ſtanding, and goes by the name of St. *Hellens*. The Beauty of its Fabriek, is a clear argument, it was built in the days of the *Conſtantinopolitan* Emperours; and though it has no Houſe neer hand it, yet great reſort is made hither for Devotion; and from time to time there never wants a *Papas* to ſay the Prayers of the Church in it.

There are beſides theſe three already nam'd, a great many little Villages ſcatter'd up and down through the whole Iſland, which for the number of Houſes, are larger of extent than thoſe in *Samos*; for here every Houſe is environ'd with its proper Garden, Orchard; but the Houſes in *Samos* are commonly built cloſer, and their Gardens, and Orchards at a greater diſtance.

The whole Iſland is for the moſt part Mountainous, and Rocky. The Valleys are few, and little in compaſs; ſo that with great labour, and

and difficulty, they force out of ſo barren a Soil, that little Corn they have; which is not ſufficient to feed the Inhabitants above one half the year; and lays a neceſſity upon the *Nicarians* to traffick abroad for ſupplies elſewhere. But principally they trade to *Scio* for Corn, whither they carry Wood from *Samos*, and the neighbouring parts of *Natolia*. They are very expert in making Boats, and ſmall Veſſels, which are in ſuoh eſteem, that they are bought up by all their Neighbours. Beſides their Traffick in Wood and ſmall Veſſels, they vend good ſtore of Sheep and Goats, wherewith their Mountains are well ſtor'd. And yet their care to keep them is ſo ſmall, that without either milking them, or driving them into Coats, or Folds, or making any limits or bounds, they only viſit them twice a Year, to count the number of their Flocks, and to imprint the Marks of the proper Owners. Some there are, and thoſe of the

Richeſt,

Richest, that are at the trouble of milking so many, as may supply their Family with Cheese. They vend likewise good store of Swines Flesh. Wax, and Honey they have great plenty of, but their Honey is in no great esteem, because of that bitterness of taste which it receives from their Bees feeding upon Firr leaves, which Tree that Island abounds with.

The most commendable thing of this Island is their Air and Water, both so healthful, that the People are very long liv'd, it being an ordinary thing to see persons in it of an 100 years of Age, which is a great wonder, considering how hardily they live. There is not a Bed in the Island, the Ground is their Tick, and the cold Stone their Pillow, and the Cloaths they wear is all the Coverlet they use. They provide no more Apparel than what they wear all at once, when that is past wearing any longer, then think of a new Suit. Betwixt their ordinary times of Eating,

Eating, there is not a piece of Bread to be found in the Isle. A little before Dinner, they take as much Corn as will serve that Meal, grind it with a Hand-Mill, bake it upon a flat Stone; when 'tis Bak'd, the Master of the Family divides it equally among the Family; but a Woman with child has two shares. If any Stranger comes in, every one parts with a Piece of his own share to accommodate the Stranger. Their Wine is always made with a third part Water, and so very weak and small. When they drink it, so much as is thought sufficient is put into one large Bowl, and so passes round. The *Nicarians* are the only Islanders of all the *Archipelago*, that neither keep Wine to sell, nor lay it up in Wooden Vessels, but in long Jars, cover'd all over in the Ground. When they have a mind to Tap it, they make a Bung-hole in the top, and draw it out with Canes. Their Houses are so plain, that all the Furniture you can see is an Hand-

Hand-Mill, besides this, there is nothing but bare Walls: That little they have besides is all hid under Ground; not so much for fear of the *Corsairs* (from whom their Poverty is a sure guard) as out of Custome. Nor are they all so poor, as not to be able to buy Beds, but custom has brought them into a contempt of Beds, as meerly superfluous; insomuch, that when they Travel into other Islands, they refuse the offer of a Bed. A Priest of *Nicaria* coming into *Samos*, was courteously entertain'd by those of his Order, and at Night was offer'd a Bed to lye in; he thank'd them, but refus'd, nor could by any importunity be prevail'd upon, but told them the Earth was his Mother, from whence he would not keep a distance; besides he was afraid of being Sick, if he should lye in a Bed; and therefore if they had a kindness for him, they must give him the liberty of sleeping after his own Country way.

When I went to visit them as Arch-

Arch-Bishop, and ignorant of the custom of the Country, carry'd no Bed. At Night, where I first lodg'd, asking for a Chamber, they told me they had no other than that where I first came; then asking for a Bed, they told me it was not the Custom of the Country; then desiring to borrow some Bed Cloaths for Love or Money, all they brought me was one Smock made of course Dimity.

They have no great communication one with another, any farther than the publick times of Sacred Solemnities, or Civil Business doth cause them to come together. At other times they keep strictly within the narrow Sphere of their own affairs. Formal Visits, Treats, and Entertainments, are things unknown. If any business do put them upon a Visit to their Neighbour, they come not close to his Door, but stand off at a great distance, and call aloud to him; If he make them answer, they discourse the Business they came about, standing

ſtanding off at the ſame diſtance; except they be earneſtly invited to come in. And this way of diſcourſing at a diſtance they practice more in the Fields and Mountains; their Voices being ſo ſtrong, that 'tis ordinary to talk at a Miles diſtance; ſometimes at four or five, where the Valleys interpos'd between two hills, give advantage to the Voice. Sometimes they can diſcourſe at that diſtance, that the carriage of the Sound through the Winding of the Valleys, ſhall require half a Quarter of an Hours time; and yet they make diſtinct, and proper Anſwers, both audible and intelligible, without the help of a *Stentorophonical* Trumpet.

Their Habit for the Men, is a Shirt, and over it a ſhort Caſſock, down to the Knees, to which, in Winter they add only a ſhort Veſt, that reaches a little below the middle. Stockings they never wear. There Shoes are only a piece of thin Copper, bow'd to the ſhape of their Feet, and every one is his own Shoe-maker. The Women have nothing but one Smock, but so large, that they wrap it double, or treble down to the Girdle, but below the Girdle single. The Priests, for greater reverence in the Church, ty two Towels about their Legs, the one is their usuall Bonnet, and the other their Girdle: so that they perform sacred Offices unguirt, as well as uncover'd.

Of all the Isles of the *Archipelago*, this only admits of no mixture with strangers in Marriage, nor admits any stranger to settle with them: They being, as they pretend, all descended of the Imperial Blood of the *Porphyrogenneti*, must not stain their noble Blood with inferiour Matches, or mixtures with *Choriats*, or Peasants, for so they term all the other Islanders.

Porphyrogenneti, were those of the Blood Royal, in the Days of the *Greek* Emperours, so call'd, from their wearing of Purple, which was a Badge of Royalty, and allow'd only to Princes of the Blood;

Blood; and not from an house call'd *Porphyra*, where the Empresses were wont to *lie in*. But Purple was throughout the East, the known Badge of Royalty. Hence came that unsanctify'd Wit, and learned'st Writer that ever oppos'd the *Christian* Religion with his Pen, to be call'd *Porphyrius*: For his true name in the Language of *Syria*, his native Country, was *Malchus*, or King; but the *Greeks* did paraphrase it *Porphyrius*, or Purple-robed; that being a Colour peculiar to Kings. Not so.

They have a great Happiness, by reason of their poverty, in not being molested by the *Turks*, who think it not worth their while to come among them, nor if they should, were they likely to enjoy any quiet, without keeping a stronger Guard than the Revenues of the Isle would maintain. Once they slew a *Caddee*, sent by the Grand Signior, and being summon'd to Answer for their Crime, they by common consent own'd the Fact, but would name no particular Man. So that the *Turkish* Officers looking upon their beggerly Cloaths, thought there was neither gain nor glory in punishing such Miscreants, and that in Justice, they must punish all, or none, dismiss'd them untouch'd. From that time no *Turk* ever troubled them: For they take all courses imaginable to seem poor; and wheresoever they come abroad, they count it no shame to beg Alms: Yet they make a shift every year to levy 300 Crowns for the Arch-Bishop. They are govern'd by a *Proesti* of their own chusing, who also levys their Haratch or Tribute to the Grand Signior, and takes care to carry it to the *Aga* of *Scio*. As for their Religion, it is the same with that of *Samos*; but their Priests are more ignorant.

Thus you have an account of a small Island, the Poorest, and yet the Happiest of the whole *Ægæan* Sea. The Soil is Barren, but the Air is Healthful; their Wealth is

but,

but ſmall; but their Liberty and Security is great. They are not moleſted with the Tyrannous Inſolence of a *Turkiſh* Officer, nor with the frightful Incurſions of barbarous and mercileſs Pirates. Their Diet and Apparel is below the Rate of Beggars in other Countrys, and their Lodging is a thing of no more care, or coſt, than that of the Beaſts of the Field, yet their Bodies are ſtrong and hardy, and the People generally long liv'd. They live with as little forecaſt, as if they expected not to ſurvive a Day, being contented to ſatisfy the preſent neceſſities of Nature. They do properly *In diem vivere*, or as we ſay, From Hand to Mouth. They have but little, yet they never Want. Their Ignorance is equal to their Poverty, and contributes much to their content. And how well they eſteem of their own condition, their contempt of their Neighbouring Iſlands, and ſcorning to mix with them in Alliance by Marriage, is a manifest sign. Whence we may learn, that they approach the nearest to Contentedness is this Life; whose desires are contracted into the narrowest compass.

A DESCRIPTION Of the ISLE of PATMOS.

THe Isle of *Patmos*, now call'd *Patino*, is 36 Miles in compass, 40 Miles from the Continent of *Asia*, towards *Ephesus*; as many Miles distant from *Samos* North East of it; 30 from *Nicaria*, North; 60 from *Paros*, and *Naxos*, West; 60 from *Amurgos*, South.

The Figure is neither round nor square, but irregular, by reason of unequal Promontories and Bays. It is furnish'd with very commodious Havens, to which it owes its being inhabited, though not so well as in former times, as appears by the many and great Ruins in it.

This Iſland was eminent for thoſe wonderful Revelations which the Bleſſed Apoſtle, and Evangeliſt St. *John* had in it, during his baniſhment thither in the time of the Perſecution under *Domitian*. The ſubſtance of what is related in that Life of St. *John*, that goes under the Name of *Prochorus*, is generally believ'd in *Patmos* to this day. And though the Author might be of later years than *Prochorus*, the Diſciple of St. *John*, as the moſt judicious Hiſtorians of later days do pronounce him to be: Yet that the whole contents of that Book ſhould be a meer Fable, and nothing but the Product of the Authors invention and fancy, is very improbable. For though he might take great liberty in the Manner and Circumſtance of what he relates, yet the Matter and Subſtance were built upon ſome foundations of real Truth, and ſuch as many Books now not extant, and the Streams of Tradition then nearer the Fountain, but now run dry, might acquaint

quaint him with. That the Island, at St. *John*'s first coming were all Idolaters, had people possessed with Devils, and were mis-led with Magicians, is more than probable. That St. *John*'s casting a Devil out of young *Apollonides*, had a great influence on the peoples Conversion, and rais'd him the Enmity of a Magician, and all that he could draw after him, is a thing reasonably credible. The Name of *Cynops* the Magitian, is known to all the People to this day; yea, not without some very improbable circumstances of the Story, that St. *John* should cause him to jump twice into the Sea, and the second time to be turn'd into a Rock, which now bears his name. However it is no small credit to a Place, otherwise very inconsiderable, that that great Apostle, once the peculiarly beloved Disciple; who of all the Apostles, did alone survive our Saviours judicial coming into his Kingdom of Power and Vengeance upon the *Jewish* Nation: that he

should

ſhould be for no ſmall time an Inhabitant of this Iſland, and there Pen that Myſterious and Sublime Book, which to him indeed was *Apocalypſe*, but to all others *Apocrypha*, to him a Revelation, but to us yet an hidden Myſtery: like the former Prophecies of the Old Teſtament, that were never rightly underſtood till actually fulfill'd. The Tradition of this Iſland is very poſitive, that he writ his Goſpel here likewiſe, and that upon the Requeſt of the Iſlanders, who at his departure, after ſeven years abode in the Iſland, did importune him to leave them in writing what they ought to believe: Whereupon he ſtaid eight days longer, to dictate the Goſpel to his Diſciples that writ it.

They add more, that as he was beginning the Work, there happened a great Thunder and Earthquake, whereupon, looking up to Heaven, he ſpake thoſe words; Ἐν ἀρχῇ ἦν ὁ λόγος: *In the beginning was the Word.* Beſides, it is a moſt confirm'd confirm'd Tradition, that the Cavern, which now goes by the name of the Holy *Grotto*, was made by the Rupture of the Earth, in that Earthquake.

The Original of this Iſland, as it is at this day, is aſcribed to St. *Chriſtodoulus*, in the Days of *Alexius Comnenus*.

It was *Alexius Comnenus*, the firſt of that name, in whoſe dayes began the Holy War, who reigned the 20 laſt years of the tenth Century, and the 18 firſt of the eleventh, and was contemporary with *William* the Conquerour, and *Godfrey* of *Bulloigne*. This *Chriſtodoulus* was Abbot of *Latros*, and had juriſdiction over ſome 20 Monaſteries in *Aſia*, near a great Lake about a days Journey and half from *Epheſus*. He being moleſted by the *Turks*, (whoſe power now mightily encreas'd in *Aſia*) obtained leave of the Emperour to build a Monaſtry in *Patmos*: Whither having tranſported his Wealth and Family, he built a Monaſtry near the Port of of *Neſtia*, and named it *Rouvali*. But not liking the place, (and as the Tradition goes, being warned by a Viſion, and a Voice from Heaven,) he quitted that Monaſtry, and built another in the higheſt part of the Iſland, and fortifi'd it with a ſtrong Caſtle, environ'd with high and ſtrong Walls: And there he built a Church. The Inhabitants that lay ſcatter'd in the Iſle, deſired leave to build Huts neer the Monaſtry, for their better Shelter, and defence, in caſe of any ſudden Attaque by Pirats. In proceſs of time, theſe Huts were chang'd into fair Houſes, and by Trade and Commerce, became a great Town, to the number of 800 Houſes, and there Inhabited by rich Merchants, that traded into all parts. But the many Revolutions that have happen'd ſince, have eclips'd the former Glory of the place: And their Ships of Merchandiſe are all dwindl'd into ſmall Fiſher Boats, and the Inhabitants are all extremely poor.

About

About half a mile from this place stands the Holy *Grotto*, where St. *John* the Evangelist is said to have writ the *Apocalypse*. Here is a small Monastry, under the Jurisdiction of a *Caloir*. The Inhabitants of the neighbouring Borough, pay great Devotion to this place. They talk here of a Fig-Tree, whose Figs have naturally the Characters of the Word Ἀποκάλυψις. *Apocalypsis*. Near the *Grotto* is a stone Font, where St. *John* the Evangelist is said to have baptiz'd.

The best Port of this Island, and of all the *Archipelago*, on the West side towards *Naxos*, is call'd *Scala*, or the *Wharf*, because of a Wharf built of stone for the convenient lading or un-lading of Ships. That which renders it free from annoyance of Winds are certain little Islands that shelter it from the East and North-east Winds. The *Venetian* Fleet were wont to winter here during the War of *Candy*.

Besides this Port, stands an entire Village, call'd *Phocas*, without an Inhabitant.

Inhabitant. Here is likewise among old Ruins, a Church yet standing, which they say was built in St. *John*'s days, and they shew something like a Pulpit, where they say St. *John* us'd to Preach. 2. *Merike*, whose neighbouring Hills are well stored with Vine-yards. 3. *Leukes*, fortify'd with a Castle for the Retreat of the Labourers in the Vine-yards, and well supply'd with fresh Fish, from a neighbouring Lake. 4. *Myrsini*, from the growth of Myrtles hereabouts. Here is a Fountain of excellent Water, which the People call Ἁγίασμα, *Hagiasma*, or *Holy-Well*. 5. St. *Nicholas*, from a Church here dedicated to that Saint. 6. St. *George*'s from a Church here dedicated to that Saint: This is a convenient place for Ships to take in fresh Water at. Two Miles hence are the Ruins of an old Town call'd πλάτυς ἀιγίαλος, *Platys Gialos*, or the *Broad shore*; but now it is cover'd with the shrub *Arbutus*, which the *Greeks* call *Coumara*, in old *Greek*

Greek Κώμαρον: it bears a Fruit like a Strawberry, but much bigger. 7. *Turcolimnionos*, or the *Turks* Port, because it is frequented by the *Corsairs*. Betwixt this place and Port *Scala*, a rich Merchant *Nicholas Mathas* did lately build a Tower at *Livadi*; it being a convenient place for Vine-yards and Fishing. 8. *Agrio Livadi*, before which lies St. *Thecla*'s Isle with a little Church, dedicated to that Saint. 9. Port *Sapsila*, before which lies a little Island, with a Church in it, dedicated to St. *Luke*. 10. Port *Gricou*, next to *Scala* for commodiousness. The Island *Tragonesi*, or Isle of *Goats*, defends it from all Winds. 11. *Diacopti*, famous for Salt Pits, which belong to the *Caloirs*. Besides this Port, is a steep Rock of a very great height, which they call *Cynops*, from the Magician in St. *John*'s days, whom the People report to have lodg'd in a great Cave in this Rock; which Cave they yet believe to be haunted by Devils. For once letting down a Man

Man into't by a Cord for curiosity, to see what was in the Cave, they pull'd him up dead. 12. *Meloi*, a Mile from Port *Scala*. And so we have finish'd the Circuit of the Island, in naming the Ports.

The Inland Villages are 1. *Livadi*. 2. *Vagie*, well beset with Vines and Figtrees. 3. *Megalocampos*, rich in the same Fruits, and accommodated with a Lake well stor'd with Fish. 4. *Hagio Theophanes*, from a Church there dedicated to that Saint, and built by St. *Christodoulos*. 5. *Sazousa*, close by the Sea, near to which are hot Springs of Water, that cure many Diseases. The Island is well stored with Vines, Figg-Trees, Lemon and Orange Trees, and Corn sufficient for the Inhabitants, if they could keep what they have free from the Robbery of Pirats, as well *Christian* as *Mahometan*, that often pillage the poor People, who have no other remedy but patience, and sometimes the pleasure of seeing them perish at Sea, that have been so so injurious to a Shore. The *Patmians* complain more of the Cruelty of the *Christian* Pirats, than of the *Turks*. And though the Islanders have procur'd Charters and Patents from the Pope; the King of *France*; from the State of *Venice*; from the Dukes of *Tuscany*; from the Grand Master of *Maltha*, to secure them from the Injuries of *Christian Corsairs*; it is so far from prevailing upon them to withhold their hands from rapine, that it does but provoke them to more fierceness. Yet these Pirats sometimes are made the visible objects of Divine Vengeance. About six years ago, the Marquess de *Fleury*, that carry'd away not only the Grazing, but the Working Cattle, had got no further than *Paros*, 'till his Ship sunk in the Port, and he was taken Prisoner, and clapt into custody at *Corfou*, by the *Venetians*. Another that pillag'd the Monastry of *Liptos*, had no sooner put to Sea, but meeting with some *Saiks*, to which he gave earnest Chase, he run himself a Ground, and there perish'd he, and all his Company.

Let us now return to the State and Government of the Place. The whole Island was given by (a) *Alexius Comnenus* to *Christodoulus*, and his successours in the Monastry, and the Islands near about, that were not inhabited. And what Culture they bestow on the little Islands, or what Cattle they put to Grazing there, becomes all a Prey to the *Corsairs*; so that the Revenues of this Monastry are now much diminish'd, and the Monks become extremely poor. And his Son *Calo Johannes*, gave also fourteen Villages in *Candie*: But the *Turks* left them but one small Hospital in *Candie*, which yields them 200 Dollars a Year, whereas their Revenues before were at least 13000. Besides the great Monastry, there is a little Nunnery, containing 40 Nuns. This was built but an age ago. They purchase their living by their labour, for they have no Revenues; only the Abbot of the great Monastry

Circiter annum Christi 1100.

stry is oblig'd to supply them with a Reverend Ancient Monk, to do all Sacred Offices among them. Besides these, there are some small Hermitages that maintain some few Monks. 1. The Hermitage of the Holy *Grotto* of St. *John* the Divine. 2. The Hermitage of the *Parasceve*. 3. Of the Annuntiation of the Blessed Virgin, lately built by a Bishop in this last Century. 4. The Hermitage, called *Asomati*. Lastly, in a place called the Gardens, which furnish the Monks Kitchin with all necessaries. They have certain Chappels consecrated for the Labourers, at certain Hours, to hear Prayers, and so return to their Work.

And this is the present Condition of the Isle of *Patmos*, once famous for the Residence of that great Apostle St. *John*, and for the great and mysterious Revelation he had in it. But now groaning under the Yoke of such Lords as are common enemies to the Christian Faith, by whom they are both kept in great awe, and ſlaviſh obedience, and yet ill protected againſt the violent Incurſion of Pirats and Robbers: ſo that Poverty is their beſt Protection againſt Rapine, and Patience the only Remedy againſt the grievous Yoak of Tyrannical Oppreſſion.

A

A DESCRIPTION OF MOUNT *ATHOS*.

MOunt *Athos* is a demy-Isle, or Chersonese, lying betwixt the Gulf of *Strymon*, from a River of that name on the North, and the Gulf of *Singus*, from the Town *Singus*, on the South. The *Isthmus*, or Neck of Land that parts them, is not much above a Mile broad: It is called by the *Greeks* Ἅγιον ὄρος, and *Athonas*, by the *Franks*, (or Western *Christians*) *Monte Santo*. It is 170 Miles in compass. *Lemnos* stands directly East of it, some 40 Miles distant, and a little before Sun-set is overshadow'd by it. *Thassos* is 30 Miles distant to the

North-east. *Thessalonica* is four days Journey to the West, and *Philippopoli* as many to the North. On the Land side there stands erected a great Wooden Cross, beyond which all Women are forbidden to pass. Because the *Caloirs*, the only Inhabitants of the place, are forbidden all communication with Women, as the principal Rule of their Profession.

Not far from this Cross, without the Bounds, on the Water-side, stands a Village call'd *Alladiava*. The Inhabitants live most upon Fishing, and bring their Fish to sell to the *Caloirs*. If perchance their Wives, or any Women of their Family come along with the Men, they are left in the Boat, and not suffer'd to step a Shore, for fear of Excommunication; for the highest Rule of Discipline, and the most strictly observed, is that of not conversing with Women. And for more caution, and better security of preserving this Rule inviolable, they suffer no other

Female

Female Creature of what kind soever, nor any Children, or young men, that are Beardless to come within the Mount.

In describing the place, we cannot pass from Town to Village, but only from Monastrys to Hermitages.

1. The first, and most ancient, (a) St. *Laura*, built by *Athanasius*, who obtained special License of the Emperour of *Constantinople* to retire hither, and found a College of Monks; so called, from that Monastry of *Laura* of *Bethlehem*, where St. *Saba* liv'd, and his Disciple *John*, once Bishop of *Colonia* in *Armenia*, and afterwards Monk, after the Discipline of St. *Saba*; whose Disciples, from a peculiar Rule of Silence, which they did solemnly profess, and strictly practice, were call'd *Silentiarii*. Of this Order was *Anastasius* the Emperour, before he was advanc'd to the Imperial Dignity: Of whom *Baronius* relates, that in the Year of our Lord, 491, he was from a

(a) Saint Laura's *Monastry*.

Professour of silence, made a Soveraign Prince, *Ex Silentiario factus Imperator.* The Monks of the place have a long Story, how this *Athanasius*, wanting Money to go on with the great Church of the Monastry, which he had begun, was met with by the Blessed Virgin, who took his staff from him, and smote a Rock, 'till it sent out a Spring of Water, that runs at this day; then thrusting his staff into the Ground, it became a Tree, and sent forth Boughs and Leaves. Then she bid him take no care for necessaries, she would provide, and did avow her self to be the Patroness of that Monastry, and of the whole Mountain. This Monastry is about a Mile from the Sea, on the East side, and hath a convenient Channel, that brings up Vessels to their very Walls; where they have a strong Magazin, and a Sentinel perpetually standing to give notice of any *Corsairs*. It hath likewise a very fair Church, and in their Hall, where they eat in common,

common, there is a large Marble Table, where 600 Monks sit down together.

2. The Monastry of (a) *Caracale*, the Name of its Founder, who did consecrate it to the Apostles St. *Peter* and St. *Paul*. This is eight Miles from the former, towards the North. It maintains 500 Monks. The Gate of the Monastry is adorn'd with an exceeding high Tower. Here is likewise a Cistern cut out of a Rock 26 Fathoms deep. This also being near the Sea, has upon the shore a Watch Tower, a Magazin, and a little Port.

(a) *Caracale.*

3. (b) *Philothe*, from the Founders name. This maintains but 50 Monks, though well stor'd with Orchards and Gardens, with its Watch Tower, and Magazin also by the Sea side. Their Church is dedicated to the Annuntiation of the Blessed Virgin.

(b) *Philothe.*

4. (c) *Imberus*, by the name of its Founder. This Monastry is in great repute for a Picture of the Virgin *Mary* upon the Gate, which Picture,

(c) *Imberus.*

Picture, by the report of Tradition, was found floating by the Shore. This Monastry has good Revenues in *Imbrus*, and maintains 400 Monks.

(a) *Coutulmousi*, 5. (a) *Coutulmousi* maintains 300 Monks; it is commodiously surrounded with Gardens, and has a fair Church dedicated to the Transfiguration of our Saviour.

6. *Porpat.* Here is the general Assembly of all the Monastries in this Mountain; hither every Monastry sends a Deputy under the name of *Proesti*, whose business is to reside in the place, and to be ready to consult of all affairs that concern the publick Good. Here is every *Saturday* a publick Market, and the only Market within the whole circumference of the Mount. Here also dwells the *Aga*, with two or three other *Turks*, who protects them from all injuries of other *Turks*, especially of the Sea-men from *Barbary*, whom they call *Levents*. The *Bostangy-Basha* appoints this Officer from amongst the *Bostangies*,

stangies. He is to stay in his Office two years, and then another succeeds him. He is maintained at the common charge of the *Caloirs*, who give him a yearly Pension. And besides, upon every Church Festival, he is invited from Monastry to Monastry, by course, and there, besides the Entertainment of him and his Retinue, he is always presented with a Purse of Money, according to the abilities of the Monastry.

7. *Stauro-Nikita*, or *The Conquering Cross.* This maintains but 30 Monks. Their Church is dedicated to St. *Nicholas*, where they have in great estimation his Picture upon a Board, that was found ready painted, as a Wreck, and devoutly taken up by the Monks of this Covent.

8. *Pantocratoras* maintains 200 Monks; their Church is dedicated to the Transfiguration of our Blessed Saviour.

9. *Vatopedi* maintains 300, their Church is dedicated to the Blessed Virgin.

10. *Tou-*

10. *Tousimenou* has but 80 Monks; the Church is dedicated to the Ascension. It is the poorest of all the Monastry, not for want of Lands, but of Men to cultivate them. For the soil about, is the best in all the Mount. It bears Olives of a singular largeness, and wants no other sort of Fruit Trees. But the number of the Monks in it amount but to 80, who being not able to make the best advantage of so much good ground continue poor in a plentiful Soil.

In the middle of all the Mount stands 11. *Chiliantary*, a Monastry of the *Bulgarians*, who speak here their own Language, and have their Prayers (though the same with the *Greek*) in the *Bulgarian* Language. This is the largest Monastry of the whole Island, and maintains 800 Monks. They have much Land abroad, which they send their own Monks to cultivate.

12. *Touzographou*, or the *Painters Convent*, from the Founder, who was

was a Painter. The Church is consecrated to St. *George*, it maintains 200 Monks, all *Bulgarians*. There is a little Church not far from this Monastry, that stands alone, and now is useless; but having a fair Picture of St. *George* in it, the Monks thought fit to bring it into their own Church; but to no purpose, for so often as they brought it, so often it takes its leave, and is found the next day in the Church.

13. *Xenophon*, a *Burgarian* Monastry, has but 30 *Caloirs*.

14. *Castamoniti* has not above six, or seven Monks at most, yet it hath a Chappel dedicated to St. *Steven*.

15. *Archangeli*, which had before another name, but changed to this upon this occasion. A young *Caloir*, that was tilling the Ground abroad, found a Treasure in an old Urn, and brought the news of it to the Superiour of the Convent; he sent with the young Man two other *Caloirs*, who finding the Treasure, agreed between themselves

ſelves to kill the Boy, and ſhare it betwixt them; and ſo they ty'd a Stone about his neck, and caſt him into the Sea, and hiding the Treaſure, came to the Superiour, and told him the Boy had deceiv'd them, and was run away. Next morning the Sexton found the Boy and the Stone about his neck in the Church, who diſcover'd all, and told that the Angels *Gabriel* and *Raphael* brought him thither. The two *Caloirs* thus convicted, were baniſh'd, and this ſtone ſet up as a Monument to this day.

16. The Monaſtry of *Ruſſicon* has a Church dedicated to *Panteleimon*, and maintains 20 *Caloirs*.

17. *Xeropotamou*, dedicated to the Memory of 40 Martyrs that were drowned in the Lake of *Sebaſte*. This Monaſtry has 300 Monks, and being by the Sea ſide, has a Magazin and a great Watch-Tower. Over againſt this Monaſtry, on the Continent of *Macedonia*, ſtands a great Village of Hermits and religious Perſons, though without

without the bounds of the *Caloirs*.

18. *Simo-Petra*, so called, from the Founder and the Foundation. It is situate on a Rock, and was founded by one *Simon*, an Hermit, who by his Prayers having cured the Daughter of a Governour of *Cassandria*, did move him to bestow enough for to build this Monastry, and 200 Monks. They shew here an hand for a sacred Relique of St. *Mary Magdalen*'s body, but the Fingers of it are extraordinary great.

19. *Gregorios*, near the Sea, and much infested with Pirats for want of Fortification, and men to defend it, having but 60 Monks.

20. *Dionisiou*, consecrated to St. *John Baptist*, whose Forehead they pretend to shew here as a sacred Relique. Besides they shew the Bones of one *Nymphus*, once Patriarch of *Constantinople*, who being weary of publick employment, retir'd hither, unknown to any who he was; so they looking upon him as a poor Vagabond, that wanted work,

work, employ'd him as their Muleteer, to fetch in their wood; in which employment he continued with great humility and faithfulness many years, not offering to ride any of the Mules going or coming, and kept all the Church Fasts strictly in the midst of all his drudgery. At his death-bed he discover'd to the Superiour who he was, and that he chose that manner of Life to mortifie his proud Flesh. Whereupon, looking upon him as a Saint, they keep his Bones as a sacred Relique.

21. *Hagios Paulos*, so named from the Founder, who was reputed a Saint. It maintains 200 Monks, all *Bulgarians*.

Pass we now to the Hermitages, which are very small, but commonly so neer one another, as to make the appearance of a Village. There are two places where they lye in great numbers. 1. *Hagia Æna*, or St. *Ain*, from a Church dedicated to that Saint. These are the retiring places of such Hermits as live by by Manufacture, as particularly, the making of Crosses and Figures that represent our Saviours Passion, and Seals and Marks proper for the consecrated Bread. The *Caloirs* that are sent abroad to confess People, and to gather Alms for pious Uses, buy up all these Manufactures to present unto people among whom they come. These Hermits live more retired and melancholly, being not above two or three, sometimes but one in an House. And they do imitate the Lives of those antient Monks in *Ægypt*, about *Thebais*, that were imitators of St. *Anthony*, who did himself, as did all his followers, live and maintain themselves by hand labour and manufactures, though of a very mean sort, yet enough to earn them Food and Raiment. This St. *Anthony* was the first *Christian* Monk of the World, his Food was only Bread and Water; yet he liv'd 150 years: His fame was so great, that *Helen*, the Mother of *Constantine* the Great, did by letters sent to him, recommend Her ſelf and her Son to his Prayers. He dy'd in the Wilderneſs. *An. Dom.* 361. 2. *Keraſia*, another plot of Ground, all ſtrew'd with ſuch Hermitages as are at St. *Aine*, and they live in the very ſame manner.

Beſides theſe Hermitages that lye ſo neer in voiſinage, there are above 1000 more diſperſed up and down the Iſland, which do all belong to ſome one of the Monaſtries. If a Man deſire to live in a Cell, he gives a certain Rate to that Monaſtry to which it belongs, and ſo is empowr'd to enjoy that Cell, and the Land belonging to't for his life: when he dies, it returns to the Monaſtry, and the Monaſtry is Heir to all that he leaves behind him. There are Cells of all rates, from 5 Dollers to 150. One thing is very remarkable, that Idleneſs is utterly baniſh'd here, no man lives in the Iſle, who is not ſome way employ'd.

As for the maintenanee of theſe Monaſtries, though their Lands be ſufficient to feed them, and their

Moun-

Mountain furnish them with Wine enough to drink; yet as the matter is order'd, they commonly want Money to pay their *Haratch*, or yearly Tribute of 3 Dollers *per* Poll, and buy themselves Cloaths and Furniture for tilling their Land. So that every year they select some of their *Caloirs* to go abroad, and beg the Charity of *Christian* People, towards the relief of the respective Monastry. And these are always by two and two together. And the Monastries agree before-hand to what particular places they will send their respective Emissaries, who continue ordinarily two or three years in their perambulation. At their coming home, the Money is delivered to the *Skenaphylax*, or the Steward of the Monastry; for it is against the Rule of their Order, to meddle with Money. He layes it out upon necessary occasions, and what is left, is kept to defray the Charge of another Voyage. They have a Register of those that bestow any thing, and they pray for them constantly in the Monastry.

When they are chosen to go abroad, the Chief of the Monastry names one of the *Caloirs*: The Person named, in token of his obedience, doth prostrate himself on the Ground before the Superiour of the Monastry, and rising, kisses the Superiours hand. Then the Person first nam'd, names those that shall go along with him, who in like obedience, first prostrate themselves before the Superiour, and kiss his hand, then do the like to the *Caloir* first nam'd by the Convent, and own him for their Father and Superiour, to whom they owe all obedience during their mission. When they go abroad, they first apply themselves to the *Metropolite* of the Diocese, and shew him their Letters of Obedience from their Superiours. Whereupon the *Metropolite* gives them Letters of Permission to ask Charity, and confess Penitents throughout his Diocese. Where they Confess any, they exact nothing of them by way of pecu-

niary

niary Penance, but only receive what in charity they freely bestow.

The beginning of Monks in Mount *Athos*, was from the time that the *Mahometans* invaded *Ægypt* and *Syria*, where the Monks in those places enjoying no security of their lives, came into *Greece*, and desired of the Emperour a Place to live in, according to their Monastick way. He appointed them Mount *Athos*, and *Athanasius* forementon'd, was the first that founded a College here. They professed at first the imitation of St. *Anthony* of *Ægypt*, and St. *Sabas*; but now the Rules of their Order are taken from St. *Basil*.

At their first coming to Mount *Athos*, they were a Colony of the Monks of the *Holy Land*, who follow'd the Rules of St. *Anthony* of *Ægypt*, and St. *Sabas*; but chiefly the Rules of St. *Sabas*, who liv'd long after St. *Anthony*, when Monkery began to alter its mode and fashion, and from a casual Retirement of some few men to a rude and simple way of life in the Wilderneſs, to become ſubject to Rules and Orders, to incorporate into Societies, to change their Caves into Cloiſters, and to remove from Deſerts to good dwelling Houſes, and places of better convenience and accommodation. This St. *Sabas*, by his eminent and ſingular ſtrictneſs, did highly advance the Fame and Admiration of a Monaſtick life. He was by birth a *Cappadocian*, of the Village of *Mutalaſca*, in the Dioceſe of *Cæſarea*, and being left Heir to a good Eſtate, under the Care of his Uncle *Hermias*, the perverſeneſs of his Aunt made him quit that Uncles Houſe, and go to *Scandos*, to live with another Uncle, whoſe name was *Gregory*. This breeding a Diſſention between the two Uncles, he, to avoid all occaſion of diſcord, betook himſelf to the Monaſtry of *Flaviana* near *Mutalaſca*; whence at the eighteenth year of his Age, he went to *Jeruſalem*, to viſit thoſe places which our Bleſſed Saviours life and death hath made ſo so memorable. At that time the Fame of *Euthymius*, then Abbot of *Laura* by *Bethlehem*, was very great in the *Holy Land*. This enflam'd young *Sabas* with great desire to be admitted into his Monastry: Wherefore one day as *Euthymius* was going to receive the Sacrament, he fell down at his feet, begging leave to be entred into his College: But *Euthymius* gave him the Repulse, telling him it was not fitting that so young a Man should be admitted into *Laura*; yet he would recommend him to a smaller Monastry hard by, where St. *Theoctistes* was Abbot: Where having stay'd ten years, *Euthymius* admitted him into a Cave by his own Monastry for five years. Then *Euthymius* selected him, and *Domitian* to vye *asketick* Severities in a solitary Place for four years, which having perform'd to great admiration, about the Fortieth year of his Age he retir'd to a Cave by the Brook of *Siloe*. By that time he had liv'd here five years he had a College of Disciples, to the number of 70, amongst whom was *John* the Silentiary, Bishop of *Colonia* in *Cappadocia*, before he entred into his Monastick life, and afterwards Abbot of this College, which was call'd *Nova Laura*. There were afterwards more Monastries of this name in *Palæstin*. *Laura Pyrgiorum* by *Jordan*, built by one *Jacobus*. *Laura Malischæ*, built by *Firminus*, and *Laura Marichæ*, by *Severianus*, and *Laura Elcerebæ*, by *Julianus*. But this *Laura*, built by St. *Sabas*, was the most Famous, where in his life-time the number of his Monks encreas'd to 150. He was eminent in the time of *Anastasius*, *Justinus*, and *Justinianus*, Emperours of *Constantinople*, and dy'd in the 94th year of his Age. His name is yet very remarkable among the Eastern *Christians*, especially at Mount *Athos*, whose first Monks were but a Colony of his Disciples, and whose ancientest College is called *Laura*, from his *Laura* in *Palæstine*.

Their constant morning Prayer is three hours before day; their evening ſevening Prayer at Sun-ſet. On *Sundays* they go to Prayers five hours before day in the morning, and before great Holy-days their Prayers continue all night. They have likewiſe other ſet hours of Prayer for the day-time.

They that enter into this profeſſion, are kept ſix months Probationers; during which time they are put to all the Exerciſe they muſt undergo in their Profeſſion. After the ſix months are expired, the Novitiat chuſeth among the Old *Caloirs* a God-father to introduce him, and to inſtruct him in the Ceremony of his Admiſſion. This God-father brings him to the Church door, where he is ſtrip'd to his Shirt, and proſtrates himſelf, then he makes a ſecond proſtration in the middle of the Church, and a third at the Altar, and a fourth to the Superiour. Then upon his knees he anſwers to all the Interrogatories made him by the Superiour, which are commonly theſe.

Sup. My Brother, what motives have

have you to come to this Altar, and to this Assembly?

Nov. *A desire to live a Monastick life.*

Sup. Do you come of your free choice, without any constraint?

Nov. *Yes.*

Sup. Will you for ever stay in the Monastry, and observe its rules?

Nov. *Yes.*

Sup. Will you keep Chastity, Temperance, and Godliness?

Nov. *By the Grace of God.*

Sup. Will you all your life be obedient to the Superiour, and his fraternity in Jesus Christ?

Nov. *By the Help of God.*

After these and some more Questions of like nature, some Prayers are said out of the *Euchologion*, and the Superiour shewing him the Book of the Gospel, doth conjure him by it, if he come to that Profession of his own proper motion. He answering in the Affirmative, the Superiour gives him a pair of Sciffers, bidding him deliver them back into his hand: Which done, the

the Superiour cuts off a little of his hair in the form of a Cross, saying, **Our Brother N. N. hath his head shaven, in the name of the Father, the Son, and the Holy Ghost.** The rest that stand by say three times *Kyrie Eleeson.* Then his Monastick habit is put on in order.

1. his *Cassock*, whereat the Superiour says, **Our Brother N. puts on the Garment of gladness, in the name of the Father,** &c. The Company say thrice *Kyrie Eleeson.*

2. His Girdle with these words. **Our Brother girds his reins with the strength of truth, to mortifie his Body, and to renew his Spirit, in the name of the Father,** &c. Then follows the *Kyrie Eleeson* thrice.

3. His Bonnet with these words. **Our Brother puts on the Helmet of Hope and Salvation, in the name of the Father,** &c.

4. His Mantle, with these words: **He puts on the Mantle as the earnest**

earnest of Angelique apparel; and of incorruptible Glory, in the name of the Father, &c.

5. His Sandals, with these words. He puts on the Shoes of the preparation of the Gospel of Peace, in the name of the Father, &c. with the *Kyrie Eleeson* thrice, as in all the rest. Then after the rehearsal of an Epistle and Gospel, and some Prayers, they put a Cross into his hand with these words: Our Saviour saith, if any man will be my Disciple, let him deny himself, and take up his Cross, and follow me. Then a Candle lighted is put into his hands, with these words.

Our Lord hath said, Let your Light so shine before men, that they seeing your good works, may glorifie your Father who is in Heaven.

This done, the other *Caloirs*, every one salute him with a Kiss, and so the Ceremony is ended.

The Rules are these,

1. To renounce the World, and

all

all that is near, and dear to them in it, as a Father and Mother, *&c.* according to that of our Saviour.

2. To continue in the Monaſtry in obedience to the Superiour and his Brethren.

3. To ſuffer all afflictions, and torments for the Love of God.

4. To have nothing of their own, but all in common among their Brethren.

5. To keep themſelves unſpotted from all carnality.

6. To be always ready to go to Prayers at the appointed Hours. At Midnight; before Day; at Noon; at three a Clock after Noon; at Sun-ſet; and after Supper: And after all this, when they go to their Cells, where they lye, to make 60 Proſtrations, which they call *Metánoia's*, or Pennances, with a ſhort Prayer to every one for the Superiour; for their Brethren; for the Benefactors of the Monaſtry, and in general, for all *Chriſtians.*

7. Not to eat or drink in ſecret; but

but in common with their Brethren; and this is so observ'd, that in case they are pinch'd with thirst betwixt Meals, they drink at the Window, or Door of the Cell, that all may see them, and before they drink, they cry aloud, Ἐυλογεῖ, i. e. *Give thanks.*

8. Not to eat Flesh all their lives, which is so strictly observed in Mount *Athos*, that in no sickness they are permitted to break this rule; but the Monks that Travel, in case of sickness, may eat Flesh, if the Physician advise them to't. But in Mount *Athos* they are allow'd on *Sundays*, *Tuesdays*, *Thursdays*, and *Saturdays*, to eat Eggs, Butter, Cheese, and Fish; the other days they eat none of these, nor drink any thing but Water only; and those other days they have only a Dinner, at Night they eat a piece of Bread, and drink a little water at the Church-door, and so to Prayers, and thence to their Cells, where they remain in great silence. But the Sick, Aged, and

and ſuch as have newly come from a Journey, are allow'd to eat in the common Refectory.

For the better Government of the Monaſtry, the Superiour goes in perſon to every man's Cell, accompanied with ſome of the elder *Caloirs*, and if he find any man out of his Cell, or two or three together in another man's Cell, this is a Crime, after three reproofs very puniſhable. The younger *Caloirs* ſtand in great dread of this nocturnal Perambulation, and have that ſaying of St. *Pauls* very much inculcated. *Heb.* 13. 17.

The Burying of the Dead is much like the way of Burying, deſcribed at *Samos*, with this difference, that a Year after Interment, they take up the Scull, and waſh it with Wine, and put it in a Charnel, inſcribing the name of the Deceaſed upon the Charnel.

Thus much of Mount *Athos*, wherein is a thing remarkable, beyond all example, that in a ſpace

ſpace of ground, 160 Miles in compaſs, where no leſs than 6000 men conſtantly live, there ſhould not be ſeen a Woman.

FINIS.

Bibliography

Manuscript Sources

Brussels, Bibliothèque Albert Ier
MS II 5359

Buenos Aires, Archivo General de la Nación
Sala IX, legajo, 48–8–2

Cambridge, MA, Houghton Library
Marquess of Bute, broadsides A 193, 195

Leicestershire, Belvoir Castle
Archives, Add. 7: Letters from Grace, Lady Chaworth
Volume headed: Haddon: Mr Edwd Sympsons Act … 1678–1679

London, British Library
Additional MS, 10130, 22910, 22910, 22912, 22914, 32095, 38142, 38847
Additional MS, 70263, Portland MS, Harley Papers, File 11

London, Guildhall Library
MS 3047/2, Tylers and Bricklayers Search Book 1650–1680

London, House of Lords Record Office
HL/PO/JT/1/1
Ms Journal of House of Lords
Ms Minute Book

London, London Metropolitan Archives
SC/PZ/WE/01/0276, 0288, 0293, 0294

London, National Archives
KB 27/2040
PC 2/64, 66, 67
SP 44/40A; 44/46; 44/51
31/3/141; 31/9/100A

London, Westminster Archives Centre
F404, Churchwardens' Accounts St Martin in the Fields
F2004 Vestry Minutes St Martin in the Fields

Matlock, Derbyshire County Record Office
D 239 M/O 1604

Oxford, Bodleian Library
MS Ashmole F.1 no. 74
MS Carte 130
MS Rawlinson A 136
MS Smith viii–lx
MS Tanner 33
MS Wood 417, F 40
University Archives, WPB/21/5: Vice Chancellor's Accounts 1666–97

Paris, Bibliothèque Nationale
Ancien Fonds Grec., 86 and 118

Wiltshire, Longleat
Coventry papers, vols xi, xxxiii, lxix,

Printed Sources and Secondary Works

Abbot, G. F., *Under the Turk in Constantinople: A Record of Sir John Finch's Embassy, 1674–1681* (London, 1920).
Amory, H., *Bute Broadsides in the Houghton Library, Harvard University: Guide and Index to Microfilm Coll.* (Woodbridge, CN, 1981).
Anderson, S. P., *An English Consul in Turkey: Paul Rycaut at Smyrna, 1667–1678* (Oxford, 1989).

Angelini, A., *Gian Lorenzo Bernini e i Chigi, tra Roma e Siena* (Siena, *c.*2000).
Baan, I., *Theophanes Mavrogordatos (1626–1688), Metropolitan of Paronaxia and Administrator of Munkacs* (Nyiregyhaza, 2012).
Bakalopoulos, E., *Historia tou Neou Hellenismou*, 4 vols (Thessaloniki, 1961–73).
Baratier, E., ed., *Histoire de Marseille* (Toulouse, 1973).
Barbounes, M. G., *Laikē latreia kai threskeutikē symperiphora tōn katoikōn tēs Samos* (Athens, 1992).
—— *Oi Mones tēs Samou* (Athens, 2006).
Barres, A. des, *L'estat present de l'Archipel* (Paris, 1678).
Barron, J., 'Archbishop Joseph Georgirenes and the Prehistory of the Greek College', in Peter M. Doll, ed., *Anglicanism and Orthodoxy 300 Years after the 'Greek College' in Oxford* (Oxford, 2006), pp. 79–112.
—— 'The Sixth-Century Tyranny at Samos', *Classical Quarterly*, n.s. xiv (1964), pp. 210–29.
Bauden, F., ed., *Le Voyage a Smyrne: un manuscript d'Antoine Galland: contenant Smyrne ancienne et moderne et des extraits du Voyage fait en Levant* (Coll. Magellane: Paris, 2000).
Belon, P., *Les Observations de plusieurs Singularitez et choses memorables* (Paris, 1553).
Benedicti p. XIV Bullarum, 4 vols (Venice, 1778).
Bent, J. T., *The Cyclades, or Life among the Insular Greeks* (London, 1885), ed. G. Brisch (Oxford, 2002).
—— *Early Voyages and Travels in the Levant* (Hakluyt Society, London, 1893).
Bere, E. S. de, ed., *The Diary of John Evelyn*, 6 vols (London, 1955).
Bey, K., *The Evils of the East: Or, Truths about Turkey* (London, 1888).
Bezodis, P. A., 'The Greek Church … and St Martin's Almshouses', in *Survey of London*, xxxiii: *The Parish of St Anne Soho*, ed. F. H. Sheppard (London, 1966), pp. 278–87.
Birchall, C., *Embassy, Emigrants, and Englishmen: The Three-Hundred-Year History of a Russian Orthodox Church in London* (Jordanville, NY, 2014).
Blet, H., *Histoire de la colonisation française: naissance et déclin d'un empire* (Paris, 1946).
Bluche, F., *Louis XIV*, trans. M. Greengrass (Oxford, 1990).
Boardman, J., *The Greeks Overseas*, 4th edn (London, 1999).
Bowie, T. R., *The Carrey Drawings of the Parthenon Sculptures* (Bloomington, IN, 1971).
Bradley, S. and N. Pevsner, *London 6, Westminster, The Buildings of England*, founding ed. N. Pevsner, rev. edn (New Haven, CT and London, 2003).
Brown, H., 'Un cosmopolite du grand siècle: Henri Justel', *Bulletin de la Societe de l'Histoire du Protestantisme Francais*, lxxxii (1933), pp. 187–20.
Browning, A., *Thomas Osborne Earl of Danby*, 3 vols (Glasgow, 1944–51).
Browning, R., 'Some Early Greek Visitors to England', in *Essays in Memory of Basil Laourdas* (Thessaloniki, 1975), pp. 387–95.

Calamy, E., *Abridgement of Mr Baxter's History of his Life and Times*, 1st edn (London, 1702).

—— *An Account of the Ministers, Lecturers, Lecturers, Masters and Fellows of Colleges and Schoolmasters, who were Ejected or Silenced after the Restoration in 1660* (London, 1713).

Calendar of State Papers, Dom. Ser., 1685, ed. F. Bickley (London, 1960).

Calendar of State Papers, Domestic, 1673–1675, ed. F. H. Blackburne Daniell (London, 1904).

Calendar of State Papers Domestic, 1677–78, ed. F. H. Blackburne Daniell (London, 1911).

Calendar of State Papers Domestic 1680–81, ed. F. H. Blackburne Daniell (London, 1921).

Calendar of State Papers Domestic, 1685, ed. F. Bickley (London, 1960).

Calendar of State Papers, Venetian, 1673–1675, ed. Allen B. Hinds (London, 1940 [1943]).

Camariano, N., *Alexandre Mavrocordato, le grand drogman (1673–1709)* (Thessaloniki, 1970).

Cantemir, D., *History of the Growth and Decay of the Othman Empire*, trans. N. Tindal (London, 1734).

Carmina Graeca rhythmica gratulatoria de reditu serenissimi, sacratissimi & principis Caroli II Magnae Britanniae, Galliae & Hiberniae Regis (Oxford, A. & L. Lichfield, 1660), reproduced by E. Legrand, ed., *Le retour de Charles II, roi d'Angleterre: poème grec du prince Constantin Rodocanacis, publié d'après l'edition de 1660* (Paris, 1873).

Carpenter, E., *The Protestant Bishop* (London, 1956).

Celebi, E., *Odoiporiko stēn Ellada (1668–71)*, ed. D. Loupes and K. Koutsika (Athens, 1994).

—— *An Ottoman traveller: Selections from the Book of Travels of Evliya Celebi*, trans. R. Dankoff and S. Kim (London, 2010).

—— *Seyahatnamesi*, trans. J. von Hammer as *Narrative of Travels in Europe, Asia and Africa in the Seventeenth Century*, vol. i, pts 1–2 (London, 1834–46; repr. New York, 1968).

Cesinale, R. da, *Storia dei missioni dei Cappuccini*, 3 vols (Paris and Rome, 1867–73).

Christie, W. D., ed., *Letters addressed from London to Sir J. Williamson while Plenipotentiary at the Congress of Cologne in the years 1673 and 1674*, 2 vols (Camden Soc., n.s. viii–ix, 1894).

Clement, P., *Histoire de la vie et de l'administration de Colbert* (Paris, 1846).

Clement, P., ed., *Lettres, instructions et memoires de Colbert*, 7 vols (Paris, 1861–2).

Collison-Morley, L., *Italy after the Renaissance: Decadence and Display in the Seventeenth Century* (New York, 1930).

Comnene, M.-A., *Cargese, une colonie grecque en Corse* (Paris, 1959).

Congregatio de Propaganda Fide, *Acta Sacrae Congegationis.*

—— *Scritture originale riferite nelle Congregazioni Generali.*
—— *Scritture riferite nei Congressi.*
Coronelli, P., *Isolario dell'atlante Veneto*, parte 1 (Venice, 1696).
Covel, J., *Some Account of the Present Greek Church* (Cambridge and London, 1722).
Crichton-Stuart, J. P., 3rd Marquess of Bute, *A List of Broadsides and Satires, ... illustrative of English History and Social Life* (London, 1892).
Crusius, M., *Graecae et Latinae Linguae, cum Oratoria, in Acad. Tybing. Professoris, Annalium Suevicorum Dodecas tertia, ab anno Christi MCCXIII usque ad MDXCIIII annum perducta, adiecto paraleipomeno variorum plurimarumque rerum libro: in quo hodiernum quoque Turcicum Bellum, a 1590 usque ad 1596 Domini annum diligenter describitur* (Frankfurt, 1596).
Dally, P., 'Les Justel: II. Henri Justel (1620–1693)', *Bulletin de la Societé de l'Histoire du Protestantisme Français*, lxxix (1930), pp. 9–32.
Darrouzes, J., 'Liste des Protes de l'Athos', in *Le Millénaire du Mont Athos, 963–1963, Études et Mélanges*, 2 vols (Chevetogne, 1963), i, pp. 407–47.
Dawkins, R. M., *The Monks of Athos* (London, 1936).
Debates of the House of Commons from the Year 1667 to the Year 1694, 1, ed. A. Grey, 10 vols (London, 1769).
Dennis, G., *Cities and Cemeteries of Etruria*, 2 vols (rev. edn London, 1879).
Diaz, F., *Il Granducato di Toscana, i Medici* (Turin, 1976).
Dima-Drağan, C., 'Le patriarche Chrysanthe Notaras et le docteur Jean Comnène – étudiants à Padoue', *Revue des Études Sud-Est Européennes*, vii (1969), pp. 691–3.
A discourse in the praise of antimonie, and the virtues thereof (London, 1664).
Doll, P. M., ed., *Anglicanism and Orthodoxy 300 Years after the 'Greek College' in Oxford* (Oxford, 2006).
Dowling, T. E., and E. W. Fletcher, *Hellenism in England* (London, 1915).
Dunbabin, T. J., *The Western Greeks* (Oxford, 1948).
Durrell, L., *The Greek Islands* (London, 1978).
Elliott, G. P., ed., *Diary of Dr Edward Lake*, Camden Soc. xxxix (*Camden Miscellany* i), 1847, pp. 1–32.
Emperors, Patriarchs and Sultans of Constantinople: An Anonymous Greek Chronicle of the Sixteenth Century, trans. M. Philippides (Brookline, MA, 1990).
Fabris, G., 'Professori e scolari greci all'università di Padua', *Archivio Veneto*, xxx (1942), pp. 121–65.
Fortescue, A., *The Orthodox Eastern Church* (London, 1920).
—— *The Uniate Eastern Churches: The Byzantine Rite in Italy, Sicily, Syria and Egypt*, ed. G. D. Smith (London, 1923).
Fouquère, A.-M., *Synodus Jerosolymitana: Adversus Calvinistas haereticos, orientalem ecclesiam de Deo rebusque divinis haeretice cum ipsis sentire mentientes, pro reali potissimum praesentia, anno MDCLXXII sub patriarcha Jerosolymorum Dositheo*

celebrata: Interprete domno Michaele Fouquere e congregatione Sancti Mauri, ordinis Sancti Benedicti (Paris, 1676, revised 1678).
Fraser, A., *Charles II* (London, 1979).
Frazee, C. A., *Catholics and Sultans: The Church and the Ottoman Empire* (London, 1983).
Freely, J., *Istanbul: The Imperial City* (London, 1996).
Frittelli, U., *Albero genealogico della nobile famiglia Chigi patrizia senese* (Siena, 1922).
Furlong, S. J. Guillermo, 'El arzobispo de Samos y su extrana comitiva en la Buenos aires de fines del siglo 17', *Criterio* 22 May 1947), pp. 505–8.
—— 'Introduction', in *Manuel Querini S. J. y sus 'Informes al Rey' 1747–1750*, ed. Guillermo Furlong, S. J. (Buenos Aires, 1967), pp. 7–15.
Galland, A., *Journal pendant son séjour à Constantinople, 1672–3*, ed. C. Schefer, 2 vols (Paris, 1881).
—— *Voyages inédits*, ed. M. Couvreur and D. Viviers (Paris, 2001).
Gams, P. B., *Series Episcoporum Ecclesiae Catholicae* (Regensburg, 1873–86; repr. Graz, 1957).
Geanakoplos, D. J., *The Emperor Michael Palaeologus and the West, 1258–1282* (Cambridge, MA, 1959).
Gennadins, J., *Hellenism in England* (London, 1915).
Georgirenes, J., *A Description of the Present State of Samos, Nicaria, Patmos, and Mount Athos*, trans. H. Denton (London, 1677).
—— *From the Arch-Bishop of the Isle of Samos in Greece, An Account of his building the Grecian Church in So-hoe Feilds, and the disposal thereof by the Masters of the Parish of St Martin's in the Feilds*, broadsheet (London, 1682).
Ghobrial, J.-P., 'The Secret Life of Elias of Babylon and the Uses of Global Microhistory', *Past and Present*, ccxxii (2014), pp. 51–93.
Grey, A., *Debates of the House of Commons, 1667–94*, 10 vols (London, 1769).
Guerin, V., *Description de l'Ile de Patmos et de l'Ile de Samos* (Paris, 1856).
Hadjiantoniou, G. A., *Protestant Patriarch: The Life of Cyril Lucaris (1572–1638), Patriarch of Constantinople* (Richmond, VA, 1961).
Hamilton, A., 'Henry Denton (c.1640–1681)', in *ODNB*, xv, p. 853.
Harris, J., *The End of Byzantium* (London, 2010).
—— 'The Grecian Coffee House and Political Debate in London 1688–1714', *London Journal*, xxv (2000), pp. 1–13.
—— 'Silent Minority: The Greek Community of Eighteenth-Century London', in D. Tziovas, ed., *Greek Diaspora and Migration since 1750: Society, Politics and Culture* (Aldershot, 2009), pp. 31–43.
Hartig, E., and K. Meyer, *The Monastery of the Great Mother of God on the Island of Samos* (Rodermark, 2004).

Hasluck, F. W., *Athos and its Monasteries* (London, 1924).
—— 'The First English Traveller's Account of Athos', *The Annual of the British School at Athens*, xvii (1910–11), pp. 103–31.
Haynes, J., *The Humanist as Traveler: George Sandys's Relation of a Journey Begun in An. Dom. 1610* (London and Toronto, 1986).
Heath, M., 'Unholy Alliance: Valois and Ottomans', *Renaissance Studies*, iii (1989), pp. 303–15.
Hennessy, G., *Novum Repertorium Ecclesiasticum Parochiale Londinense* (London, 1898).
Henning, B. D., *History of Parliament: The House of Commons, 1660–1690*, 3 vols (London, 1983).
Hetherington, P., *The Greek Islands: Byzantine and Medieval Buildings* (London, 2001).
Hinds, P., *'The Horrid Popish Plot': Roger L'Estrange and the Circulation of Political Discourse in late Seventeenth Century London* (Oxford, 2010).
Historical Manuscripts Commission, *Fourth Report, Manuscripts of the Marquis of Bath at Longleat*, Part i (London, 1874).
Historical Manuscripts Commission, *Seventh Report*, Appendix pt i, *Manuscripts of Sir Henry Verney, Bart.* (London, 1879).
Historical Manuscripts Commission, *Eleventh Report*, Appendix pt. ii, *Manuscripts of the House of Lords, 1678–1688*, ed. E. Fairfax Taylor and F. Skene (London, 1887).
Historical Manuscripts Commission, *Manuscripts of the Duke of Rutland at Belvoir Castle*, 4 vols (London, 1888–1905).
Historical Manuscripts Commission, *Twelfth Report*, Appendix, pt. v, *Papers of the Duke of Rutland*, ed. H. C. Maxwell Lyte (London, 1889).
Historical Manuscripts Commission *Thirteenth Report*, Appendix, pt vi, *Manuscripts of Sir William Fitzherbert, Bart.* (London, 1893).
Historical Manuscripts Commission, *Manuscripts of the Duke of Portland at Welbeck Abbey*, 10 vols (London, 1894–1931).
Historical Manuscripts Commission, *Fourteenth Report*, Appendix, pt viii, *Manuscripts of Lincoln ... Lichfield ... etc.* (London, 1895).
Historical Manuscripts Commission, *Manuscripts of his Grace the Duke of Rutland*, iv (London, 1905).
Historical Manuscripts Commission, *Calendar of the MSS of the Marquess of Ormonde, KP*, iv (London, 1906).
Historical Manuscripts Commission, *Report on the Manuscripts of the late Allan George Finch Esq., of Burley-on-the-Hill, Rutland*, ii (London, 1922).
Hofmann, G., 'Athos e Roma', *Orientalia Christiana Analecta*, v.2 (1925), pp. 137–83.
—— 'Rom und Athoskloster', *Orientalia Christiana Analecta*, viii (1926), pp. 4–39.

—— 'Rom und der Athos: Briefwechsel zwischen dem Missionar auf dem Athos Nikolaus Rossi und der Kongregation de Propaganda Fide, Quellenausgabe mit Einfuhrung', *Orientalia Christiana Analecta*, cxlii (1954).

Hooke, R., *The Diary of Robert Hooke MA MD FRS 1672–1680*, ed. H. W. Robinson and W. Adams (London, 1935; repr. 1968).

Hopkirk, M., *Queen over the Water* (London, 1953).

Horton, G., *Home of Nymphs and Vampires: The Isles of Greece* (Indianapolis, IN, 1929).

Hunting, P., *They Built London: History of the Tylers and Bricklayers' Company* (London, 2016).

Inwood, S., *The Man Who Knew Too Much* (London, 2002).

Iorga, N., *Byzance après Byzance* (Paris, 1992, reprint).

Isolario dell' atlante Veneto, del P. Coronelli, Parte 1 (Venice, 1696).

Jardine, L., *The Curious Life of Robert Hooke* (London, 2003).

—— *On a Grander Scale: The Outstanding Career of Sir Christopher Wren* (London, 2002).

Jensen, D. L., 'The Ottoman Turks in Sixteenth-Century French Diplomacy', *Sixteenth Century Journal*, xvi (1985), pp. 451–70.

Journals of the House of Commons, 1667–1687, vol. ix (London, 1803).

Journals of the House of Lords, 1675–1681, vol. xiii (London, n.d.).

Kadas, S., *Mount Athos* (Athens, 1998).

Kenyon, J. P., *The Popish Plot* (London, 1972; 2nd edn, 1983).

Kienast, H. J., 'Der Turm des Sarakini auf Samos', *Deutsches Archäologisches Institut: Archaologischer Anzeiger* (2001), pp. 525–57.

Kiminas, D., *The Ecumenical Patriarchate: A History of its Metropolitanates with Annotated Hierarch Catalogs* (Rockville, MD, 2009).

Knights, M., 'London's "Monster" Petition of 1680', *Historical Journal*, xxxvi (1993), pp. 39–67.

Kokkinos, G. N., *Ē paradosiakē katoikia tēs Ikarias, kai to idiomorpho ktisto petiballon tou nēsiou* (Athens, 2005).

Komninos, J., *Prosonetarion tou Agiou Orous tou Athonos* (2nd edn, Venice, 1864).

Korolevskij, P. S., 'Italo-Greci ed Italo-Albanesi nell' archivio di Propaganda Fide: documenti esistenti nell' archivio', *Archivio Storico per la Calabria e la Lucania*, xvi (1947), pp. 113–53.

Laborde, L. marquis de, *Athènes aux xve, xvie et xviie siècles* (Paris, 1854).

Layton, E., 'Nikodemos Metaxas: The First Greek Printer in the Eastern World', *Harvard Library Bulletin*, xv (1967), pp. 140–68.

Legrand, E., *Bibliographie hellénique … des ouvrages publiés par des Grecs au dix-septième siècle*, 5 vols (Paris, 1894–1903).

—— ed., *Le Retour de Charles II, roi d'Angleterre: poeme grec du prince Constantin Rodocanacis, publie d'apres l'edition de 1660* (Paris, 1873).

Lemerle, P., ed., *Actes de Kutlumus, Archives de l'Athos* II 2 (Paris, 1988).
Lillywhite, B., *London Coffee Houses* (London, 1963).
Lithgow, W., *The Totall Discourse of the Rare Adventures and Painfull Peregrinations* (Glasgow, 1906).
Llewellyn Smith, M., *The Great Island* (London, 1965).
Loch, S., *Athos: The Holy Mountain* (London, 1957).
Lough, J., ed., *Locke's Travels in France, 1676–1679* (Cambridge, 1953).
Lyna, F., *Catalogue des manuscrits de la Bibliothèque Royale de Belgique*, xi (Brussels, 1927).
McClain, M., *Beaufort: The Duke and his Duchess, 1657–1715* (New Haven, CT and London, 2001).
Magni, C., *Quanto di piu curioso, e vago ha potuto raccorre C. M. nel primo biennio da esso consumato in viaggi* (Parma, 1679).
Magrath, J. R., *The Queen's College*, 2 vols (Oxford, 1921).
Manousakas, M. I., 'Structure sociale de l'hellénisme postbyzantin', *Jahrbücher der österreichischen Byzantinistik*, xxxi (1981), pp. 791–821.
Mansel, P., *Constantinople: City of the World's Desire, 1453–1924* (London, 1995).
Margarones, M., *Geographia Nomou Samou* (Karlovasi, 1966).
Marshall, A., *The Strange Death of Edmund Godfrey: Plots and Politics in Restoration London* (London, 1999).
Martin, M. E., 'Some Western Images of Athos in Early Modern Times', *Byzantine and Early Modern Greek Studies*, xxii (1998), pp. 51–74.
Marvell, A., *Account of the Growth of Popery, and Arbitrary Government, in England* (London, 1677).
Melas, I., *Istoria tes Nesou Ikarias*, 2 vols (Athens, 1953–8).
Mendieta, E. A. de, *Le presqu'île des caloyers: le Mont-Athos* (Brussels and Bruges, 1955), new and revised ed., trans. M. R. Bruce as *Mount Athos, the Garden of the Panaghia* (*Berliner Byzantinistische Arbeiten*, xli, Berlin and Amsterdam, 1972).
Mettis, C., 'Josef Georgerines o Melios, proen Archiepiskopos Samou, idrytes tes protes Ellenikes koinotetas tou Londinou to 1677', *The Orthodox Herald* (magazine of the Greek Orthodox Archdiocese of Thyateira and Great Britain), vol. ix (1997), July/August, pp. 11–17; September/October, pp. 10–19; November/December, pp. 18–24.
—— *Oi Rizes tou Paroikiakou Ellenismou ste Megale Vretania* (London, 1998).
Meyer, P., *Die Haupturkunden für die Geschichte der Athosklöster* (Leipzig 1894).
Miller, J., *Charles II* (London, 1991).
—— *James II* (Hove, 1978).
—— *James II: A Study in Kingship*, rev. edn (London, 1989).

—— *Popery and Politics in England, 1660–1688* (Cambridge, 1973).
Montagu, Lady Mary Wortley, *The Complete Letters*, ed. Robert Halsband, 3 vols (Oxford, 1965–7).
Mordhorst, S., *Guida alla Val di Cecina* (Siena, 1996).
Newton, C. T., *Travels and Discoveries in the Levant*, 2 vols (London, 1865).
Nicholls, J. F., and J. Taylor, *Bristol Past and Present*, 3 vols (Bristol, 1882).
North, R., *The Lives of The Right Hon. Francis North ... The Hon. Sir Dudley North ... and The Hon. and Rev. John North*, ed. A. Jessop, 3 vols (London, 1890).
Nouvelle biographie générale, ed. M. Hoefer, 46 vols (Paris, 1855–66).
Œuvres de Louis XIV, ed. P. A. Grouvelle and P.-H. Grimoard, 6 vols (Paris, 1806).
Omont, H., *Athènes au XVIe siècle: dessins des sculptures du Parthenon attributés à J. Carrey et conservés a la Bibliothèque Nationale, Paris* (Paris, 1898).
—— 'Martin Crusius, George Dousa et Theodore Zygomalas', *Revue des Etudes Grecques*, x (1897), pp. 66–70.
—— *Missions archéologiques françaises en Orient aux XVIIe et XVIIIe siècles*, 2 vols (Paris, 1902).
Osbat, L., 'Clemente X, Papa', in *Dizionario biografico degli italiani* 26 (1982), pp. 293–302.
Oxford Dictionary of the Christian Church, by E. A. Livingstone after F. L. Cross, 3rd edn (Oxford, 1997).
Oxford Dictionary of National Biography, ed. H. C. G. Matthew and B. Harrison, 61 vols (Oxford, 2004).
Papademetriou, T., *Render unto the Sultan: Power, Authority and the Greek Orthodox Church in the Early Ottoman Centuries* (Oxford and New York, 2015).
Papadopoulos, Th., 'Maniates apoikoi stēn Italia tou 17° aiona', *Lakonikai Spoudai*, iv (1979), pp. 396–474.
Papalas, A. J., *Ancient Icaria* (Wauconda, IL, 1992), Greek trans. with additional illustrations by A. Kalokairinos, *Archaia Ikaria* (Ikaria, 2002).
—— *Rebels and Radicals, Icaria 1600–2000* (Wauconda, IL, 2005).
Papalas, I., *Ē Ekklesia tēs Samou apo tēs idreuseōs autēs mechri sēmeron* (Samos, 1976).
Paris, R., *De 1660 à 1789, le Levant*, v, in G. Rambert, ed., *Histoire du commerce de Marseille*, 7 vols (Paris, 1949–66).
Patterson, W. B., 'Cyril Lukaris, George Abbot, James VI and I, and the Beginning of Orthodox–Anglican Relations', in P. M. Doll, ed., *Anglicanism and Orthodoxy 300 Years after the 'Greek College' in Oxford* (Oxford and Berne, 2006), pp. 39–55.
Paulus, H. E. G., *Sammlung der merkwürdigsten Reisen in den Orient* (Jena, 1799).
Pearson, J. B., *A Biographical Sketch of the Chaplains to the Levant Company, maintained at Constantinople, Aleppo and Smyrna, 1611–1706* (Cambridge, 1883).

Perry, C., *A View of the Levant: Particularly of Constantinople, Syria, Egypt and Greece* (London, 1743).

Pettegree, A., *Foreign Protestant Communities in Sixteenth-Century London* (Oxford, 1986).

Philippson, A., *Die griechischen Landschaften*, 4 vols (Frankfurt a.M., 1950–9).

Pinnington, J., *Anglicans and Orthodox: Unity and Subdivision 1559–1725* (Leominster, 2003).

Plested, M., 'Athos and the West: Benedictines, Crusaders and Philosophers', *Friends of Mount Athos, Annual Report 2007* (Oxford, 2008).

Podskalsky, G., *Griechische Theologie in der Zeit der Turkenherrschaft (1453–1821)* (Munich, 1988).

Porfyriou, H., 'La presenza greca in Italia tra cinque e seicento: Roma e Venezia', in D. Calabi and P. Lanaro, eds, *La città italiana e i luoghi degli stranieri XIV–XVIII secolo* (Rome, 1998), pp. 21–38.

Rambert, G., *Histoire du Commerce de Marseille*, 7 vols (Paris, 1949–66).

Randolph, B., *The Present State of the Islands in the Archipelago* (Oxford, 1687).

Recopilación de Leyes de los Reynos de las Indias (Madrid, 1681).

Rhodocanaces, C., *Alexicacus, spirit of salt of the world, which vulgarly prepar'd is call'd the spirit of salt, or, The transcendent virtue of the true spirit of salt ...* (London, 1662; repr. St Peter Port, 1977).

Riley, A., *Athos, or the Mountain of the Monks* (London, 1887).

Roberti, G. M., *Disegno storico dell' ordine de' Minimi*, 3 vols (Rome, 1902–22).

Robinson, N. F., *Monasticism in the Orthodox Churches* (London and Milwaukee, WI, 1916).

Rodota, P. P., *Dell' origine, progresso, e stato presente del rito Greco in Italia, osservato dai Greci, monaci basiliani, e albanesi*, 3 vols (Rome, 1758–63).

Runciman, S., *The Great Church in Captivity: A Study of the Patriarch of Constantinople from the Eve of the Turkish Conquest to the Greek War of Independence* (Cambridge, 1968).

Rycaut, P., *The Present State of the Greek and Armenian Churches in 1678* (London, 1679).

Sandys, G., *A Relation of a Journey Begun in An. Dom. 1610* (London, 1615).

Sauger, P., *Historia tōn archaiōn doukōn kai tōn loipōn hēgemonōn tou Aigaiou pelagous*, trans. A. M. Karales (Hermoupolis, Syros, 1878).

Schreiner, Peter, *Die byzantinischen Kleinchroniken*, ed. Peter Schreiner, Corpus Fontium Historiae Byzantinae 12, 3 vols (Vienna, 1975–7).

Schwartz, S., 'The Greek Gunners and the Spanish Conquest', in A. N. Zahareas and Y. Andreadis, eds, *Grecia en España, España en Grecia: Hacia una historia de la cultura mediterránea* (Madrid, 1999), pp. 337–41.

Seggiano, I. da, 'Documenti inediti sull' apostolato dei Minori Cappucini nel vicino Oriente (1623–1683)', *Collectanea Franciscana*, xviii (1948), pp. 118–244; xxii (1952), pp. 339–86; xxiii (1953), pp. 297–338.

—— *L'opera dei Cappuccini per l'unione dei Cristiani nel vicino Oriente durante il secolo XVII*, *Orientalia Christiana Analecta* 163 (Rome, 1962).

Sella, D., *Italy in the Seventeenth Century* (London and New York, 1997).

Setton, K. M., *Venice, Austria and the Turks in the Seventeenth Century* (Philadelphia, 1991).

Sheppard, F. H. W., ed., *Survey of London*, vols xxxiii–xxxiv, *The Parish of St Anne, Soho* (London, 1966).

Sherrard, P., *Athos, the Mountain of Silence* (London, 1960).

Skouvaras, V., in A. Martinos, ed., *Threskeutikē kai Ethikē Enkyklopaidia*, 12 vols (Athens, 1965), vii, col. 125.

Smith, T., *An Account of the Greek Church* (London, 1680).

—— *Collectanea de Cyrillo Lucario* (London, 1707).

—— *De Graecae Ecclesiae hodierno statu epistola* (Oxford, 1676; London, 1678).

—— *Miscellanea, in quibus continentur Paemonitio ad Lectorem de infractum Communione apud Graecos*, etc. (London, 1686).

—— *Remarks upon the manners, Religion and Government of the Turks, together with a Survey of the Seven Churches of Asia as they now lie in ruins* (London, 1678).

—— *Some Account of the Present Greek Church, with Reflections on their present Doctrine and Discipline, Particularly in the Eucharist and the Rest of their Seven Pretended Sacraments* (Cambridge, 1722).

Smyrnakes, G., *To Agion Oros* (Athens, 1903).

Speake, G., *Mount Athos: Renewal in Paradise* (New Haven, CT and London, 2002).

Speliotakis, K. K., 'Neotera Stoicheia peri tes metoikeseos ton medikon tes Manes eis Toskanen (1670–1671)', *Lakonikai. Spoudai*, i (1972), pp. 199–211.

Spencer, T. J. B., *Fair Greece, Sad Relic: Literary Philhellenism from Shakespeare to Byron* (London, 1954).

Spon, J., *Voyage d'Italie, de Dalmatie, de Grèce et du Levant, fait és années 1675 & 1676 par Iacob Spon, Docteur Médécin Aggregé à Lyon, & George Wheler, Gentilhomme Anglois* (Lyon, 1678).

Stamatiades, E. I., *Epistolimaia diatribē peri Ioseph Georgeirenou, Archiepiskopou Samou 1666–1671* (Samos, 1892).

—— *Samiaka etoi Historia tes nesou Samou*, 5 vols (Samos, 1881–7).

State Trials, ed. W. Cobbett and T. C. Howell, 34 vols (London, 1809–28).

Tappe, E. D., 'The Greek College in Oxford', in P. M. Doll ed., *Anglicanism and Orthodoxy 300 Years after the 'Greek College' in Oxford* (Oxford and Berne, 2006), pp. 153–74 and 415–20.

Terzorio, C. da, *Le missioni dei Minori Cappuccini*, 10 vols (Rome, 1913–38).

Theocharides, P. L., *Photography on Mount Athos*, iv: *Monasteries and sketes of the Holy Mountain ... 1870* (bilingual, Thessaloniki, 1996).

Thévenot, Jean de, *Voyages de Mr de Thevenot en Europe, Asie & Afrique*, 3rd edn, 3 pts in 5 vols, i: *Voyage du Levant* (Amsterdam, 1727).

Tournefort, J. Pitton de, *Relation d'un voyage du Levant, fait par ordre du Roy* (Lyon, 1717).

—— *A Voyage into the Levant: Perform'd by Command of the late French King*, trans. John Ozell, 2 vols (London, 1718).

The Travels of Lord Charlemont in Greece and Turkey, 1749, ed. W. B. Stanford and E. J. Finopoulos (London, 1984).

Treby, G., *Collection of Letters and other Writings relating to the Horrid Popish Plot. from the Originals in the Hands of George Treby Esq.* (London, 1681).

Trevor-Roper, H., 'The Church of England and the Greek Church in the time of Charles I', in D. Baker, ed., *Religious Motivation: Biographical and Sociological Problems for the Church Historian* (Oxford, 1978), pp. 213–40.

Tsakos, K., *Samos: A Guide to the History and Archaeology* (Athens, 2003).

Tsirpanles, Z. N., 'Ekloge metropolite Italias apo tous Ellenes tes Ankonas', *Dodone*, ii (1973), pp. 61–76.

—— 'Gia tēn eklogē metropolitē Italias sta mesa tou 16 aiēnas (Prosthēkē kai diorthōseis)', *Dodone*, iii (1974), pp. 143–50.

—— 'Oi Maniotes tēs Toskanēs kai tēs Periochēs tou Taranta (b miso tou 17ou ai.)', *Lakonikai Spoudai*, iv (1979), pp. 105–59.

Tsourkas, Cleobulo, *Gli scholari greci di Padova nel rinnovamento culturale dell'oriente ortodosso* (Padua, 1959).

Vakalopoulos, A. E., *Historia tou Neou Hellēnismou*, 4 vols (Thessaloniki, 1961–63).

Valakou, P., 'Monē Osias Theoktistēs', *Archaiologikon Deltion*, liv (2006 for 1999), B' Chronika, p. 829.

Valle, P. della, *The Pilgrim: The Travels of Pietro della Valle*, trans. George Bull (London, 1989).

Vandal, A., *L'Odyssée d'un ambassadeur: les voyages du Marquis de Nointel (1670–1680)* (Paris, 1900).

Vaporis, N. M., 'A Study of Ziskind Ms No. 22 of the Yale University Library: Some Aspects of the Ecumenical Patriarchate of Constantinople in the Seventeenth and Eighteenth Centuries', *Greek Orthodox Theological Review*, xii (1967), supplement, 1–40.

Wheler, G., *A Journey into Greece* (London, 1682).

Williams, G., *The Orthodox Church of the East in the Eighteenth Century, Being the Correspondence between the Eastern Patriarchs and the Nonjuring Bishops* (London, 1868).

Wood, A., *Athenae Oxonienses, to which are added the Fasti*, ed. P. Bliss, 4 vols (London, 1813–20).

—— *Life and Times of Anthony Wood, antiquary of Oxford, 1632–1695, described by himself*, ed. A. Clark, 4 vols (Oxford Historical Society, 1891–5).

Wood, A. C., 'The English Embassy at Constantinople, 1660–1762', *English Historical Review*, xl (1925), pp. 533–61.

Zapheiriou, N. I., *Archeiōn Samou: Syngramma periodikon kata trimēnian ekdidomenon* (Athens, 1946).

Zerlentos, P. G., *Sēmeiōmata peri Hellēnōn ek tōn Martinou Krousiou Souebikōn Chronikōn, Historikē Bibliothēkē tōn apo Halōseōs Chronōn* (Athens, 1922).

Map 1: Greece and the Aegean Sea, c. 1670

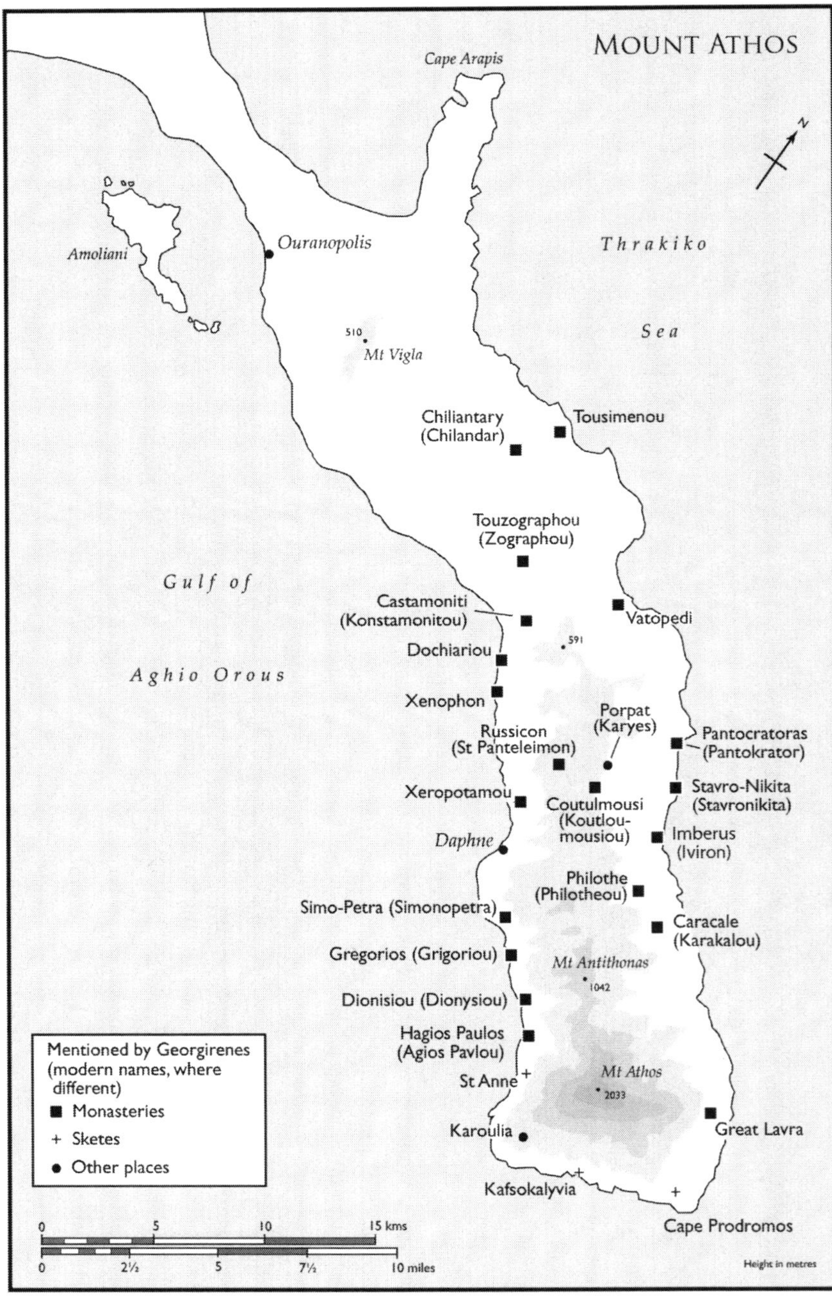

Map 2: Mount Athos, c. 1670

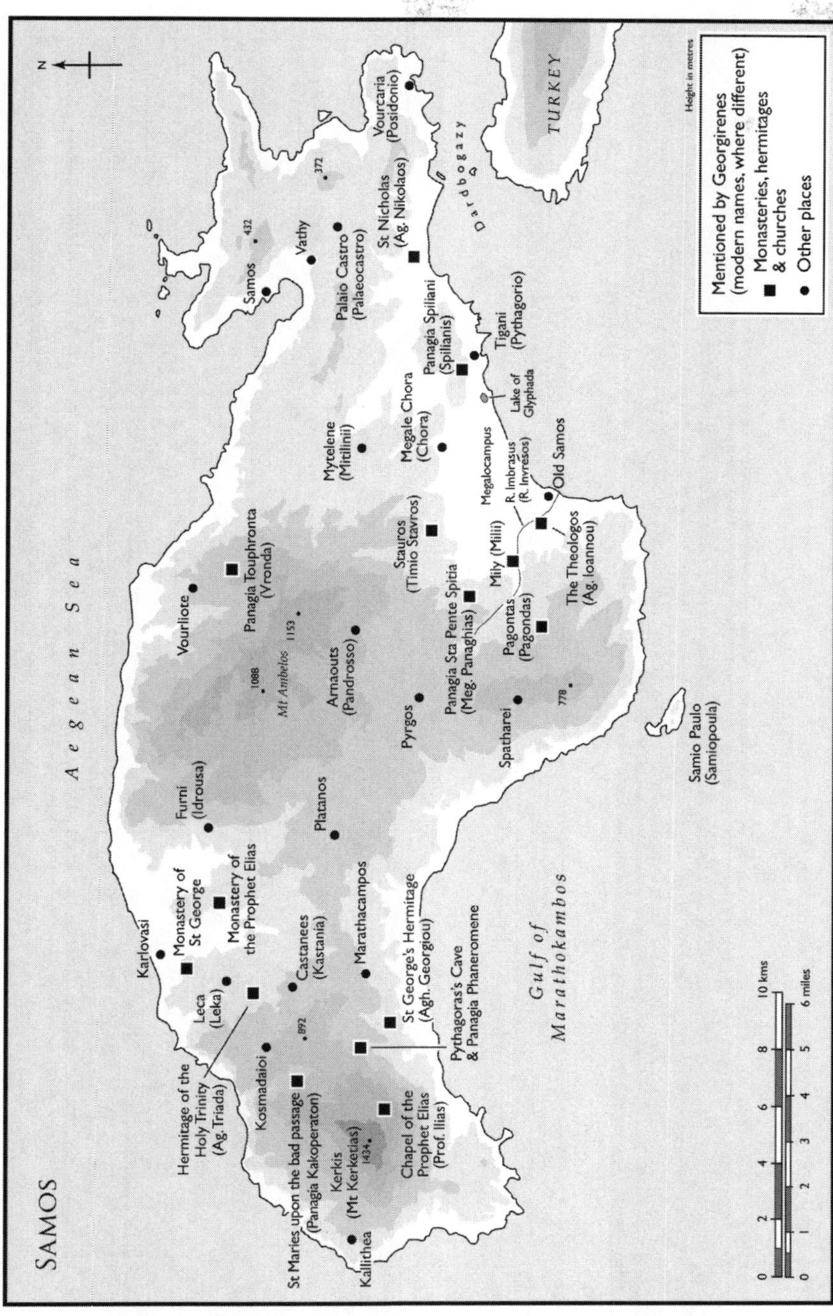

Map 3: The Island of Samos, c. 1670

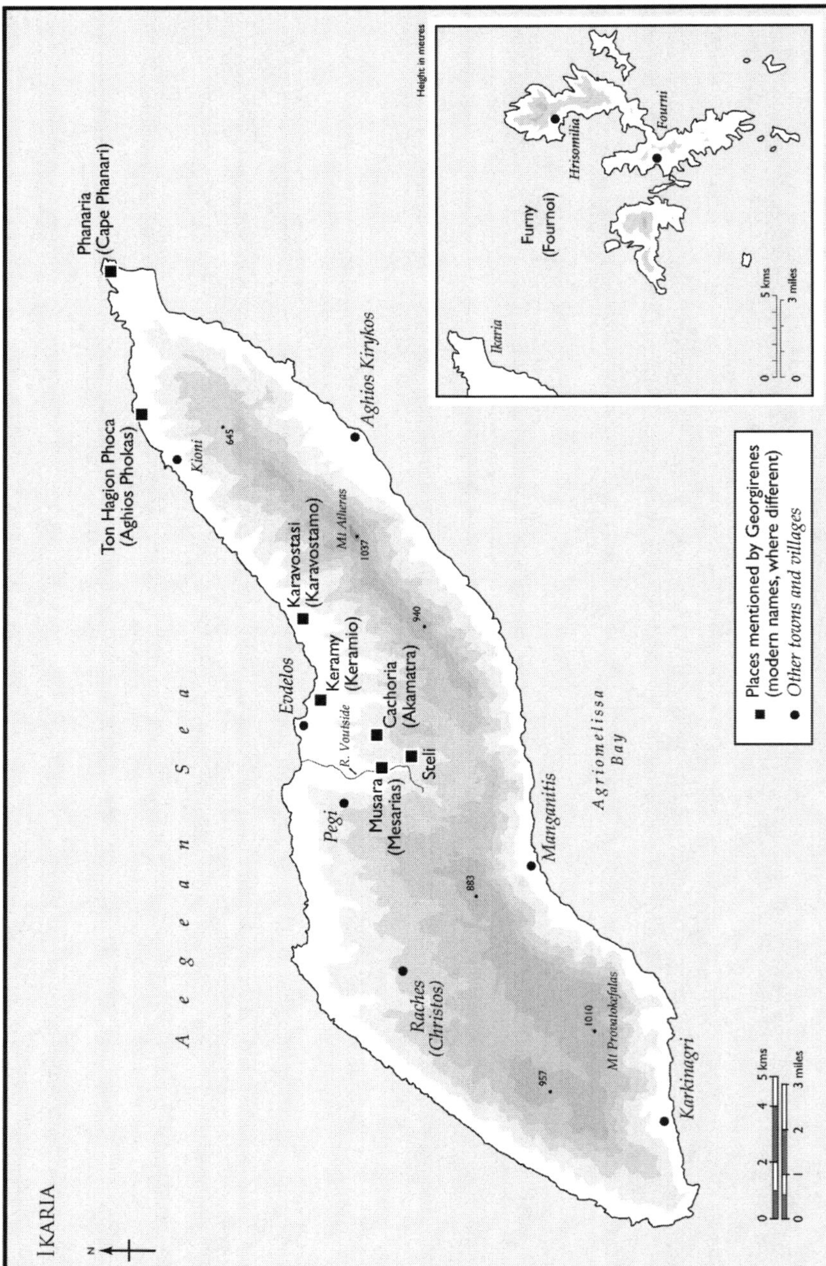

Map 4: The Island of Ikaria, c. 1670

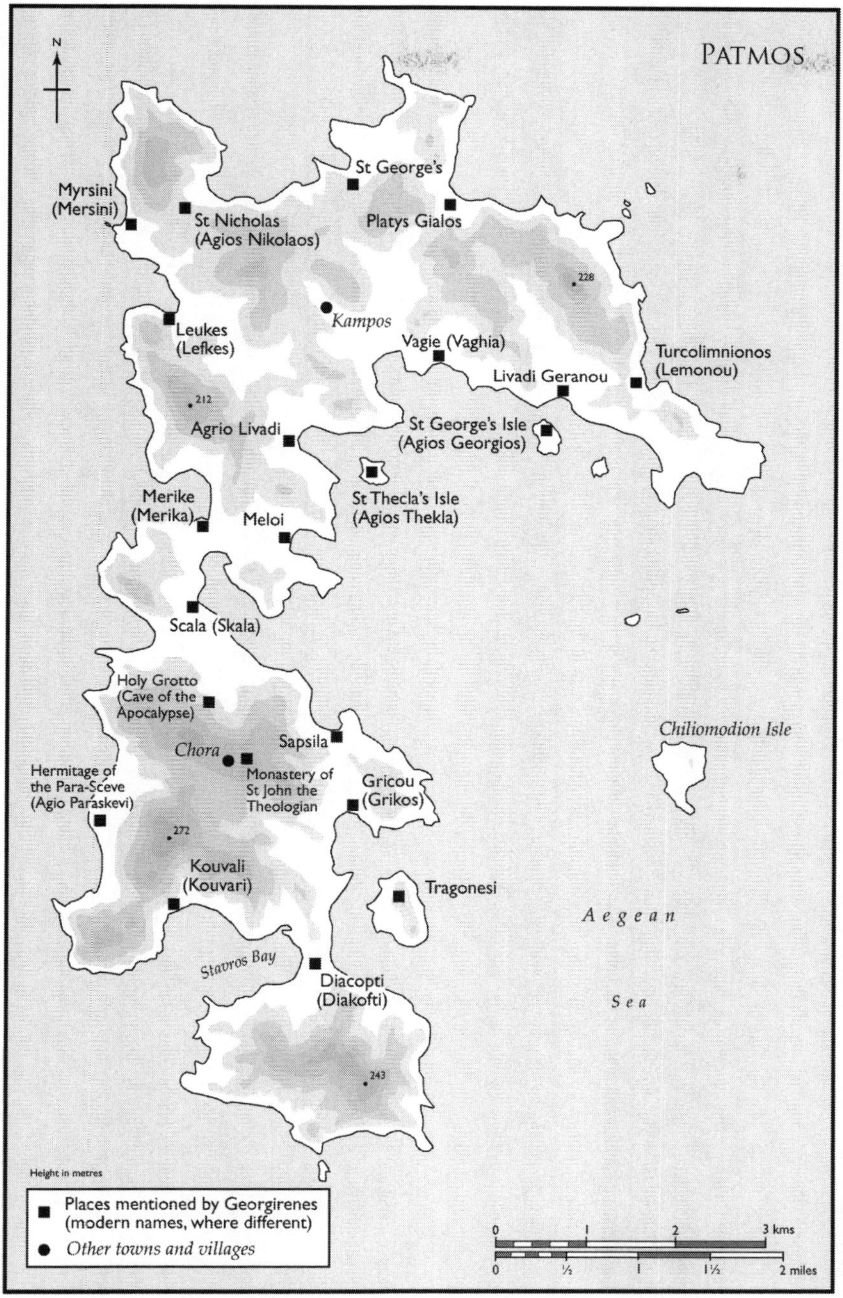

Map 5: The Island of Patmos, c. 1670

Index

This index relates only to the main text and not to the reprinted pamphlet.

Byzantine and Neohellenic Studies

Edited by

Andrew Louth FBA, Professor Emeritus of Patristic and Byzantine Studies, University of Durham.

David Ricks, Professor of Modern Greek and Comparative Literature, King's College London.

This series encompasses the religion, culture, history, and literary production of the Greek-speaking world and its neighbours from the fourth century AD to the present. It aims to provide a forum for original scholarly work in any of these fields, covering cultures as diverse as Late Antiquity, the Byzantine empire, the Venetian empire, the Christian communities under Ottoman rule, and the modern nation states of Greece and Cyprus. Submissions in English are welcomed in the form of monographs, annotated editions, or collections of papers.

Volume 1 Anthony Hirst, *God and the Poetic Ego: The Appropriation of Biblical and Liturgical Language in the Poetry of Palamas, Sikelianos and Elytis*.
425 pages. 2004. ISBN 3-03910-327-X

Volume 2 Hieromonk Patapios and Archbishop Chrysostomos, *Manna from Athos: The Issue of Frequent Communion on the Holy Mountain in the Late Eighteenth and Early Nineteenth Centuries*.
187 pages. 2006. ISBN 3-03910-722-4

Volume 3 Liana Giannakopoulou, *The Power of Pygmalion: Ancient Greek Sculpture in Modern Greek Poetry, 1860-1960.*
340 pages. 2007. ISBN 978-3-03910-752-0

Volume 4 Irene Loulakaki-Moore, *Seferis and Elytis as Translators.*
392 pages. 2010. ISBN 978-3-03911-918-9

Volume 5 Maria Mandamadiotou, *The Greek Orthodox Community of Mytilene: Between the Ottoman Empire and the Greek State, 1876–1912.*
270 pages. 2013. ISBN 978-3-0343-0910-3

Volume 6 Eugenia Russell, *St Demetrius of Thessalonica: Cult and Devotion in the Middle Ages.*
213 pages. 2010. ISBN 978-3-0343-0181-7

Volume 7 Ivan Sokolov, *The Church of Constantinople in the Nineteenth Century: An Essay in Historical Research.*
1041 pages. 2013. ISBN 978-3-0343-0202-9

Volume 8 Forthcoming

Volume 9 Bernard Mulholland, *The Early Byzantine Christian Church: An Archaeological Re-assessment of Forty-Seven Early Byzantine Basilical Church Excavations Primarily in Israel and Jordan, and their Historical and Liturgical Context.*
245 pages. 2014. ISBN 978-3-0343-1709-2

Volume 10 Maximilian Lau, Caterina Franchi and Morgan Di Rodi (eds), *Landscapes of Power: Selected Papers from the XV Oxford University Byzantine Society International Graduate Conference.*
323 pages. 2014. ISBN 978-3-0343-1751-1

Volume 11 Dimitrios Konstadakopulos, *From Pax Ottomanica to Pax Europaea: The growth and decline of a Greek village's micro-economy.*
375 pages. 2014. ISBN 978-3-0343-1749-8

Volume 12 John Penrose Barron, *From Samos to Soho: The Unorthodox Life of Joseph Georgirenes, a Greek Archbishop.*
418 pages. 2017. ISBN 978-3-0343-1788-7

Volume 13 Forthcoming.

Volume 14 Kirsty Stewart and James Moreton Wakeley (eds), *Cross-Cultural Exchange in the Byzantine World, c.300–1500 AD: Selected Papers from the XVII International Graduate Conference of the Oxford University Byzantine Society.*
210 pages. 2016. ISBN 978-3-0343-2258-4